Clinical Advances in Cognitive Psychotherapy

THEORY AND APPLICATION

Biographies

E. Thomas Dowd is Professor of Psychology at Kent State University in Ohio, USA. He was President of the International Association for Cognitive Psychotherapy, is President of the American Board of Behavioral Psychology, and is a Fellow of the American Psychological Association in two divisions. He holds board certification (diplomates) in Behavioral Psychology and Counseling Psychology. He is the author of *Cognitive Hypnotherapy,* published in 2000 by Jason Aronson, and several other book chapters and articles on the topic, including one in the *Handbook of Clinical Hypnosis* and another in the *Casebook of Clinical Hypnosis,* both published by APA Press. His research interests are in hypnotherapy, psychological reactance, and social influence processes. He has presented at numerous conferences in the USA, Europe, the Middle East, and South America.

Robert Leahy (B.A., Ph.D., Yale) is the Editor of the *Journal of Cognitive Psychotherapy* and the President-elect of the International Association of Cognitive Psychotherapy. He serves on the executive committees of the International Association of Cognitive Psychotherapy and the Academy of Cognitive Therapy. Dr. Leahy is the Founder and Director of the American Institute for Cognitive Therapy in New York City (www.CognitiveTherapyNYC.com) and he is currently Associate Professor of Psychology in the Department of Psychiatry at Weill-Cornell Medical School. Dr. Leahy's books include *Cognitive Therapy: Basic Principles and Applications, Practicing Cognitive Therapy, Treatment Plans and Interventions for Depression and Anxiety Disorders* (with Stephen Holland), *Overcoming Resistance in Cognitive Therapy* and *Bipolar Disorder: A Cognitive Therapy Approach* (with Newman, Beck, Reilly-Harrington and Gyulai).

Clinical Advances in Cognitive Psychotherapy

THEORY AND APPLICATION

Robert L. Leahy, PhD
E. Thomas Dowd, PhD, ABPP
Editors

 Springer Publishing Company

Springer Publishing Company, Inc.
536 Broadway
New York, NY 10012-3955

Acquisitions Editor: Sheri W. Sussman
Production Editor: Janice Stangel
Cover design by Susan Hauley

01 02 03 04 05 / 5 4 3 2 1

Library of Congress Cataloging-in-Publication-Data

Clinical advances in cognitive psychotherapy : theory and application / Robert
  L. Leahy, E. Thomas Dowd, editors.
     p. cm.
  Includes bibliographical references and index.
  ISBN 0-8261-2306-6
     1. Cognitive therapy.   2. Psychotherapy.   I. Leahy, Robert L.
  II. Dowd, E. Thomas.
  [DNLM: 1. Cognitive therapy—methods. WM 425.5.C6 C6408 2002]
  RC489.lC63 C575 2002
  616.89'142—dc21

                                                                    2001049300

Printed in the United States of America by Sheridan Books

To Helen
RLL

To Therese, Kathleen, Jon, and Michael—
"the ones who remind me what it's all about"
ETD

Contents

Part II Applications

Contributors

Lyn Y. Abramson, PhD
Professor
Department of Psychology
University of Wisconsin
Madison, Wisconsin

Lauren B. Alloy, PhD
Professor
Department of Psychology
Temple University
Philadelphia, Pennsylvania

Anthony Bates
Jonathan Swift Clinic
St. James Hospital
Dublin, Ireland

Aaron T. Beck, MD
Professor
Department of Psychiatry
University of Pennsylvania
President, Beck Institute for
    Cognitive Therapy
Philadelphia, Pennsylvania

David M. Clark, MD
University of Oxford
Department of Psychiatry
Warneford Hospital
Oxford, England

**Myra J. Cooper, MA, DPHIL,
    CPSYCHOL**
Research Tutor
Organiser of Research Training,
    Teaching and Supervision
Isis Education Centre
Warneford Hospital
Oxford, United Kingdom

Karen Courchaine, PhD
Clinical Program Coordinator
Florida Recovery Center
Shands at Vista, Florida
and
Clinical Assistant Professor
University of Florida
Gainesville, Florida

Constance Dancu, PhD
Former Director (deceased)
Center for Cognitive and
    Behavioral Therapy
Wilmington, Delaware

Patricia Donovan, MA
Senior Research Specialist
Department of Psychology
University of Wisconsin
Madison, Wisconsin

Anke Ehlers
Department of Psychology
Philipps University
Marburg, Germany

Karen Fleming, PhD
Psychologist
Coleman Professional Service
Kent, Ohio

Edna B. Foa, PhD
Department of Psychiatry
Medical College of Philadelphia
Philadelphia, Pennsylvania

Tyler J. Gabriel, MA
Department of Counseling
    Psychology
Graduate School of Education
University of California
Santa Barbara, California

Vicki L. Gluhoski
Department of Social Work Research
Memorial Sloan-Kettering Cancer
    Center
New York, New York

Rebecca Heikkinen, PhD
Psychologist in Private Practice
Kent, Ohio

David P. Himle, PhD
Former Professor (deceased)
University of Michigan
School of Social Work
Ann Arbor, Michigan

Michael E. Hogan, PhD
Senior Data Base Administrator
Department of Psychology
University of Wisconsin
Madison, Wisconsin

Karen Kayser, PhD
Associate Professor
Graduate School of Social Work
Boston College
Chestnut Hill, Massachusetts

Michael D. Lindemann, PhD
Cognitive Therapy Center
New York, New York

Giovanni Liotti
Association for the Research on the
    Psychopathology of the
    Attachment System
Rome, Italy

William J. Lyddon, PhD
Professor and Director of Training
Counseling Psychology and
    Doctoral Program
University of Southern Mississippi
Hattiesburg, Mississippi

Michael J. Mahoney, PhD
Professor
Department of Psychology
University of North Texas
Denton, Texas

Lata K. McGinn, PhD
Associate Professor
Department of Psychology
Ferkauf Graduate School of Psychology
Yeshiva University
New York, New York

Jeanne M. Miranda, PhD
Department of Psychiatry
Georgetown University
Washington, DC

Robert A. Neimeyer, PhD
Professor
Department of Psychology
University of Memphis
Memphis, Tennessee

Cory F. Newman, PhD, ABPP
Director
Center for Cognitive Therapy; and
Associate Professor of Psychology
Department of Psychiatry
University of Pennsylvania
Philadelphia, Pennsylvania

Catherine Panzarella, PhD
Psychologist
Philadelphia Behavioral Health
    System
Philadelphia, Pennsylvania

Jacqueline B. Persons, PhD
Associate Clinical Professor
Department of Psychiatry
University of California
San Francisco, California

James L. Pretzer, PhD
Director
Cleveland Center for Cognitive
    Therapy
Beachwood, Ohio

Stanley Rachman
Professor Emeritus of Psychology
University of British Columbia
Vancouver, Canada

David Raniere, PhD
Program Director and Psychologist
Two Brattle Center
Cambridge, Massachusetts

Simon A. Rego
Staff, Alcohol Services
Department of Clinical Psychology
Rutgers University
Piscataway, New Jersey

Donna T. Rose, PhD
Psychologist
Counseling Associates of Madison
Madison, Wisconsin

William C. Sanderson, PhD
Associate Professor
Department of Clinical Psychology
Rutgers University
Piscataway, New Jersey

Mervin R. Smucker, PhD
Associate Clinical Professor and Director
    of Cognitve Behavioral Training
Medical College of Wisconsin
Milwaukee, Wisconsin

Gillian Todd
Addenbrookes Hospital
Cambridge, United Kingdom

Robin Weill, PhD
Psychologist in Private Practice
Visiting Lecturer
Department of Psychology
University of Houston
Houston, Texas

Marjorie Weishaar, PhD
Clinical Associate Professor
Department of Psychiatry &
    Human Behavior
Brown University
Providence, Rhode Island

Adrian Wells
The University of Manchester
Department of Clinical Psychology
Manchester Royal Infirmary
Manchester, United Kingdom

Wayne G. Whitehouse, PhD
Adjunct Associate Professor
Data Systems Manager
Temple University
Philadelphia, Pennsylvania

Jeffrey E. Young, PhD
Psychologist
Cognitive Therapy Center
New York, New York

The Life of Aaron T. Beck, MD

Marjorie Weishaar

Aaron T. Beck, MD, is himself a lot like cognitive therapy—active, direct, pragmatic, creative, and optimistic about change. For nearly 40 years, he has formulated his theory of psychotherapy, applied it to various clinical problems and populations, and subjected it to empirical testing. He encourages feedback from colleagues and students and, in turn, fosters their work as well. In a time of professional specialization, he is a leader in both psychiatry and psychology, a researcher with deft clinical skills, and a teacher whose training grants have educated a generation of researchers and hundreds of clinicians. As a result of his intelligence, energy, and skillful intermingling of empirical research and clinical practice, Beck has made cognitive therapy one of the most robust and fastest growing psychotherapies today. He has written more than 400 published articles and 14 books, from reports of outcome studies and theoretical developments to a recent book, *Prisoners of Hate* (Beck, 1999), which he describes as "political psychology."

Many of the characteristics that have made him a great scholar, clinician, and researcher can be traced to Aaron Beck's early life in Providence, Rhode Island. Born the youngest child of Russian Jewish immigrants, Aaron Temkin Beck was raised in a politically active family that valued education. His father, Harry Beck, was a printer in the Ukraine where he set type in Ukrainian, Hebrew, Russian, German, and Yiddish. After moving to the United States, Harry taught himself English by working in print

shops. Within five years of immigrating, he had established his own business, H. Beck & Company. Harry Beck was also a Socialist and a sup-
porter of the labor union movement. He held the unusual position of
being both a business owner and a member of the typographical union.

Harry Beck also had a commitment to intellectual pursuits. During his
printing apprenticeship, he delivered playbills to Russian officers at the
theater. He would stay to watch performances and thus learned about the
great Russian playwrights as well as about Shakespeare. His home was a
meeting place for discussing literature, politics, and philosophy. Throughout his life he wrote poetry, and later in life he would send his poems to
his grandchildren and ask for feedback. Dr. Judith Beck, now director of
the Beck Institute, remembers exchanging poems with her grandfather.

Aaron Beck and his brothers, Maurice and Irving, were raised to love
literature, writing, and ideas. (Maurice and Aaron were both on the staff
of the Brown University newspaper during college; and Irving, the eldest,
was a James Joyce scholar as well as a revered physician of internal
medicine.) Aaron subscribes to more than 25 journals and magazines in
addition to his professional subscriptions. His teaching style encourages
the open exchange of ideas and feedback from students, a style that
seems to come naturally to him.

Beck's mother, Elizabeth (Lizzie) Temkin Beck, became the matriarch
of her family when her own mother died shortly after their immigration
to the United States. Lizzie raised eight younger brothers and sisters
while helping to run the family grocery store. Two of her brothers grad-
uated from Brown University and one from Harvard Law School, but her
own ambitions to become a physician went unfulfilled. She was active in
the community as president of several organizations and was assertive
speaking her opinion at public meetings. Her sons remember her as forceful, outspoken, and moody. It is likely that she suffered periodically from
depression, which began when her only daughter, Beatrice, died in the
influenza epidemic of 1919. Many family members think that Aaron's
birth in 1921 relieved her depression.

As a consequence of the deaths of Beatrice and a son earlier, Lizzie
was overprotective of her youngest child. Her anxieties were compound-
ed when a playground accident and consequent infection nearly killed
him when he was about seven years old. He also developed anxieties
then, for he was told that he would be briefly separated from his mother
to have x-rays taken and instead was taken to surgery, where the surgeon
began cutting before the anesthesia had taken effect. Beck believes that
this trauma established his fears of abandonment and surgery. He sur-
vived the illness, but was held back in school because he had missed so

much while hospitalized. Because of this he saw himself as "genetically and inalterably inferior" (Weishaar, 1993, p.10). Through study, however, he not only caught up with his classmates, but surpassed them. He believes this experience taught him the value of persistence and how to turn a disadvantage into an advantage.

After graduating from high school, Aaron Beck enrolled at Brown University, as had his brothers before him. He delivered newspapers, worked in the library, worked for an urban planner, and sold brushes door-to-door to help pay college expenses. He majored in English and political science and, graduating magna cum laude, won awards for oratory and essay writing. As he began his studies at Yale University School of Medicine, he had some interest in psychiatry, but found the Kraeplinian approaches nihilistic and unrewarding and the psychodynamic approaches esoteric and unsubstantiated, particularly compared to internal medicine. He did a rotating internship at Rhode Island Hospital to get as broad a background in medicine as possible. In the end, he chose to specialize in neurology, for he was attracted to its precision and discipline.

As he was to begin his residency in neurology at Massachusetts General Hospital, Beck learned that he would have to wait a year because veterans returning from World War II needed placements. Rather than waiting, he went to Cushing Veterans Administration Hospital in Framingham, Massachusetts. At Cushing, however, all neurology residents had to complete a six-month rotation in psychiatry because of a shortage of psychiatry residents. Aaron Beck thus began his career in psychiatry.

His psychiatry training at Cushing was primarily influenced by the Boston Psychoanalytic Institute. He struggled with psychoanalytic formulations and continued to find them unscientific, and his classmates told him he wasn't relating to the material because of his own resistance. He believed that his pragmatism and rebelliousness might be getting in the way of his acceptance of psychoanalysis, so he went into analysis himself, in part to evaluate psychoanalysis fairly. He completed his analytic training in 1958.

While an intern, Beck met Phyllis Whitman, a student at Pembroke, the women's college at Brown. They married in 1950. Now a superior court judge in Pennsylvania, Phyllis Beck has a master's degree in social work as well as a law degree, which she earned while raising four children.

Following his residency and a two-year fellowship at the Austin Riggs Center in Stockbridge, Massachusetts, Beck worked at the Valley Forge Army Hospital in Pennsylvania for two years. He became the chief of psychiatry and used imagery to treat posttraumatic stress disorder in combat veterans.

Board certified in psychiatry in 1953, Aaron Beck became an instructor in psychiatry at the University of Pennsylvania Medical School in 1954. He is now professor emeritus of psychiatry at Penn. Other faculty appointments have included visiting professor at Harvard University in 1982 and visiting professor at Oxford University in 1985. Since 1995, he has been president of the Beck Foundation for Cognitive Therapy and Research as well as continuing his research at the University of Pennsylvania.

In 1959, he received a grant to conduct dream research, which he thought would help confirm the psychoanalytic hypotheses that he had found unscientific. According to psychoanalytic theory, depressed persons experienced anger turned inward as the result of an earlier loss of a loved object. However, in this initial study, Beck did not find greater hostility in the dream content of depressed persons compared to nondepressed persons. The depressed subjects did, however, have more dreams in which they were rejected, disappointed, or criticized. These themes also appeared in their waking thoughts. Further studies were conducted to investigate whether these themes represented a masochistic "need to suffer," a core feature of the psychodynamic model of depression. Word completion and card-sorting tasks were manipulated so that subjects were predetermined to succeed or fail. Depressed subjects who "succeeded" were found to have improved moods and improved self-confidence, not a need to fail. In addition, depressed subjects seemed more sensitive to "failure;" that is, they had a lower estimate of success on future tasks and poorer self-evaluations. Beck proposed that the dream content, sensitivity to failure, and negative expectations simply revealed how the patients viewed themselves, that such symptoms were due to cognitive patterns that "negatively biased their judgments of themselves, their environment, and their future" (Beck, 1967, p. 185). The dreams were not motivated by a need to suffer, but rather were a reflection of a person's thinking. The model of depression was thus reformulated, no longer based on motivation but on how a person processes information in a negatively biased way.

Beck's concurrent observations from his private practice helped him develop his own form of psychotherapy. Several incidents with patients revealed to him that while free-associating in sessions, patients were also having a second stream of thoughts, a running commentary or internal monologue. They were having thoughts about Beck and the session that they were not reporting. These "automatic thoughts" were immediate, plausible, and, in the case of depressed patients, negatively biased.

As he was reformulating the theory of depression, he found his greatest encouragement from psychologists, associates at the University of Pennsylvania, and writers elsewhere, particularly George Kelly. Karen Horney and Alfred Adler were also influential. He views the period of 1960 through 1963 as the most important time for him professionally, for during those years he laid the groundwork for cognitive therapy. He says, "there's nothing that I've been associated with since 1963 the seeds of which were not in the 1962 to 1964 articles. That was the critical period: changing from psychoanalysis and developing a new theory of therapy. It was very exciting. I even had trouble sleeping sometimes, I was so excited about this thing" (Weishaar, 1993, p. 21).

In 1963, Albert Ellis, the founder of rational emotive behavior therapy, read Beck's article on thinking and depression in the *Archives of General Psychiatry* and, recognizing the commonalities of their therapies, contacted him. They have maintained a professional relationship since. Beck credits Ellis with introducing the fundamental concept that people's beliefs are accessible, and Ellis views Beck's research as a major contribution to psychotherapy.

Beck continued his research and teaching at the University of Pennsylvania and was promoted to associate professor in 1967. However, when he got only a 1-year renewal on his depression research grant, he lost his office on campus. He decided to work from his home and wrote his formulation of depression, *Depression: Clinical, Experimental and Theoretical Aspects* (Beck, 1967), later published as *Depression: Causes and Treatment* (Beck, 1972). He believes he was mildly depressed at the time and found writing the book therapeutic. Indeed, his own experiences with depression (once brought on by hepatitis) and phobias (blood and injury, public speaking, suffocation, heights, and abandonment) have given him insight into those disorders. He begins developing his theories with observations, and sometimes he has observed his own reactions.

By the late 1960s, Beck's psychologist colleagues had left the University of Pennsylvania, so he traveled to the State University of New York at Stony Brook to share ideas with Gerald Davison. With the encouragement of Davison and other psychologists, in 1970 Beck published an article on cognitive therapy and its relation to behavior therapy in the journal *Behavior Therapy*. With this article, Beck joined the "cognitive revolution" in psychology, which created a paradigm shift in behavior therapy from conditioning models to ones emphasizing the role of information-processing in human behavior and behavior change. Cognitive therapies, of which there were and are several types, combined a return to the patient's inner world with empirically based interventions. Beck's research, particularly his use of patients rather than college student volunteers as subjects, gave credibility to the cognitive movement. Throughout these fruitful years, Beck was influenced by many psychologists, especially Albert Bandura, Marvin Goldfried, Gerald Davison, Arnold Lazarus, Michael Mahoney, Donald Meichenbaum, and Albert Ellis.

The journal *Cognitive Therapy and Research* was launched in 1977. The first issue featured an article by Beck and some of his students (Rush, Beck, Kovacs, & Hollon, 1977) describing an outcome study that found cognitive therapy to be superior to imipramine in the treatment of unipolar depression. The treatment manual for that study was further developed and published as *Cognitive Therapy of Depression* (Beck, Rush, Shaw, & Emery, 1979), now a classic in the field of depression research and the first explicit description of what goes on in therapy of any kind.

Throughout his prolific research career, Beck has followed a specific strategy for understanding and treating psychological problems. First, he begins to conceptualize disorders through observations of patients. Next, he develops inventories for measuring these observations. The Beck Depression Inventory (Beck, Ward, Mendelson, Mock, & Erbaugh, 1961), for example, grew out of the need for a diagnostic tool for depression in his early studies. He then conducts research to test the validity of his conceptualization. If his observations are validated, he designs interventions and conducts clinical trials. This procedure, repeated with each extension of cognitive therapy into new psychological territory, has yielded treatment manuals and books on the cognitive therapy of depression, anxiety disorders, couples' problems, substance abuse, suicidal behavior, and personality disorders. His inventories, most notably the Beck Depression Inventory, have been used in hundreds of outcome studies, and the Beck Hopelessness Scale (Beck, Weissman, Lester, & Trexler, 1974) has been found to be predictive of eventual suicide for both inpatients and outpatients.

Beck has conducted suicide research since the early 1970s, when he was asked to head a National Institute of Mental Health task force on suicide. This research has produced a taxonomy of suicidal behaviors; assessment scales for measuring suicide ideation and intent, hopelessness, and self-concept; and a model of suicidality that identifies hopelessness as the key psychological variable. Beck has received several awards for his work in suicide, including one from the American Suicide Foundation for Outstanding and Innovative Research into the Detection and Treatment of Suicidal Individuals, and the Louis I. Dublin Award for Lifetime Contributions to Suicidology from the American Association of Suicidology. He is the recipient of a MERIT award from the National Institute of Mental Health for his suicide research.

In 1979, the American Psychiatric Association awarded Beck the Foundation Fund Prize for Research in Psychiatry for his work on depression and the development of cognitive therapy. In the same year, preparation began for the National Institute of Mental Health's collaborative research program on the treatment of depression, a multisite study designed to compare the efficacies of two short-term therapies, interpersonal psychotherapy and cognitive therapy, and pharmacotherapy in the treatment of unipolar depression. The primary difficulty with the NIMH study was the lack of skilled cognitive therapists to implement the treatment. Whereas interpersonal psychotherapy, derived from analytic therapy, had a large pool of skilled therapists, cognitive therapy was too new to have enough experienced therapists. Beck wanted therapists who were highly skilled and committed to cognitive therapy, but NIMH disagreed that this was necessary. Unfortunately, the cognitive therapists in the study barely reached minimal levels of competence. The process was a great disappointment to Beck. Despite the finding that there were no significant differences in mean scores and recovery rates among the four groups (including placebo plus clinical management), subsequent research has suggested that cognitive therapy may reduce the risk of relapse.

In 1982, Beck was named one of the ten most influential psychotherapists by the *American Psychologist.* In the same year, he received an honorary doctorate of medical science from Brown University. By the early 1980s, his work was being very well-received in Europe because of its strong empirical base. He was a Visiting Scientist at Oxford in 1986 and was named a Fellow of the Royal College of Psychiatrists in 1987.

In the 1980s, Beck's contributions were wide-ranging. He reconceptualized his model of depression to include various types and etiologies of depression (Beck, 1987); he completed longitudinal studies of suicidal inpatients and outpatients (Beck, Steer, Kovacs, & Garrison, 1985; Beck, Brown, Berchick, Stewart, & Steer, 1990) that established the importance of hopelessness as a suicide risk factor; he co-edited a casebook on cognitive therapy (Scott, Williams, & Beck, 1989); and he wrote a book for general readership on couples' problems, *Love Is Never Enough* (Beck, 1988). Even in view of all this, it can be argued that the 1980s is most associated with the extension of the cognitive model to anxiety disorders.

As he had with depression, Beck investigated the cognitive features of anxiety—the biases that distorted a person's thinking when anxious, the dominant themes in thoughts and beliefs, and the role of interpretations of symptoms in escalating anxiety. Together with Gary Emery and Ruth Greenberg, he wrote his theoretical treatise and treatment strategies for the treatment of various anxiety disorders, *Anxiety Disorders and Pho-*

bias: A Cognitive Perspective (Beck, Emery, & Greenberg, 1985). Anxiety research proliferated among cognitive therapy researchers in the 1980s in the United States and Europe, particularly in England. Beck first demonstrated in the early 1970s (Beck, Laude, & Bohnert, 1974) that anxiety states have ideational content, and the research in the 1980s looked at the importance of cognitions in perpetuating anxiety. Behavioral techniques such as exposure were used for cognitive change. Thus, anxiety was reduced not necessarily by counterconditioning, but because certain beliefs related to threat and danger were disproved. Patients were taught to challenge their catastrophic beliefs and bolster their coping abilities by recognizing their resources and realistically assessing risks in a situation.

In 1989, Beck received the Distinguished Scientific Award for the Applications of Psychology from the American Psychological Association. The citation states: "His pioneering work on depression has profoundly altered the way the disorder is conceptualized, assessed, diagnosed, and treated. His influential book *Cognitive Therapy of Depression* is a widely cited, definitive text on the subject. The systematic extension of his approach to conditions as diverse as anxiety and phobias, personality disorders, and marital discord demonstrates that his model is as comprehensive as it is rigorously empirical. He has provided alternative psychological treatment for a variety of conditions that had largely been treated by medication" (*American Psychologist,* 1990, p. 458). With this award, Aaron Beck became the only person to win the highest research awards from both the American Psychiatric Association and the American Psychological Association.

The William Rogers Alumni Recognition Award from Brown University, awarded that same year, also recognized the application of cognitive therapy to couples' therapy and anxiety disorders in addition to depression. As cognitive therapy was extended to address different clinical problems, it was modified to deal with the specific cognitive complexities of each disorder. In anxiety, for example, the cognitive themes (assumptions and core beliefs) are different from those in depression (e.g., themes of threat and danger as opposed to deprivation, loss, defeat, and defectiveness). Although the general goals may be similar (e.g., teaching patients to test their beliefs logically and empirically, problem-solving, etc.), the specific, therapeutic strategies are based on the cognitive profile for each disorder and the individualized case conceptualization for each patient.

The cognitive model underwent further modifications as it addressed personality disorders. It became (a) longer in order to change the long-standing, dysfunctional behavior patterns characteristic of personality disorders; (b) more inclusive of childhood experiences to understand the development and functions of core beliefs; and (c) more extensive in its use of imagery and experiential techniques. Cognitive therapy had always gathered data on patients' early life experiences in order to understand the origins of core beliefs. In working with personality disorders, however, that early childhood experience was often relived through imagery and modified through role play. Imagery—used extensively in the treatment of anxiety for such things as the identification of fears and the reshaping of intrusive memories—became even more important in gaining access to core beliefs and emotions. With some of his former students, Beck published *Cognitive Therapy of Personality Disorders* in 1990 (Beck, Freeman & Associates, 1990).

A dissection of cognitive therapy occurred in the 1990s as researchers tested aspects of cognitive theory. Haaga, Dyck, and Ernst (1991) conducted an extensive review of the data supporting or refuting aspects of the cognitive theory of depression. Recently, Clark, Beck, and Alford (1999) published a comprehensive review of the current status of the cognitive model of depression, *Scientific Foundations of Cognitive Theory and Therapy of Depression.* Thus Beck continues to examine the veridicality of his theory as well as the efficacy of his treatments. Beck says he is especially proud of this volume, which investigates the scientific basis of numerous hypotheses derived from the cognitive theory of depression and presents his thinking after 40 years of research.

Beck's extensive interests continued in the 1990s. Since the mid-1970s, he had received research grants to study substance abuse, and in 1993 he coauthored *Cognitive Therapy of Substance Abuse* (Beck, Wright, Newman, & Liese, 1993). *Cognitive Therapy with Inpatients: Developing a Cognitive Milieu* was also published in 1993 (Wright, Thase, Beck, & Ludgate, 1993). The modern movement for psychotherapy integration, begun in the late 1970s, also spurred Beck to write that cognitive therapy can serve as *the* integrative psychotherapy because of its blend of techniques shared with other modalities and its cohesive theory (Beck, 1991). Beck, along with Brad Alford, expands this argument in *The Integrative Power of Cognitive Therapy* (Alford & Beck, 1997). Turning to a cognitive perspective on violence, Beck wrote *Prisoners of Hate: The Cognitive Basis of Anger, Hostility and Violence* (Beck, 1999). Written for professionals and nonprofessional alike, Beck describes how cognitive biases and rigid thinking contribute to hostile behaviors, from individual acts of crime to stereotypes and group prejudice to war and genocide.

Beck has been continuously recognized for his professional achievements throughout the past decade. He received honors from the New York Academy of Medicine, Albert Einstein College of Medicine, the American Psychological Society, the Institute of Medicine of the National Academy of Sciences, and the Society for Research in Psychopathology. In 1995, he received an honorary doctor of letters degree from Assumption College, and in 1998 he received the Lifetime Achievement Award from the Association for the Advancement of Behavior Therapy.

Beck describes his current research interests as the psychopathology of psychiatric disorders, the prediction of suicide, and cognitive therapy of depression and other disorders. He has two major projects under way. The first is developing the cognitive model of schizophrenia. In recent years, he has reexamined the symptoms of schizophrenia and finds them quite amenable to a cognitive model. In three papers soon to appear, Beck rebuts traditional perspectives on the illness. He believes his new perspective will create a paradigm shift in how schizophrenia is conceptualized and treated. The second project continues his suicide research with a study of the efficacy of a brief treatment for those who attempt suicide. The study is very important clinically because the subjects are recruited from hospital emergency rooms following their suicide attempts. They tend to have multiple problems, such as substance abuse, PTSD, and histories of childhood abuse. Thus, they represent a high-risk group for whom few interventions have been studied.

Aaron Beck's late brother, Irving, once described him as far more creative than ambitious. His creative energies and sense of rebellion led him to question traditional theories in psychiatry and to develop new models of human behavior based on observation, testing, and empirical validation. He has always been more intent on learning the truth than on perpetuating any dogma, and his openness has allowed his creativity to be fed by the contributions of his students and colleagues. He enjoys the exchange of ideas, and when he felt isolated with his new paradigm in the 1960s, he sought out psychologists, who welcomed him and his scientific methodology. He has been increasingly productive with age and, as his most recent research demonstrates, not afraid to tackle difficult questions. It is no surprise that he is held in esteem and in gratitude for his contributions and his immense goodwill.

REFERENCES

Alford, B. A., and Beck, A. T. (1997). The integrative power of cognitive therapy. New York: Guilford Press.

American Psychologist. (1990). *Distinguished scientific award for the application of psychology, 1989, 45,* 458–460.

Beck, A. T. (1987). Cognitive models of depression. *Journal of Cognitive Psychotherapy: An International Quarterly, 1,* 5–37.

Beck, A. T. (1991). Cognitive therapy as the integrative therapy: Comment on Alford and Norcross. *Journal of Psychotherapy Integration, 1,* 191–198.

Beck, A. T. (1967). Depression: Clinical, experimental, and theoretical aspects. New York: Harper and Row. Republished as Depression: Causes and treatment. Philadelphia: University of Pennsylvania, 1972.

Beck, A. T. (1988). Love is never enough. New York: Harper and Row.

Beck, A. T. (1999). Prisoners of hate: the cognitive basis of anger, hostility, and violence. New York: Harper Collins.

Beck, A. T., Brown, G., Berchick, R. J., Stewart, B. L., and Steer, R. A. (1990). Relationship between hopelessness and ultimate suicide: a replication with psychiatric outpatients. *American Journal of Psychiatry, 147,* 190–195.

Beck, A. T., and Emery, G. with Greenberg, R. (1985). Anxiety disorders and phobias: a cognitive perspective. New York: Basic Books.

Beck, A. T., Freeman, A., and Associates. (1990). Cognitive therapy of personality disorders. New York: Guilford Press.

Beck, A. T., Laude, R., and Bohnert, M. (1974). Ideational components of anxiety neurosis. *Archives of General Psychiatry, 31,* 456–459.

Beck, A. T., Rush, A. J., Shaw, B. F., and Emery, G. (1979). Cognitive therapy of depression. New York: Guilford Press.

Beck, A. T., Steer, R. A., Kovacs, M., and Garrison, B. (1985). Hopelessness and eventual suicide: a ten-year prospective study of patients hospitalized with suicidal ideation. *American Journal of Psychiatry, 142,* 559–563.

Beck, A. T., Ward, C. H., Mendelson, M., Mock, J., and Erbaugh, J. (1961) An inventory for measuring depression. *Archives of General Psychiatry, 4,* 561–571.

Beck, A. T., Weissman, A., Lester, D., and Trexler, L. (1974). The measurement of pessimism: the hopelessness scale. *Journal of Consulting and Clinical Psychology, 42,* 861–865.

Beck, A. T., Wright, F. D., Newman, C. F., and Liese, B. S. (1993). Cognitive therapy of substance abuse. New York: Guilford Press.

Clark, D. A. and Beck, A. T. with Alford, B. A. (1999). Scientific foundations of cognitive theory and therapy of depression. New York: John Wiley & Sons.

Haaga, D. A. F., Dyck, M. J., and Ernst, D. (1991). Empirical status of cognitive therapy of depression. *Psychological Bulletin, 110,* 215–236.

Rush, A. J., Beck, A. T., Kovacs, M., and Hollon, S. D. (1977). Comparative efficacy of cognitive therapy and pharmacotherapy in the treatment of depressed outpatients. *Cognitive Therapy and Research, 1,* 17–37.

Scott, J., Williams, J. M. G., and Beck, A. T. (Eds.) (1989). Cognitive therapy in clinical practice: An illustrative casebook. New York: Routledge.

Weishaar, M. E. (1993). Aaron T. Beck. London: Sage Publications.

Wright, J. H., Thase, M. E., Beck, A. T., and Ludgate, J. W. (Eds.) (1993). Cognitive therapy with inpatients: The cognitive milieu. New York: Guilford Press.

PART I

General Theory

CHAPTER 1

History and Recent Developments in Cognitive Psychotherapy

E. Thomas Dowd

THE HISTORY AND RECENT DEVELOPMENTS IN COGNITIVE PSYCHOTHERAPY

Cognitive psychotherapy, a relative newcomer on the therapeutic scene, has shown an amazing ability to provide an overarching and encompassing theory of psychological development and change. Perhaps more than any other extant system, it shows promise as an integrative therapy (Alford, 1995; Alford & Beck, 1997). In this chapter, I will trace the history and derivation of cognitive psychotherapy and give some recommendations for its future development.

In one sense, we owe everything to Sigmund Freud. Although several of his concepts were more culture-specific than they appeared to be at the time and some have been demonstrated to be in error, many of his central concepts have heavily influenced and become part of western culture. Two of his ideas—the theory of unconscious processes and motivation and the developmental antecedents of behavior—were truly revolutionary and caused him considerable difficulty with both religious and secular authorities of the time. To understand just how revolutionary these concepts really were, recall that until that time it was assumed that humans were rational creatures who always understood why they did what they did. Furthermore, the whole idea of human development was unknown; children were assumed to be miniature adults and the concept of adolescence was unknown. Another important Freudian idea was that of repression and resistance. Certain ideas were so unacceptable that they could not be allowed in consciousness; however, they continued to influence human actions and attitude, generally in a negative manner. These repressed cognitions could be accessed by a combination of free association and interpretation.

In the United States especially, there was a reaction against the more mentalistic concepts in experimental and applied psychology that was known as behaviorism. Behavioral psychologists argued that human cognitions, although they undeniably existed, were not important in understanding human psychology. All that mattered, and indeed all that could be studied, was externally observable behavior and the environmental contingencies that shaped and maintained it. Behaviorism has been very influential in the United States for decades and even today is an important aspect of many clinical-psychology training programs although many of its techniques were focused on special populations such as people with the mental retardation. More cognitive concepts have steadily infiltrated behaviorism in recent years. Recognizing this, the European Association for Behaviour Therapy changed its name several years ago to the European Association for Behaviour and Cognitive Therapies. On the other hand, its American counterpart, the Association for Advancement of Behavior Therapy defeated a move to add "and Cognitive" to its title.

From the cognitive side, Beck (1976) and Ellis (1962), both in reaction to different aspects of psychoanalysis, independently developed cognitive approaches to psychotherapy. Beck was interested in depression and attempted to validate psychoanalytic themes assumed to be implicated in that disorder. Rather than uncovering themes of inverted anger and hostility, as postulated by analytic thinking he discovered themes of loss and sadness. From these beginnings, Beck developed the cognitive model of depression (negative thoughts of self, the world, and the future) and the cognitive processing distortions (such as arbitrary inference and selective abstraction) that underlie this and other psychological disorders. Becks's cognitive therapy has undergone extensive modifications over the years and has been extended to anxiety and phobias (Beck & Emery, 1985), personality disorders (Beck, Freeman, & Associates, 1990), substance abuse (Beck, Wright, Newman, & Liese, 1993), suicide (Freeman & Reinecke, 1993), and bipolar disorder (Basco & Rush, 1996), in addition to other more specific psychological problems (e.g., Freeman & Dattilio, 1992). Although cognitive therapy has developed a rich armamentarium of techniques (see, for example, Freeman, Pretzer, Fleming, & Simon, 1990; McMullin, 1986), the process of identifying and challenging automatic thoughts is probably the most commonly used technique.

Ellis likewise identified cognitive processing errors which he described as irrational thoughts (for isntance, "awfulizing," and jumping to conclusions.). One of Ellis's major contributions is the distinction between rational and irrational thoughts, the former expressed as preferences and the latter expressed as demands (or "musts"). Another important contribution follows from the A-B-C model, wherein emotional consequences (C) are thought to be caused by one's beliefs about upsetting events, not by the events themselves. Therefore, these emotional consequences can be changed by "vigorously disputing" the beliefs (B) about the situation (A). Rational-Emotive-Behavior therapy (REBT) likewise has been applied to a large variety of problems (Ellis & Bernard, 1985) and although it includes a large number of techniques (e.g., Ellis & MacLaren, 1998), the central intervention is the identification and disputation of irrational thoughts that are thought to be responsible for the original emotional upset. Ellis also distinguishes between *elegant REBT,* which involves a profound philosophical shift towards healthier thinking and *inelegant REBT,* which involves only an application of rational thinking to more circumscribed problems without generalization necessarily to other concerns. Over the years and in response to criticisms, Ellis has modified his thinking away from a strictly cognitive approach; in the process changing the name of his therapy from *rational therapy* (RT) to *rational-emotive therapy* (RET) to *rational-emotive-behavior therapy* (REBT) to reflect these shifts.

From the behavioral side, Albert Bandura and Donald Meichenbaum were the seminal figures. Although originally a behaviorist, Bandura (1977a, 1977b) developed social learning theory, based on the principle of reciprocal influence or counterconditioning. Essentially, he was able to demonstrate that individuals are not only shaped by their environment, they also shape that environment, indicating that behavioral influence was not unidirectional. Second, his research showed that a *perceived* reinforcer was more reinforcing than an *actual* reinforcer that was not perceived to be reinforcing. Third, he found that individuals did not have to be directly reinforced for performing a behavior in order for it to occur; it was sufficient to observe another person being reinforced for performing that behavior. These empirical findings indicated that the behavioral assumption of an invariant and automatic connection between reinforcer and response was not necessarily true. Internal cognitive processes appeared to mediate this connection.

Donald Meichenbaum, who was originally trained as a behaviorist, made an important discovery in the early 1970s. People talk to themselves. This private speech, which at first is overt in young children and is later covert, serves as an important regulator of behavior. Although he began his work with training impulsive children to be less impulsive by instructing themselves about a task to be performed, he later broadened his theory to include adults. Meichenbaum (1977) developed a three-stage model of psychological change. In the first stage, clients become aware of their behavior and their internal dialogue about it. For example, clients may approach any difficult task with "I-can't-manage-this" type of internal dialogue. They are then trained to emit incompatible behavior and the internal dialogue that is associated with it. In other words, they are trained do things differently and to talk to themselves differently about it. Finally, they are trained to exhibit this new behavior in their environment and to think differently about it.

Meichenbaum's theory is still behavioral in nature because he advocated changing behavior first and the internal dialogue about it afterwards. He saw the change in the internal dialogue within the psychotherapeutic relationship as learning to think differently about events and problems, as the client's language system comes to more closely resemble the therapist's. He stated: "As a result of therapy a *translation* process takes place . . . The translation is from the internal dialogue the client engaged in prior to therapy to a new language system that emerges over the course of treatment" (1977, p. 217). Thus, Meichenbaum can be seen as a precursor of what has come to be called *constructivism,* which will be discussed later.

THE CURRENT STATUS OF COGNITIVE PSYCHOTHERAPY

Cognitive therapy and rational-emotive-behavior therapy have both been criticized for being too nonhistorical in nature, whereby only the current maintaining causes of irrational thinking and dysfunctional cognitions are examined and changed. Ellis in particular has argued that consideration of a client's developmental history and its role in creating and maintaining irrational beliefs amounts to practicing psychoanalysis. As Beck extended his cognitive therapy to personality disorders, however, he modified his theory to take into account clients' developmental histories and the cognitive distortions arising from them. This is well illustrated in the recent work on identifying and changing *intermediate beliefs* and *core beliefs,* as well as the childhood experiences that led to these beliefs (e.g., J. S. Beck, 1995). Intermediate beliefs are considered to lie somewhere between automatic assumptions about specific situations and core beliefs, and they are generally expressed as "if-then" statements (for example, "*If* I don't do as well as others, *then* I'm a failure" or "*If* I trust others, *then* I will be hurt"). Core beliefs are tacit beliefs about the nature of reality that cannot be expressed verbally without considerable help from the therapist. Because they are largely inexpressible and are part of the client's "deep cognitive structure," clients are often unwilling or unable to examine the evidence against their validity. Core beliefs are experienced by people, if they consciously think about them at all, as "just the way things are."

J. S. Beck (1995) has divided core beliefs into two domains, *helpless core beliefs* and *unlovable core beliefs,* corresponding to A. T. Beck's vulnerability domains of *autonomy* and *sociotropy* (Beck, Epstein, & Harrison, 1983). However, other core beliefs can be hypothesized, such as, "I must always be on guard against others" or "I must fight for everything I get." These intermediate and core beliefs are then connected with relevant childhood data that are hypothesized to lead to the beliefs, along with compensatory strategies that enable clients to cope with the beliefs. Finally, along with problematical situations, automatic thoughts arising from them, the meaning of these thoughts, and subsequent emotions and behavior, all are developed into a rich and elaborate client cognitive conceptualization diagram (J. S. Beck, 1995).

In Italy, Vittorio Guidano (1987) also examined the influence of early cognitive organization on subsequent thoughts and behaviors. Guidano introduced two concepts that were soon to become important; motor theories of the mind and tacit knowledge. Motor theories assume that the mind is not simply an information-processing organ, as the early cognitive therapists appear to have believed, but that it actively constructs reality through its interaction with incoming stimuli and its interpretation and classification of those stimuli, based on prior organizing cognitive constructs. Tacit knowledge consists of deep, abstract, unverbalized rules that organize an individual's perception of self and the world. Guidano developed the concept of personal cognitive organization (P.C.Org.), the specific organization of personal knowing processes, and applied this construct to an analysis of the cognitive organizations behind several psychological problems.

An alternative theory for the assessment of clients' core cognitive structures and the modification of these structures in therapy has been developed by Jeffrey Young (1994, 1996), called schema-focused therapy. A schema can be defined as "a cognitive structure for screening, coding, and evaluating the stimuli that impinge on the organism" (Beck, 1967) and is an organizing process to differentiate, categorize, screen in, and screen out the large number of stimuli impinging on the sensory receptors of any organism. No one can pay attention to *everything,* and a schema functions like a cognitive map to determine what is noticed and processed and what is not. It allows individuals to categorize and interpret experiences meaningfully. Schemas act as screening templates, created by one's experiences and in turn determining how subsequent experiences are processed and interpreted. Because of this self-reflexive nature, wherein schemas are both caused by interpretation of experiences and in turn determine the interpretation of subsequent experiences, they are very resistant to alternative constructions of reality and tend to be self-perpetuating (Lewicki, Hill, & Czyzewska, 1992).

Central to Young's (1994; 1996) theory is the concept of early maladaptive schema (EMS). EMS's are dysfunctional schemas that develop as the result of early experiences with significant others, such as caregivers or peers. Because they are developed early, sometimes before the acquisition of formal language structures, they are a form of tacit knowledge (Dowd & Courchaine, 1996) and cannot be easily observed, much less evaluated. They therefore are a form of core beliefs and are generally quite resistant to change.

Young (1994) has developed an assessment categorization system and instrument (the Schema Questionnaire) for early maladaptive schemas. Currently there are 18 EMS's, organized into five themes: disconnection and rejection; impaired autonomy and performance; impaired limits; other-directedness, and overvigilance and inhibition. The initial phase of schema-focused therapy is devoted to an assessment of the client's specific EMS's. Young states that clients typically possesses two or three EMS's.

Because these early maladaptive schemas are a form of core beliefs or tacit knowledge, techniques other than traditional verbal cognitive psychotherapy may be necessary. Young (1994; 1996) has suggested imagery, the "life review," schema (two-chair) dialogue, and schema flash cards. However, more traditional methods are also used, such as performing new behaviors and examining schemas triggered within the therapy relationship. Because these schemas are very entrenched and resistant to change, more repetition is required than in traditional cognitive therapy. In general, these techniques depend less on verbal (left-brain) processing and more on imaginal (right-brain) processing.

Resistance is a psychological phenomenon that has intrigued and baffled psychologists since Freud. Even when apparently willing (and sometimes desperately wishing) to change, clients often sabotage the very therapeutic process designed to help them. Therapists of may persuasions have had different explanations for this paradox, from unconscious client conflicts to inappropriate therapeutic techniques. These various views of resistance explicitly or implicitly assume that it is an undesirable expression of neurotic needs and is therefore something to be worked on and overcome. However, a cognitive view of resistance sees it as both necessary and inevitable. In this view, the therapeutic task is to work with and accept resistance. Mahoney (1988a; 1988b) states that resistance is self-protective and often adaptive. He argues that "resistance to change serves as a natural and often healthy function in protecting core organizing processes (and hence systemic integrity) from rapid or sweeping reconstructive assault" (1988b, p. 300). Similarly, Liotti (1987) argues that therapeutic resistance arises primarily from the individual's natural resistance to the displacement of old meaning structures by new ones, including a sense of personal identity. The resistance to change is a function of its past ability to predict events along with its centrality to the individual's experience and personal identity. Those self-schemas that have been highly predictive or very central to an individual's meaning system are more resistant to change. Meichenbaum and Gilmore (1982) state that resistance is a reluctance to consider data that do not confirm one's preexisting view of the world, a point that is supported by Lewicki et al. (1992), as discussed earlier. Certain individuals, especially those for whom a strong sense of personal autonomy and identity are important, may be especially resistant (Dowd, 1999).

Thus, resistance to change is a necessary part of the integrity of the human cognitive system, which is deeply conservative and preservative. Core beliefs (core cognitive schemas) are an aspect of tacit or implicit knowledge, which can be defined as knowledge that exists out of conscious awareness and recall. Rather than factual knowledge, which is explicit knowledge, implicit knowledge can be expressed as tacit rules for living, such as, "The world is a dangerous place" or "People can't be trusted." Insofar as people can think and talk about their implicit knowledge, it is experienced simply as "the way things are." One's culture is an important aspect of one's tacit knowledge base and people's cognitive structures are shaped by the cultural assumptions of their society; indeed, the very definition of "irrational" thoughts and how they differ from "rational" ones may be partially culturally based. The difference between explicit and implicit knowledge can be expressed as the difference between "knowing that" and "knowing how" (Tataryn, Nadel, & Jacobs, 1989). Implicit knowledge occurs faster than explicit knowledge, is laid down early in life, and thereafter is only elaborated upon; therefore, it is particularly resistant to change (Dowd & Courchaine, 1996). Indeed, Seger (1994) found that when explicit learning was opposed to conflicting implicit knowledge, the former tended to be disregarded. Clients, as well as other individuals, tend to discount ideas that are strongly opposed to what they already believe, so repeated cognitive disputes and challenges are necessary to modify these entrenched cognitive structures. This is especially true when these structures are culture-based.

The modification of core cognitive structures may require some additional techniques. Hypnosis in particular has been thought to access early developmental schemas and to bypass conscious resistance (Dowd, 1997b). In addition, Dowd and Courchaine (1996) discuss consciousness streaming (similar to free association), mirror time (examining oneself in a mirror for an extended period of time), divided consciousness, and the matching of the client's current mood to the mood at the time of original learning as ways of changing core cognitive structures.

The focus on core cognitive structures fits well with the increasing interest in constructivism (Dowd, 1998; Mahoney, 1995a), which argues that reality is socially constructed rather than strictly representational. Constructivism is a philosophical alternative to logical positivism and is often referred to as postmodernism, since it rests on a different epistemological base (Lyddon & Weill, 1997). Reality is considered created rather than apprehended and understood. The "truth" of a therapeutic system therefore is not in its objective reality but whether it is useful to the client. Thus, utility rather than immutable truth is the criterion. Michael Mahoney has stated the following:

> Constructive metatheory, on the other hand, (a) adopts a more proactive (versus reactive and representational) view of cognition and the organism, (b) emphasizes tacit (unconscious) core ordering processes, and (c) promotes a complex systems model in which thought, feeling, and behavior are interdependent expressions of a life span developmental unfolding of interactions between self and (primarily social) systems. (1995a, p 8)

Constructivism involves a fundamental shift from the assessment and modification of irrational (by cultural definition) cognitions to an examination of the client's existing tacit assumptions and meaning structures and the co-creation (with the therapist) of new meaning structures.

Some empirical evidence for a constructivistic explanation of therapeutic change has been shown, for example, by Claiborn and Dowd (1985) who found that the content of an interpretation made little difference in therapeutic outcome. Discrepancy, or the difference between the therapist's and the client's interpretation of an event did, however; a moderate discrepancy between the two was more productive that either a high or low discrepancy. The important point is that the therapist should consistently lead the client with a moderate interpretation discrepancy.

Narrative cognitive therapy (Goncalves, 1994; Russell, 1991) is a natural expression of a constructivistic approach. Narrative therapy assumes that people mentally represent information about themselves and the world by narratives that they construct about their lives and their place in the world. Individuals are seen as storytellers who create narrative structures to explain their life structures. These stories are metaphorical and imaginative. Therapy then becomes the creation of alternative narratives and consequently alternative meaning structures to explain the past and create the future.

FUTURE DEVELOPMENTS

In its short history, cognitive psychotherapy has moved from a relatively nonhistorical examination of an individual's current self-statements or automatic assumptions to a broader and deeper examination of the developmental antecedents of those self-statements and the core ordering processes behind them. In addition, the explanatory mechanism behind cognitive psychotherapy has shifted from an information-processing metaphor to a socially and culturally construction metaphor. Though it appears that an analysis and modification of these self-statements can have significant therapeutic benefit, more lasting results may occur from a consideration of the precursors of the cognitive themes behind these self-statements. This appears to be especially true when dealing with long-standing problems and personality disorders, rather than acute psychological distress. The term cognitive-developmental therapy might be more appropriate for these concepts and the interventions derived from them.

What does the future hold? There appear to be several trends emerging that might indicate future directions for cognitive psychotherapy. First, although cognitive psychotherapy has been applied to an increasing number of psychological disorders (cf. Salkovskis, 1996), almost all of the research and theoretical development has been conducted with individual psychotherapy in mind. Very little has been written, for example, about cognitive psychotherapy in groups or with families. However, as Mahoney (1995b) notes, constructivism has heavily infiltrated the family therapy movement. Cognitive psychotherapy, especially its more constructivist approach, could easily be applied to families and group. Mahoney has also discussed the application of cognitive psychotherapy models to the analysis of change events within the psychotherapy process.

Second, there has been very little written about cognitive psychotherapy applied to questions of *ultimate* meaning, the kind usually left for religious practitioners. There are potentially significant points of contact between religion and psychotherapy (cf Dowd, 1997c) that could profitably be explored further. Questions of meaning, at different levels, are common to religion and psychotherapy and both must deal constantly with these expressions of the human condition.

Third, more work needs to be done to connect the large literature on cognitive psychotherapy with the equally vast literature on cognitive psychology. The two domains have been surprisingly separate and only a few attempts have been made to bridge the gap (for example, Dowd & Courchaine, 1996; Fleming, Heikkinen, & Dowd, 1992; Stein & Young, 1992; Tataryn et al., 1989). Cognitive psychology has acquired much data to inform the cognitive psychotherapist about the mechanisms and resistance to psychological and behavioral change.

Fourth, cognitive psychotherapy, like many other systems of psychological change, has a boundary problem. As can be seen from the previous discussion, the concepts and techniques in cognitive psychotherapy have steadily expanded from a focus on immediate self-statements and automatic assumptions to include an examination of core cognitive schemas and their developmental antecedents as well as the constructivist model. In addition, cognitive psychotherapy has begun to incorporate a constructivist and narrative epistemological framework. Cognitive psychotherapy has even been proposed as an integrating theory of psychotherapy (Alford, 1995). This expansionist movement has had its critics (for an examination of this controversy, see the special issue of the *Journal of Cognitive Psychotherapy* on cognitive psychotherapy and postmodernism [Lyddon & Weill, 1997]). As the theory and techniques expand to include concepts and techniques formerly thought to belong to other systems of psychotherapy, it becomes more difficult to determine what is cognitive psychotherapy and what is not. However, if cognitive psychotherapy does not continue to change and develop, it risks becoming static and ossified and may lose influence. The difficulty is in continuing to expand its boundaries without creating a situation in which everything is seen as cognitive psychotherapy.

Fifth, although cognitive psychotherapy has been consistently demonstrated as more effective than a no-treatment control condition, it has not been shown to be consistently more effective than a variety of other treatments. Although the evidence is mixed, it does appear to be consistently more effective that control or placebo effects, at least as effective as (and occasionally more effective than) alternative treatments, and especially helpful in preventing relapse. Furthermore, it is at least as effective with anxiety disorders as depression and shows considerable promise with the more entrenched personality disorders and substance abuse. There is also evidence that cognitive psychotherapy may be differentially effective with different types of clients (Beutler et al., 1991). Externalizing clients and low-defensive clients improved more with cognitive psychotherapy whereas the reverse was true for supportive therapy. These client X treatment interaction effects may be one reason why some studies have found no overall outcome differences among different treatments. In addition, there are some indications that different outcome rates in different treatment sites in the NIMH collaborative study may have resulted in lower outcome rates for cognitive therapy (Jacobson & Hollon, 1996). Jacobson and Hollon also argue that studies involving pill-placebo conditions might make the results more interpretable because they can then account for nonspecific effects. Finally, Ollendick (1998) argues that the use of manualized treatment procedures may be one reason why cognitive behavior therapy procedures may not be more effective. He found evidence among those who had been classified as failures using manualized treatment procedures that the subsequent use of individualized treatment procedures resulted in an increase in the percentage of individuals responding to CBT for school refusal, PTSD, and specific phobias for animals.

Cognitive psychotherapy has shown tremendous growth in the last 25 years and promises to be influential in the future. Although equivocal comparative results have been found for depression, the differential effectiveness of cognitive therapy appears somewhat stronger for the anxiety disorders. In addition, cognitive therapy appears to significantly reduce relapse and show promise for other disorders. Substantial work remains to be done to define its boundaries and through further investigations to show its effectiveness in treating a variety of disorders, yet substantial progress has already been made. Cognitive (behavioral) psychotherapy has been shown to be at least as effective as many pharmacological interventions and to be more or as effective as most psychosocial interventions. I expect future work to demonstrate cognitive therapy's ability to treat a variety of psychological disorders and to show that it is truly an integrative therapy.

REFERENCES

Alford, B. A. (Ed.). (1995). Psychotherapy integration and cognitive psychotherapy [Special issue]. *Journal of Cognitive Psychotherapy: An International Quarterly, 9,* 147–212.

Alford, B. A., & Beck, A. T. (1997). *The integrating power of cognitive therapy.* New York: Guilford.

Bandura, A. (1977a). Self-efficacy: Toward a unifying theory of behavior change. *Psychological Review, 84,* 191–215.

Bandura, A. (1977b). *Social learning theory.* Englewood Cliffs, NJ: Prentice-Hall.

Basco, M. R., & Rush, A. J. (1996). *Cognitive-behavioral therapy for bipolar disorder.* New York: Guilford.

Beck, A. T. (1967). *Depression: Clinical, experimental, and theoretical aspects.* New York: Harper & Row.

Beck, A. T. (1976). *Cognitive therapy and the emotional disorders.* New York: International Universities Press.

Beck, A. T., & Emery, G. (1985). *Anxiety disorders and phobias: A cognitive perspective.* New York: Basic Books.

Beck, A. T., Epstein, N., & Harrison, R. (1983). Cognitions, attitudes, and personality dimensions in depression. *British Journal of Cognitive Psychotherapy, 1,* 1–16.

Beck, A. T., Freeman, A., & Associates (1990). *Cognitive therapy of personality disorders.* New York: Guilford.

Beck, A. T., Wright, F. D., Newman, C. F., & Liese, B. S. (1993). *Cognitive therapy of substance abuse.* New York: Guilford.

Beck, J. S. (1995). *Cognitive therapy: Basics and beyond.* New York: Guilford.

Beutler, L. E. et al. (1991). Predictors of differential response to cognitive, experiential, and self-directed psychotherapeutic procedures. *Journal of Consulting and Clinical Psychology, 59,* 333–340.

Claiborn, C. D., & Dowd, E. T. (1985) attributional interpretations in counseling: Content versus discrepancy. *Journal of Counseling Psychology, 32,* 188–196.

Dowd, E. T. (1997a). The use of hypnosis in cognitive-developmental therapy. In R. Leahy (Ed.), *Practicing cognitive therapy* (pp. 21–36). New York: Jason Aronson.

Dowd, E. T. (1997b). What makes people really change (and what stops them from changing)? Symposium presentation at the 27th Congress of the European Association for Behaviour and Cognitive Therapies, Venice, Italy.

Dowd, E. T. (Ed.). (1998). Social construction in counselling psychology. *Counselling Psychology Quarterly, 11,* 133–222.

Dowd, E. T. (1999). Why don't people change? What stops them from changing? An integrative commentary on the Special Issue on resistance. *Journal of Psychotherapy Integration, 9,* 119–131.

Dowd, E. T. (in press). Toward a briefer therapy: Overcoming resistance and reactance in the therapeutic process. In W. J. Matthews & J. Edgette (Eds.), *Current thinking and research in brief therapies: Solutions, strategies, narratives (Vol. III).* New York: Brunner/Mazel.

Dowd, E. T., & Courchaine, K. E. (1996). Implicit learning, tacit knowledge, and implications for stasis and change in cognitive psychotherapy. *Journal of Cognitive Psychotherapy: An International Quarterly, 10,* 163–180.

Ellis, A. (1962). *Reason and emotion in psychotherapy.* Secaucus, NJ: Citadel.

Ellis, A., & Bernard, M. E. (1985). *Clinical applications of rational-emotive therapy.* New York: Plenum.

Ellis, A., & MacLaren, C. (1998). Rational-emotive-behavior therapy: A therapist's guide. San Luis Obispo, CA: Impact.

Fleming, K., Heikkinen, R., & Dowd, E. T. (1992). Cognitive therapy: The repair of memory. *Journal of Cognitive Psychotherapy: An International Quarterly, 6,* 155–174.

Freeman, A., & Dattilio, F. M. (1992). *Comprehensive casebook of cognitive therapy.* New York: Plenum.

Freeman, A., & Reinecke, M. A. (1993). *Cognitive therapy of suicidal behavior.* New York: Springer.

Freeman, A., Pretzer, J., Fleming, B., & Simon, K. M. (1990). *Clinical applications of cognitive therapy.* New York: Plenum.

Goncalves, O. F. (1994). Cognitive narrative psychotherapy: The hermeneutic construction of alternative meanings. *Journal of Cognitive Psychotherapy: An International Quarterly, 8,* 105–125.

Guidano, V. F. (1987). *Complexity of the self: A developmental approach to psychopathology and therapy.* New York: Guilford.

Jacobson, N. S., & Hollon, S. D. (1996). Cognitive-behavior therapy versus pharmacotherapy: Now that the jury's returned its verdict, it's time to present the rest of the evidence. *Journal of Consulting and Clinical Psychology, 64,* 74–80.

Lewicki, P., Hill, T., & Czyzewska, M. (1992). Nonconscious acquisition of information. *American Psychologist, 47,* 796–801.

Liotti, G. (1987). The resistance to change of cognitive structures: A counterproposal to psychoanalytic metapsychology. *Journal of Cognitive Psychotherapy: An International Quarterly, 1,* 87–104.

Lyddon, W. J., & Weill, R. (1997). Cognitive psychotherapy and postmodernism: Emerging themes and challenges. *Journal of Cognitive Psychotherapy: An International Quarterly, 11,* 75–90.

Mahoney, M. J. (1988a). Constructive metatheory I. Basic features and historical foundations. *International Journal of Personal Construct Psychology, 1,* 1–35.

Mahoney, M. J. (1988b). Constructive metatheory II. Implications for psychotherapy. *International Journal of Personal Construct Psychology, 1,* 299–316.

Mahoney, M. J. (1995a). Theoretical developments in the cognitive and constructivistic psychotherapies. In M. J. Mahoney (Ed.), *Cognitive and constructive psychotherapies: Theory, research, and practice.* New York: Springer.

Mahoney, M. J. (1995b). The cognitive and constructive psychotherapies: Contexts and challenges. In M. J. Mahoney (Ed.), *Cognitive and constructive psychotherapies: Theory, research, and practice.* New York: Springer.

McGinn, L. K., & Young, J. E. (1996). Schema-focused therapy. In P.M. Salkovskis (Ed.), *Frontiers of cognitive therapy.* New York: Guilford.

McMullin, R. E. (1986). *Handbook of cognitive therapy techniques.* New York: Norton.

Meichenbaum, D. (1977). *Cognitive-behavior modification: An integrative approach.* New York: Plenum.

Meichenbaum, D., & Gilmore, B. (1982). Resistance: From a cognitive-behavioral perspective. In P. Watchel (Ed.), *Resistance in psychodynamic and behavioral therapies.* New York: Plenum.

Ollendick, T. H. (1998). Functional analysis and manualized treatments. Symposium presentation at the annual meeting of the *Association for Advancement of Behavior Therapy,* Washington D.C.

Russell, R. L. (Ed.). (1991). Narrative [Special issue]. *Journal of Cognitive Psychotherapy: An International Quarterly, 5,* 239–304.

Salkovskis, P. M. (Ed.). (1996). *Frontiers of cognitive therapy.* New York: Guilford.

Seger, C. A. (1994). Implicit learning. *Psychological Bulletin, 115,* 163–196.

Stein, D. J., & Young, J. E. (1992). *Cognitive science and clinical disorders.* San Francisco: Academic Press.

Tataryn, D. J., Nadel, L., & Jacobs, W. J. (1989). Cognitive therapy and cognitive science. In A. Freeman, K. M. Simon, L. E. Beutler, & H. Arkowitz (Eds.), *Comprehensive handbook of cognitive therapy* (pp. 85–98). New York: Plenum.

Young, J. E. (1994). *Cognitive therapy for personality disorders: A schema-focused approach* (Rev. ed.). Sarasota, FL: Professional Resource Press.

CHAPTER 2

Cognitive Models of Depression

Aaron T. Beck, M.D.

The cognitive theory of depression is based essentially on an information-processing model. A pronounced and prolonged negative biasing of this process is manifest in the characteristic thinking disorder in depression (selective abstraction, overgeneralization, negative self-attributions).

It is apparent that the original elaboration of cognitive processes in depression needs expansion. Indeed, the variety of ways in which the cognitive processes in depression have been conceptualized warrants the presentation of six separable but overlapping models. The *cross-sectional* model states that the systematic negativity that pervades the cognitive processes is a necessary (but not sufficient) component of depression. The *structural* model stipulates that certain negatively biased schemas become hypervalent in depression and shift the cognitive processes suffi-ciently to produce a systematic bias in the abstraction of data, interpreta-tion, short-term memory, and long-term memory. The *stressor-vulnerability* model stipulates that specific patterns of schemas make a person sensitive to specific stressors. The *reciprocal-interaction* model focuses on the ways that interaction with key figures is relevant to the predisposition, precipitation, aggravation, prolongation, and recurrence of depression. The *psychobiological* model integrates genetic, neurochemical, views cogni-tive processes and biological processes as different sides of the same coin. Further, this model integrates genetic, neurochemical, physiologi-cal, psychological, affective, and behavioral aspects of this disorder. The *evolutionary* model views depression as an atavistic mechanism or program that may have been adaptational in a prehistoric environment but is not adaptive in our current milieu.

In order to function in the myriad of life situations, we are continuously dependent on observing, taking in, interpreting, and storing data from our environment. Further, we rely on feedback to inform us as to the accuracy or utility of our interpretations and the outcome of the actions we take in response to these interpretations. Without a reasonable method of abstracting and appraising the information regarding the nature and demands of a particular situation, we could not marshal the appropriate behaviors to deal with it. The various gross and fine adjustments necessary for smooth adaptation, moreover, require continuous processing of feedback. Without this type of adjustment and readjustment, we would walk around like zombies and would eventually get killed or die of starvation.

The usual processes for utilizing information are modified in depression. The depressive shows deviations not only in the initial appraisal of the signs and signals he observes, but also in his interpretation of feedback regarding his behavior. Although the cognitive processing system does not deviate sufficiently to produce death (except from suicide), it is dysfunctional enough to lead to vast amounts of misery. I have previously proposed a cognitive model to explain the dysfunctional and distressing phenomena of depression (Beck, 1963, 1964, 1967). With the large number of studies of depression in recent years, it has become apparent that the original model is insufficient to account for all of the recent findings and needs to be expanded. Articles by Krantz (1985) and by Coyne and Gotlib (1983), for example, have prompted a further expansion of the model to encompass the role of social factors in predisposing, precipitating, and maintaining depression as well as facilitating relapse. Depending on the unit of observation and the level of analysis, this model can be viewed from various perspectives: cross-sectional, structural, stressor-vulnerability, interactive, psychobiological, and evolutionary. In a sense, these perspectives constitute independent models, which can be tested separately from each other or in various combinations. The elaboration of the perspective may help to clarify a number of important issues raised by Krantz (1985) and Coyne and Gotlib (1983).

Before reviewing the specific cognitive models of depression, it would be helpful to make a distinction between descriptive models, explanatory models, and causal or etiological models. Much of the literature on the psychology of depression is misleading because a clear distinction between each of these models is often lacking. At times, for instance, description and explanation are confused with each other and both are confused with causality. The *descriptive* cognitive model simply stipulates that a group of affective, cognitive, and behavioral phenomena tend to covary in such a manner as to constitute a syndrome, a pattern of reaction, or a disorder. The model stipulates that cognitive processes or abnormalities are an intrinsic part of depression (Beck, 1963).

The *explanatory* model attempts to arrange the various symptoms of depression in such a way as to establish some kind of pattern by ordering them into a particular sequence or describing them as part of a mechanism. The various symptoms of depression, for example, could be attributed to the increased salience of negative cognitive structures. The *causal* or etiological model delineates the distal (or predisposing) factors and the proximal (or precipitating) factors in the genesis of depression. The kinds of determinants, for instance, could be expanded to include a wide variety of genetic, developmental, hormonal, physical, and psychosocial factors. These factors combine in varying proportions in a given case to form the final common pathway that leads to the activation of depression.

CROSS-SECTIONAL MODEL

Negativity and Exclusivity Hypotheses

This model asserts that negative cognitive content is an integral part of the depressive symptomatology and is as much a symptom as the affect of sadness or the behavioral impairments or deficiencies. The descriptive model was based initially on a systematic evaluation of 966 psychiatric patients (Beck, 1967), which demonstrated a pervasive negativity in the thought content of depressed patients. The intensity of those negative evaluations increased in a stepwise progression with an increase in other manifestations of depression. Thus, highly depressed patients showed a high level of self-criticism, negative expectations, and a negative view of past experience.

Another aspect of the negativity was the observation that a high proportion of these patients experienced negative "automatic thoughts" that were repetitive, persistent, and not readily controllable (Beck, 1963). These negative thoughts at times dominated the patient's consciousness to the point that it was difficult for him to concentrate on anything else. Finally, there appeared to be a decrement in positive ideas and recollections almost to the point of expunging any personally favorable evaluations.

The clinical observation regarding the pervasiveness of negative themes in the ideation of depressed patients has been borne out by a number of studies. A recent study by Eaves (1982), for example, showed that the Automatic Thought Questionnaire (Hollon & Kendall, 1980) was able to separate correctly 97% of depressives from normal subjects and did not misidentify any of the normals as depressed. This questionnaire was designed to assess the prevalence of negative automatic thoughts experienced by depressed patients. Eaves's study would tend to support the universality of these cognitions in depression. Since this study did not attempt to assess automatic thoughts in other psychopathological groups, it is not possible to confirm to what degree nondepressed psychiatric patients might also experience this type of ideation.

However, a more recent study by Beck, Brown, Riskind, and Steer (1986), using the Cognition Checklist (CCL), showed high correlations of depressive-type cognitions with clinical ratings of depression and of danger-type cognitions with ratings of anxiety. Further, the depression and anxiety scales of the CCL clearly differentiated depression and anxiety. Additional support for the relevance of cognitive factors to depression was provided by a study showing that, compared to anxious patients, depressed patients assigned high probabilities to a negative outcome of their specific problems and low probabilities to a positive outcome (Beck, Riskind, Brown, & Sherrod, 1986). Finally, Beck, Brown, and Steer (1986) showed that the cognitive items accounted for more of the variance in the Hamilton Rating Scale of Depression than did the affective and somatic items.

The cross-sectional model stipulates further that these negative cognitive phenomena are present in all types of depression. Whether it is a bipolar, unipolar, endogenous, reactive, or organic depression, the same cognitive factors will appear; these various subtypes of depression are indistinguishable on the basis of the cognitive symptomatology (Eaves & Rush, 1984).

The cognitive manifestations have not traditionally been considered to be part of the symptomatology of depression, probably because they are not in themselves painful (as is sadness), nor do they seem to represent an obvious disability in the same sense that psychomotor retardation is a disability. Furthermore, since the patients regard the negative evaluations as plausible and reasonable, it does not occur to them to report them as symptoms. Nonetheless, since negative thinking appears to be universal in depression and leads to sadness and behavioral difficulties, it should be accorded the rank of a diagnostic sign. The negativity hypothesis simply implies a pervasiveness of negative cognitions; it does not take a position on whether they are accurate. The exclusivity hypothesis refers to the automatic exclusion of positive self-evaluations (and the retention of negative evaluations). Schwartz and Garomoni (1986) have presented an intriguing thesis regarding the relative proportion of positive and negative cognitions in nondepressed and depressed persons. Nondepressed people show a ratio of approximately 1.7 to 1.0 of positive to negative cognitions (the "normal dialogue"), whereas the depressed show a monopoly of negative cognitions (the "depressive dialogue").

The numerous clinical observations of the depressives' tendency to downgrade their personal attributes and performance, exaggerate the insolubility of problems, and forecast negative outcomes have been supported by many studies (see Rush & Beck, 1978).

The Negative Bias and Primacy Hypotheses

When we move from simple observations of depressive thinking to an understanding of the principles underlying the depressive phenomena, we need to rely more on abstractions and inferences from our observations. I have proposed that depressive thinking represents not simply a mirror of depressives' negative experiences, but a biased sample of these experiences (Beck, 1967, pp. 228–240). This bias appears more at the level of the patient's interpretation of his experiences rather than at the level of his observation and in part is an inevitable outcome of *selective focusing* on the negative aspects and excluding the positive aspects of experience. Thus, while the depressed patient might be accurate in extracting the *negative* details of an event or situation, this type of exclusivity leads to a variety of negative interpretations and elaborations that extend far beyond, and are not justified by, the actual data composing the situation. Furthermore, many of the meanings the patients attach to the experiences are idiosyncratic and are discrepant with the types of meaning that would be attached by nondepressed individuals or by the patients themselves when they are in a nondepressed state (for example, "I'm slowed down; therefore, I'm worthless"; "My thinking is sluggish; therefore, my brain is deteriorating").

This perspective, to some degree, is in disagreement with Krantz's (1985) thesis that the conclusion of a depressed patient may be close to the conclusions that would be reached by others regarding "multiple ongoing problems." We see clinically that recovered depressives often view the same—or worse—problems in a much more benign light than they did during the depression. The different types of deviant thinking led me to postulate the premise of a *thinking disorder*, manifested by selective abstraction, overgeneralization, dichotomous categorization, and personalization (Beck, 1963). This type of thinking occurs not only in the depressive's appraisal of himself and his problems, but also, to a lesser extent, in nondepressed states.

Another way of viewing these thinking problems is in terms of a systematic bias that is manifested by an increasingly distorted cognitive processing process. Thus the various "deviations" may be viewed as successive stages in a chain reaction. The following sequence illustrates the chain of cognitive responses of a depressed woman who attended a social function with her fiancé. During the party her fiancé socialized with the other guests—although he did spend time with the patient. The "information processing" apparently followed this sequence:

Selective Abstraction: "Jerry spent time with the other guests."
Biased Interpretation: "He cared more about them than about me."
Dichotomous Thinking: "He doesn't like me anymore."
Self-Attribution: "I must bore him."
Overgeneralization: "I am a boring person; nobody likes me."
Negative Prediction: "I will always be alone and unhappy."

Note how each conclusion forms the basic assumption for the next conclusion. Of course, the sequence occurs so rapidly that the patient may report only the final conclusion, "I will always be alone, etc." Broad negative appraisals of the self and future may already be built into the cognitive apparatus and, thus, may tend to "draw out" the kind of sequencing illustrated above. In fact, after the depression has settled in, the patient may jump almost immediately from an observation of "being neglected" to the conclusion, "Nobody likes me." The ultimate conclusion may reflect a core schema ("I am unlovable" or "I am weak and helpless") that is activated in moderate to severe depression. Consequently, the progression from an observation to a grim conclusion may be inevitable; the depressive schema organizes the logical processes.

The explanatory model assigns a central role to the cognitive processes in the generation of the affective and behavioral symptoms. The *primacy* hypothesis suggests that if the cognitive or information processing is biased in some way, there is going to be a corresponding modification in the affective responses and in the individual's behavior.* The affective reactions and behavioral responses are congruent with the individual's faulty

---

*The primacy hypothesis simply assigns a note to the various components of the disorder after the depression has developed. It seems unwarranted to assert that "cognitions cause depression." Such statements would be akin to saying that "delusions cause psychosis." I view deviant cognitive processes as intrinsic to the depressive disorder, not a cause or consequence.

appraisal of a situation, not with the situation itself. Thus, if a depressed patient interpreted a spouse's behavior as rejecting he would be prone to feel bad even though the spouse had in actuality been neutral or positive. The cognitive bias, thus, would lead to or intensify other symptoms, such as inappropriate or excessive sadness, inertia, dependency, or suicidal wishes.

The role of the "cognitive triad"—namely the negative view of experience (past and present), the negative view of the future, and the negative view of the self—in activating the other symptoms of depression has been supported by many studies. (For a review see Fleming, Simon, & Pretzer, 1986). One line of inquiry, for example, investigated which psychosocial characteristics would predict ultimate suicide among depressed patients. It was found that the best predictor of subsequent suicide among depressed inpatients (Beck, Steer, Kovacs, & Garrison, 1985) or depressed outpatients (Herold, Beck, Berchick, Brown, & Steer, 1986) was hopelessness, as measured by the Hopelessness Scale and the pessimism item of the Beck Depression Inventory.

Although an accurate view of reality may, in some instances, precipitate or activate a depression, I would argue that the exaggerated negative meanings attached to ongoing experiences are responsible for the buildup and maintenance of the noncognitive symptoms of depression. The adverse reality may serve to start the chain reaction, but the development of a full-blown depression depends on the progressive activation of a specific cluster of depressive cognitive structures. The persistence of negative interpretations and predictions throughout the course of depression may be best understood in terms of the operation of the resulting "negative cognitive set."

In depression the negative cognitive set may remain fixed across most or all situations. Thus, it is operative even though the patient may enter a situation that ordinarily would be considered positive or self-enhancing. In these cases, the preformed set determines the type of data that will be processed rather than the situation determining the nature of the cognitive set, as occurs normally. Whereas an affectionate greeting may generally evoke a self-enhancing set, depressives do not assimilate the positive signals because their set does not change in keeping with the situation. They will selectively attend to negative signs and will weave them into some kind of conclusion relevant to their presumed undesirability or unworthiness. Furthermore, even if a patient acknowledges that a smile indicates affection, he is prone to discount it with such thoughts as, "If she really knew what I was like she would not accept me" or "I'm unworthy of her affection."

When a depressed person receives continuous positive feedback, why does the dysphoria not improve or disappear? Following a disappointment, we ordinarily feel better if we find that initially disappointing information was incorrectly communicated and was actually positive rather than negative, if we get reassurance from another person, or if something good happens to us that overshadows the disappointing event.

Depressed patients, however, are locked into the notion that nothing matters, that nothing will ever really work out, that their plight is hopeless. The sense of futility pervades or hovers over every cognitive appraisal. Thus, even though the depressive may be reasonably accurate in a cognitive appraisal (for example, "They seem to like me"), the overall meaning is still a negative one: "if they knew how worthless I was, they would not like me." Even though situations may be favorable and indeed may temporarily reduce dysphoria and introduce some satisfaction, the overall set of futility persists. As long as the negative set persists, the dysphoria will persist and the patient will be stripped of motivation to engage in any goal-directed activity because of the sense of futility.

To summarize, depressed patients' thinking is characterized by the following:

1. Predominant emphasis on the negative aspects of life events, a pervasive preoccupation with the possible adverse meanings or consequences of events, and a blotting out of positive aspects, meanings and consequences. There is a negation of the self-serving bias that often enables people to mobilize themselves to more effective functioning.

2. Self-attribution for problems across all situations. Thus, while it is possible that the patients may be responsible for a few of their mishaps, it is hardly credible that they "cause" every single event for which they blame themselves.

3. Secondary elaboration. The patients not only attribute responsibility to themselves, but devalue their self-worth, adequacy, and lovability and then criticize themselves for falling short of their standards.

4. Overgeneralization. Any particular errors, mishaps, or deficiencies are generalized into a broad spectrum of failure and deficiency that extends not only into the past and present but also into the future— and across all situations.

5. A "blind alley" view of problems. The patients see themselves coming to a dead stop when there is a problem and do not see that the problem can be resolved or ameliorated either spontaneously or by the efforts of themselves or others. Further, there seems to be a reduction in available capacity for generating solutions to problems (see Roy-Byrne, Weingartner, Bierer, Thompson, & Post, 1986).

The combination of these tendencies leads to a one-sided negative self-concept and negative expectancies. This exclusively negative generalized life-view constitutes the real cognitive distortion in depression and is responsible for the all-pervasive sense of futility. It is a view that is not sustained by the patient in the nondepressed state or by objective observers of his state.

Differentiation from Other Disorders

We can contrast syndromes such as depression and anxiety. In depression the patient takes his interpretation and predictions as facts. In anxiety they are simply possibilities. The depressive automatically adjusts his expectations to a low level. In a sense he shuts off his engine since it is "futile" to keep striving. In anxiety, the patient sees the negative consequences as a possibility, but he does see options of better things occurring and also of possible coping, even though the coping strategies may not be immediately available. So he keeps his engine running, as it were, and is in a continuous state of readiness.

In other psychopathological states we can see the same attribution of causality as well as predictions. In hostile or paranoid states the subject reads negative motives into the behavior of other people and tends to disqualify information that would be likely to exculpate the other person. Unlike the depressive, whose distal and ultimate explanations have to do with his own wrongness or badness, the hostile or angry person ascribes wrongness and badness to the other person. In the case of the depressive, he believes that he deserves blame, that the cause of difficulties resides inside him. In the case of the hostile or paranoid person, the cause is in the other individual, who is perceived as wrong and bad. Thus, after an identical interaction, the depressed patient may conclude, "I am no good." And the hostile person may conclude, "He has wronged me; he is bad." Once the direction of the "wrong" is determined, then the appropriate affect is energized. As soon as the hostile person establishes that "He has wronged me," he feels angry. As soon as the depressed patient concludes that "I am wrong," he feels bad.

STRUCTURAL MODEL

The Cognitive Continuum

An important aspect of the structural perspective is the concept of "the cognitive continuum." This particular construct suggests that a specific cognitive set or bias influences information processing from the early stages of perception through working memory, interpretation, recall, and long-term memory. The information processing can be viewed as dependent on the operation of functional units, labeled "schemas (Beck, 1964, 1967).

The Role of Schemas

I have postulated the existence of structures (schemas) to account for the repetitiveness of the same type of thinking in a given individual with each recurrence of the depression and for the striking similarities of the nature of the thinking pattern from one depressed individual to another (Beck, 1963). The idiosyncratic schemas determine the biases in information processing and ultimately shape the interpretations of experience and expectations. Further, the depressive constructions are predominantly "schema-driven" rather than "data-driven," as in normals.

The schemas that are prepotent during depression have a content such as "Since people don't like me, I am nothing" or "Since I failed, I am worthless." These schemas shape the conceptualizations of a particular experience and in turn are reinforced by these biased interpretations. At the deepest level the conditional phrases starting with "since" are dropped out of the rule, and the "core schema" consisting of an absolute concept, such as I am nothing," mold the interpretations of situations. These core schemas appear to be embedded in the cognitive apparatus at an earlier developmental stage, and their effect on self-concept is apparent only in the deeper levels of depression (Beck, 1967).

The personality organization is made up of clusters of attitudes that may, under certain circumstances, increase a person's susceptibility to depression. These "predisposing attitudes" are reflected in relatively stable schemas that reflect the individual's enduring orientations, rules, and behavioral inclinations. Krantz's (1985) view of the schemas as "the basic rules that are relatively independent of current life circumstances" is a welcome refinement of previous presentations of the depressive's rules (Beck, 1976). These rules or schemas have a conditional content ("if" or "when") and become operative when the conditional event occurs.

The reversal in behavior in depression is mediated by the negative cognitive schemas. The generalized negative schemas are pressed onto broad segments of life, work, play, and interpersonal relations. Consequently, the large behavioral systems relevant to these segments are vitiated. The content of the schemas is represented by broad negative attitudes that are accessible to probing. The continuous activation of these schemas can account for the prolonged lassitude, sadness, and chronic inactivity. Thus, we do not have to look for a specific negative automatic thought, prediction, or interpretation to account for the relatively durable negative affects and behavioral deficits. Characteristics can therefore be attributed to the continuous operation of the negative cognitive schemas as reflected in the nihilistic attitudes and sense of futility. Negative attitudes such as "Nothing will work out" promote *loss of initiative;* "It's not worth the effort" fosters *fatigability;* "I can't be happy without somebody to share it with" accentuates *anhedonia;* and "My whole life is empty and meaningless" leads to *apathy.*

In the nondepressed state the prospect of engaging in meaningful activities usually evokes positive affects (enthusiasm, joy); the depressive, however, has already discounted the value of all activities. Hence, his affect is consistent with his cognitive appraisal: apathetic, discouraged. Although the cognitive schemas directly regulate behaviors by deactivating behavioral systems, these *negative affects* also play a role. When sadness, frustration, or apathy emerge when constructive action is contemplated or undertaken by the depressed person, these negative affects enhance the negative expectations, such as the anticipation of more pain.

Cognitive Deficits in Depression

A number of studies have concentrated on the form and adequacy, as opposed to the content, of the thinking of depressed patients. Braff and Beck (1974), for instance, found that hospitalized depressed patients, like schizophrenics and unlike age-matched controls, showed concrete responses to the Gorham Proverbs Test and a test of abstraction ability (Shipley-Hartford Test). Since that time, a number of other investigators have conducted studies of the capacity of depressed patients to engage in a variety of cognitive tests. This work seems to indicate that depressives show a consistent impairment when confronted with cognitive tasks that require "effortful processes" (Clark, Clayton, Andreasen Lewis, Fawcett, & Sheftner, 1985; Roy-Byrne, Weingartner, Bierer, Thompson, & Post, 1986). Free recall of a previously presented list of words, for example, would be considered effortful, as contrasted with recognition of these words, which would not be considered effortful.

Hasher and Zacks (1979) have described the differences between "effortful" and "automatic" processes in cognition. They label as "automatic" those operations that "drain minimal energy from our limited-capacity attentional mechanism." These automatic processes occur without intention and do not interfere with other ongoing cognitive activity. Some of these processes are regarded by the authors as genetically "prepared" and encoded with the fundamental aspects of the flow of information. Other automatic processes develop through practice and "function to prevent the subcomponents of complex skills from overloading our limited-capacity system." These authors found that mild "depression" in college students affected effortful but not automatic learning.

It is possible to postulate a unified explanation for the coexistence of generalized problems in concentration and effortful thinking and the preoccupation with negative meanings found in depressives. We can consider, first of all, whether the negative cognitive set (schemas) is so powerful that it draws off attention that might be available for other cognitive processes such as effortful recall or problem solving. By way of analogy, if we should suddenly be exposed to a life-threatening scene, all of our attention could be so riveted to that scene that other factors in the environment would be precluded from conscious awareness. Further, if our attention is totally fastened on this dramatic scene, we might not be able to engage in other reflective activities. It might be difficult, for example, to assess whether the scene is truly life-threatening. For example, when movie clips of simulated mutilation were shown to subjects their subjective and physiological responses were of the same quality as they would have been if the mutilation had been real (Lazarus & Folkman, 1984). Clearly the subjects were not able to mobilize reality testing sufficiently to dispel the realism of the film.

It could be speculated that the depressive set focuses attention so intensely on the negative configurations and on the automatic negative interpretations that the patients have minimal remaining attentional capacity available to reflect on and reappraise the content and validity of their interpretations. Hence, because of this *fixation* and consequent depletion of available attention, the negative interpretations pass without further interruption into "working memory."

In cognitive therapy, this process is reversed. The strong external stimulation provided by the confrontation and challenges draws the patient's attention away from the negative thinking and onto the task proposed by the therapist. This procedure, by loosening the grip of automatic thinking, also frees up the attention for more reflective thinking.

Another approach to the connection between the rigid negative content of the preoccupation in depression and the problems in abstract thinking is to reconceptualize the negative cognitive set in depression. Once the set (or constellation of schemas) is in place, it shows the following characteristics. First, there is a fixation on certain aspects of external events, namely the negative components. Associated with this is the fixation on the negative interpretation of those events. Negative stimuli are processed automatically and subsequently become conscious. Second, the cognitive set directs much or most of the attention to the negative interpretations, so that minimal attentional capacity is available for higher-level, more complex, effortful cognitive tasks. One of the cognitive functions that suffers is the reappraisal of the negative interpretations. In nondepressed states people may make either reasonable or unreasonable negative interpretations, but are able to "reality-test" them and dismiss them if they appear unreasonable. In depression, however, this capacity to "reality-test" is diminished and the patients are stuck with the negative interpretations that work their way into the working memory and long-term memory.

Is the reduction of abstraction capacity a generalized property of depressive cognition, or is it a secondary consequence of the fixation on the negative? The psychobiological tests certainly suggest a generalized impairment (Braff & Beck, 1974; Clark et al., 1985; Roy-Byrne et al., 1986). If so, the generalized impairment could instigate or aggravate a depression because of the patients' inability to view their negative productions objectively. However, the coincidence of negative thinking and reduction of abstraction capacity needs to be explained. The work of Clark and associates (1985) would seem to suggest that there is no connection between the severity of negative cognitive content and cognitive impairment in the depressed patient. They found no correlation between the degree of low self-esteem, for example, and cognitive impairment. Their finding, however, does not exclude the possibility of a connection between negative cognitive content and cognitive impairment. One of the major characteristics of negative cognitive processing is the increased *plausibility* of the depressive conclusions, a reflection of the reduction in objectivity. If this is the case, we could consider the following formulation: Once the depressive cognitive set is activated, there is a concomitant concentration of attention on the negative appraisals and so forth. Because of this fixation, there is minimal capacity remaining for higher-order functions, whether they are directed toward evaluating the veridicality of the negative conclusions, or determining abstract meanings of proverbs (Braff & Beck, 1974), or trying to recall words that they had previously seen. Future research might concentrate on determining the relationship between the loss of objectivity and the overall impairment of abstraction ability.

Another possible explanation for the coincidence of selective negative content and reduction of evaluative capacity should be considered, however. Experiments with the binocularscope have indicated that when each eye is exposed briefly and simultaneously to a different picture, the image in one eye is suppressed. Depressives tend to be more sensitive to unhappy images and thus are more prone to "see" an unhappy image and to suppress a happy image than are nondepressed patients (Gilson, 1983). It could be speculated by analogy that, when there is an intense fixation on a particular scene or concept such as reappraisal, other processes are inhibited. According to this line of reasoning, the depressive's problems in engaging in difficult mental processes may be related to an automatic *reflex inhibition* of these processes. Although there is no experimental evidence at the present time to support this explanation, it should be amenable to testing.

Neurochemical Correlates

As I have pointed out, the literature indicates that depressed patients are impaired in a variety of cognitive operations, specifically those that require effort and that presumably involve different mechanisms from those used for automatic, more superficial information processing. Other studies using the same cognitive paradigm suggest that the dopaminergic system may preferentially control effortful as opposed to automatic learning. For example, Newman, Weingartner, Smallberg, and Calne (1984) administered levodopa to normal elderly controls and found an improvement in the normal baseline level of free recall (effortful processing) without any change in automatic processing (specifically, remembering how often an event had occurred).

Weingartner, Burns, Diebel, and Lewitt (1984) showed that patients with Parkinson's disease had a selective defect in effort-demanding learning and memory similar to that seen in depressed patients, but no impairment for tasks that required superficial information processing. Since the dopaminergic system is defective in Parkinson's disease, this would seem to suggest a connection between this deficit and the selective deficit in effort-demanding learning. By analogy, the dopaminergic deficit can be seen as a causal agent for, or as a correlate of, the abstraction difficulty on the psychological level.

Other convergent evidence may be seen in demonstrations that depressed patients, when treated with catecholamine agonists (such as dextroamphetamine), improve on effort-demanding learning and memory tasks. This biological evidence is consistent with the theories that implicate dopaminergic dysfunction in the pathophysiology of depression and dopaminergic effects on the therapeutic action of various antidepressant drugs (Jimerson & Post, 1984).

In summary, putting together these various findings provides us with two contrasting hypotheses. First, the negative cognitive set in depression is so salient that it preempts the conscious cognitive capacity and thus makes effortful functions, such as reappraisal of the conclusions or performance on effort-demanding tests, more difficult. The second hypothesis would be that because of a basic neurochemical deficiency in depression, the negative cognitive set that goes with this condition becomes fixed; or, alternatively, because of the basic neurochemical malfunction the depressed individual loses the cognitive capacity to reality-test his negative interpretations and so progresses in the downward cycle so typical of depressed thinking.

These findings are relevant to a psychobiological model of depression and present an exciting area for further research on the interface of psychological and biological correlates of depression.

Role of Personality

The schemas that are prepotent in depression seem to be relatively dormant when the depression is not present (Beck, 1967), although specific experiences of deprivation or defeat may activate them even during nondepressed periods. During depression the negatively toned schemas emerge from the predepressive personality of the patient. Thus, a sociotropic person who always placed a high premium on interpersonal relations and judged his own worth according to the amount of acceptance and affection he received would be primed (when depressed) to respond negatively to situations relevant to social acceptability and personal attractiveness. Such patients are bombarded with such thoughts as, "Nobody cares for me. I am ugly. I have no personality. I made a fool of myself."

The autonomous personality, on the other hand, greatly prizes independence, freedom of action, privacy, and self-determination. When depressed, such individuals are particularly sensitive to situations that they perceive as encroaching on their autonomy, mobility, or physical or mental functioning and respond with such thoughts as, I am defeated. I am incompetent. I will never be able to do what I need to do."

A clinical example illustrates the relationship between personality and depressive responses. A 50–year-old depressed businessman had a high-ranking position in an organization that he himself had helped to build. When referred for treatment for his depression, he felt that he could not continue his treatment because he did not have sufficient funds. A review of his actual life situation indicated that he had assets of over $500,000 and was making close to $100,000 a year. When asked why he believed that this was not sufficient to sustain him, he reported the following preoccupations: "My investments could all fail . . . The bond market could go down . . . My wife could get sick and use up all of our health insurance . . . I am getting old and am deteriorating . . . The business has not been growing recently and could start to fail . . . I have been having some quarrels lately with the chief executive officer and I might have to leave."

The patient viewed each of these hypothetical outcomes as being highly probable. In fact, he *expected* each unfortunate event to occur. Further, the anticipated depletion of his financial resources meant that he could not afford to pay for his treatment and thus (according to his thinking) he would never get over his depression.

After making a detailed analysis of his problems at home, we were able to uncover the typical "dead-end" thinking that precluded any type of problem solving. As we shall see, each of these problems affected an important aspect of his personality.

The pattern of seeing negative events as irreversible or irremediable was evident in all areas of his life. He was an autonomous individual who, characteristically, relied on himself to make repairs and called in specialists only when a job was too large for him to handle. When depressed, however, he seemed to operate on the idea that he had to take care of all problems by himself and, if he could not, then some disaster would occur. For example, one day he had some problem in starting his expensive sports car. He jumped to the conclusion that the engine had "burned out." He felt too slowed down to be able to examine the engine himself (he had installed his own automotive equipment in his garage). He did not trust mechanics because he believed that they would ruin the car; however, because he was depressed, he could not fix it himself. Therefore, he became saddened by the notion that the car was useless and worthless.

On another occasion, he noted that one of the outside beams in his house seemed loosened. He immediately jumped to the conclusion that the side of the house would eventually collapse. Since he was too depressed to tighten the beam, and he had ruled out the possibility of employing a carpenter, the entire house was "doomed."

The patient was disturbed because he was informed that the township was planning to install some utilities on an easement on his property. He perceived this as an act that would greatly destroy the appearance and value of the land. He was not able, on his own, to figure out that it was possible to minimize the amount of damage to his landscaped yard, that the shallow ditch would be filled in, and that the grass could be replaced.

During his depression, several other incidents occurred that led to the patient's feeling more depressed and hopeless. First, he had to have a medical examination for suspected gallstones. He reacted very negatively to "being probed, pummeled, and pounded." He perceived the medical examination as a violation of his privacy and personal integrity, as an invasion of his physical boundaries. He became agitated over a one-week stay in the hospital, which he regarded as an incarceration. Similarly, a psychiatric examination by a psychopharmacologist elicited a strong negative reaction: He was bothered by the "probing" into his private life.

As his condition improved and he was able to drive, he complained bitterly about the slowness of the traffic; he was being "blocked" by the other drivers. He also complained of being stymied by the executive director of his organization, who questioned him periodically about his work. He asserted that he could not be creative since he was accountable to somebody else. It is apparent that whenever the patient perceived that a "vital zone" was encroached on—autonomy, mobility, self-sufficiency, individuality, privacy—he made a catastrophic interpretation. Thus, being hospitalized curbed his mobility and was interpreted as "incarceration"; physical or mental examination by doctors was an invasion of his boundaries; heavy traffic blocked his freedom of movement; being questioned by a superior infringed on his individuality. The impact of these situations on the particular facets of his personality is described below.

It is interesting to note that when the patient recovered from his depression, he observed that the business had indeed been doing well, that the differences with the chief executive officer were minor and that, in fact, his superior had come around to his way of thinking, and that his health insurance was more than adequate to pay for his treatment as well as any foreseeable treatment for his wife, particularly since he had taken out several million dollars worth of "catastrophic insurance." The loose beam in the house was easily repaired by a handyman. Finally, when he took his car to a garage, he learned that there was a minor problem in the timing of the engine, which was fixed in just a few minutes.

Two characteristics of his depressive state of thinking disappeared when his depression cleared. First, not only did his focus on negative outcomes change to a positive outlook, but he was able to find quick solutions to problems. Second, the exaggerated emphasis on mobility, autonomy, and self-sufficiency shifted to a more moderate set of attitudes. Although clinicians tend to observe an increase in dependent attitudes during depression, we often find, as illustrated by this case, an accentuation of autonomous attitudes in the autonomous personalities.

STRESSOR-VULNERABILITY MODEL

The Vulnerability Hypothesis

It has been observed clinically that the events or sets of circumstances that precipitate depression vary considerably from person to person. The class of events that are depressogenic for a given individual depends on his specific vulnerabilities. Part of the structural perspective stipulates that an individual's vulnerability will be dependent, to a large extent, on his specific personality organization. An individual who is largely individualistic, for example, may be hypersensitive to situations that appear to encroach on his autonomy (or mobility) and thus prevent him from obtaining the types of payoffs or gratification that he would ordinarily get from individualistic achievement. A person with a strong investment in sociotropic concerns, on the other hand, will be particularly susceptible to events that appear to close off the intake of social supplies. For example, physical closeness appeals to the predominantly sociotropic person but might be threatening to the predominantly autonomous individual. Distancing from family members could be traumatic to the sociotropic type but liberating to the autonomous person.

Thus, the analysis of which circumstances are depressogenic for a given person needs to take into account the particular features of his personality makeup. The same event (for example, separation from a spouse, being furloughed from a job) may trigger euphoria in one person and depression in another. The types of events that ordinarily receive a negative label will have a variable effect depending on the patient's personality characteristics and life situation.

The individual's personality organization contains clusters of attitudes or schemas that reflect certain dimensions, such as autonomy or sociotropy (Beck, 1983). These dimensions are represented in attitudes such as, "I must be loved in order to be happy" (sociotropy) or "I must be a success in order to be worthwhile" (autonomy). Such attitudes are latent (unconscious) during the depressed period but, nonetheless, exert an influence in the patient's preferences and satisfactions. Given a particular set of circumstances that impinge on these attitudes, the individual becomes conscious of their importance and begins to operate according to a syllogism such as this:

1. "I need to be loved in order to be happy."
2. "David doesn't love me."
3. "Therefore, I cannot be happy."

It should be emphasized that the predisposing schema ("I need to be loved in order to be happy") becomes salient only after the person makes the judgment that he or she is not loved by a particular key person. In cases of anxiety disorder, the same schema ("I need to be loved . . .") I becomes dominant when there is a perceived danger of losing the loved person. If the judgment shifts from being threatened with the loss to actually experiencing the loss, then the depressive schema—"I can never be happy"—becomes dominant.

The longitudinal perspective addresses some of the questions raised by Krantz (1985) regarding the presence of more than average negative circumstances (i.e., more negative than that encountered by nondepressives) in precipitating and maintaining depression. The vulnerability hypothesis postulates that certain latent attitudes become operative when these precipitating factors impinge on the individual's *specific vulnerability*—like a key fitting into a lock.

There is considerable evidence that chronic stress or distress, per se, does not precipitate clinical depression. For example, Breslau and Davis (1986) studied a group of 310 mothers of children with congenital disabilities. These mothers were subjected to comparatively great amounts of stress in the form of life-threatening exacerbations of the children's chronic conditions and consequent financial, occupational, and family crises. In fact, these mothers showed a significantly higher divorce rate (12.2%) than did a control group of mothers from the community. Despite the presence of more symptoms of distress in the mothers of disabled children, they did not show a higher incidence of depression than did the control group.

The role of acute stressors in leading to depression has been supported by a number of studies, most of which emphasize the importance of loss or "exits" from the patient's social field. These stressors could react directly on the individual's specific vulnerabilities to create new problems, intensify preexisting problems, or bring into focus, "the unfavorable implications of one's continuous life problems" (Breslau & Davis, 1986). In any event, my theory would dictate that the life stressors, chronic or acute, primary or secondary, will have their greatest depressogenic effect if they impinge on the specific vulnerabilities. Ultimately, a combination of chronic or acute nonspecific stressors and a specific stressor might work to undermine the general coping mechanisms and at the same time activate the specific vulnerability schemas. In this context, a social support system might help to shore up the nonspecific coping mechanisms, even though it might not be capable of neutralizing an acute loss.

Some persons are more vulnerable to depression than others because their latent predisposing schemas are more rigid and more substantial. For example, a person who has had an accretion of negative life experiences, providing the matrix for a later negative attitudinal structure, might be especially vulnerable to negative experiences that impinged on this cluster.

Family studies indicate that certain individuals are genetically predisposed to depression. One can speculate that certain innate structural precursors provide a nucleus that facilitates the accretion of negative learning experiences. By the same token, some people (as a result of the embedding of positive attitudinal clusters or of coping structures) may be able to ward off, neutralize, or compensate for this negativity. In a sense, these individuals are "prepared" by the genetically based structures to react selectively to these negative experiences and consequently to form negative schemas that predispose them to depression. It is conceivable, furthermore, that familial tendencies toward suicide may be the consequence of the enhanced development of schemas relevant to hopelessness.

Absence of Stressors

Any comprehensive explanation of the predisposition to and the precipitation of depression needs to take into account the fact that some cases of depression have been induced by drugs and other cases appear to be initiated without any relevance to external social influences. Certain cases of bipolar depression, for instance, appear in a cyclical fashion, particularly following a manic episode, and have no consistent relevance to the social environment.

The longitudinal cognitive model should probably be restricted to the so-called reactive depressions; that is, those that are brought about by socially relevant events. We would then postulate that although the *negative cognitive processing* is similar for all types of depression, the factors precipitating the various disorders vary widely. Whether nonsocial (e.g., biological) factors are more likely to have a selective effect on those persons who have a psychological predisposition to depression can only be speculated on at this point. Clinically, however, it does appear that a person with a psychological vulnerability is more likely to be susceptible to such a drug reaction than is a person lacking the psychological disposition.

Role of Developmental Experiences

One more question remains: Are some individuals more disposed, as a result of developmental events, experiences, circumstances, and so forth, to develop substantial negative self-schemas? I have argued elsewhere (Beck, 1967) that some children exposed to a number of negative influences and judgments by significant figures would be prone to extract such negative attitudes and incorporate them into their cognitive organization.

Although these attitudes might subsequently become latent, they would be continuously present, remaining to be activated by a series of events that impinge on the person's vulnerabilities. There are data, for example, supporting the notion that irrevocable losses in childhood might sensitize an individual so that he or she would react very drastically to somewhat analogous losses in adulthood (Beck, 1967). On the basis of a study showing that depressed patients are more likely to have experienced the loss of a parent in childhood than are nondepressed patients, I suggested that childhood experiences of this nature might cement the belief that all losses are irreversible, noncompensable, and irretrievable (Beck, Sethi, & Tuthill, 1963). Some of the work by George Brown and his colleagues (Brown & Harris, 1978) add support to this notion.

RECIPROCAL-INTERACTION MODEL

Although we observed in our clinical work that depressed patients interacted with significant figures in ways that could be either beneficial or detrimental, these observations were not explicitly incorporated into a specific model until relatively recently (Beck, Rush, Shaw, & Emery, 1979). One of the reasons for not concentrating on the adverse effects of counterproductive behavior by significant others was that we found that when the patients learned to deal more effectively with their own psychological problems and their cognitive distortions, they seemed to cope better with other people. Furthermore, even when there was clear evidence of the noxious influence of a partner, the working through of the negative interaction in therapy, combined with practice in coping strategies, was often sufficient to promote recovery from the depression.

In order to extend the theoretical network beyond the intrapsychic formulation to encompass interactions with the social environment, we have formulated a reciprocal interaction model (Beck et al., 1979, p. 17). In a given set of interactions, it is difficult to state whose behaviors (patient's, spouse's) may have started the downhill slide. As a starting point, we could observe that the patients' depressive behaviors (crying, complaining, immobility, avoidance, retardation, cheerlessness, withdrawal of affection, nonresponsiveness, solemn expression, pessimism, impaired performance, loss of initiative and spontaneity) often appear to evoke negative responses from significant persons* (nagging, criticism, impatience). Subsequently, a characteristic "external vicious cycle" is created.

*I use the term "significant persons" to denote those individuals who play the most important role in the life of the patient; for example, spouse, other members of family, lover, close friend.

It should be noted that not all of the depressive behaviors are necessarily noxious to the partners. Some partners react negatively to clinging dependency, others react positively. Some feel sympathetic toward crying; others may be scornful. Moreover, the negative response of the partner is not always adverse. A disapproving reaction to a patient's inertia may mobilize him or her into engaging in constructive activity, which may serve to arrest the downward course of the depression. Finally, in many instances the behavior of the partner may be benign but have little influence in mitigating the severity of the depression.

It is important to note that the discordant or noxious behavioral interactions reflect the mutually reinforcing interactions of beliefs of the individuals. To take an example, suppose a depressed man believes that he is helpless and nothing can be done to help him. This cognitive structuring is reflected in his sinking into inertia and ignoring attempts to cheer him up. The wife reacts to the overt *behavior* (not to the underlying hopelessness) and concludes, for example, that he is *intentionally* being unresponsive, uncooperative, and manipulative. She then conveys her belief to him through verbal and nonverbal behavior—scolding, criticism, frowning, and so forth. The consequence of the wife's reactions is that he sees his situation as even more hopeless and thus he is likely to sink into a more profound state of lethargy. Consequently, the vicious cycle is aggravated.

The reciprocal interaction model is most applicable to the escalation or the maintenance of the depression. However, the same model could cast light on the precipitation of depression. A series of noxious interactions could produce a sequence of nonadaptive responses in the vulnerable partner that leads to further aversive behavior on the part of the spouse. Thus, a housebound mother who is being criticized by her husband may experience a drop in self-confidence and a spurt of hopelessness that would be reflected in a decreased level of performance in her domestic and maternal role. This reaction might then evoke further criticism that could gradually push her to the edge of a clinical depression.

Some experimental work by Sacco (1986, personal communication) provides further clues as to the nature of the interaction. He found, as expected, that depressed patients tend to make "internal, stable and global attributions for failure, and external, unstable, and specific attributions for success." That is, they tended to blame themselves for a failure and attribute it to a generalized personality trait, whereas they explained away successes as due to chance or momentary luck. Sacco's important additional finding was that others tended to categorize the patient's failures and successes in precisely the same way. Thus, we have further evidence of a kind of *folie à deux.*

PSYCHOBIOLOGICAL MODEL

One of the problems in focusing on psychological, behavioral, and environmental approaches to depressive phenomena is that other equally important aspects may be neglected or completely overlooked.

To understand depression fully, however, it is necessary to realize that the type of data collected will influence the type of conclusions. Thus, an investigator collecting introspective data will derive a model quite different from that of an investigator who tests the effect of drugs on animals' brains or measures the amount of neuroendocrine metabolites in the blood or other fluids of the depressed patient. The methods of sampling obviously determine the form and content of interpretations made by the investigator. Moreover, a researcher pursuing one line of investigation exclusively may find it difficult to reconcile his findings with those of another investigator working at a different level.

The psychobiological perspective prompts the theorist or researcher to consider whether the biological and the cognitive data represent different perspectives of the *same* phenomenon. Thus, a negative interpretation of a situation would be reflected in some neurophysiological change. Similarly, a chronic negative cognitive set would be represented in some deviation in neurochemical process. From this perspective, the cognitive and biological phenomena represent different sides of the same coin.

Although this formulation may smack of philosophical dualism, it actually provides a framework for *integrating* neurochemical and psychological observations. We may find, for example, that a definable psychological process, such as information processing, represents the key element in the depressive disorder. The information processing can then be studied concurrently from two perspectives: cognitive and neurochemical. Remediation, as well as precipitation of faulty processing, can be investigated in terms of the reactions to verbal stimuli and pharmacological agents. Since information processing can be demonstrably upset by drugs (as in the toxic psychoses), it does not seem farfetched to consider that they can improve the processing of information. Thus, depending on the nature of the disorder and the accessibility of the patient, the therapist can treat the patient either cognitively or pharmacologically. Some evidence for this concept is found in studies that demonstrate that when depressed patients start to improve clinically, they show improvement in their negative thinking and negative attitudes—irrespective of whether they received drug therapy or cognitive therapy (Simons, Murphy, Levine, & Wetzel, 1986).

Negative interpretations of reality may be related less to the direct impact of the negative environment per se than to the effect of drugs, toxins, or hormones that make the individual sensitive or hypersensitive to the adverse environmental circumstances. Thus, the individual who responds with depression to a generally negative situation (for example, unemployment) may be the one person whose cognitive organization has become destabilized or sensitized by organic (as opposed to interpersonal) factors such as those listed above. The observer—or the patient himself—can notice only the external event and its effect but cannot see what may be a more crucial determinant of a profound depressive response; namely, the psychobiological sensitivity.

EVOLUTIONARY MODEL OF DEPRESSION

The Paradoxes of Depression

A satisfactory explanation for the ubiquitousness of depressive disorders has eluded theorists for the past two millennia. The various theories, ranging from the notion of an excess of black bile to the concept of early oral fixation, have failed to clarify the puzzling and paradoxical features.

Perhaps, as I have suggested elsewhere, "Depression may some day be understood in terms of its paradoxical features" (Beck, 1967, p. 3). The overall behaviors of the depressed patients—verbal and nonverbal—seem to contradict the most hallowed notions of human nature. According to the pleasure principle, the patients should seek to maximize their satisfactions and minimize their pain. Yet because of their self-criticisms and negative interpretations, their pain increases. Their former pleasure in their favorite activities turns to distaste. In defiance of the time-honored concept of the instinct of self-preservation, they think of terminating rather than prolonging their lives. Further, the mandate of other basic drives seem to be violated: parenting "instinct," herd "instinct," sexual drive, appetite, and sleep.

A satisfactory theory of depression has to account not only for these paradoxes but also for the more particular changes observed in the switch from a nondepressed to a depressed state: from affection to loss of feeling or revulsion; from gratification to anhedonia; from enthusiasm to indifference; from amusement to mirthlessness; from curiosity to loss of interest. Further, a host of other changes requires clarification: avoidance, withdrawal, self-neglect, fatigability, passivity, suicidal wishes, selfdevaluation, and hopelessness.

The usual explanations for this variety of symptoms do not provide a framework on which to hang more than a fraction of these characteristic features. Yet if we step back from the data and try to fit our observations into the scenario of the development of our species, we can discern a consistent pattern.

The Unifying Principle: An Evolutionary Strategy

A unifying principle of depression can be teased out when we focus on two broad features of depression: the abandonment of major areas of emotional involvement and the damping down of major behavioral systems. Among the broad segments of living that appear to be stripped of their emotional investment are activities relevant to interpersonal attachments and achievements: bonding, mating, parenting, camaraderie, aggressive activity, work, competition, exploration.

The proposed unifying principle is based on the notion that depression represents a kind of atavistic program or strategy that had some important survival value in the wild but that is maladaptive in our current environment. The characteristics of depression are strongly suggestive of an underlying mechanism designed to conserve energy by slowing down the entire psychobiological apparatus. The loss of appetite and loss of sexual interest discourage foraging for food and sexual competition. The loss of gratification from usual activities encourages passivity-another hedge against energy depletion. The reduction of interest in mating, parenting, socializing with friends, and achieving may similarly reflect a broad principal of conservation.

One biological component of the syndrome—namely, early morning awakening—may not seem to fit into the picture of generalized inactivity or even retardation. Moreover, this component seems inconsistent with the "conservation principle." However, as we shall see later, the phylogenetic hypothesis of depression stipulates that, following defeat, an individual withdraws from the group and consequently forgoes its protection. Similarly, loss of a parent strips a juvenile of protection. In this context, the insomnia would represent the necessity for vigilance as daylight approaches because the individual, stripped of the usual protectors, is more vulnerable to attack by others.

In considering this formulation, an important question naturally arises: What possible survival value could have been achieved by the enforced slowdown or cessation of activity? Under what circumstances could the conservation principle have been adaptational? For clarification of these issues, we need to distinguish between "adaptational" and "adaptive." An adaptational mechanism automatically regulates the individual's behavior in order to maintain the continuity of his or her lineage. Consequently, this mechanism operates by maximizing the probabilities of passing genes from the previous to the subsequent generation. These probabilities are maximized if the individual (the gene carrier) is compelled by automatic mechanisms to withdraw from activities that might ultimately jeopardize this process. For example, if individuals have been engaging in activities that could increase their vulnerability (for example, persevering in a life-and-death struggle against a victorious adversary or in a futile foraging for food), an automatic mechanism that would compel them to withdraw from the struggle, to give up for a prolonged period, would tend to reduce the risk of depletion of energy or death. Such a mechanism would have been useful to undermine the frenetic pursuit of some unattainable goal that might eventually deplete their internal resources and make them vulnerable to disease or attack—unless some conservation—like mechanism forced them to slow down. (The subjective feeling of lethargy or lack of energy in the early stage of depression may be a safeguard against the ultimate depletion of energy.)

Relation of the Conservation Principle to Depression

At this point, it might seem impossible to relate the hypothesized sequence of reactions in an ancestral habitat to our observations of what actually happens to people in our contemporary environment. It is obvious that depression, with all its pain and dysfunction, is hardly adaptive in the present scene—and it may not be clear as yet how it can be adaptational. (I use the term "adaptive" to refer to those processes or behaviors that promote our dealing with *present* environment demands and satisfying our basic requirements for living. I consider these adaptive behaviors to be far more under voluntary conscious control than the adaptational mechanisms.) But we should bear in mind that evolutionary changes may not have caught up with environmental changes, and what may have been adaptational in the wild may not be so today. We can get some inkling as to how adaptational principles that regulated the behavior of our prehistoric ancestors might still be operating today if we examine the types of situations that often precipitate depression. These situations are obviously far removed from the typical circumstances characteristic of the early development of our species.

I have previously categorized the common classes of precipitants of depression as "defeat" and "deprivation" (Beck, 1983). Certain events, such as a person's failure to reach a career objective, inability to perform up to his or her standards, or a setback in a competitive enterprise, could be perceived as a catastrophic loss of status; for individuals who have a large investment in individualistic achievement or self-sufficiency (autonomous personality), such events could precipitate depression.

Similarly, persons who place a large premium on close relationships and attach great significance to disruptions of these ties (sociotropic personality) would be more likely to become depressed after a loss of a loved person. Thus the two major axes relevant to predisposition to depression are concerned with status and bonding, and the precipitation revolves around perceived loss of status or of a relationship. In the wild, status and bonding represent major conduits for satisfying basic survival requirements; namely, access to food and protection. In this context, the precipitation of depression may be viewed in terms of the activation of a primordial organization—an evolutionary strategy—designed to conserve energy.

Pain and Pleasure in Everyday Life

In order to understand the workings and psychobiological function of this involuntary strategy, we now have to turn our attention to the automatic mechanisms that regulate our behavior in everyday life. We need to acknowledge, first of all, that although a good part of our behavior appears to be under voluntary control, even our conscious volition is influenced by automatic processes. When we reach a goal, for instance, we are generally "rewarded" with feelings of pleasure; when we fail, we are "punished" with feelings of dysphoria. The experience of pleasure and sadness serves a useful adaptive purpose. Gratification reinforces (among other things) behaviors that ultimately promote our survival and reproduction. We experience pleasure when we master a problem, develop a skill, secure a relationship. Conversely, we experience dysphoria when we engage in unrewarding behaviors. The unpleasant feelings associated with disappointment prompt us to change either our expectations or our behavior: relinquish the goal, change our tactics, or try harder. Lacking the painful experience of disappointment, we might burn ourselves out in repetitious assaults on an unattainable goal—without regard to the costs. Our internal mechanisms seem to guard against such an eventuality by forcing an automatic reduction in activity before we have depleted our energy. (As we shall see, these mechanisms are analogous to those that produce the more pronounced dysphoria and inactivity in depression.)

In order to understand fully the internal system of reward and punishment, we need to look not only at the events or situations themselves, but also at their symbolic meanings. If we catalogue the various events leading to pleasure versus pain, we find that they would fall into the classes of gains versus losses, benefits versus costs. However, the ingredients of the events producing dysphoria (and ultimately depression) are not actual losses or costs so much as *symbols* of the loss. The events that produce the most dysphoria are those that symbolize the loss or erosion of significant resources (health, power, intimate relationships, group membership, or status). A new relationship pleases us because it symbolizes an addition to our "support group"; a rejection saddens us because it signifies a reduction. Ultimately, sadness and pleasure are directed toward maintaining an optimal reserve of internal resources (health, skill, energy) and external resources (support, protection). We draw on these reserves when we seek to expand our domain, mate, and propagate. The perception of an increase in our available resources produce gratification; the perception of a decrease produces dysphoria. The potential availability of resources is represented by a variety of symbolic events or situations; for example, the approach of a loved person, elicitation of a smile from a stranger, the receipt of an award. Since each of these situations symbolizes a potential source of support, protection, or status, it can produce gratification. Conversely, events with negative meaning (a frown, the exit of a loved person, failure to win an expected prize) represent a subtraction of available resources and thus produce dysphoria.

Pleasure and pain ebb and flow from minute to minute in the course of our daily life. When we perceive a continuing negative balance between the negative and positive symbols of supplies, we are likely to experience prolonged dysphoria (even though we may receive intermittent positive inputs). A major factor in the formation of this balance is the amount of effort that is expended (cost) in relationship to the actual or anticipated rewards (gains). Thus, if we expend a great deal of energy in pursuing a goal such as prestige or possessions and receive only a fraction of the anticipated return on this investment, we experience an upset in the give-get balance and we are likely to feel sad.

Give-Get Imbalance in Depression

The give-get imbalance that automatically leads to sadness and possibly a reduction, or at least a change, in activity in our everyday lives can be extended to the more profound discrepancy between gains and costs that sometimes lead to depression. In terms of the adaptational principle, depression represent a "conservation program" that is activated in order to prevent continued depletion of resources. The individual has to adapt to an economy of scarcity by adjusting his intake to the level of "available" supplies and by reducing his output to the minimal level consistent with survival. Long-term investments in bonding and procreation are abandoned for a time-limited period in favor of conservation of resources—in order to prevent further "cost overruns."

Thus, the depressive mechanism reduces not only behaviors relevant to consumption (e.g., feeding) but also behaviors that will consume or exhaust internal resources (energy supplies): working toward a goal and interaction with significant others, the group, or strangers. Consequently, the individual does not expect "supplies" from others and does not give as much to them.

In one of the clearest set of circumstances logically leading (occasionally) to depression, an individual expends a great deal of time and effort in an attempt to reach a given goal; when the time comes for him to receive the reward, it turns out to have much less symbolic value or utility than he had anticipated. If the expenditure of energy has been considerable and the proportionate reward has been substantially less, it may take a significant period of time for the individual to overcome his disappointment and return to a normal hedonic state. During the period of disappointment he is prone to be less responsive to positive symbols and, in fact, is inclined to see things somewhat more negatively. It is as though the negative schemas that were activated in order to process the disappointing experience remain active for a period of time and thus continue to process new information in a negative way.

The precipitation of depression in many cases seems to be based on the perception, at some level, of a continued and prolonged discrepancy between input and output, gains and costs. The decrease in perceived or anticipated input and the expectation that this decline will not be reversed is analogous to the situation of an individual marooned on a desert island. Since resources are in very short supply, he has to adjust his expectations of input to what is available and reduce his output of energy to the minimal level necessary to exploit the scarce supplies. This means forsaking other former sources of gratification for the amount and quality immediately available.

When we can identify a specific precipitating event in a depressive episode, it does not necessarily turn out to be an overwhelming loss. The effect of such a precipitating event may be an upset in the balance between anticipated income and expenditure, or it may produce other problems that lead to such an upset. The examples, par excellence, are the peripartum depressions. In these cases the increased demands prior to and following the birth may not be compensated for by increased support from, say, the spouse. The relative lack of support in the context of increased expenditures may symbolize a substantial loss, just as a desertion or death would.

There seems to be some kind of mechanism for automatically regulating expenditure of energy when there is a perceived threat of total exhaustion of internal resources. The mechanism operates by reducing activity before the point of total depletion of energy occurs. Presumably a total depletion would lead to a collapse of the various systems responsible for survival and reproduction. We have seen patients exhausted by manic activity, for example, die from infections resulting from their lowered resistance.

In the setting of potential depression, the threat of total depletion occurs when the individual perceives an increased demand on and a drainage of internal resources (as in the perinatal period in females) or a shut down of external resources (e.g., death of or desertion by a caretaker). In our contemporary society, the threat does not consist of an actual deprivation of food supplies or protection, but is of a symbolic nature. That is, those symbols (expressions of love or camaraderie) that stand for continued access to resources (namely, caretakers or peers, status within the group) have been replaced by negative symbols representing loss of support or protection: desertion or rejection (by significant persons), death (of a loved person), defeat, the absence of status symbolized by defeat. With the reversal of the sign of the symbols, the appearance of plenty has been replaced by the specter of scarcity.

The impact of the symbolic meaning of the precipitating events can best be understood if we consider their effect in the primitive conditions confronting our ancestors. In those circumstances certain symbolic events would be predictive of a long-range threat to existence. In the wild, the loss of a parent or a peer could be followed by a prolonged reduction in availability of food supplies, since individuals hunted and foraged in pairs and groups. Similarly, the loss of status as a result of a hierarchical defeat would relegate the individual to a subordinate position that would, in itself, presage a reduced claim on the supplies obtained by the group. Under the circumstances (loss of a significant person or position in the group) the depressive mechanism would automatically reduce the requirement for food consumption as well as the motivation to explore. In sum, the primitive symbols predicting prolonged deprivation trigger the depressive program.

The symbols, however, are just symbols and not the real thing. Thus in contemporary life the loss of a parent or peer does not generally lead to an irreversible loss of supplies. The loss of position in the social group does not automatically cast the individual into outer darkness. Nonetheless, the psychobiological reaction to the symbolic loss appears to prepare the individual for such a prolonged period of deprivation. It should be emphasized that pain and suffering per se are not precipitants—only symbols—of prolonged deprivation.

The cognitive aspects of depression can now be fitted into the notion of perceived scarcity. The patient perceives the loss (if there is any) as representing the deprivation of an essential ingredient for satisfaction, for pursuing an objective. In fact, the symbol generally represents the objective itself: being taken care of, loved, admired. The patient's belief that the loss is irreversible and noncompensable and that the future is hopeless further enhances the desirability of *giving up.* Finally, the attribution to the self of deficiency removes any expectation of succor and reinforces the sense of *futility.* Thus, the cognitive content would tend to promote prolonged inactivity.

The generalized negative attitudes apply to broad segments of life, work, play, and interpersonal relations; thus the large behavioral systems relevant to these segments are vitiated. Negative attitudes such as, "Nothing will work out" reduce initiative; "It's not worth the effort" leads to *fatigability;* "I can't be happy without somebody to share my experiences with" promotes *anhedonia;* and "My whole life is empty and meaningless" elicits *apathy.*

Although cognitive structures directly regulate behaviors by deactivating behavioral systems, affects such as dysphoria play a role by becoming more salient when constructive action is contemplated or undertaken. The feedback of these affects reinforces the negative cognitive schemas. The feedback mechanism is analogous to pain. You attempt something. You get hurt. You stop what you are doing.

It is possible to draw an analogy between an economic and a psychological depression. In both cases there is the expectation of a prolonged reduction in income (material or psychic). Increased productivity would result in only a further depletion of resources with no payoff. The only solution is to damp down activity until the conditions obviously improve.

In summary, cognitive and neurochemical disturbances may be viewed as the same phenomenon represented at different levels of organization. Alternatively, the cognitive and neurochemical changes can be regarded as interactive: a chemical disturbance, for example, undermines cognitive functioning so that the individual is more susceptible to negative experiences; the resulting upset is manifest in further neurochemical activity that aggravates the cognitive problem.

REFERENCES

Beck, A. T. (1963). Thinking and depression: 1. Idiosyncratic content and cognitive distortions. *Archives of General Psychiatry, 9,* 324–333.

Beck, A. T. (1964). Thinking and depression: 2. Theory and therapy. *Archives of General Psychiatry, 10,* 561–571.

Beck, A. T. (1967). *Depression: Clinical, experimental, and theoretical aspects.* New York: Harper & Row. Republished (1972) as *Depression: Causes and treatment.* Philadelphia, PA: University of Pennsylvania Press.

Beck, A. T. (1976). *Cognitive therapy and the emotional disorders.* New York: International Universities Press.

Beck, A. T. (1983). Cognitive therapy of depression: New perspectives. In P. Clayton (Ed.), *Treatment of depression: Old controversies and new approaches* (pp. 265–290). New York: Raven Press.

Beck, A. T., Brown, G., Riskind, J. H., & Steer, R. A. (1986, April 17–20). *Development and validation of the Cognition Checklist.* Paper presented at the Annual Meeting of the Eastern Psychological Association, New York, NY. Beck, A. T., Brown, G., & Steer, R. A. (1986). *Thoughts for differentiating anxiety from depression.* Unpublished manuscript, University of Pennsylvania, Philadelphia, PA.

Beck, A. T., Riskind, J. H., Brown, G., & Sherrod, A. (1986, June 17–21). *A comparison of likelihood estimates for imagined positive and negative outcomes in anxiety and depression.* Paper presented at the Annual Meeting of the Society for Psychotherapy Research, Wellesley, MA.

Beck, A. T., Rush, A. J., Shaw, B. F., & Emery, G. (1979). *Cognitive therapy of depression.* New York: Guilford Press.

Beck, A. T., Sethi, B., & Tuthill, R. (1963). Childhood bereavement and adult depression. *Archives of General Psychiatry, 9,* 295–302.

Beck, A. T., Steer, R. A., Kovacs, M., & Garrison, B. E. (1985). Hopelessness and eventual suicide: A ten-year prospective study of patients hospitalized with suicidal ideation. *American Journal of Psychiatry, 142,* 559–563.

Braff, D. L., & Beck, A. T. (1974). Thinking disorder in depression. *Archives of General Psychiatry, 31,* 456–459.

Breslau, H., & Davis, G. C. (1986). Chronic stress and major depression. *Archives of General Psychiatry, 43,* 309–314.

Brown, G. W., & Harris, T. 0. (1978). *Social origins of depression.* London, England: Tavistock.

Clark, D. C., Clayton, P. J., Andreasen, N. C., Lewis, C., Fawcett, J., & Sheftner, W. A. (1985). Intellectual functioning and abstraction ability in major affective disorders. *Journal of Comprehensive Psychiatry, 26,* 313–325.

Coyne, J. C., & Gotlib, 1. H. (1983). The role of cognition in depression: A critical appraisal. *Psychological Bulletin, 94,* 472–505.

Eaves, G. (1982). *Cognitive patterns in endogenous and nonendogenous unipolar major depressions.* Unpublished doctoral dissertation, University of Texas, Health Science Center, Dallas.

Eaves, G., & Rush, A. J. (1984). Cognitive patterns in symptomatic and remitted unipolar major depression. *Journal of Abnormal Psychology, 33*(1), 31–40.

Fleming, B., Simon, K. M., & Pretzer, J. L. (1986). *Beck's cognitive theory of depression: Current status of the empirical literature.* Manuscript submitted for publication.

Gilson, M. (1983). *Depression as measured by perceptual bias in binocular rivalry.* Unpublished doctoral dissertation, Georgia State University. (University Microfilms No. AAD83-27351).

Hasher, L., & Zacks, R. T. (1979). Automatic and effortful processes in memory. *Journal of Experimental Psychology General, 108,* 386–388.

Herold, R. C., Beck, A. T., Berchick, R. J., Brown, G., & Steer, R. A. (1986). *Hopelessness as a predictor of long-term suicide in psychiatric outpatients.* Manuscript submitted for publication.

Hollon, S. D., & Kendall, P. C. (1980). Cognitive self-statements in depression: Development of an automatic thoughts questionnaire. *Cognitive Therapy and Research, 4*(4), 383–395.

Jimerson, D. C., & Post, R. M. (1984). Psychomotor stimulants and dopamine agonists in depression. In R. M. Post & J. C. Ballenger (Eds.), *Neurobiology of the Mood Disorders* (pp. 619–628). Baltimore, MD: Williams & Wilkins Co.

Krantz, S. E. (1985). When depressive cognitions reflect negative realities. *Cognitive Therapy and Research, 9,* 61–77.

Lazarus, R., & Folkman, S. (1984). *Stress appraisal and coping.* New York: Springer Publishing Co.

Newman, R., Weingartner, H., Smallberg, S. A., & Caine, D. (1984). The dopamine system in memory. *Neurology, 34,* 805–807,

Roy-Byrne, P. P., Weingartner, H., Bierer, L. M., Thompson, K., & Post, R. M. (1986). Effortful and automatic cognitive processes in depression. *Archives of General Psychiatry, 43,* 265–267.

Rush, A. J., & Beck, A. T. (1978). Adults with affective disorders. In M. Hersen & A. S. Bellack (Eds.), *Behavior therapy in psychiatric settings* (pp. 286–330). Baltimore, MD: William & Wilkins.

Sacco, W. P. (1986). Personal communication.

Schwartz, R. M., & Garomoni, G. (1986). A structural model of positive and negative states of mind: Asymmetry in the internal dialogue. In P. C. Kendall (Ed.), *Advances in cognitive-behavioral research and therapy* (Vol. 5) pp. 1–62. New York: Academic Press.

Simons, A. D., Murphy, G. E., Levine, J. L., & Wetzel, R. D. (1986). Cognitive therapy and pharmacotherapy of depression: Sustained improvement over one year. *Archives of General Psychiatry, 43,* 43–48.

Weingartner, H., Burns, S., Diebel, R., & Lewitt, P. A. (1984). Cognitive impairments in Parkinson's disease: Distinguishing between effortful and automatic cognitive processes. *Psychiatry Research, 11,* 223–235.

CHAPTER 3

Treating Dysfunctional Beliefs: Implications of the Mood-State Hypothesis

Jacqueline B. Persons and Jeanne Miranda

The mood-state hypothesis proposes that underlying dysfunctional beliefs are more available for therapeutic interventions when patients are in a negative mood state than when they are in a positive one. After briefly reviewing evidence that supports the mood-state hypothesis, this chapter will offer recommendations for treating dysfunctional beliefs. First, when patients begin therapy in a clinically depressed state, we recommend working on underlying dysfunctional beliefs early in treatment when the presence of negative mood enhances the patient's ability to report the beliefs. Second, when symptoms have remitted and the mood is positive and the underlying beliefs are not readily reported, we discuss four ways to obtain information about those beliefs: direct accessing strategies, the therapeutic relationship, homework, and the case formulation. Finally, when patients experience recurrent pronounced mood shifts, we recommend teaching them to anticipate corresponding shifts in thinking.

   Treatment of underlying dysfunctional beliefs is an important goal of cognitive therapy. According to the cognitive theory, pathological patterns of mood, behavior, and thinking are produced by these beliefs (Beck, 1976); therefore, cognitive therapy is designed to identify and correct the dysfunctional beliefs (Beck, Rush, Shaw, & Emery, 1979). Effective treatment of underlying dysfunctional beliefs has been shown to be associated with a lower relapse rate (Simons, Murphy, Levine, & Wetzel, 1986) in depressed patients.

Recent findings suggest that individuals who hold dysfunctional beliefs that make them vulnerable to depression have difficulty reporting those beliefs unless they are experiencing a negative mood state (Miranda & Persons, 1988; Miranda, Persons, & Byers, 1990; Teasdale & Dent, 1987). The proposition that negative mood facilitates the reporting of dysfunctional beliefs comes directly from Bower's (1981) associative network model of mood and memory; we call it the mood-state hypothesis. We believe this hypothesis has important implications for both the cognitive theory itself (Persons & Miranda, 1990) and for therapeutic work devoted to changing dysfunctional beliefs. We briefly describe evidence that supports the mood-state hypothesis and outline recommendations for treating dysfunctional beliefs based on the knowledge that dysfunctional thinking varies with current mood state.

THE EVIDENCE

Miranda and Persons have directly tested the hypothesis that reports of dysfunctional beliefs depend on current mood state in two samples. A volunteer sample of 43 nondepressed women reported changes in mood and dysfunctional thinking following a mood induction (Miranda & Persons, 1988), and depressed psychiatric patients reported changes in mood and dysfunctional thinking during spontaneous diurnal mood fluctuations (Miranda et al., 1990). Furthermore, dysfunctional beliefs have been shown to be mood-state-dependent for vulnerable individuals only. In 2 nondepressed volunteer samples included in the studies just cited, individuals who had a history of depression showed elevated scores on a measure of dysfunctional beliefs if they were in a negative mood state at the time they were assessed; however, nonvulnerable individuals did not show this effect. These studies provide direct support for the mood-state hypothesis.

In addition to these studies that directly test the hypothesis that reporting of dysfunctional beliefs depends on current mood state, three types of evidence collected for other purposes provide indirect support for the mood-state hypothesis.

1. Several longitudinal studies (with one exception that of Eaves & Rush, 1984) show that as depressive symptoms remit, underlying dysfunctional beliefs, attributions, or schema "remit" as well (Hamilton &

Abramson, 1983; Hammen, Miklowitz, & Dyck, 1986; Persons & Rao, 1985; Reda, 1984; Silverman, Silverman, & Eardley, 1984; Simons, Garfield, & Murphy, 1984). The mood-state hypothesis would predict that when subjects' moods improve as their depression remits, they are less likely to report pathological underlying beliefs.

2. Comparisons of normals and recovered depressives find (except for Dobson & Shaw, 1986) that these groups do not differ in underlying dysfunctional attitudes (Hamilton & Abramson, 1983; Hollon, Kendall, & Lumry, 1986; Silverman et al., 1984). The mood-state hypothesis would predict that although underlying pathological cognitions are present in recovered depressives, the cognitions would not be reported when the individuals are in a positive mood.

3. Findings in cognitive and clinical psychology showing that recall of life events, perception of ambiguous pictures, free associations to neutral words, and other cognitive processes depend on mood state (see reviews by Bower, 1981; Singer & Salovey, 1988; Teasdale, 1983) also support the mood-state hypothesis.

Although some evidence supports the hypothesis that reporting of underlying dysfunctional beliefs depends on mood state, much more evidence is needed. However, if the mood-state hypothesis is correct, it has important implications for the practice of cognitive therapy.

CLINICAL IMPLICATIONS

We will describe implications of the mood-state hypothesis for therapeutic work in three types of situations. First, we examine work with clinically depressed patients. Next, we outline four approaches to obtaining information about underlying dysfunctional attitudes when negative mood is not present during therapy sessions. Finally, we consider treatment of dysfunctional attitudes when patients experience recurrent intense mood fluctuations.

When Patients are Depressed, Elicit Underlying Beliefs Early

When treating severely depressed patients, therapists often focus first on increasing pleasant activities; asking a severely depressed patient to challenge distorted cognitions may seem too demanding. However, if the patient recovers prior to uncovering the distorted cognitions, the beliefs may become much less accessible. We recommend eliciting the beliefs early in therapy.

Once the dysfunctional beliefs have been elicited, it may be possible to begin working to change them. This viewpoint is consistent with those of Greenberg and Safran (1987) who argue that emotion, including powerful negative emotion, plays a central role in therapeutic change. However, as Beck et al. (1979) point out, some severely depressed patients are unable to perceive alternatives to their negative world view. For example, an elderly woman with serious medical problems stated that life was not worth living. The therapist's attempts to alter this hopeless view met with extreme resistance. Finally, the therapist distracted the patient momentarily by asking about her grandchildren and other more positive aspects of her life. The patient's mood shifted, and within a few minutes she was able to counter the hopelessness and suicidality that had overwhelmed her earlier. Thus, the therapist may need to work actively to produce a mood change or wait until the patient's mood has improved before challenging the dysfunctional beliefs.

Even if underlying dysfunctional beliefs cannot be treated directly early in treatment, we argue that it is important to get as much possible information about them early on. Murphy, Simons, Wetzel, and Lustman (1984) reported that their depressed subjects (in all treatment groups) showed a dramatic drop in Beck Depression Inventory (BDI) score by week 4 (approximately session 8) of a 16-week treatment protocol. Fennell and Teasdale (1987) reported that, on average, 17 cognitive therapy patients showed a marked response to treatment after 2 weeks of therapy (maximum of 3 sessions), with an average BDI score dropping from approximately 30 to 15 during that interval. The mood-state hypothesis proposes that later in treatment, when the patient's mood state is improved, retrieval of important information about the beliefs—including memories of traumatic incidents in which the beliefs were learned—is likely to be more difficult. To some degree this may be due to the fact that when she has begun feeling better, the patient is reluctant to retrieve painful memories because she knows how badly she feels when this material is activated.

When Mood is Positive, Work Actively to Uncover Dysfunctional Beliefs

The cognitive theory proposes that individuals can hold dysfunctional beliefs at times when they are unaware of and unable to report them, particularly when they are in a positive mood state. For example, a dependent person who is depressed following the breakup of the relationship with his girlfriend may "cure" his depression by getting another girlfriend. The new relationship alleviates his depressive symptoms but does not change his underlying dysfunctional belief ("Unless I'm loved, I'm worthless"), leaving him vulnerable to future depression following the breakup of an important relationship.

If one of the goals of treatment is the prevention of relapse, then treatment of latent dysfunctional attitudes is indicated before terminating therapy. To accomplish this, we outline four strategies that are useful in uncovering the latent dysfunctional beliefs: direct accessing, homework, the therapeutic relationship, and the case formulation.

Direct Accessing Strategies

Dysfunctional attitudes can be elicited by arranging for the patient to directly confront situations that evoke negative mood, pathological thinking and maladaptive behaviors. Direct accessing techniques are well known to behavior therapists who treat phobias and anxiety (e.g., Foa & Kozak, 1986; Marks, 1981). This is probably a result of the natural way in which pathological fear responses tend to be limited to specific situations. Thus, a person who is afraid of cats usually does not show a fear response or report distorted cognitions about cats unless in the presence of live or imagined cats. As a result, a major component of the behavioral treatment of fears and phobias includes active procedures to access pathological fear. Similarly, we recommend the use of active procedures to access pathological depression and underlying dysfunctional beliefs.

The therapist may be able to activate hidden dysfunctional beliefs by asking patients to focus on current difficulties and problems that they are avoiding. Guided by the therapist's hypothesis about the patient's problematic underlying beliefs, careful questioning may be necessary to reveal these patterns of avoidance. In other cases, the nature of the avoidance behavior is readily apparent. For example, the lover described earlier may spend all his time with his new girlfriend, avoiding solitude at all costs because he feels lonely, unwanted, and worthless unless he is receiving infusions of love and caring. To expose the dysfunctional belief that is causing these feelings, the therapist could ask him to spend some time alone recording his mood and automatic thoughts or to come early to the therapy session and spend some time alone in the waiting room, so that the therapist can work with him on the negative thoughts and feelings that emerge.

The downward arrow technique (Burns, 1980) can be used to uncover the pathogenic beliefs underlying the patient's emotional upset and automatic thoughts. That is, the therapist can ask repeatedly, "Why is this situation upsetting to you? What does it mean to you?" After answering this question several times, the sequence often "bottoms out" at the irrational underlying belief, "This situation is upsetting because I'm alone, and if I'm alone that means no one cares about me, and if no one cares about me I'll be alone forever, and if I'm alone forever, it means I'm unwanted, bad, and worthless."

The therapist can also ask the patient to focus on and recall previous upsetting experiences and can help the patient re-create and reexperience these events in the session. The patient can be asked to provide details of the situation and to focus on how he or she felt at the time and why the event was so upsetting. Again, the therapist can guide the patient through this material to uncover underlying dysfunctional attitudes.

Some patients may not be able to report dysfunctional attitudes even when they confront distressing situations. The therapist may be able to evoke the attitudes by focusing on the aspects of the situation (mood, behavior) that the patient does recall. Sometimes a probe for a feeling elicits a cognition, as when the therapist asks, "How did you feel when the boss put you in charge?" and the patient responds, "I felt I couldn't do a good job." The therapist might also ask the patient to imagine the details of the problematic situation as vividly as possible: What furniture was in the room? Who else was there? What were they wearing? What were they doing? As Beck et al. (1979) and Edwards (1989) point out, some patients retrieve important material when they focus on images rather than on cognitions.

Role-playing can also be quite helpful in uncovering dysfunctional beliefs. A patient reported distress at the thought of being assertive but was unable to report automatic thoughts that hampered her ability to speak up. She was asked to role-play being assertive with her husband. As the role-play progressed, the patient's mood plunged and she reported the belief, "I must never reveal my feelings to others—if I do, I'll get hurt."

Therapists can also help patients access their dysfunctional beliefs by taking advantage of spontaneously occurring mood states. Therapists can encourage patients to schedule therapy sessions or to telephone the therapist at times of acute emotional distress. Sessions conducted at times when the negative material is readily available can be extremely profitable and powerful. (This intervention may be counter-therapeutic for patients who believe "I am weak and fragile and I can't tolerate any emotional distress" or "I can't solve problems on my own—I must get help or I won't survive.")

A variety of techniques, including confronting, recalling, or enacting situations that evoke negative mood, and scheduling therapy at times of distress can be used to directly access dysfunctional attitudes that are not spontaneously reported in therapy sessions.

Homework

Homework assignments can be used to provide valuable information about underlying beliefs during the times when those problems are powerfully activated and available for inspection (Burns, Adams, & Anastopoulos, 1985). For example, a physician sought treatment for vague, amorphous feelings of anxiety and distress that "came out of the blue." Repeated attempts during therapy sessions to collect more information about her symptoms proved futile. To determine the origins of the anxiety, the patient carried out a homework assignment in which she recorded her thoughts and feelings whenever this vague feeling occurred. After several weeks of record keeping, she came to therapy and said, "I realize I'm afraid that my husband is going to leave me, and I feel I can't survive without him!" In therapy sessions, where she felt calm and protected by the therapist, she was unable to experience and describe this fear, but when she kept careful logs at home of her feelings and their precipitants (her husband's business trips), the nature of her fear became clear.

In therapy groups for medical patients in the depression clinic at San Francisco General Hospital, a homework assignment called working backward is used to treat dysfunctional beliefs. Patients are asked to keep daily mood logs so that they become aware of changes in their mood. Next, they are asked to note periods of intense negative mood and are taught to work backward from the negative mood to access the distorted thoughts. That is, they first become aware of the mood; they next note the situation creating the mood; and finally they note the thoughts that are most prominent during the negative mood.

The Therapeutic Relationship

Interactions with the therapist can elicit negative mood states, irrational cognitions and attitudes, and maladaptive behaviors (Goldfried, 1985). This material can provide valuable clues about the patient's underlying beliefs and a powerful setting in which to work on these beliefs. For example, when his therapist arrived 5 minutes late to his session, a young teacher became panicky and angry. When the therapist asked him to report the automatic thoughts that were causing these feelings, the patient reported the following: "You don't care about me, You're not committed to the therapy, I'll never get well, I'll be starved, beaten, and abandoned." This interaction elicited the patient's central fears, and a very productive session was spent working on them. Although no research evidence is available yet to support this notion, we suggest that in vivo cognitive-behavior therapy conducted when the interaction with the therapist activates intense mood states, distorted thinking, and problematic behavior patterns is particularly effective at changing underlying pathogenic cognitions; similar ideas have been outlined by others (Goldfried, 1985; Jacobson, 1989; Safran & Greenberg, 1986).

Nearly every aspect of the patient-therapist interaction, including fee-setting, scheduling appointments, billing procedures, and the patient's responsiveness to the therapist's interventions, can be informative and provide a basis for useful work on the underlying beliefs. For example, patient-therapist interactions involving homework can bring up patients' beliefs about competence or independence. Although every interaction with the therapist does not point to an underlying pathogenic belief, those that are highly emotionally charged or involve a frequently repeated theme deserve careful inspection from this point-of-view.

The Case Formulation

This method (Persons, 1989; Turkat, 1985; Turkat & Maisto, 1985) offers another route to uncovering and working on underlying beliefs. The case formulation model proposes that over/psychological symptoms and problems stem from and reflect an individual's central underlying pathogenic beliefs. This model is based directly on the cognitive theory of depression, which proposes that depressive symptoms originate in underlying pathological beliefs (Beck, 1983). The case formulation model simply extends the cognitive theory and uses it to understand all of the patient's problems and difficulties, not just depressive symptoms.

For example, a woman who believes her needs don't count and that she is only worthwhile if she's helping others may avoid depression by doing laundry for her grown children, meeting the needs of an alcoholic spouse, and spending many hours doing volunteer work at church. Although she is not clinically depressed, the patterns of her behavior provide important clues about her underlying belief and the therapist who includes these behaviors in a careful assessment may be able to develop a hypothesis (formulation) about the nature of the underlying belief. To activate the belief and point it out to the patient, the therapist might in the following way suggest a behavioral change that challenges the belief:

T: Suppose you said to the people at church, "No, I won't be able to help with that." How would you feel?

P: No, I couldn't do that! I'd feel too guilty!

T: I see. And what thoughts would you be having that would be making you feel guilty?

P: I'd think, If they need me to do it, then I should do it for them.

T: Suppose they need you to do it, but you don't do it—what would that mean?

P: (long pause) It would mean I'm bad.

Other strategies for obtaining information about patients' central irrational beliefs are provided by Persons (1989) and by Safran, Vallis, Segal, and Shaw (1986).

Mood Swings are Likely to be Accompanied by Cognitive Swings

Some patients experience recurrent dramatic shifts in mood and equally dramatic shifts in thinking. The knowledge that mood and cognitions are covariant can be quite helpful to the therapist. It can help the therapist maintain a stabilized viewpoint instead of passively following the patient's swings in mood and thinking. It also reminds the therapist that the patient's dysfunctional thinking has probably not dramatically changed, even though it appears to have shifted overnight. That is, the lover who feels vulnerable to abandonment probably retains the belief "Unless I'm loved, I'm worthless" even during periodic positive moods that occur when he is involved in a relationship. In fact, the intensity of the positive mood the patient experiences at these times can serve as a clue to the presence of the underlying irrational belief; if questioned about his positive mood, the patient may report the distorted cognition that "Because I'm loved, I'm a good person." Therefore, additional work on the patient's pathogenic beliefs is indicated even though the patient's mood and thinking has shifted.

The patient also can learn that dysfunctional thinking and negative mood are linked and may be able to use this information to maintain a more stabilized self-concept and behavior plan. For example, the patient who begins feeling bad and then believes that no one likes her may have a tendency to avoid others, thus reinforcing her view that she is undesirable and destined to be alone. If, on the other hand, she learns to say to herself, "When I am in a bad mood I believe that others will reject me, but when I am in a good mood I know that I have friends who love me," she may be able to distance herself from the negative thoughts, continue to interact with friends, and receive positive feedback that contradicts her irrational belief that others will reject her.

The notion that dramatic mood swings are accompanied by dramatic cognitive swings seems particularly helpful when working with individuals who have personality disorders, such as borderline and narcissistic disorders. For these individuals, environmental events may trigger vast mood swings and resultant severe changes in dysfunctional thinking. In fact, dramatic mood swings and accompanying shifts in thinking and behavior may explain why these individuals find it difficult to develop a stable identity and to persevere in careers and relationships.

CONCLUSIONS

Although further empirical evidence is needed, the mood-state hypothesis has important implications for psychotherapy with depressed patients. We hope the ideas presented here will stimulate this work.

The role of mood in cognitive and therapeutic processes is controversial and has been discussed by others. For example, the mood-state hypothesis is consistent with Reda's (1984) views about the effects of antidepressant medication on underlying irrational beliefs: "My hypothesis is that the tricyclic antidepressants. . . modify the negative emotional state that may be the cause . . . of the emergence of the depressive beliefs. . . ." (p. 134). Like Reda, we speculate that the apparent remission in dysfunctional attitudes that is seen in patients who are treated with antidepressants (e.g., Simons et al., 1984) results from medication-induced mood improvements that prevent subjects from reporting dysfunctional attitudes that are still actually present. Other writers, including Segal (1988), Segal and Shaw (1986), and Teasdale (1983), have also suggested that mood may play a role in activating latent dysfunctional beliefs.

Riskind (in Kuiken, 1989) offers a slightly different proposal. He suggests that what appear to be the effects of mood on cognitive processing are actually cognitive effects. For example, he argues that mood inductions may activate cognitive priming that affects other cognitions. Whether the effects of mood change are a result of mood per se or cognitive priming, the point we want to make is that some type of activation procedure may be necessary for full and effective assessment and treatment of underlying dysfunctional attitudes

Although we focus this discussion primarily on depression and anxiety, irrational underlying beliefs may also play a role in other pathological phenomena such as addictive behaviors. Evidence that a negative mood state is a major contributor to relapse in drinking, smoking and other addictive behaviors (Marlatt 1985) can be understood through the mood-state hypothesis. Negative mood may be linked to irrational cognitions and maladaptive behavioral patterns, so that when the mood state changes, thinking and behavior change in tandem. Most discussions of cognitive therapy focus on the way in which negative cognitions produce negative mood. We suggest that attention to the way in which negative mood elicits negative cognitions can be therapeutically useful as well. Of course as Teasdale (1983) points out, causal influences probably flow in both directions.

ACKNOWLEDGMENT

We thank Aaron T. Beck for helpful comments on an earlier version of this material.

REFERENCES

Beck, A. T. (1976). *Cognitive therapy and the emotional disorders.* New York: International Universities Press.

Beck, A. T. (1983). Cognitive therapy of depression: New perspectives. In P. J. Clayton & J. E. Barreu (Eds.), *Treatment of depression: Old controversies and new approaches.* New York: Raven Press.

Beck, A. T., Rush, A. J., Shaw, B. F., & Emery, G. (1979). *Cognitive therapy of depression.* New York: Guilford.

Bower, G. H. (1981). Mood and memory. *American Psychologist, 36,* 129–148.

Burns, D. D. (1980). *Feeling good: The new mood therapy. New* York. William Morrow.

Burns, D. D., Adams, R. L., & Anastopoulos, A. D. (1985). The role of self-help assignments in the treatment of depression. In E. E. Beckham & W. R. Leber (Eds.), *Handbook of depression* (pp. 634–669). Homewood, IL: Dorsey Press.

Dobson, K. S., & Shaw, B. F. (1986). Cognitive assessment with major depressive disorders. *Cognitive Therapy and Research, 10,* 13–29.

Eaves, G., & Rush, A. J. (1984). Cognitive patterns in symptomatic and remitted unipolar major depression. *Journal of Abnormal Psychology, 93,* 31–40.

Edwards, D. J. A. (1989). Cognitive restructuring through guided imagery: Lessons from Gestalt therapy. In A. Freeman, K. M. Simon, L. E. Beutler, & H. Arkowitz (Eds.), *Comprehensive handbook of cognitive therapy* (pp. 283–298). New York: Plenum Press.

Fennell, M. J. V., & Teasdale, J. D. (1987). Cognitive therapy for depression: Individual differences and the process of change. *Cognitive Therapy and Research, 11,* 253–271.

Foa, E. B., & Kozak, M. J. (1986). Emotional processing of fear: Exposure to corrective information. *Psychological Bulletin, 99,* 20–35.

Goldfried, M. (1985). In-vivo intervention or transference? In W. Dryden (Ed.), *Therapists' dilemmas* (pp. 63–74). London: Harper & Row.

Greenberg, L. S., & Safran, J. D. (1987). *Emotion in psychotherapy.* New York: Guilford.

Hamilton, E. W., & Abramson, L. Y. (1983). Cognitive patterns and major depressive disorder: A longitudinal study in a hospital setting. *Journal of Abnormal Psychology, 92,* 173–184.

Hammen, C., Miklowitz, D. J., & Dyck, D. G. (1986). Stability and severity parameters of depressive self-schema responding. *Journal of Social and Clinical Psychology, 4,* 23–45.

Hollon, S. D., Kendall, P. C., & Lumry, A. (1986). Specificity of depressotypic cognitions in clinical depression. *Journal of Abnormal Psychology, 95,* 52–59.

Jacobson, N. S. (1989). The therapist-client relationship in cognitive behavior therapy: Implications for treating depression. *Journal of Cognitive Psychotherapy, 3,* 85–96.

Kuiken, D. (Ed.). (1989). *Journal of Social Behavior and Personality, 4,* 173–184.

Marks, I. M. (1981). *Cure and care of neuroses: Theory and practice of behavioral psychotherapy.* New York: Wiley.

Marlatt, G. A. (1985). Relapse prevention: Theoretical rationale and overview of the model. In G. A. Marlatt & J. R. Gordon (Eds.), *Relapse prevention* (pp. 3–70). New York: Guilford.

Miranda, J., & Persons, J. B. (1988). Dysfunctional attitudes are mood-state dependent. *Journal of Abnormal Psychology, 97,* 76–79.

Miranda, J., Persons, J. B., & Byers, C. N. (1990). Endorsement of dysfunctional beliefs depends on current mood state. *Journal of Abnormal Psychology, 99,* 237–241.

Murphy, G. E., Simons, A. D., Wetzel, R. D., & Lustman, P. J. (1984). Cognitive therapy and pharmacotherapy: Singly and together in the treatment of depression. *Archives of General Psychiatry, 41,* 33–41.

Persons, J. (1989). *Cognitive therapy in practice: A case formulation approach.* New York: Norton.

Persons, J. B., & Miranda, J. (1990, June). *Cognitive theories of vulnerability to depression: Reconciling negative evidence.* Paper presented at meetings of the Society for Psychotherapy Research, 1990, Wintergreen, VA.

Persons, J. B., & Rao, P. A. (1985). Longitudinal study of cognitions, life events, and depression in psychiatric inpatients. *Journal of Abnormal Psychology, 94,* 51–63.

Reda, M. A. (1984). Cognitive organization and antidepressants: Attitude modification during amitriptyline treatment in severely depressed individuals. In M. A. Reda & M. J. Mahoney (Eds.), *Cognitive psychotherapies: Recent developments in theory research, and practice* (pp. XX). Cambridge, MA: Ballinger

Safran, J. D., & Greenberg, L. S. (1986). Hot cognition and psychotherapy process: An information processing/ecological approach. In P. C. Kendall (Ed.), *Advances in cognitive-behavioral research and therapy, Vol. 5.* (pp. XX). New York: Academic Press.

Safran, J. D, Vallis, T. M., Segal, Z. V., & Shaw, B. F. (1986). Assessment of core cognitive processes in cognitive therapy. *Cognitive Therapy and Research, 10,* 509–526.

Segal, Z. V. (1988). Appraisal of the self-schema construct in cognitive models of depression. *Psychological Bulletin, 103,* 147–162.

Segal, Z. V., & Shaw, B. F. (1986). Cognition in depression: A reappraisal of Coyne and Gotlib's critique. *Cognitive Therapy and Research, 10,* 671–693.

Silverman, J. S., Silverman, J. A., & Eardley, D. A. (1984). Do maladaptive attitudes cause depression? *Archives of General Psychiatry, 41,* 28–30.

Simons, A. D., Garfield, S. L., & Murphy, G. E. (1984). The process of change in cognitive therapy and pharmacotherapy for depression. *Archives of General Psychiatry, 41,* 45–51.

Simons, A. D., Murphy, G. E., Levine, J. L., & Wetzel, R. D. (1986). Cognitive therapy and pharmacotherapy for depression: Sustained improvement over one year. *Archives of General Psychiatry, 43,* 43–48.

Singer, J. A., & Salovey, P. (1988). Mood and memory: Evaluating the network theory of affect. *Clinical Psychology Review, 8,* 211–251.

Teasdale, J. (1983). Negative thinking in depression: Cause, effect, or reciprocal relationship? *Advances in Behavior Research and Therapy, 22,* 549–552.

Teasdale, J. & Dent, (1987). Cognitive vulnerability to depression: An investigation of two hypotheses. *British Journal of Clinical Psychology, 26,* 113–126.

Turkat, I. D. (Ed.) 1985. *Behavioral case formulation.* New York: Plenum.

Turkat, I. D., & Maisto, S. A. (1985). Personality disorders: Application of the experimental method to the formulation and modification of personality disorders. In D. H. Barlow (Ed.), *Clinical handbook of psychological disorders: A step-by-step treatment manual* (pp. 502–570). New York: Guilford.

CHAPTER 4

Cognitive Vulnerability to Depression: Theory and Evidence

Lyn Y. Abramson, Lauren B. Alloy,
Michael E. Hogan, Wayne G. Whitehouse,
Patricia Donovan, Donna T. Rose,
Catherine Panzarella, and David Raniere

According to the cognitive vulnerability hypothesis of two major cognitive theories of depression, Beck's (1967; 1987) theory and the hopelessness theory (Abramson, Metalsky, & Alloy, 1989), negative cognitive styles provide vulnerability to depression, particularly hopelessness depression (HD), when people encounter negative life events. The Temple-Wisconsin Cognitive Vulnerability to Depression (CVD) Project is a two-site, prospective longitudinal study designed to test this hypothesis as well as the other etiological hypotheses of Beck's and the hopelessness theories of depression. We present findings from the CVD Project suggesting that the hypothesized depressogenic cognitive styles do indeed confer vulnerability for clinically significant depressive disorders and suicidality. In addition, we present evidence about the information processing and personality correlates of these styles. Finally, we discuss preliminary findings about the developmental origins of cognitive vulnerability to depression.

COGNITIVE VULNERABILITY HYPOTHESIS OF DEPRESSION ONSET

Why are some people vulnerable to depression whereas others never seem to become depressed? According to the cognitive theories of depression, the way people typically interpret or explain events in their lives, their cognitive styles, significantly affects their vulnerability to depression. Thus, as a complement to work emphasizing biological or genetic risk for depression, the hopelessness theory (Abramson, Metalsky, & Alloy, 1989) and Beck's theory (Beck, 1967; 1987) highlight cognitive risk for depression.

For example, according to the hopelessness theory (Abramson et al., 1989), people who (1) characteristically attribute negative life events to stable (likely to persist over time) and global (likely to affect many areas of life) causes, (2) infer that further negative consequences will follow from a current negative life event, (3) and believe that the occurrence of a negative event in their lives means that they are fundamentally flawed or worthless are hypothesized to be more likely to develop episodes of depression—particularly the subtype of "hopelessness depression" (HD)—when they confront negative life events than people who don't exhibit these inferential styles. The logic here is that people who exhibit this hypothesized depressogenic inferential style should be more likely to make negative inferences about the cause, consequences, and self-implications of any particular negative life event they confront, thereby increasing the likelihood that they will develop hopelessness and, in turn, the symptoms of depression, particularly HD.

In Beck's theory (Beck, 1967; 1987) negative self-schemata revolving around themes of inadequacy, failure, loss, and worthlessness are hypothesized to provide cognitive vulnerability to depressive symptoms. Such negative self-schemata often are represented as a set of dysfunctional attitudes or self-worth contingencies such as "If I fail partly, it is as bad as being a complete failure" or "I am nothing if a person I love doesn't love me." When they encounter negative life events that impinge on their cognitive vulnerability, individuals exhibiting such negative self-schemata or dysfunctional attitudes are hypothesized to develop negatively biased construals of the self (low self-esteem), world, and future (hopelessness) and, in turn, depressive symptoms. Thus, both the hopelessness theory and Beck's theory can be conceptualized as vulnerability-stress theories in which negative inferential styles provide cognitive vulnerability to depression through their effect on the interpretation or processing of personally relevant negative life events.

TESTING THE COGNITIVE VULNERABILITY HYPOTHESIS: THE BEHAVIORAL HIGH-RISK DESIGN

A powerful strategy for testing the cognitive vulnerability hypothesis is the "behavioral high-risk design" (e.g., Depue et al., 1981). Similarly to the genetic high-risk paradigm, the behavioral high-risk design involves studying participants who do not currently have the disorder of interest but who are hypothesized to be at high or low risk for developing it. In contrast to the genetic high-risk paradigm, in the behavioral high-risk study individuals are selected on the basis of hypothesized psychological, rather than genetic, vulnerability or invulnerability to the disorder. Thus, to test the cognitive vulnerability hypotheses of depression, one would want to select nondepressed people who were at high versus low risk for depression based on the presence versus absence of the hypothesized depressogenic cognitive styles. One would then compare these cognitively high-and low-risk groups on their likelihood of exhibiting depression both in the past, in a retrospective version of the design, and in the future, in a prospective version of the design. The prospective version of the design is superior to the retrospective version because the cognitive "vulnerability" that is assessed in the latter might actually be a scar of a prior depressive episode (Rohde, Lewinsohn, & Seeley, 1991) rather than a causal factor in that prior episode (Gotlib & Abramson, in press).

The results of studies that have used methods less optimal than the behavioral high-risk design to test the cognitive vulnerability hypothesis of depression have been equivocal (see Barnett & Gotlib, 1988). In contrast, recent studies using or approximating a behavioral high-risk design have obtained considerable support for the cognitive vulnerability hypothesis of depression. For example, using a retrospective behavioral high-risk design, Alloy, Lipman, and Abramson (1992) tested the attributional vulnerability hypothesis of the hopelessness theory for clinically significant depression. In this study, currently nondepressed college students who either did or did not exhibit attributional vulnerability for depression with low self-esteem were compared on the likelihood that they had experienced major depressive disorder, as well as the hypothesized subtype of HD, over the past 2 years. Consistent with the cognitive vulnerability hypothesis, attributionally vulnerable students were more likely to have exhibited major depressive disorder and the syndrome of HD over the previous 2 years and to have experienced a greater number of episodes of these disorders than attributionally invulnerable students. Moreover, recent studies that have used variants of the prospective behavioral high-

risk design consistently have found that people who exhibit the hypothesized cognitive vulnerability are more likely to develop depressive moods
and/or depressive symptoms when they experience negative life events
than are individuals who do not show this vulnerability (Alloy &
Clements, 1998; Alloy, Just, & Panzarella, 1997b; Metalsky, Halberstadt, & Abramson, 1987; Metalsky & Joiner, 1992; Metalsky, Joiner,
Hardin, & Abramson, 1993; Nolen-Hoeksema, Girgus, & Seligman,
1992).

THE TEMPLE-WISCONSIN COGNITIVE VULNERABILITY TO DEPRESSION (CVD) PROJECT

The ongoing Temple-Wisconsin Cognitive Vulnerability to Depression
(CVD) Project is a collaborative, two–site study that uses a prospective
behavioral high-risk design to test the cognitive vulnerability and other
etiological hypotheses of hopelessness and Beck's theories of depression
for both depressive symptoms and clinically significant depressive episodes. In the CVD project, first-year college students at either high or low
cognitive risk for depression who were nondepressed and had no other
current Axis I psychopathology at the outset of the study were followed
every six weeks for two and a half years with self-report and structured
interview assessments of stressful life events, cognitions, and symptoms, and
diagnosable episodes of psychopathology. The participants then were followed for an additional 3 years, with assessments occurring every 4
months.

Because the cognitively high-risk (HR) participants were required to
score in the highest quartile on measures of the cognitive vulnerabilities
featured in both the hopelessness theory (Cognitive Style Questionnaire
[CSQ]; Abramson, Metalsky, & Alloy, 1998) and Beck's theory (expanded Dysfunctional Attitude Scale [DAS]; Weissman & Beck, 1978), and
the cognitively low-risk (LR) participants were required to score in the
lowest quartile on both of these measures, the CVD project provides a
broad test of a "generic" cognitive vulnerability hypothesis. A strength of
this study is that the two sites permit a built-in assessment of replicability
of results. Whereas the University of Wisconsin sample has a high representation of Caucasian individuals from rural, farming, small-town, and
suburban backgrounds, the Temple University sample is more urban, with
a high representation of minority (largely African Americans) and lower
socioeconomic participants. Notably, all of the results reported below
replicated across the two sites.

COGNITIVE VULNERABILITY AND THE PREDICTION OF DEPRESSION AND SUICIDALITY

The CVD Project behavioral high-risk design allows for retrospective and prospective tests of the cognitive vulnerability hypothesis. We now review findings on the predictive validity of the hypothesized negative cognitive styles for depressive disorders and suicidality.

Retrospective Lifetime History of Depression

Based on the cognitive vulnerability hypothesis and evidence that attributional styles exhibit some stability over the lifespan (Burns & Seligman, 1989); Alloy et al., 1998a) examined the lifetime prevalence rates of DSM-III-R and RDC depressive disorders, the syndrome of HD, and other Axis I disorders in HR versus LR participants. Consistent with the cognitive vulnerability hypothesis, Alloy et al. (1998a) found that the HR group showed greater lifetime prevalence than the LR group of major depressive disorder, DSM and RDC (39% vs. 17%); RDC minor depressive disorder (22% vs. 12%); HD (40% vs. 12%); and depressive spectrum disorders such as RDC labile personality (8% vs. 1%) and subaffective dysthymia (4% vs. 0%). Indeed, the HR group showed double the rate of lifetime major depression than the LR group, and triple the rate of HD. Moreover, these HR-LR differences were specific to depressive disorders. The groups did not differ on lifetime prevalence rates of anxiety disorders, alcohol and drug abuse, or other Axis I disorders. These findings suggest that depressogenic cognitive styles may indeed confer risk for full-blown, clinically significant depressive disorders and for HD, and that the risk may be specific to depression.

One possible confound in interpreting these lifetime history findings is that the risk group differences may be due to differential residual depressive symptoms associated with HR status (even though no one with current episodes of psychopathology was allowed in the final sample). To rule out this possibility, Alloy et al. (1998a) examined the Beck Depression Inventory (BDI; Beck, Rush, Shaw, & Emery, 1979) scores at the time of the cognitive vulnerability assessment as a covariate. With the exceptions of RDC minor depression and the depressive spectrum disorders, the significant risk group differences on lifetime history of major depression and HD were maintained, even with BDI scores controlled. Note that the use of the BDI as a covariate in these analyses provides a very conservative test of the cognitive vulnerability hypothesis because any of the variance in depressive diagnoses that is shared between cognitive risk status and current BDI is allocated to the BDI even though the cognitive theories predict that such shared variance should exist.

Alloy et al. (1998a) also examined several other hypothesized cognitive vulnerability factors for depression, including self-consciousness (Ingram, 1990), sociotropy and autonomy (Beck, 1987), and inferential style for positive events (Alloy, Reilly-Harrington, Fresco, Whitehouse, & Zechmeister, in press). These other variables did not predict lifetime history of depressive disorders (major, minor, and HD) and moreover, the HR-LR differences in lifetime prevalence of major, minor, and HD remained when these other hypothesized vulnerability factors were used as covariates. (The only exception to this pattern is that when sociotropy was used as a covariate, HR-LR differences in lifetime prevalence of minor depression no longer were significant.) Thus, these results support the importance of the cognitive vulnerabilities featured in hopelessness and Beck's theories.

These findings provide the first demonstration that, as predicted, negative cognitive styles may confer risk for full-blown, clinically significant depressive disorders and for the hypothesized subtype of HD. This is noteworthy because a criticism of the cognitive theories of depression is that they apply only to mild depression. Alloy et al.'s (1998a) results suggest that this criticism is inappropriate and that these theories are relevant to explaining more severe, clinically significant forms of depression. Second, the results also provide support for the hypothesis that the specific subtype of HD exists in nature and conforms to theoretical description. Of course, the major conceptual limitation of Alloy et al.'s (1998a) retrospective findings is that the causal direction of the association between cognitive vulnerability and increased lifetime rates of depressive disorders is unclear. Did the negative cognitive styles temporally precede and contribute to the onset of the past episodes of depression, or did these styles develop as a result of the past depression? To more clearly test whether negative cognitive styles actually increase risk for depression, a prospective test of the cognitive vulnerability hypotheses is needed.

Prospective Incidence of First Onsets and Recurrences of Depression

Alloy et al. (1998c) examined CVD project findings on the prospective incidence of first onsets and recurrences of depressive and anxiety disorders for the first two and a half years of follow-up at both sites. More than half of the CVD project sample entered college with no prior history of clinically significant depression. These participants could potentially experience their very first episode of clinical depression during the prospective follow-up period. Does the cognitive vulnerability hypothesis hold for these first onsets of depression?

Consistent with the cognitive vulnerability hypothesis, Alloy et al. (1998c) reported that HR participants showed a greater likelihood than LR participants of a first onset of DSM-III-R or RDC major depressive disorder (17% vs. 1%), RDC minor depressive disorder (39% vs. 6%), and the subtype of HD (41% vs. 5%). In contrast, there were no risk group differences in the development of anxiety disorders during the prospective follow-up period among this sample (7% vs. 3%). Moreover, in order to control for any residual depressive symptoms associated with HR status, Alloy et al. (1998c) used initial BDI scores as a covariate. Even with initial BDI scores controlled, the impressive risk group differences in rates of first onsets of depressive episodes were maintained. These findings provide especially important support for the cognitive vulnerability hypothesis because they are based on a truly prospective test, uncontaminated by prior history of depression. Moreover, they suggest that depressogenic cognitive styles confer specific risk for first onsets of depression, and in particular, the subtype of HD, but not for anxiety disorders.

Recall that with our selection strategy, we excluded any potential participant who exhibited any current Axis I diagnosis. However, as demonstrated by the results from our retrospective analyses, we did include participants with a past history of clinical depression as long as they were not experiencing a current episode of depression at the outset of the study. What about these participants who, though nondepressed at the outset of the CVD project, did have a prior history of clinically significant depression? This subsample allows a test of whether the cognitive vulnerability hypothesis holds for recurrences of depression which is particularly important given that depression often is a recurrent disorder (Belsher & Costello, 1988; Judd, 1997).

Alloy et al. (1998c) reported that HR participants with a past history of depression were more likely than LR participants with prior depression to develop recurrences of DSM-III-R and RDC major depression (27% vs. 6%), RDC minor depression (50% vs. 26.5%), and HD (52% vs. 22%), and these differences were maintained even when initial BDI scores were controlled. HR participants with a prior history of depression also were more likely than previously depressed LR participants to experience onsets of anxiety disorder (11% vs. 2%). Thus, the cognitive vulnerability hypothesis was upheld for both recurrences as well as first onsets, suggesting that similar processes may, at least in part, underlie the first as well as subsequent episodes of depression. The prospective CVD project results are exciting because they provide the first demonstration that negative cognitive styles, or for that matter, any hypothesized psychological vulnerability factor, indeed appear to confer vulnerability to clinically significant depressive episodes.

Of interest, Steinberg, Alloy, and Abramson (1998a) reported that cognitive vulnerability did not worsen following episodes of depression. That is, participants' inferences for stressful events did not increase in negativity from before to after each recurrence of major or minor depression, supporting the stability of depressogenic cognitive styles.

Prospective Incidence of Suicidality

The cognitive theories of depression also may be especially useful for understanding the processes giving rise to suicidality. Drawing on prior research demonstrating a powerful link between hopelessness and suicide (Beck, Brown, Berchick, Stewart, & Steer, 1990; Minkoff, Bergman, Beck, & Beck, 1973), Abramson et al. (1989) speculated that suicidality, on a continuum from suicidal ideation to completed suicide, may be a core symptom of HD. Indeed, according to both hopelessness and Beck's theories, individuals exhibiting negative inferential styles and dysfunctional attitudes, respectively, should be at risk for suicidality mediated by hopelessness. In a test of this hypothesis, Joiner and Rudd (1995) found that college students with a stable, global attributional style for negative interpersonal events showed increases in suicidality when they experienced interpersonal stressors, consistent with prediction.

Using CVD Project data from the first two and a half years of prospective follow-up, Abramson et al. (1998a) also tested the cognitive vulnerability hypothesis of suicidality. They reported that during the prospective follow-up, the HR group was more likely that the LR group to exhibit suicidality as assessed by structured diagnostic interview (28% vs. 12.6%). In addition, the HR group exhibited higher levels of suicidality than the LR participants as assessed by questionnaire self-report. Further, HR participants were more likely than LR participants to exhibit other hypothesized risk factors for suicidality not explicitly specified in hopelessness or Beck's theories, including prior history of suicidality (Beck, Steer, & Brown, 1993), personal history of depressive disorders (Hawton, 1987; Lewinsohn, Rohde, & Seeley, 1993), borderline personality dysfunction (Isometsa et al., 1996), and parental history of depression (Wagner, 1997). Given that cognitive vulnerability was related to these other hypothesized risk factors for suicidality, Abramson et al. (1998a) controlled statistically for these other risk factors and found that cognitive risk status continued to predict prospective suicidality. Finally, Abramson et al. (1998a) found that hopelessness across the two and a half year follow-up completely mediated the relationship between cognitive vulnerability and prospective suicidality as measured by both interview and questionnaire, even when controlling for prior history of suicidality. It should be noted that controlling for prior history of suicidality in tests of the cognitive vulnerability hypothesis may be overly conservative because prior history of suicidality may, itself, be a result of cognitive vulnerability in part.

CHARACTERISTICS OF COGNITIVELY VULNERABLE INDIVIDUALS

Given that depressogenic cognitive styles predict lifetime history and prospective incidence of depressive disorders and suicidality, it is important to characterize the personalities of cognitively vulnerable individuals. At the outset of the CVD project, we examined the information processing and personality correlates of cognitive vulnerability.

Cognitive Vulnerability and Self-Referent Information Processing

According to the cognitive theories of depression, people with negative cognitive styles are vulnerable to depression in part because they tend to engage in negatively toned information processing about themselves when they encounter negative life events. Thus, Alloy, Abramson, Murray, Whitehouse, and Hogan (1997a) examined whether nondepressed individuals with negative cognitive styles do, in fact, process information about themselves more negatively than do those with positive styles, based on a Self-Referent Information Processing (SRIP) Task Battery administered to the HR and LR participants in the CVD project at the outset of the study.

Consistent with prediction, Alloy et al. (1997a) found that relative to LR participants, HR participants showed preferential processing of self-referent negative depression-relevant information as evidenced by relatively greater endorsement, faster processing, greater accessibility, and better recall of content involving themes of incompetence, worthlessness, and low motivation. Even more consistent across the SRiP measures, HR participants also were less likely to process positive depression-relevant stimuli than were LR participants. These risk group differences in self-referent information-processing remained even when current levels of depressive symptoms were controlled, suggesting that the self-referent information processing differences associated with cognitive vulnerability status are not due to any residual differences in the risk groups' depressive symptoms.

These findings of HR-LR group differences in self-referent information processing are important for two reasons. First, they indicate that negatively toned self-relevant information processing previously demonstrated to be characteristic of depressed individuals (Segal, 1988) also occurs among nondepressed individuals who are vulnerable to depression by virtue of exhibiting negative cognitive styles. Second, from a methodological perspective, the findings provide converging evidence for information-processing effects of cognitive styles on laboratory tasks adapted from cognitive science paradigms and, thereby, further support the construct validity of the cognitive style questionnaire measures.

Cognitive Vulnerability and Personality Dysfunction

Aside from the tendency to engage in negative information processing about the self, what other personality characteristics cohere with cognitive vulnerability to depression? Abramson et al. (1998b) hypothesized that individuals with depressogenic cognitive styles should be especially likely to exhibit Axis II personality dysfunction. First, the comorbidity between depression and personality disorders is high (Farmer & Nelson-Gray, 1990). Second, among depressed inpatients, those with personality disorders, particularly borderline personality disorder, are more likely to exhibit cognitive vulnerability than other depressives (Rose, Abramson, Hodulik, Halberstadt, & Leff, 1994). Finally, many currently diagnosed personality disorders are associated with the cognitive profiles defining cognitive risk for depression (Beck, Freeman, & Associates, 1990), suggesting a link between cognitive vulnerability to depression and personality disorders. For example, Cluster C, the "anxious/fearful cluster," is associated with feelings of incompetence and helplessness.

To assess personality dysfunction, Abramson et al. (1998b) administered the Personality Disorder Examination (PDE; Loranger, 1988) at the outset of the CVD project. The PDE provides for DSM-III-R categorical personality disorder diagnoses as well as dimensional scores, which is important given that participants in the CVD project were young (mean age = 18) and, therefore, relatively unlikely to have developed full-blown diagnosable personality disorder by the time they entered the study. Despite their young age, Abramson et al. reported that the HR group showed a higher rate than the LR group of actual diagnosable personality disorders (5.4% vs. 1.7%).

In addition, as expected, the HR group showed greater dysfunction on personality dimensions from all three clusters, including the paranoid and schizotypal dimensions from Cluster A, the borderline, histrionic, and narcissistic dimensions from Cluster B, and the avoidant, dependent, obsessive-compulsive, and passive-aggressive dimensions from Cluster C. HR participants also showed greater dysfunction on the self-defeating dimension, but the risk groups did not differ on the schizoid, antisocial, and sadistic dimensions. With the exception of the narcissistic, passive-aggressive, and self-defeating dimensions, these HR-LR differences in personality dysfunction were maintained when participants' depressive symptom levels (BDI scores) were controlled. Abramson et al. (1998b) additionally reported that the risk group differences in lifetime prevalence of episodic unipolar depressive disorders (major, minor, and HD) reviewed above were maintained even when the personality dysfunction associated with HR status was controlled. Thus, personality dysfunction does not mediate the effect of cognitive vulnerability on development of depression.

The association between cognitive vulnerability and personality disturbance is intriguing given current theoretical controversy about the relationship between mood and personality disorders and the demonstrated comorbidity between the two (Farmer & Nelson-Gray, 1990). This finding points to the importance of interpersonal dysfunction among individuals exhibiting depressogenic cognitive styles. A shortcoming of the cognitive theories of depression is that cognitive vulnerability for depression often has been described as if it occurs in a behavioral and interpersonal vacuum. Abramson et al.'s (1998b) results begin to reveal the behavioral and interpersonal styles associated with cognitive risk for depression.

Developmental Origins of Cognitive Vulnerability to Depression

If depressogenic cognitive styles do confer vulnerability for depression and suicidality, as indicated by the CVD project findings, then it is important to understand the antecedents of these cognitive styles. What are the developmental origins of cognitive vulnerability to depression? In the CVD project, we directly studied the parents of the cognitively HR and LR participants with respect to parents' cognitive styles, parenting behaviors, psychopathology, and personality as well as the HR and LR participants' early childhood life events and neglect and maltreatment experiences.

Below, we briefly review preliminary findings from the CVD project and several related studies on possible developmental precursors of negative and positive cognitive styles. We emphasize that the CVD project findings presented in this section indeed are preliminary because analyses still are in progress. Moreover, many of our initial explorations of potential precursors of cognitive styles have relied on retrospective designs and, thus, should be construed as generating hypotheses for more definitive testing with future prospective designs.

Parental Psychopathology and Children's Cognitive Vulnerability to Depression

Prior research has demonstrated that children of depressed parents are at increased risk for depression themselves (Downey & Coyne, 1990). Parental depression may contribute to the development of depressogenic cognitive styles and, thus, cognitive vulnerability to depression in their offspring through a variety of mechanisms including genetic transmission, modeling, and negative parenting practices, among others. To explore the possible familial origins of negative cognitive styles, Abramson, Alloy, Tashman, Whitehouse, and Hogan (1998d) examined the association between CVD project participants' cognitive risk status and their parents' depression based on the participants' reports of their parents' psychiatric history using the family history RDC method (Andreason, Endicott, Spitzer, & Winokur, 1977) as well as a direct interview of the parents themselves with the SADS-L (Endicott & Spitzer, 1978). Child and parent reports of parental psychopathology showed significant, but modest, agreement, with *phi* coefficients ranging from .18 to .43 for various disorders. Based on the child (CVD participants) reports of parental psychopathology, Abramson et al. (1998d) found that HR participants' mothers were significantly more likely, and their fathers showed a trend to be more likely, to have a history of depressive disorder than were LR participants' mothers and fathers, respectively (35% vs. 18% for mothers; 18% vs. 12% for fathers). There were no HR-LR differences in the parents' rates of other disorders. With the direct interview of parents, Abramson et al. (1998d) found that mothers of HR participants had greater lifetime histories of depression than mothers of LR participants whereas fathers of HR and LR participants didn't differ. In sum, both child and parent reports about parents' depression were consistent in showing greater lifetime depression in the mothers of HR than LR individuals. These findings are consistent with the hypothesis that mothers' depression may contribute to the development of cognitive vulnerability to depression in their offspring.

Modeling, Parental Inferential Feedback, and Cognitive Vulnerability to Depression

Children may learn their cognitive styles in part from significant others, in particular their parents. If modeling of parents' styles is a contributor to the development of cognitive vulnerability versus invulnerability to depression, then children's cognitive styles should correlate with those of their mothers or fathers. In addition to modeling, the feedback parents provide to their children about causes and consequences of negative events in the child's life may contribute to the child's cognitive risk for depression. Children may be taught, implicitly or explicitly, to make the same inferences about events in their lives as those made by their parents for the children's events. If parental feedback contributes to children's cognitive risk, then parents' typical inferential communications to their children should be correlated with the children's cognitive styles.

Alloy et al. (1998b) examined the modeling and feedback hypotheses with data from the CVD Project. To test the modeling hypothesis, the same cognitive style measures (CSQ and DAS) were administered to the parents of the HR and LR participants as the participants completed themselves. To test the feedback hypothesis, parent and child report versions of the Parent Attributions for Children's Events Scale (PACE; Steinberg, Tashman, Alloy, & Abramson, 1998b), a questionnaire that assessed parents' typical feedback to their child regarding the causes and consequences of negative events in the child's life, were administered. Consistent with the modeling hypothesis, parents of HR participants had more dysfunctional attitudes than parents of LR participants. Supporting the feedback hypothesis, according to the child reports of their parents' behavior, both mothers and fathers of HR participants provided more depressogenic feedback about causes and consequences of negative life events that happened to their child than did mothers and fathers of LR participants. Thus, not only may children model the cognitive styles of their parents, but they also may be directly taught habitual ways of interpreting events by the inferential feedback they receive from their parents.

Developmental Maltreatment and Cognitive Vulnerability to Depression

Rose and Abramson (1998) hypothesized that a developmental history of maltreatment and neglect may contribute to the origins of cognitive vulnerability to depression. Noting that research on "depressive realism" suggests that depressives may not be as irrational as originally portrayed in Beck's cognitive distortion theory of depression (Alloy, Albright, Abramson, & Dykman, 1990), Rose and Abramson suggested that the negative cognitive styles exhibited by depressives might be the internal representations of maltreatment or adverse environments they actually experienced rather than cognitive distortions.

Consistent with their formulation, Rose and Abramson (1998) found that adults who exhibited marked cognitive vulnerability for depression reported growing up in environments characterized by emotional, sexual, and physical maltreatment as well as neglect. According to Rose and Abramson, emotional maltreatment may be a particularly virulent contributor to cognitive vulnerability to depression because, unlike physical or sexual maltreatment, the abuser, by definition, supplies negative cognitions to the victim. For example, the individual may be told why negative events happen ("Of course you didn't get invited to the prom. You're ugly.") and internalize these attributions. Anecdotally, Rose and Abramson noted that participants spontaneously reinforced this position while they were being interviewed about their early maltreatment. Participants who had experienced multiple forms of abuse made comments such as, "Bruises heal. Unless you end up needing reconstructive surgery, getting beaten isn't the worst thing. But I could not forget those terrible things my mother said to me. I can't get the names she called me out of my head." Of course, the correlational data obtained by Rose and Abramson (1998) cannot establish that the association between early maltreatment and cognitive risk for depression is causal; however, they are consistent with the hypothesis that developmental maltreatment predisposes cognitive vulnerability to depression and underscore the importance of future prospective tests of this hypothesis.

CONCLUSION

We have reviewed promising evidence from the CVD project and related studies indicating that the negative inferential styles and dysfunctional attitudes featured in hopelessness and Beck's theories of depression appear to confer vulnerability to clinically significant depressive disorders, particularly the subtype of hopelessness depression, as well as suicidality. We also have presented preliminary findings on the information processing and personality correlates and developmental origins of depressogenic cognitive styles.

Many important theoretical issues remain to be addressed with the CVD project data. For example, because the cognitive theories of depression are vulnerability-stress models, future analyses of CVD project data must test whether it is particularly in the face of negative life events that cognitively vulnerable individuals are more likely to become depressed than invulnerable individuals. Further, does hopelessness mediate the development of depression by cognitively vulnerable individuals confronted with negative life events? Finally, how may cognitive vulnerability change over the lifetime?

In conclusion, the findings to date from the CVD project provide strong support for the hypothesis that people's characteristic way of construing their life experiences, their cognitive styles, importantly influences their vulnerability to clinically significant depression. Given that depression often leads to considerable suffering, impairment, and economic cost, that it is recurrent, and that it can be lethal when accompanied by suicidality, the documentation of a cognitive risk factor for this disorder has considerable therapeutic and preventive significance.

ACKNOWLEDGMENTS

The research reviewed in this article was supported by National Institute of Mental Health Grants MH 43866 to Lyn Y. Abramson and MH 48216 to Lauren B. Alloy. We would like to thank the following CVD project staff for their contributions to this article: Sogoli Akhavan, Sue Amundson, Michelle Armstrong, Monica Calkins, Mark Cenite, Alexandra Chiara, Judith Cronholm, Rayna Dombro, llene Dyller, Kimberly Eberbach, Erika Francis, Teresa Gannon, Stephanie Johnson, Nancy Just, Rita Kekstas, Ray Kim, Christine Klitz, Joanna Lapkin, Alan Lipman, Susan Luelke, Gary Marshall, Laura Murray, Noreen Reilly-Harrington, Matthew Robinson, Pamela Shapiro, Janet Shriberg, Deborah Small, Laurie Teraspulsky, Sandra Tierney, Aaron Torrance, Ann Whitehouse, and Lin Zhu. The first two authors contributed equally to this article.

REFERENCES

Abramson, L. Y., Alloy, L. B., Hogan, M. E., Whitehouse, W. G., Cornette, M., Akhavan, S., & Chiara, A. (1998a). Suicidality and cognitive vulnerability to depression among college students: A prospective study. *Journal of Adolescence, 21,* 157–171.

Abramson, L. Y., Alloy, L. B., Hogan, M. E., Whitehouse, W. G., Rose, D. T., & Panzarella, C. (1998b). The Temple-Wisconsin Cognitive Vulnerability to Depression (CVD) Project: Axis II personality disorders and dimensions in individuals at high and low cognitive risk for depression. Manuscript in preparation, University of Wisconsin.

Abramson, L. Y., Alloy, L. B., Tashman, N., Whitehouse, W. G., & Hogan, M. E. (1998d). The Temple-Wisconsin Cognitive Vulnerability to Depression (CVD)

Project: Axis I and II psychopathology in the parents of individuals at high and low cognitive risk for depression. Manuscript in preparation, University of Wisconsin.

Abramson, L. Y., Metalsky, G. I., & Alloy, L. B. (1989). Hopelessness depression: A theory-based subtype of depression. *Psychological Review, 96,* 358–372.

Abramson, L. Y., Metalsky, G. I., & Alloy, L. B. (1998). The Cognitive Style Questionnaire: A measure of the vulnerability featured in the hopelessness theory of depression. Manuscript in preparation, University of Wisconsin-Madison.

Alloy, L. B., Abramson, L. Y., Hogan, M. E., Whitehouse, W. G ., Rose, D. T., Robinson, M. S., Kim, R., & Lapkin, J. B. (1998a). The Temple-Wisconsin Cognitive Vulnerability to Depression (CVD) Project: Lifetime history of Axis I psychopathology in individuals at high and low cognitive risk for depression. Manuscript in preparation, Temple University, Philadelphia, PA.

Alloy, L. B., Abramson, L. Y., Tashman, N., Whitehouse, W. G., & Hogan, M. E. (1998b). The Temple-Wisconsin Cognitive Vulnerability to Depression (CVD) Project: Parenting practices of the parents of individuals at high and low cognitive risk for depression. Manuscript in preparation, Temple University.

Alloy, L. B., Abramson, L. Y., Murray, L. A., Whitehouse, W. G., & Hogan, M. E. (1997a). Self-referent information-processing in individuals at high and low cognitive risk for depression. *Cognition and Emotion, 11,* 539–568.

Alloy, L. B., Abramson, L. Y., Whitehouse, W. G., Hogan, M. E., Panzarella, C., Robinson, M. S., Lapkin, J. B., & Rose, D. T. (1998c). The Temple-Wisconsin Cognitive Vulnerability to Depression (CVD) Project: Prospective incidence of first onsets and recurrences of Axis 1 disorders in individuals at high and low cognitive risk for depression. Manuscript in preparation, Temple University, Philadelphia, PA.

Alloy, L. B., Albright, J. S., Abramson, L. Y., & Dykman, B. M. (1990). Depressive realism and nondepressive optimistic illusions: The role of the self. In R. E. Ingram (Ed.), *Contemporary psychological approaches to depression: Treatment, research, and theory.* New York: Plenum.

Alloy, L. B., & Clements, C. M. (1998). Hopelessness theory of depression: Tests of the symptom component. *Cognitive Therapy and Research, 22,* 303–335.

Alloy, L. B., Just, N., & Panzarella, C. (1997b). Attributional style, daily life events, and hopelessness depression: Subtype validation by prospective variability and specificity of symptoms. *Cognitive Therapy and Research, 21,* 321–344.

Alloy, L. B., Lipman, A., & Abramson, L. Y. (1992). Attributional style as a vulnerability factor for depression: Validation by past history of mood disorders. Cognitive Therapy and Research, 16, 391–407.

Alloy, L. B., Reilly-Harrington, N., Fresco, D., Whitehouse, W. G., & Zechmeister, J. S. (1999). Cognitive styles and life events in subsyndromal unipolar and bipolar disorders: Stability and prospective prediction of depressive and hypomanic mood swings. *Journal of Cognitive Psychotherapy: An international Quarterly, 14,* 21–40.

Andreasen, N., Endicott, J., Spitzer, R. L., & Winokur, G. (1977). The family history method using diagnostic criteria: Reliability and validity. *Archives of General Psychiatry, 34,* 1229–1235.

Barnett, P. A., & Gotlib, I. H. (1988). Psychosocial functioning and depression: Distinguishing among antecedents, concomitants, and consequences. *Psychological Bulletin, 104,* 97–126.

Beck, A. T. (1967). Depression: Clinical, experimental, and theoretical aspects. New York: Harper & Row.

Beck, A. T. (1 987). Cognitive models of depression. *Journal of Cognitive Psychotherapy: An International Quarterly, 1,* 5–37.

Beck, A. T., Brown, G., Berchick, R. J., Stewart, B. L., & Steer, R. A. (1990). Relationship between hopelessness and ultimate suicide: A replication with psychiatric patients. *American Journal of Psychiatry, 147,* 190–195.

Beck, A. T., Freeman, A. (1990). *Cognitive therapy of personality disorders.* New York: Guilford Press.

Beck, A. T., Rush, A. J., Shaw, B. F., & Emery, G. (1979). *Cognitive therapy of depression.* New York: Guilford Press.

Beck, A. T., Steer, R. A., & Brown, G. (1993). Dysfunctional attitudes and suicidal ideation in psychiatric outpatients. *Suicide and Life-Threatening Behavior, 23,* 11–20.

Belsher, G., & Costello, C. G. (1988). Relapse after recovery from unipolar depression: A critical review. *Psychological Bulletin, 104,* 84–96.

Burns, M. O., & Seligman, M. E. P. (1989). Explanatory style across the life span: Evidence for stability over 52 years. *Journal of Personality and Social Psychology, 56,* 471–477.

Depue, R. A., Slater, J., Wolfstetter-Kausch, H., Klein, D., Goplerud, E., & Farr, D. (1981). A behavioral paradigm for identifying persons at risk for bipolar depressive disorder: A conceptual framework and five validation studies (Mono graph). *Journal of Abnormal Psychology, 90,* 381–437.

Downey, G., & Coyne, J. C. (1990). Children of depressed parents: An integrative review. *Psychological Bulletin, 108,* 50–76.

Endicott, J., & Spitzer, R. A. (1978). A diagnostic interview: The schedule for affective disorders and schizophrenia. *Archives of General Psychiatry, 35,* 837–844.

Farmer, R., & Nelson-Gray, R. O. (1990). Personality disorders and depression: Hypothetical relations, empirical findings, and methodological considerations. *Clinical Psychology Review, 10,* 453–476.

Gotlib, I. H., & Abramson, L. Y. (in press). *Attributional theories of emotion.* In T. Dalgleish & M. Power (Eds.), Handbook of cognition and emotion. New York: Wiley.

Hawton, K. (1987). Assessment of suicide risk. *British Journal of Psychiatry, 150,* 145–153.

Ingram, R. E. (1990). Self-focused attention in clinical disorders: Review and a conceptual model. *Psychological Bulletin, 107,* 156–176.

Isometsa, E. T., Henriiksson, M. M., Heikkinen, M. E., Aro, H. M., Martunnen, M. J., Kuoppasalmi, K. II., & Lonnqvist, J. K. (1996). Suicide among subjects with personality disorders. *American Journal of Psychiatry, 153,* 667–673.

Joiner, T. E., & Rudd, M. D. (1995). Negative attributional style for interpersonal events and the occurrence of severe interpersonal disruptions as predictors of self-reported suicidal ideation. *Suicide and Life-Threatening Behavior, 25,* 297–304.

Judd, L. L. (1997). The clinical course of unipolar major depressive disorders. *Archives of General Psychiatry, 54,* 989–991.

Lewinsohn, P. M., Rhode, P., & Seeley, J. R. (1993). Psychosocial characteristics of adolescents with a history of suicide attempt. *Journal of the American Academy for Child and Adolescent Psychiatry, 32,* 60–68.

Loranger, A. W. (1988). *The personality disorder examination (PDE) manual.* Yonkers, NY: DV Communications.

Metalsky, G. I., Halberstadt, L. J., & Abramson, L. Y. (1987). Vulnerability to depressive mood reactions: Toward a more powerful test of the diathesis-stress and causal mediation components of the reformulated theory of depression. *Journal of Personality and Social Psychology, 52,* 386–393.

Metalsky, G. I., & Joiner, T. E. (1992). Vulnerability to depressive symptomatology: A prospective test of the diathesis-stress and causal mediation components of the hopelessness theory of depression. *Journal of Personality and Social Psychology, 63,* 667–675.

Metalsky, G. I., Joiner, T. E., Hardin, T. S., & Abramson, L. Y. (1993). Depressive reactions to failure in a naturalistic setting: A test of the hopelessness and self-esteem theories of depression. *Journal of Abnormal Psychology, 102,* 101–109.

Minkoff, K., Bergman, E., Beck, A. T., & Beck, R. (1973). Hopelessness, depression, and attempted suicide. *American Journal of Psychiatry, 130,* 455–459.

Nolen-Hoeksema, S., Girgus, J. S., & Seligman, M. E. P. (1992). Predictors and consequences of childhood depressive symptoms: A 5–year longitudinal study. *Journal of Abnormal Psychology, 101,* 405–422.

Rohde, P., Lewinsohn, P. M., & Seeley, J. R. (1990). Are people changed by the experience of having an episode of depression? A further test of the scar hypothesis. *Journal of Abnormal Psychology, 99,* 264–271.

Rose, D. T., & Abramson, L. Y. (1998). *Developmental maltreatment and cognitive vulnerability to depression.* Manuscript in preparation, University of Wisconsin.

Rose, D. T., Abramson, L. Y., Hodulik, C., Halberstadt, L. J., & Leff, G. (1994). Heterogeneity of cognitive style among inpatient depressives. *Journal of Abnormal Psychology, 103,* 419–429.

Segal, Z. V. (1988). Appraisal of the self-schema construct in cognitive models of depression. *Psychological Bulletin, 103,* 147–162.

Steinberg, D. L., Alloy, L. B., & Abramson, L. Y. (1998a). *Predictors of relapse and recurrence of depression: The scar hypothesis and the impact of depressive episodes.* Manuscript in preparation, New York State Psychiatric Institute, New York, NY.

Steinberg, D. L., Tashman, N., Alloy, L. B., & Abramson, L. Y. (1998b). *The parent attributions for children's events scale (PACE).* Manuscript in preparation, Temple University, Philadelphia, PA.

Wagner, B. M. (1997). Family risk factors for child and adolescent suicidal behavior. *Psychological Bulletin, 121,* 246–298.

Weissman, A., & Beck, A. T. (1978). Development and validation of the Dysfunctional Attitude Scale: A preliminary investigation. Paper presented at the meeting of the American Educational Research Association, Toronto, Canada.

CHAPTER 5

An Integrative Schema-Focused Model for Personality Disorders

Jeffrey E. Young and Michael Lindemann

THEORY

Overview

In treating patients with personality disorders, many cognitive therapists have encountered difficulties that necessitate modification of the short-term cognitive techniques outlined by Beck and his associates in treating depression (Beck et al., 1979). This paper presents a schema model for conceptualizing and treating cases in which characterological issues violate the assumptions of short-term cognitive therapy. In this approach, the important innovations and advantages pioneered by Beck are augmented with affective and interpersonal strategies.

Two important characteristics of patients with personality disorders differentiate them from those with only Axis I disorders. The first is the presence of enduring, inflexible traits in personality disorders (DSM-III-R, p. 335). Millon (1981) emphasizes this point by specifying *adaptive inflexibility* and *vicious circles* as two major criteria for personality pathology: ". . . the alternative strategies the individual employs for relating to others, for achieving goals, and for coping with stress are not only few in number but appear to be practiced rigidly" (p. 9).

He elaborates as follows on the process by which such patients perpetuate their self-defeating thoughts and behaviors: "Maneuvers such as protective constriction, cognitive distortion, and behavior generalization are processes by which individuals restrict their opportunities for new learning, misconstrue essentially benign events, and provoke reactions from others that reactivate earlier problems" (p. 9).

Millon contrasts personality disorders with "symptom disorders" (Axis I disorders) such as depression. The latter "possess well-delineated clinical features that are less difficult to modify than the ingrained personal traits from which they arise" (p. 10). In addition, these traits often "feel right" (ego syntonic) to the individual who possesses them.

Avoidance is a second important distinguishing feature of personality disorders. Whereas short-term cognitive therapy assumes that patients have relatively free access to their thoughts and feelings, patients with personality disorders usually avoid painful memories, associations, and feelings. This chronic avoidance may lead to a therapeutic impasse unless additional techniques are applied.

Schema Model

The schema model proposed here includes the following four constructs as an expansion of Beck's (1979) short-term cognitive approach:

1. Early maladaptive schemas
2. Schema maintenance
3. Schema avoidance
4. Schema compensation

Our model is intended not as a comprehensive theory of personality or psychopathology, but rather as a "convenient clinical heuristic" (Segal, 1988).

Early Maladaptive Schemas

Beck (1967) emphasized the importance of schemas in depression, defining a schema as "a [cognitive] structure for screening, coding, and evaluating the stimuli that impinge on the organism" (p. 283). Segal, drawing from a consensus of many researchers, provides the following definition of schemas: "organized elements of past reactions and experience that form a relatively cohesive and persistent body of knowledge capable of guiding subsequent perception and appraisals" (1988, p. 147).

We define *early maladaptive schemas* (EMSs) as extremely broad and pervasive themes regarding oneself and one's relationships with others, developed during childhood and elaborated throughout one's life. These schemas serve as templates for the processing of later experience. They are characterized by all of the following and are:

1. Early in origin and continuing throughout life, unless treated. EMSs appear to be the cumulative result of dysfunctional early experiences with parents, siblings, and peers, rather than of isolated traumatic events.

2. Capable of generating high levels of disruptive affect, extremely self-defeating consequences, and/or significant harm to others.

3. Capable of interfering significantly with meeting core "needs" for self-expression, autonomy, interpersonal relatedness, social validation, or societal integration.

4. Deeply entrenched patterns, central to one's sense of self. They are usually self-perpetuating and display "fight for survival characteristics". EMSs are extremely difficult to change in an enduring manner using short-term techniques.

EMSs usually erupt when activated by events in the environment relevant to the schema. Since schema change poses a threat to the core cognitive organization, individuals engage in a variety of cognitive maneuvers to keep the schema intact (cf., Millon, 1981, p. 102; Guidano & Liotti, 1983, p. 88). In contrast with the underlying assumptions addressed in short-term CT, which are conditional in nature (e.g., "If I can be perfect, then I am worthwhile"), many EMSs are *unconditional* beliefs. When an EMS erupts, individuals believe that they can, at best, delay or hide the inevitably bad outcome such as rejection or punishment. We hypothesize that EMSs can lead directly or indirectly to psychological distress such as depression or panic, to loneliness or destructive relationships, to inadequate work performance,\ to addictions, or to psychosomatic disorders.

Schema-focused therapists have, to date, identified 16 EMSs which characterize almost all of the longer-term patients in our clinical practices. Table 5.1 lists these schemas with definitions.

In addition, we have identified three important schema processes: schema maintenance, avoidance, and compensation.

Table 5.1 Listing of Early Maladaptive Schemas with Definitions, Grouped by Domain

Instability & Disconnection

(Expectations that one's needs for security, safety, stability, nurturance, and empathy will not be met in a predictable manner within the context of intimate or family relationships. Typical family origin is detached, explosive, unpredictable, or abusive.)

1. Abandonment/instability

   The perceived *instability* or *unreliability* of those available for support and connection.

   Involves the sense that significant others will not be able to continue providing emotional support, connection, strength, or practical protection because they are emotionally unstable, unpredictable, unreliable, or erratically present; because they will die imminently; or because they will abandon the patient in favor of someone better.

2. Abuse/mistrust

   The expectation that others will hurt, abuse, humiliate, cheat, lie, manipulate, take advantage, or explode with violence or anger. Usually involves the perception that the harm is intentional or the result of unjustified and extreme negligence. May include the sense that one always ends up being cheated relative to others or "getting the short end of the stick."

3. Emotional deprivation

   Expectation that one's desire for a normal degree of emotional support will not be adequately met by other.

   A. Deprivation of Nurturance: Absence of attention, affection, warmth, or companionship.

   B. Deprivation of Protection: Absence of strength, direction, or guidance from others.

   C. Deprivation of Empathy: Absence of understanding, listening, selfdisclosure, or mutual sharing of feelings from others.

Impaired Autonomy

(Expectation about oneself and the environment that interferes with one's perceived ability to separate, survive, and function independently. Typical family origin is enmeshed, undermining of child's judgment, or overprotective.)

4. Functional dependence/incompetence

   Belief that one is unable to handle one's everyday responsibilities in a competent manner, without considerable help from others (e.g., take care of oneself, solve daily problems, exercise good judgment, tackle new tasks, make good decisions). Often presents as a pervasive passivity.

5. Vulnerability to harm and illness

   Exaggerated fear that disaster is about to strike at any time (natural, criminal, medical, or financial), and that one is unable to protect oneself. May include unrealistic fears that one will have a heart attack, get AIDS, go crazy, go broke, be mugged, crash, etc.

6. Enmeshment/undeveloped self

   Excessive emotional involvement and closeness with one or more significant others (often parents), at the expense of full individuation or normal social

Table 5.1 *(Continued)*

development. Often involves the belief that at least one of the enmeshed individuals cannot survive or be happy without the constant support of the other. May also include feelings of being smothered by, or fused with, others. OR Insufficient individual identity or inner direction. Often experienced as a feeling of emptiness or of floundering.

Undesirability

(The expectation that one will not be desirable to—or is different from—other people, in terms of any of the following: physical attractiveness, social skills, inner worth, moral integrity, interesting personality, career accomplishment, values, interests, masculinity/feminity, socio-economic background, etc. Typical origin is criticalness or rejection from family or peer group.)

7. Defectiveness/shame

The feeling that one is *inwardly* defective, flawed, or invalid; that one would be fundamentally unlovable to significant others if exposed; or a sense of shame regarding one's perceived internal inadequacies. Often involves excessive self-criticism, self-punishment, comparisons with others, and exaggerated expectations of rejection and blame—within *intimate* relationships.

8. Social undesirability/alienation

The belief that one is outwardly undesirable to others (e.g., ugly; sexually undesirable; low in status; poor in conversational skills; dull) OR the feeling that one is isolated from the rest of the world, different from other people, and/or not part of any group or community. Often involves self-consciousness, alienation, comparisons with others, and insecurity within social situations.

9. Failure to achieve

The belief that one will inevitably fail, or is fundamentally inadequate relative to one's peers, in areas of achievement (school, career, sports, etc.). Often involves the belief that one is stupid, inept, untalented, ignorant, etc.

Restricted Self-expression

(Inordinate restriction, suppression, or ignoring of one's emotions or daily preferences. Typical family origin is suppression of feelings and domination by adults.)

10. Subjugation

Excessive surrendering of control over one's own decisions and preferences—usually to avoid anger, retaliation, or abandonment. Involves the perception that one's own desires are not valid or important to others. Often leads to anger at the subjugator. Frequently presents as excessive compliance and eagerness to please.

11. Emotional inhibition

Excessive difficulty expressing or discussing feelings (anger, hurt, sadness, joy, etc.), because one expects their expression to result in loss of esteem, harm to others, embarrassment, retaliation, or abandonment.

Table 5.1 (*Continued*)

Restricted Gratification

(Excessive emphasis on work, status, duty, standards, responsibility to others, or the negative aspects of life—at the expense of happiness, natural inclinations, pleasure, health, optimism, or creativity. Typical family origin is grim: pain, performance, sacrifice, self-control, and negativity predominate over pleasure, playfulness, and optimism.)

---

12. Self-sacrifice/overresponsibility

Excessive focus on meeting the needs of others, at the expense of one's own gratification. The most common reasons are: to prevent causing pain to others; to avoid guilt; to gain in esteem; to maintain the connection with others perceived as needy. Often results from an acute sensitivity to the pain of others. Often involves an exaggerated sense of duty and responsibility to others. Usually leads to a sense that one's own needs are not being adequately met and sometimes to resentment of those who are taken care of.

13. Unrelenting/unbalanced standards

The relentless striving to meet high or unbalanced expectations of oneself or others, at the expense of happiness, pleasure, relaxation, spontaneity, playfulness, health, sense of accomplishment, or satisfying relationships. Usually involves undue emphasis on any of six broad areas: (1) achievement or competition; (2) money, physical appearance, or social status; (3) self-control or discipline; (4) perfectionism, order, or attention to detail; (5) control and mastery of the environment; or (6) moral, ethical, or religious precepts (other than self-sacrifice).

14. Negativity/pessimism

A pervasive, lifelong focus on the negative aspects of life (pain, death, loss, disappointment, conflict, guilt, resentment, unsolved problems, potential mistakes, betrayal, things that could go wrong, etc.) while minimizing or neglecting the positive or optimistic aspects. May include feelings of helplessness or uncontrollability, based on the expectation that one cannot prevent negative outcomes in life.

Impaired Limits

(Deficiency in internal limits, leading to difficulty respecting the rights of others or meeting one's own personal goals. Typical family origin is permissiveness and indulgence.)

---

15. Entitlement/self-centeredness

Insistence that one should be able to have whatever one wants, regardless of what others consider reasonable or the cost to others. Often involves excessive control over others, demandingness, and lack of empathy for others' needs.

16. Insufficient self-control/self-discipline

Pervasive difficulty exercising sufficient self-control and frustration tolerance to achieve one's personal goals, or to restrain the excessive expression of one's emotions and impulses.

Schema Maintenance (Rigidity)

We hypothesize that schema maintenance accounts for the rigidity char-acteristic of personality disorders. At the cognitive level, schemas are maintained by processes described by Beck (1967) as cognitive distor-tions, e.g., selective abstraction, overgeneralization, magnification, and minimization. At the behavioral level, schemas are maintained by mal-adaptive partner selection and other self-defeating activities.

Schema Avoidance

Since the eruption of EMSs is accompanied by high levels of unpleasant affect, patients develop volitional and automatic processes for avoiding schemas. These processes may include cognitive avoidance, affective avoidance, and behavioral avoidance.

Schema Compensation

We have observed that many patients adopt cognitive or behavioral styles that seem to be the opposite of what we would predict from a knowledge of their EMSs. These styles *overcompensate* for the underlying schemas. For example, some patients who have experienced significant emotional deprivation as children behave in a narcissistic manner as adults: their apparent sense of entitlement obscures the underlying deprivation. Al-though functional to a certain extent, schema compensation may ulti-mately "backfire." The narcissistic patient may end up alienating friends and reverting to a state of deprivation; the counterdependent patient may reject help and end up unable to ask for it even when appropriate. Schema compensation processes may be viewed as partially successful attempts by patients to challenge their schemas. Since it usually involves a failure to recognize the underlying vulnerability, it leaves the patient unprepared for the pain evoked when compensation fails and the schema is triggered.

Schemas Compared With Other Levels of Cognition

Schema-focused cognitive therapists are sometimes asked why they find it necessary to add the construct of EMSs rather than simply working in terms of automatic thoughts and underlying assumptions, as in the short-term cognitive approach. In our experience, there are *qualitative* differ-ences between clinical issues at the schema level and those related to

automatic thoughts and underlying assumptions. They may be summarized as follows:

1. Schemas are more *pervasive* than automatic thoughts and underlying assumptions. They concern basic life themes of autonomy, intimacy,
social adjustment, standards, and limits. These themes cut across specific
times and contexts. Therefore, working with schemas affords greater unity
and coherence, making the therapy less atomistic. In addition, the clinical
rationale is clearer to the patient.

2. *Differential therapeutic strategies* have been developed for each
EMS. Furthermore, the schemas are grouped in accordance with the developmental issues they have in common (e.g., impaired autonomy, disconnection, inhibition).

3. *Higher levels of affect* are evoked when working with schemas,
because *core human "needs"* are involved.

4. The *pain* associated with EMSs and attempts to change them is
usually so great that patients resort to schema avoidance and schema
compensation in order to protect themselves. Distinctive therapeutic strategies are required to address and counteract these processes.

5. Schemas are developed and maintained through *interpersonal experience.* Consequently, they can best be modified by working closely with the
patient's current relationships and with the therapeutic relationship, rather
than by adopting a primarily individual or "intrapsychic" cognitive approach.

6. EMSs are experienced as *a priori* truths and are thus taken for
granted by the patient. As part of the core self, they are far more *resistant
to change* than less deep levels of cognition because of the importance of
maintaining cognitive consistency. Therefore, the prospect of surrendering schemas to change is extremely threatening.

TREATMENT

Assessment

In order to illustrate the process of identifying EMSs and conceptualizing
a case in schema-focused terms, we will present a patient named Ben, a
25–year-old single man. We have simplified the presentation for the purposes of this paper by abbreviating the history and presenting symptoms,
focusing only on two interrelated schemas. In addition, we will emphasize those aspects of the case that we conceptualized and treated differently from short-term cognitive therapy, although many short-term
techniques were incorporated during this treatment.

Ben presented with (a) chronic anxiety at work, (b) inability to date since ending a relationship two years prior to consultation, and (c) a growing sense that he was being "consumed" and "drained" by his constant preoccupation with his job. In the initial consultation, he described his work as involving the preparation of administrative reports and the management of a small bureau including financial analysts and clerical workers. He explained that, although he enjoyed a reputation for being a dynamic, confident financial analyst, he experienced severe anxiety in connection with his supervisory work.

Specifically, he found it difficult to confront his staff members regarding missed deadlines or unauthorized absences. He also assumed excessive responsibility when his staff seemed unhappy or underutilized. Although well aware of his authority to issue instructions and to transfer or dismiss unsatisfactory employees, he feared acting in a harsh or unsympathetic manner. As a result, he tended to ruminate, experiencing resentment toward his employees, frustration, and growing anxiety as his office failed to meet its deadlines.

In addition, Ben reported that his social life was lonely and empty. Apart from two close friends, whom he saw occasionally, he felt that very few people would understand his internal life and troubled family history. He feared that women would perceive him as "too intense." He felt that most professional people in his age group were too materialistic to share his values, so he was attracted to bars patronized primarily by "working class" people, where he seldom found it possible to enter into a conversation.

During the initial consultation, the therapist hypothesized that Ben experienced significant difficulties in two of the six EMS domains: Restricted Gratification and Instability/Disconnection (see Table 5.1 for definitions of these two domains).

When Ben was asked to complete the Schema Questionnaire (SQ), this initial impression was confirmed. Ben scored especially high on items corresponding to two schemas: Self-Sacrifice and Emotional Deprivation. Self-sacrifice involves excessive worrying about pleasing other people, feeling guilty for letting them down, and building up anger and resentment; emotional deprivation refers to the feeling that no one will ever be really available to attend to one's needs or feelings.

Partly by means of the Multimodal Life History Inventory (Lazarus & Lazarus, 1991) and partly by follow-up questions related to the SQ, a *schema-focused life history* was compiled. This history traced the origins of Ben's Self-Sacrifice and Emotional Deprivation schemas. It emerged that a number of his close relatives had experienced mental illness during

his childhood and adolescence. In particular, his mother had a two-year
episode of major depression starting when he was 13. Shortly thereafter,
his younger sister began to display the signs of what was eventually
diagnosed as schizophrenia.

For a time, he and his father had been "the only sane people" in the
house. Ben had taken considerable pride in helping his father to run the
household. He recalled, however, that he had always felt as if he was
"treading on eggshells" and that his mother's and sister's urgent needs
had always taken priority over his own. Moreover, until his senior year,
he had felt unable to discuss his family problems with his friends at
school. His family lived in an affluent neighborhood where it was important to "maintain appearances." In his senior year, he met another student
with a family background similar to his, and together they set up an
informal "crisis team" to offer counseling and support to distressed teen-
agers in their neighborhood.

The next step in the schema-focused assessment process involved *ed-
ucating the patient* about the nature of EMSs. Although some prior explanation had been offered to Ben before he completed the SQ, at this point
the therapist provided a fuller description emphasizing the degree of
emotion connected with schemas. The therapist tried to prepare Ben for
the process of schema change by reminding him that schemas are central
to one's self-image and view of the world, and that schemas will fight
hard for survival.

Up to this point, the process used to detect the relevance of EMSs to
Ben's presenting problems had been primarily historical and rational. In
order to gain additional support for the hypothesis that Ben's symptoms
were attributable to Self Sacrifice and Emotional Deprivation schemas,
the therapist next attempted to *trigger schemas* during and outside the
session.

Imagery exercises, including *dialogues* with parents and other significant figures, provided the therapist with his primary means of triggering
Ben's schemas. He asked Ben to close his eyes and get an image of a
situation involving one of his parents. Ben responded with a detailed
image which he described as his most vivid early memory. In the image,
he was entering the living room after returning from school, where he had
a difficult day. His mother was slumped on the couch in her robe, deeply
depressed, and complaining about her illness. As the therapist prompted
Ben to explore the image in detail, he began to tremble and reported that
he felt afraid. Gradually, he recollected that the original experience had
aroused a similar sense of fear in him. Specifically, he had feared that by
talking to his mother about his day at school he would make her depres-

sion worse, and that by expressing his concern about her unkempt appearance, he would hurt her. The image ended with his quietly leaving the room. This image added support to the hypothesis that Self-Sacrifice was one of Ben's core schemas.

A second imagery exercise also served to support the hypotheses formed earlier. Ben recalled his family's arrival in their new house when he was about six years old. His elder brother and younger sister were each given attractive rooms, recently redecorated. Ben was assigned a drab bedroom which had not even been repainted. In the image, it was winter and he was sitting alone in the room, gazing out at the bare trees and feeling neglected by his family. He reported that the image made him feel "bleak and lonely." This added support to the therapist's hypothesis that Emotional Deprivation was another one of Ben's core schemas.

Both imagery exercises, therefore, provided further information about Ben's primary schemas. In expanding upon the first image (in which he had sacrificed his own needs for fear of making his mother feel worse), the therapist invited him to verbalize the feelings he had been unable to express at the time. As part of the imagery exercise, Ben told his mother how difficult it was for him to suppress his need for her guidance and support in dealing with the everyday stress of school and interactions with peers. He spoke of his fear that she would be unable to tolerate his needs. Finally, he admitted to feeling angry and cheated of the "normal childhood" his friends seemed to be having, as well as guilty for having this feeling.

The *therapeutic relationship* was another source of confirmation for the schema-focused case formulation that emerged from the early sessions of Ben's treatment. The therapist noticed that Ben bristled and became angry when the therapist tried to help him identify his cognitive distortions (recorded during a homework assignment). Upon inquiry, it emerged that Ben took this as evidence that the therapist did not fully empathize with him or understand his difficulties. Instead, he felt that the therapist was "labeling" him and applying jargon in a superficial, rote manner. The therapist conceptualized Ben's hostility as overcompensation for his Emotional Deprivation schema.

Ben's Self-Sacrifice schema was manifested in sessions by an unusually meek, polite approach to issues such as the therapist's vacation and other scheduling issues, and by his extreme concern about how tired the therapist looked at the start of late evening sessions. This alternation between meekness and anger helped illuminate how emotional deprivation was intertwined with his Self-Sacrifice schema. The sacrifice of his emotional needs for the sake of others left him feeling unsatisfied; this in turn lent further support to his belief that others would never meet his needs (emotional deprivation).

At this point, the assessment was broadened to include a discussion of current events in which Ben's core schemas had been triggered. There were a number of instances in which he reported concealing his dissatisfaction from employees for fear that he would hurt them. In particular, when his relationship with one of these people was explored, it emerged that he perceived this man as being "emotionally fragile, like (his) sister." He was afraid that confronting this man's erratic work performance— which he was perfectly capable of doing with other members of his staff—would cause this employee to "break down or explode," although Ben conceded that he lacked evidence to support this fear.

By the end of the assessment phase, Ben's presenting symptoms had been explored in a way that made their schema-driven quality explicit. His inability to make full use of his otherwise adequate interpersonal skills with a subset of employees whom he perceived as vulnerable, brittle or dependent was formulated as evidence of his Self-Sacrifice schema. He agreed with the therapist that his self-effacing manner with these people was an instance of schema maintenance. The way in which he agonized after hours about getting his work done without imposing more stringent controls on his staff, becoming anxious and "drained," reflected the price he paid for maintaining this schema.

Ben's reluctance to date women, despite feeling attracted to several, was interpreted as avoidance of situations in which his Emotional Deprivation schema could be triggered. The prospect of intimacy conveyed the threat that his strong emotional needs would be aroused and then left unfulfilled.

Schema Change

Ben's symptoms were eventually understood as the result of two EMSs which, either independently or in association, led him to behave in a consistently self-sacrificing manner and perpetuate a state of emotional deprivation. In this section we will describe the techniques used to modify Ben's Self-Sacrifice and Emotional Deprivation schemas.

Emotive Techniques

A cardinal feature of schema-focused cognitive therapy is the emphasis placed on challenging EMSs when they are actually triggered and erupt, i.e., when the patient experiences affective arousal relevant to the schema.

In Ben's case, the therapist made use of *images* from the past and imaginary *dialogues* with his parents, as well as current life experiences, to help him become aware of the full extent of his feelings. This was especially important for this patient, who tended to conceal his feelings beneath a brisk, businesslike interpersonal manner. By means of imagery exercises in which Ben played himself as he would have liked to behave during his teenage years, he was increasingly able to express the pain associated with his self-sacrifice, and the guilt and fear which he had experienced when his mother and sister were present. Imagery exercises arising from current family interactions, in which his institutionalized sister continued to be the focus of his family's attention, allowed him to verbalize his resentment and anger. Eventually, in a memorable session, Ben returned to the image of his depressed mother and was able to express his anger toward her.

Interpersonal Techniques

The therapist continued the process of schema change by working with several of Ben's current, ongoing personal relationships. These included the therapeutic relationship, the woman Ben began dating several months after starting treatment, and his family and work relationships. In this section, we describe how the therapist helped Ben translate emotive exercises, such as the imagery and dialogues described above, into his actual interpersonal behavior.

In the therapeutic relationship, the therapist began by pointing out how Ben inhibited the expression of his own needs by placing undue emphasis on those of the therapist (schema maintenance). He allowed Ben to *ventilate* his fear of encroaching upon the therapist's time or energy, and express the guilt he felt when he thought he had done so. The next step was to *empathize* with these feelings to ensure the maintenance of therapeutic collaboration. Finally, the therapist gently engaged in *reality testing* to confront Ben's distorted view of the relationship. This included a degree of self-disclosure by the therapist, as well as dialogues in which Ben played the role of his Self-Sacrifice schema while the therapist provided an alternative view. Ben presented the basic arguments and evidence supporting the schema, while the therapist argued for Ben's "healthy side," which was capable of understanding that Self-Sacrifice was not his only viable option. Later, Ben and the therapist changed roles, enabling Ben to argue against his own schema.

A similar sequence of techniques was applied to Ben's Emotional Deprivation schema as manifested in the therapeutic relationship. Here,

Ben's sharp protests against the therapist's explicit use of short-term cognitive techniques was identified as overcompensation for his underlying sense of not being genuinely heard or understood. After allowing him to ventilate, and empathizing with his feelings, the therapist pointed out the way in which he was overreacting to potentially fruitful interventions and hence running the risk of creating the barriers to collaborative work which he accused the therapist of imposing.

As Ben and the therapist made progress in confronting Self-Sacrifice and Emotional Deprivation in the therapeutic relationship, it became increasingly possible to apply similar techniques to situations he encountered at work and while visiting his family. Imagery rehearsal and role-playing were used to anticipate and prepare for these situations. In each case, the goal was to allow Ben to identify his feelings and needs, to argue against his own negative schemas, and finally to express his needs appropriately. Care was taken to evaluate the degree to which he was subsequently able to modify his behavior at work and in interacting with his family.

In addition, the therapist adopted a *reparenting role* as part of the interpersonal aspect of the treatment. By determining that Ben's early needs for nurturing had not been adequately met, and trying (within reasonable limits) to be especially nurturing, the therapist was able to counteract and help invalidate Ben's Emotional Deprivation schema.

Conjoint sessions were started with Ben and his girlfriend after several months of treatment. By this time, Ben had been dating Brenda for three months. He had begun to complain that he felt frustrated and lonely with her at times, and that there seemed to be a limit beyond which she was not attuned to his feelings.

The therapist began by pointing out the way in which Ben's *partner selection* formed part of the process of schema maintenance. Ironically, Ben reported being attracted to Brenda initially because she seemed "stable and unemotional." Although this sense of stability was important to him in view of his early experiences with emotionally fragile relatives, an additional part of the "chemistry" he experienced with her was his familiar sense of poignant neglect.

Next, the therapist clarified the way in which Ben *perpetuated* these feelings of deprivation. Here, his Self-Sacrifice schema was relevant. By paying excessive attention to Brenda's needs (self-sacrifice) and failing to communicate his own, he reduced her ability to give him what he desired. He feared imposing himself on her, and became guilty at the prospect of asking for more. As his feelings of deprivation overtook him, he tended to withdraw from her (schema avoidance).

Finally, during a series of conjoint sessions held at intervals over an extended period, the therapist helped Ben to *change his behavior* toward Brenda. Ben learned to ask her more directly for what he wanted, and to give to her in accordance with what he genuinely felt like giving rather than to avoid guilt. His anger was gradually refocused around the question of how to communicate clearly and get his needs met. In this regard, the therapist had to remind Ben frequently that Brenda was not intentionally ignoring or depriving him. This aspect of the conjoint treatment was explicitly linked with the therapeutic relationship, in which Ben's feelings of emotional deprivation had caused angry outbursts which had already been examined collaboratively.

Use of Flashcards

Although we have emphasized the use of emotive and inter-personal techniques in describing Ben's treatment, cognitive techniques were no less integral to the process of schema change. As an example of a cognitive technique, we shall describe the way in which the therapist used a flashcard to counteract Ben's Self-Sacrifice and Deprivation schemas as they applied to his relationship with Brenda. This flashcard technique served to consolidate and rehearse the gains made in the individual and conjoint sessions. It summarized the results not only of interpersonal interventions but also of cognitive techniques, such as critical review of the evidence Ben used to support his schemas, review of evidence contradicting the schemas, and illustrations of how Ben discounted this contradictory evidence.

These illustrations emerged clearly during Point-Counterpoint exercises: Ben had no difficulty playing the role of his own EMSs, but great difficulty in playing the "healthy side." In addition, the therapist helped Ben invalidate some of the evidence he used to support his EMSs by relating it to the distorted family relationships resulting from his mother's and sister's illnesses, as well as to *maladaptive expectations*. The therapist helped Ben see that these relationships and expectations could not validly be generalized to other situations.

On the basis of this work, Ben and his therapist developed the following flashcard addressing his Self-Sacrifice and Deprivation schemas in his relationship with Brenda:

Right now I feel angry, drained and ignored because schemas prevent me from expressing my needs to Brenda and make me assume that she can't really empathize with me. However, my healthy side knows that I exaggerate the risk of burdening her with my needs and underestimate her ability to respond to them. If I try to see the situation from her perspective and give her the benefit of the doubt, I can acknowledge that she may be unaware of the needs I'm holding back because of my Self-Sacrifice and Emotional Deprivation schemas. Therefore, if I withdraw or hold back until I can't help making an angry outburst, I'm likely to land in difficulties again. It would be best to find a way to tell Brenda how I feel and ask for what I want from her.

Outcome of Case

After about 13 months of schema-focused treatment, Ben reported that his anxiety at work had decreased considerably. He was able to confront his staff when necessary, and set appropriate limits with them, without his former feelings of guilt or fear of harming them. His frustration and periods of rumination had largely disappeared. His relationship with Brenda had become more satisfying as he learned to express his needs. And his fears of being unable to find an empathic partner no longer preoccupied him.

SUMMARY

We have attempted to demonstrate that schema-focused cognitive therapy offers an integrated set of strategies for dealing with the high degree of rigidity, avoidance, and interpersonal dysfunction characteristic of personality disorders. The focus on specific core schemas for each patient provides continuity to treatment over time. Furthermore, this approach encourages the gradual refinement of specific treatment strategies geared to each of the 16 schemas, as we gain more experience working with each one.

We have also emphasized the need to include affective strategies to cope with the high levels of emotion generated by maladaptive schemas, and interpersonal strategies to deal directly with the relationships within which schemas are maintained. Although many short-term cognitive and behavioral techniques have been retained, we have systematically integrated them with affective and interpersonal strategies.

REFERENCES

Beck, A. T. (1967). *Depression: Causes and treatment.* Philadelphia: University of Pennsylvania Press.

Beck, A. T., Rush, A. J., Shaw, B. F., & Emery, G. (1979). *Cognitive therapy of depression.* New York: Guilford Press.

Guidano, V. F., & Liotti, G. (1983). *Cognitive processes and emotional disorders.* New York: Guilford Press.

Lazarus, A. (1980). *Multimodial life history questionnaire.* Kingston, NJ: Multimodal Publications, Inc.

Millon, T. (1981). *Disorders of personality.* New York: John Wiley & Sons.

Segal, Z. (1988). Appraisal of the self-schema: Construct in cognitive models of depression. *Psychological Bulletin, 103,* 147–162.

Young, J. (1990). *Cognitive therapy for personality disorders: A schema-focused approach.* Sarasota, FL: Professional Resource Exchange, Inc.

CHAPTER 6

Constructivism and the Cognitive Psychotherapies: Conceptual and Strategic Contrasts

Robert A. Neimeyer

Cognitive therapies have continued to develop along both quantitative and qualitative lines. One important qualitative development has been the emergence of a constructivist trend, which has suggested that both conceptual realignments and new strategic emphases for theorists and practitioners of cognitive therapy have been an important and qualitative development. This paper reviews several informative contrasts between traditional cognitive therapies and their constructivist alternatives, both at the level of epistemology and at the level of clinical practice.

Since the "cognitive revolution" of the mid-1970s, psychotherapies influenced by this perspective have continued to develop along both quantitative and qualitative lines. At a quantitative level, the sheer volume of research and scholarship in the cognitive-behavioral tradition has grown, to a point that nearly defies systematic review and evaluation. The burgeoning number of cognitive models of specific disorders (Beck & Greenberg, 1988; Beck, Rush, Shaw, & Emery, 1979; Kendall, 1993; Wilson & Fairbairn, 1993), assessment techniques targeting various cognitive structures and processes (Clark, 1988; R. Neimeyer & Feixas, 1992), and distinguishable schools of therapy within the cognitive behavioral fold (cf. Dryden & Golden, 1987; Kuehlwein & Rosen, 1993) provide further testimonies to the vitality of the field.

Cognitive therapies have also undergone an "evolution within the revolution" (Mahoney, 1991) as they have matured, since some schools, models, and practitioners have experienced significant qualitative change as well as quantitative growth. Among the more profound shifts at this qualitative level is the emergence of a clear "constructive-developmental trend" (Goncalves, 1989), involving both fundamental philosophical realignments and the elaboration of new therapeutic procedures. My goal in the present article is to survey these developments by highlighting some of the informative contrasts between traditional cognitive-behavioral approaches and those influenced by the constructivist trend. These remarks will then set the stage for a more detailed consideration of particular conceptual and practical contributions to the cognitive therapies in the remaining articles in this series.

SOME INFORMATIVE CONTRASTS

As Anderson (1990; p. 137) has noted,

> Constructivist therapy is not so much a technique as a philosophical context within which therapy is done, and more a product of the zeitgeist than the brainchild of any single theorist. . . . These approaches work with a part of the human psyche that is surprisingly neglected in many schools of therapy—the form-giving, meaning-making part, the narrator who at every waking moment of our lives spins out its account of who we are and what we are doing and why we are doing it.

As this argument implies, constructivist approaches to clinical practice comprise a "fuzzy set" whose indistinct boundaries include at least four distinct traditions of psychotherapy: personal construct theory (e.g., Kelly, 1955; R. Neimeyer & G. Neimeyer, 1987), structural-developmental approaches (e.g., Guidano & Liotti, 1983; Mahoney, 1991), narrative psychology (e.g., Russell, 1991; White & Epston, 1990), and constructivist family therapy (e.g., Boscolo, Cecchin, Hoffman, & Prata, 1987; Efran, Lukens, & Lukens, 1990; see R. Neimeyer, 1993a, for a review of each tradition). The boundaries between constructivist and traditional "rationalist" (cf. Mahoney, 1988b) or "objectivist" (cf. R. Neimeyer & Feixas, 1990) approaches to cognitive therapy are similarly fuzzy. Thus, while constructivist approaches can be philosophically distinguished from conventional psychotherapies, especially at the level of epistemology (Feixas, 1990), these distinctions are approximate rather than absolute. This is particularly the case in the domain of the cognitive therapies, where both traditional cognitive-behavioral approaches and their constructivist alternatives share a number of features, e.g., attention to the client's belief system, use of behavioral "experiments" (cf. Goldfried, 1988) while differing in other respects. Even rational-emotive therapy, regarded as a prototypically rationalist approach by many constructivists (Lyddon, 1990; Mahoney & Gabriel, 1987; R. Neimeyer, 1985), may include features often associated with constructivist therapies, such as the attempt to foster deep-going philosophical change in a client's outlook (Ellis, 1992). For this reason, it may prove more fruitful to use the *rationalist (or objectivist) vs. constructivist* distinction as a dimension for measuring developments *within* a given school of therapy, rather than as a classificatory principle for drawing boundaries *between* approaches. The following discussion therefore outlines contrasting features of constructivist and traditional cognitive-behavioral therapies, acknowledging that these distinctions are matters of emphasis rather than inherent opposition. Indeed, to the extent that cognitive therapies generally are evolving in a constructivist direction, the boundaries between these two "camps" might be expected to become still fuzzier across time.

Epistemological Contrasts

Table 6.1 presents several distinguishing emphases of constructivist theory and metatheory vis-à-vis more traditional forms of cognitive therapy. Because constructivist approaches focus on the quest for personal knowledge in the social context, these philosophical commitments are epistemological in two senses, insofar as they bear on both an abstract theory of knowledge, and a set of guiding assumptions about the knowing processes of actual human subjects. My discussion here will necessarily be synoptic; a fuller treatment of these issues has been provided elsewhere (Mahoney, 1991; R. Neimeyer, 1993a).

Human Mentation

Most traditional approaches to cognitive behavioral therapy are fundamentally Lockean in orientation, viewing the human "mind" as a repository of stimulus-response-outcome relationships originating in the environment. Sometimes the behavioristic ancestry implied in this reactive theory of human mentation is explicit, as in the stress placed by cognitive behavior modification on verbal "rules" conceived as "contin-

Table 6.1 Epistemological Contrasts: Traditional vs. Constructivist Therapies

Assumption	Traditional emphasis	Constructivist emphasis
Human mentation	reactive; "map" of actual events and relationships; mediational	proactive; "plan" for organizing activity; predicational
Basic cognitive unit	concept or schema assimilating events on basis of similar inherent "features"	establishing meaning through contrast
Relations between cognitions	associationist; series of isolated self-statements or rules	systematic; hierarchical architecture of personal knowledge
Validation of knowledge	correspondence theory of truth; veridical matching between cognitions and real word as revealed through senses	coherence theory of truth; pursuit of viable knowledge through internal consistency and social concensus
Nature of truth	singular, universal, ahistorical, incremental	multiple, contextual, historical, paradigmatic

gency-specifying stimuli" that signal reinforcing or punishing outcomes (Jaremko, 1987; Meichenbaum, 1977). But more often, the relative passivity of this model is implicit, as in assumption that individuals form "cognitive maps" in an attempt to mirror event relationships observed in the world (cf. Beck et al., 1979). In either case, cognition is seen as essentially a *mediational* process (Rychlak, 1990), a (sometimes flawed) representation or conveyer of environmental "input" which in turn influences the individual's emotional and behavioral response.

In contrast, constructivism is more Kantian in its leanings, emphasizing the active, form-giving nature of human knowing. Construction processes are seen as inherently anticipatory (Kelly, 1955) or proactive (Mahoney, 1988a), envisioning hypothetical or possible worlds as a means of regulating one's activity. In this sense, human beings are viewed as self-organizing entities, determined more by the structure of their own systems than by environmental perturbations (Maturana & Varela, 1987). From this perspective, cognition is necessarily a *predicational* process (Rychlak, 1990), an act of framing, affirming, or denying a broader pattern of meaning in a specific experiential context.

Basic Cognitive Unit

For many cognitive-behavioral theorists, the basic "building block" of thought is the *schema,* a prototypical abstraction that serves to assimilate events on the basis of their similar "features." Schemas are said to be induced "from the 'bottom up,' based on repeated past experiences involving many examples of the complex concept it represents" (Goldfried, 1988, p. 320). For many constructivists, on the other hand, the fundamental process of knowing is the act of *framing a distinction,* literally "making a difference" to segment the flow of experience in personally and communally meaningful ways (Bateson, 1972). The processing and relating of these distinctions gives rise to a complex system of differentiations, formulated by Kelly (1955) as a system of bipolar personal constructs. Importantly, as von Foerster (1981) recognized, these distinctions are not contained in the environment, but are imposed on it by the human knower. As such, this basic construing activity is a "top-down" rather than "bottom-up" process, which has been found to structure memory in a number of cognitive science studies (Millis & R. Neimeyer, 1990; Rychlak, 1992).

Relations Between Cognitions

Historically, cognitive therapists have been criticized for their failure to pay sufficient attention to subtle interactions among cognitions (Sarason, 1979), instead treating them as a series of relatively isolated "self-statements" that are at most bound together by principles of association. This tendency has in turn opened cognitive therapy to the charge that it oversimplifies the process of therapeutic change, metaphorically suggesting that discarding "faulty cognitions" might be as simple a procedure as identifying and replacing malfunctioning spark plugs. By contrast, constructivists emphasize the interdependence of our beliefs, likening them to "life forms in a complex ecology. The therapist cannot arbitrarily add a construct and expect it to thrive unless it is compatible with the current system. Removal of a construct that appears 'irrational' or 'distorted' to the clinician may likewise upset this delicate ecological balance, with unexpected results" (R. Neimeyer & Harter, 1988, p. 177). Constructivists thus tend to view cognition in systemic terms, with more peripheral hypotheses and activities organized around a "hard core" of assumptions about self and world that resist invalidation (Liotti, 1987). This "nuclear structure" of our knowledge systems (Mahoney, 1991) is being adopted by increasing numbers of cognitive therapists (Persons, 1989; Safran, Vallis, Segal, & Shaw, 1986), thereby edging them closer to a constructivist paradigm (R. Neimeyer, 1991).

Validation of Knowledge

In keeping with its "sensory metatheory of mind" (Weimer, 1977), rationalist cognitive therapy assumes a correspondence theory of truth: beliefs are considered true or valid to the extent that they match external reality (e.g., Beck et al., 1979; Bums, 1980). Forms of cognitive therapy that emphasize cognitive "distortions" or poor "reality contact" as the source of psychological disturbance are therefore the inheritors to a long tradition of realism in the mental health field, in which "the perception of reality is called mentally healthy when what an individual sees corresponds to what is actually there" (Jahoda, 1958; p. 6). Constructivists, on the other hand, subscribe to a coherence theory of truth: knowledge claims are judged "true" to the extent that they are viable, internally consistent, and consensually validated (cf. von Foerster, 1981; Kelly, 1955). This key epistemological contrast implies important pragmatic differences between the two corresponding styles of therapy, therapeutic goals, and preferred methods of "disputation."

Nature of Truth

These two respective sets of criteria for validation of personal knowledge suggest equally distinctive theories of truth or reality. Traditional cognitive therapists lean toward the conviction that truth is singular, universal, ahistorical, and incremental, in the sense that it can be "accumulated" through the collection of factual observations across time (Mahoney & Gabriel, 1987). Like Platonic truths, the reality sought by therapists with this orientation is assumed to be revealed by the correct application of reason (Ellis, 1973), with differences between observers representing unfortunate "error variance" to be controlled or corrected. Constructivist theorists, however, view truths as multiple, contextual, historical, and paradigmatic (Kelly, 1955; Steenbarger, 1991). From this perspective, "anything said is always said by an observer" (Maturana & Varela, 1987), with intraobserver consistencies established largely by their immersion in a common language system or set of social conventions. Again, this carries implications for the role of the counselor or therapist, something that we will explore in greater detail in the remainder of this article.

Strategic Contrasts

Constructivist approaches to psychotherapy are sometimes criticized for being "long on theory and short on practice," as a result of their emphasis on abstract theoretical assumptions, rather than their applications in the counseling context. For example, Minuchin (1991, p. 48), in an article entitled *The Seductions of Constructivism,* has cautioned,

> Much has been written about the theoretical underpinnings for constructivist psychotherapy . . . but they have produced almost nothing about how to put these theories into practice, how to intervene in what feels like real families with real problems.

Even advocates of constructivism sometimes echo these sentiments, contending that

> The weakness of many of the texts of postmodern thought is that, for all their analytical brilliance, they tend to be rather abstract about the human experience involved . . . They are short on practical ideas about [what] is to be done. The task of therapists is to turn some of postmodernism's vague celebrations of multiplicity and change into lived experience (O'Hara & Anderson, 1991, p. 25).

In fairness, however, these critiques represent only a half-truth. For while it is true that constructivist scholars have engaged in a good deal of epistemological reflection in establishing a conceptual foundation for their work, they have been equally creative in exploring its implications for the helping relationship. The strategies and techniques associated with this approach to assessment and psychotherapy have been presented in case study format in a variety of recent books and videotapes (e.g., Guidano & Liotti, 1983; Kuehlwein & Rosen, 1993; Neimeyer, 1993; R. Neimeyer & G. Neimeyer, 1987; see Note 1), and are represented in several of the articles in this series. To provide the backdrop for understanding these techniques, I will consider some of their common strategic similarities, once again contrasting them with the more familiar emphases of traditional cognitive therapy approaches (Table 6.2).

Assessment Focus

Cognitive assessment in the clinical context usually relies on some form of self-report questionnaire, to which the subject responds by endorsing a limited range of numerical options (cf. Merluzzi, Glass, & Genest, 1981).

Table 6.2 Strategic Contrasts: Traditional vs. Constructivist Therapies

Assumption	Traditional emphasis	Constructivist emphasis
Assessment focus	frequency or typicality of self-statements	implicative relationships among constructs
Assessment intent Goal of therapy	neutral, non-reactive promote rational, realistic appraisal of self and situations; corrective	change-generating promote elaboration of construct system, meaningful personal narratives; creative
Treatment of (negative) emotion	controlled as by-product of dysfunctional cognitions	respected as integral to meaning-making process
"Level" of intervention	automatic thoughts	core-ordering processes; structural coupling
Therapist's cognitive style	"tight," logical, accurate	"loose," metaphorical, approximate
Characteristic focus systemic	individualistic	individualistic to
Group work	psychoeducational instruction, mutual "problem-solving"	psychodramatic exploration

Most such methods require the client to report the *frequency* or *typicality* of separate cognitions or self-statements, as in the Automatic Thought Questionnaire (Hollon & Kendall, 1980) or the Crandell Cognitions Inventory (Crandell & Chambless, 1986). While questionnaires are sometimes employed by constructivist therapists as well (e.g., Lyddon & Alford, 1993), they are more likely to use interview techniques that pen-nit deeper examination of the organization of belief systems. Many of these methods focus on the implicative relationships among an individual's personal constructs, as in repertory grid technique (Kelly, 1955; G. Neimeyer & R. Neimeyer, 1981), or laddering and downward arrow methods, which enable the "vertical" exploration of progressively more central beliefs (R. Neimeyer, 1993). The kind of personal journal work encouraged by many constructivist and narrative therapists represents a still greater departure from the typical methods employed by cognitive therapists, allowing free-form qualitative self-examination on the part of the client (cf. Mahoney, 1991). When journal entries are selectively shared with the therapist in the course of counseling, they function as a means of both monitoring and fostering change.

Assessment Intent

This suggests another distinction between the two models of therapy, namely, the presumed neutrality of assessment from a cognitive standpoint (e.g., Genest & Turk, 1981), a position that is radically questioned by constructivists (G. Neimeyer & R. Neimeyer, 1993). Therapists of the latter orientation reject the assumption that any form of measurement can be wholly "nonreactive," and instead embrace the change-generating possibilities of even the most basic of "assessment" techniques—therapist generated questions (Tomm & Lannamann, 1988). Likewise, more elaborate methods such as "mirror time" and "stream of consciousness" methods (Mahoney, 1991) erase the distinction between assessment and therapy, fostering new awareness on the part of both client and therapist.

Goal of Therapy

In keeping with their epistemological assumptions, cognitive therapists typically associate successful therapeutic outcome with the development of rational, realistic, or "scientific" client appraisals of self and situation (Beck et al., 1979; Dryden & Ellis, 1987). In this sense, therapy is viewed as essentially corrective, serving to eliminate those irrational beliefs or cognitive distortions that are considered the wellsprings of psychological disturbance. Constructivist therapy, however, is more creative than corrective (R. Neimeyer & Harter, 1988), insofar as it promotes the elaboration of the construct system through the entertainment of hypothetical, "as if" worlds (Vaihinger, 1924). Narrative therapies that attempt to increase the coherence or power of a client's personal narrative (Russell, 1991; White & Epston, 1990) or account of life transitions (Harvey, Orbuch, Weber, Merbach, & Alt, 1992) also express this elaborative goal.

Treatment of (Negative) Emotion

From the standpoint of objectivist cognitive therapies, emotion—especially negative emotion—is viewed primarily as a problem to be controlled through the attainment of greater rationality and the elimination of cognitive distortions (Beck et al., 1979, Ellis, 1973). Constructivists, on the other hand, view emotions as integral to the meaning-making process (Carlsen, 1988), and therefore view it as something to work with rather than against (Mahoney & Gabriel, 1987). This perspective has been reinforced recently by qualitative research on psychotherapeutic change processes conducted by Clark (1991).

"Level" of Intervention

Any practicing therapist is aware that counseling consists of an endless series of "choice points," moments of decision in which the therapist must determine what to pursue and how. Cognitive and constructivist therapists differ in their modal response to such choice points, with the former more frequently opting to pursue the "automatic thoughts" that are relatively accessible to a client's conscious report (Beck et al., 1979; Bums, 1980), and the latter choosing to focus on "core ordering processes" that may be less easily reported in an explicit fashion (Mahoney, 1991). These core processes—often thematizing one's deepest sense of self (Guidano, 1991)—may be amenable only to exploratory strategies that make extensive use of idiosyncratic images or metaphors (Mair, 1989).

Style of Intervention

Several of the above strategic emphases imply that different styles of intervention may be preferred by cognitive and constructivist counselors. At their most forceful, rationalist therapists may "vigorously and persistently attack" the client's "old crooked thinking," taking special care to "attack and uproot" any defenses and resistances (Ellis, 1973, p. 309). Even in their more collaborative roles, cognitive-behavioral therapists typically provide an authoritative, Socratic, and instructional context designed to move the client closer to principles of "right thinking" (Lewinsohn, Steinmetz, Antonuccio, & Teri, 1984; Weishaar & Beck, 1987). Constructivists, in contrast, are likely to eschew this form of "information giving," instead attempting to promote "structural coupling" with a client's own meaning system (Efran, Lukens, & Lukens, 1990) in order to promote change from within. For this reason, such therapists tend to practice a less directive, almost "reverential" form of therapy (Leitner, 1988), which more strongly emphasizes the developmental roots of a client's current outlook (Guidano & Liotti, 1983; Lyddon, 1993; Mahoney, 1988b; Wessler & Hankin-Wessler, 1987).

Therapist's Cognitive Style

To a considerable extent, therapists' own "cognitive styles" mirror their therapeutic models. Thus, it is not surprising that cognitive therapists are often characterized by their precise, logical, and systematic approach to a client's complaints, a style that corresponds to their therapeutic goal to promote a clear, accurate, and objective self-evaluation on the part of their clients (c.f. Beck, 1986). Constructivists also display a characteristic way of thinking, one that is more metaphoric, approximate, and intuitive, modeling the exploratory, "as if" style they more frequently encourage in their clients (R. Neimeyer & G. Neimeyer, 1987).

Characteristic Focus

Although it has been expanded into the treatment of couples and groups (Freeman, 1983), cognitive therapy is usually quite individualistic in its focus, in keeping with its emphasis on thinking patterns that lead to dysfunctional emotional and behavioral responses. Constructivist therapy can also be highly individualistic and personal (Kelly, 1955; Leitner, 1988; Mair, 1989), but it has been more extensively integrated with therapies targeting couples and larger family systems. Just as important, it has developed means of conceptualizing and measuring clinically relevant "emergent properties" of shared belief systems, which are not reducible to the individual outlooks of the family members involved (Harter, Neimeyer, & Alexander, 1989; G. Neimeyer, 1985; Ryle, 1981). In fact, the field of constructivist family therapy is one of the most vigorous areas of development in constructivist thinking over the last ten years (Feixas, 1990; Hoffman, 1988; Procter, 1987).

Group Work

Finally, these two orientations to therapeutic practice emphasize and mobilize rather different processes in the group therapy context. Group therapists in the cognitive-behavioral tradition are typically more psychoeducational (Lewinsohn et al., 1984; Yost, Beutler, Corbishley, & Allender, 1986), often engaging the group in carefully regulated "problem solving" according to specified techniques (Platt, Prout, & Metzger, 1987). By comparison, constructivist group leaders tend to make heavier use of psychodramatic methods that encourage the enactment of thematic issues that involve multiple group members (Epting & Nazario, 1987; Morris, 1977). When more structured forms of group interaction are employed, they are used to facilitate the nonthreatening disclosure and exploration of alternative "realities" held by various group members (Landfield, 1979; R. Neimeyer, 1988).

In summary, the constructivist emphasis that is now influencing cognitive therapy differs from the traditional rationalist or objectivist emphasis in several respects, both at the level of epistemological assumptions and at the level of psychotherapeutic strategy. As increasing numbers of cognitive therapists begin to survey the territory of the helping relationship through a constructivist lens, we can expect that they will reveal new horizons of psychotherapeutic theory, research, and practice.

Conclusion

As an expression of a postmodern mindset that has accepted the linguistic, cultural, and personal relativism of social realities (Anderson, 1990), constructivism has begun to permeate numerous fields of contemporary psychology (R. Neimeyer, 1993a). With fields such as cognitive science (Agnew & Brown, 1989; K. Ford & Adams-Webber, 1991), developmental psychology (Berzonsky, 1990; D. Ford, 1987), and cultural studies (Bruner, 1990) adopting increasingly constructivist tenets, cross-fertilization of these areas with psychotherapeutic scholarship is likely to occur. Even more likely is the prospect of exchange among clinical traditions such as psychoanalysis (Soldz, 1988), family therapy (Alexander & G. Neimeyer), cognitive-behavioral therapy (Goldfried, 1988), and existential-humanistic therapies (Leitner, 1988), as each tradition participates in and absorbs aspects of this postmodern mindset. For this reason, constructivism is well-positioned to contribute to a systematic integration of the psychotherapies, promoting the articulation of a more inclusive model of therapy that remains theoretically consistent but technically diverse (R. Neimeyer, 1993c; R. Neimeyer & Feixas, 1990). The convergence of cognitive and constructivist traditions in the present Special Issue both expresses and contributes to this trend.

NOTE

1. Information on the availability of training videotapes in constructivist psychotherapies can be obtained from Psychoeducational Resources, P.O. Box 141231, Gainesville, FL, 32614.

REFERENCES

Agnew, N. M., & Brown, J. L. (1989). Foundations for a model of knowing: 1. Constructing reality. *Canadian Psychology/Psychologie Canadienne, 30,* 152–167.

Alexander, P. C., & Neimeyer, G. J. (1989). Constructivism and family therapy. *International Journal of Personal Construct Psychology, 2,* 11–122.

Anderson, W. T., (1990). *Reality isn't what it used to be.* San Francisco: Harper & Rowe.

Bateson, G. (1972). *Steps to an ecology of mind.* New York: Dutton.

Beck, A. T. (1986). *Three approaches to psychotherapy III: Cognitive therapy.* Psychological and Educational Films, E. L. Shostrum, producer.

Beck, A. T., & Greenberg, R. L. (1988). Cognitive therapy of panic disorder. In A. J. Frances & R. E. Hales (Eds.). *Review of psychiatry* (vol. 7) pp. 571–583. Washington: American Psychiatric Press.

Beck, A. T., Rush, J., Shaw, B., & Emery, G. (1979). *Cognitive therapy of depression.* New York: Guilford.

Berzonsky, M. D. (1990). Self-construction over the lifespan. In G. J. Neimeyer & R. A. Neimeyer (Eds.), *Advances in personal construct psychology* (vol. 1), Greenwich, CT: JAI Press, 155–186.

Boscolo, L., Cecchin, G., Hoffman, L., & Penn, P. (1987). *Milan systemic family therapy.* New York: Basic.

Bruner, J. (1990). *Acts of meaning.* Cambridge, MA: Harvard University Press.

Burns, D. (1980). *Feeling good.* New York: Signet.

Carlsen, M. B. (1988). *Meaning makings: Therapeutic processes in adult development.* New York: Norton.

Clark, D. A. (1988). The validity of measures of cognition: A review of the literature. *Cognitive Therapy and Research, 12,* 1–20.

Clark, D. A. (1991). A performance model of the creation of meaning event. *Psychotherapy, 28,* 395–401.

Crandell, C. J., & Chambless, D. L. (1986). The validation of an inventory for measuring depressive thoughts: The Crandell Cognition Inventory. *Behaviour Research and Therapy, 24,* 403–41 1.

Dryden, W., & Ellis, A. (1987). Rational-emotive therapy (RET.). In W. Dryden & W. Golden (Eds.), *Cognitive-behavioral psychotherapy.* New York: Hemisphere, 129–168.

Dryden, W., & Golden, W. (1987). *Cognitive-behavioural approaches to psychotherapy.* New York: Hemisphere.

Efran, J. S., Lukens, M. D., & Lukens, R. J. (1990). *Language, structure and change.* New York: Norton.

Ellis, A. (1973). Rational-emotive therapy. In R. Jurjevich (Ed.), *Direct psychotherapy.* Coral Gables, FL: University of Miami Press.

Ellis, A. (1992). First-order and second-order change in rational-emotive therapy: A reply to Lyddon. *Journal of Counseling and Development, 70,* 449–451.

Epting, F. R., & Nazario, A. (1987). Designing a fixed role therapy. In R. A. Neimeyer, & G. J. Neimeyer (Eds.), *Personal construct therapy casebook.* New York: Springer.

Feixas, G. (1990). Personal construct theory and the systemic therapies: Parallel or convergent trends? *Journal of Marital and Family Therapy 16,* 1–20.

Ford, D. H. (1987). *Humans as self-constructing living systems.* Hillsdale, NJ: Lawrence Erlbaum.

Ford, K. M., & Adams-Webber, J. R. (1991). Structure of personal construct systems and the logic of confirmation. *International Journal of Personal Construct Psychology, 4,* 15–42.

Freeman, A. (1983). Cognitive therapy with couples and groups. New York: Plenum.

Genest, M., & Turk, D. C. (1981). Think aloud approaches to cognitive assessment. In T. Merluzzi, C. Glass, & M. Genest (Eds.), *Cognitive assessment.* New York: Guilford, 233–269.

Goldfried, M. (1988). Personal construct therapy and other theoretical orientations. *International Journal of Personal Construct Psychology, 1,* 317–328.

Goncalves, O. F. (1989). The constructive-developmental trend in the cognitive therapies. In O. F. Goncalves (Ed.), *Advances in the cognitive therapies.* Porto, Portugal: APPORT.

Guidano, V. F. (1991). *The self in process.* New York: Guilford.

Guidano, V., & Liotti, G. (1983). *Cognitive processes and emotional disorders.* New York: Guilford.

Harter, S., Neimeyer, R. A., & Alexander, P.C. (1989). Personal construction of family relationships. *International Journal of Personal Construct Psychology, 2,* 123–142.

Harvey, J. H., Orbuch, T. L., Weber, A. L., Merbach, N., & Alt, R. (1992). House of pain and hope: Accounts of loss. *Death Studies, 16,* 99–124.

Hoffman, L. (1988). A constructivism position for family therapy. *Irish Journal of Psychology, 9,* 110–129.

Hollon, S. D., & Kendall, P. C. (1980). Cognitive self-statements in depression: Development of an Automatic Thoughts Questionnaire. *Cognitive Therapy and Research, 4,* 383–395.

Jahoda, M. (1958). *Current concepts of positive mental health.* New York: Basic Books.

Jaremko, M. (1987). Cognitive-behavior modification: The shaping of rule-governed behavior. In W. Dryden, & W. Golden (Eds.), *Cognitive behavioural approaches to psychotherapy.* New York: Hemisphere, 31–60.

Kelly, G. A. (1955). *The psychology of personal constructs.* New York: Norton.

Kendall, P. C. (1993). Cognitive approaches to children's problems. *Journal of Consulting and Clinical Psychology, 61,* 235–247.

Kuehlwein, K. T., & Rosen, H. (1993) (Eds.). *Cognitive therapy in action: Evolving innovative practice.* San Francisco: Jossey-Bass.

Landfield, A. W. (1979). Exploring socialization through the Interpersonal Transaction group. In P. Stringer, & D. Bannister (Eds.), *Constructs of sociality and individuality.* London: Academic, 133–15 1.

Leitner, L. M. (1988). Terror, risk and reverence: Experiential personal construct therapy. *International Journal of Personal Construct Psychology,* 251–261.

Lewinsohn, P. M., Steinmetz, J., Antonuccio, D., & Teri, L. (1984). Cognitive-Behavioral with youth. *International Journal of Mental Health, 13,* 833.

Liotti, G. (1987). Structural cognitive therapy. In W. Dryden, & W. Golden (Eds.), *Cognitive-behavioral approaches to psychotherapy.* New York: Hemisphere.

Lyddon, W. J. (1990). First- and second-order change: Implications for rationalist and constructivist cognitive therapies. *Journal of Counseling and Development, 69,* 121–127.

Lyddon, W. J. (1993). Developmental constructivism: An integrative framework for psychotherapy practice. *Journal of Cognitive Psychotherapy, 7* (3).

Lyddon, W. J., & Alford, D. J. (1993). Constructivist assessment: A developmental-epistemic perspective. In G. J. Neimeyer (Ed.), *Casebook of constructivist assessment.* Newbury Park, CA: Sage.

Mahoney, M. J. (1988a). Constructive metatheory 1: Basic features and historical foundations. *International Journal of Personal Construct Psychology, 1,* 299–315.

Mahoney, M. J. (1988b). Constructive metatheory 11: Implications for psychotherapy. *International Journal of Personal Construct Psychology, 1,* 299–315.

Mahoney, M. J. (1991). *Human change processes.* New York: Basic.

Mahoney, M. J., & Gabriel, T. J. (1987). Psychotherapy and cognitive sciences: An evolving alliance. *Journal of Cognitive Psychotherapy, 1,* 39–59.

Mair, M. (1989). *Between psychology and psychotherapy.* London: Routledge.

Maturana, H., & Varela, F. (1987). *The tree of knowledge.* Boston: New Science Library.

Meichenbaum, D. (1977). *Cognitive-behavior modification.* New York: Plenum.

Merluzzi, T., Glass, C., & Genest, M. (1981). *Cognitive assessment.* New York: Guilford.

Millis, K. K., & Neimeyer, R. A. (1990). A test of the dichotomy corollary: Propositions versus constructs as basic cognitive units. *International Journal of Personal Construct Psychology, 3,* 167–181.

Minuchin, S. (1991). The seductions of constructivism. *Family Therapy Networker, 15,* 47–50.

Morris, J. B. (1977). The prediction and measurement of change in a psychotherapy group using the repertory grid. In F. Fransella, & D. Bannister, *A manual for repertory grid technique,* 120–148. London: Academic.

Neimeyer, G. J. (1985). Personal constructs in the counseling of couples. In F. Epting, & A. Landfield (Eds.), *Anticipating personal construct psychology.* Lincoln: University of Nebraska Press.

Neimeyer, G. J. (Ed.) (1993). *Handbook of constructivist assessment.* New York: Sage.

Neimeyer, G. J., & Neimeyer, R. A. (1981). Personal construct perspectives on cognitive assessment. In T. Merluzzi, C. Glass, & M. Genest (Eds.), *Cognitive assessment.* New York: Guilford, 188–232.

Neimeyer, G. J., & Neimeyer, R. A. (1993). Intervening in meaning. In G. J. Neimeyer (Ed.), *Casebook of constructivist assessment.* Newbury Park, CA: Sage.

Neimeyer, R. A. (1985). Personal constructs in clinical practice. In P. Kendall (Ed.), *Advances in cognitive-behavioral research and therapy (Vol. 4),* New York: Academic.

Neimeyer, R. A. (1988). Clinical guidelines for conducting Interpersonal Transaction groups. *International Journal of Personal Construct Psychology, 1,* 181–190.

Neimeyer, R. A. (1991). Edging toward a constructivist psychotherapy. *International Journal of Personal Construct Psychology, 4,* 215–218.

Neimeyer, R. A. (1993a). An appraisal of constructivist psychotherapies. *Journal of Consulting and Clinical Psychology, 61,* 221–234.

Neimeyer, R. A. (1993b). Constructivist approaches to the measurement of meaning. In G. J. Neimeyer (Ed.), *Casebook of constructivist assessment*. Newbury Park, CA: Sage.

Neimeyer, R. A. (1993c). Constructivism and the problem of psychotherapy integration. *Journal of Psychotherapy Integration, 3,* 133–234.

Neimeyer, R. A., & Feixas, G. (1990). Constructivist contributions to psychotherapy integration. *Journal of Integrative and Eclectic Psychotherapy, 9,* 4–20.

Neimeyer, R. A., & Feixas, G. (1992). Cognitive assessment in depression: A comparison of some existing measures. *European Journal of Psychological Assessment, 8,* 47–56.

Neimeyer, R. A., & Harter, S. (1988). Facilitating individual change in personal construct therapy. In G. Dunnett (Ed.), *Working with people*. London: Routledge.

Neimeyer, R. A. & Neimeyer, G. J. (1987). *Personal construct therapy casebook*. New York: Springer.

O'Hara, M., & Anderson, W. T. (1991). Welcome to the postmodern world. *Family Therapy Networker, 15,* 18–25.

Persons, J. B. (1989). *Cognitive therapy in practice*. New York: Norton.

Platt, J., Prout, M., & Metzger, D. (1987). Interpersonal cognitive problem-solving therapy. In W. Dryden & W. Golden (Eds.), *Cognitive behavioural approaches to psychotherapy*. New York: Hemisphere, 261–289.

Procter, H. G. (1987). Change in the family construct system. In R. A. Neimeyer & G. J. Neimeyer (Eds.), *Personal construct therapy casebook*. New York: Springer.

Russell, R. L. (1991). Narrative in views of humanity, science, and action: Lessons for cognitive therapy. *Journal of Cognitive Psychotherapy 4,* 241–256.

Rychlak, J. F. (1990). George Kelly and the concept of construction. *International Journal of Personal Construct Psychology, 3,* 7–19.

Rychlak, J. (1992). Oppositionality and the psychology of personal constructs. In G. J. Neimeyer & R. A. Neimeyer (Eds.), *Advances in personal construct psychology* (Vol. 2). Greenwich, CT: JAI Press.

Ryle, A. (1981). Dyad grid dilemmas in patients and control subjects. *British Journal of Medical Psychology, 45,* 375–382.

Safran, J. D., Valis, T. M., Segal, Z. V., & Shaw, B. F. (1986). Assessment of core cognitive processes in cognitive therapy. *Cognitive Therapy and Research, 10,* 509–526.

Sarason, I. G. (1979). Three lacunae of cognitive therapy. *Cognitive Therapy and Research, 3,* 223–235.

Soldz, S. (1988). Constructivist tendencies in recent psychoanalysis. *International Journal of Personal Construct Psychology, 1,* 329–348.

Steenbarger, B. N. (1991). All the world is not a stage: Emerging contextualist themes in counseling and development. *Journal of Counseling and Development, 70,* 288–296.

Tomm, K., & Lannamann, J. (1988). Questions as interventions. *Family Therapy Networker, 12,* 38–41.

Vaihinger, H. (1924). *The philosophy of "as if."* London: Routledge.

vonFoerster, H.(1981). Observing systems. Seaside, CA: Intersystems Publications.

Weimer, W. B. (1977). A conceptual framework for cognitive psychology: Motor theories of the mind. In R. Shaw & J. Bransford (Eds.), *Acting, perceiving, and knowing,* 267–311. Hillsdale, NJ: Erlbaum.

Weishaar, M. E., & Beck, A. T. (1987). Cognitive therapy. In W. Dryden & W. Golden (Eds.), *Cognitive-behavioral approaches to psychotherapy.* New York: Hemisphere.

Wessler, R. L., & Hankin-Wessler, S. (1987). Cognitive appraisal therapy. In W. Dryden & W. Golden (Eds.), *Cognitive-behavioural approaches to psychotherapy.* New York: Hemisphere, 196–223.

White, M., & Epston, D. (1990). *Narrative means to therapeutic ends.* New York: Norton.

Wilson, G. T., & Fairbairn, C. (1993). Cognitive treatments of eating disorders. *Journal of Consulting and Clinical Psychology, 61,* 261–269.

Yost, E., Beutler, L. E., Corbishley, M. A., & Allender, J. R. (1986). *Group cognitive therapy.* New York: Pergamon Press.

CHAPTER 7

Psychotherapy and the Cognitive Sciences: An Evolving Alliance

Michael J. Mahoney and Tyler J. Gabriel

The "cognitive revolution" in psychology is now well on its way, and the future of the cognitive sciences seems to be one of continuing heuristic promise. Modern cognitive therapies are hardly "finished," however, as is evident in several recent expressions in the field. The continuing differentiation of cognitive theories is a case in point, and developments in constructivism, evolutionary epistemology, autopoiesis, and attachment and social learning theories appear to reflect accelerating theoretical evolution in late twentieth-century mind sciences. This article will trace historical aspects of this evolution, examine recent developments in the field, and discuss selected implications for the practice of psychotherapy.

A BRIEF HISTORY OF THE COGNITIVE REVOLUTION

Historical Contexts

Cognitive psychology and the ongoing "cognitive movement" may be framed within the longstanding philosophical debate between structuralism and functionalism. Functionalist thinking is apparent in current theories of behaviorism, in which the functional effects of behavior are the focus of analysis. Structuralism, by comparison, seeks to understand the organizational processes of human experience that place restrictions on the functional capabilities of the organism. This dichotomy appears to have been resolved by theorists in evolutionary biology and complex phenomena who have recently proposed that structure and function are interdependent and isomorphic (Guidano, in press; Hayek, 1964; Mahoney, 1987, in press; Varela, 1979; Weimer, 1982).

As a tradition, functionalism has emphasized a *reactive* portrayal of human nature. Thus, in the writings of Watson, Skinner, Wolpe, and other behaviorists, one encounters frequent references to the axiom that behavior is a function of its environment [$B = f(e)$]. Such perspectives explicitly argue for the necessity and sufficiency of environmental modification in any endeavor of behavior modification. In this article we will elaborate some recent challenges to this portrayal and prescription. Specifically, we will argue that environments (including stimuli, contingencies, and consequences) are *proactively construed* by the individual. The relationship between an organism and its world entails a complex and dynamic reciprocity of influence. Cognitive theorists, as we will illustrate, have challenged extreme environmentalism and the implied linear model of causality by asserting that humans respond only to their dynamic representational models of the world, rather than to any "true" reality as such. We will now summarize some of the major developments during the emergence of the cognitive therapies.

Cognitive Psychology in the 1960s and 1970s

During the early 1960s, it was tempting to divide psychotherapists into two groupings—those who focused on internal and those who focused on external determinants of adaptation. As each group became increasingly aware of the limitations of their own approach, however, they began to challenge and transcend their self-imposed boundaries. Insight-oriented therapists were often frustrated with their inability to induce behavioral change, while behavior therapists found themselves able to achieve behavioral changes only in specific contexts (Mahoney, 1977). Underlying both schools was an adherence to a linear, or unidirectional, model of causality, with dichotomous views on the appropriate focus for intervention. Behaviorists focused on external influences on a person's actions. Intrapersonal therapists emphasized internal events or the interaction between the individual and environment in determining behavior. Common to both was their treatment of behavior as a dependent variable rather than as an interdependent factor (Bandura, 1978; Mahoney, 1984a).

Cognitive learning theory was a major departure from the above themes in that it emphasized an interactive, or reciprocal, model of determinism. These cognitive theories could thus account for the importance of private events and intrapersonal factors while simultaneously emphasizing the role of environmental variables in influencing personal phenomenology and performance. Some of the contributors who gave an initial boost to the emergence of the cognitive trend were Kelly (1955), Rotter (1954), Beck (1963), Ellis (1962), and Bandura (1969). These theorists all invoked central cognitive and symbolic mechanisms as necessary for behavior change, and some utilized behavioral procedures in their therapy.

The emergence of cognitive approaches was met with considerable controversy, and the initial reactions of many influential writers were denial and diminishment (Ledwidge, 1978; Skinner, 1971, 1974; Wolpe, 1976). The most ardent protests came from within the ranks of behavioral theorists, who perceived the introduction of mediational processes as "blasphemous" (Mahoney, 1974). Recent archival records reflect, for example, that early volumes in "cognitive behavior modification" were actually banned at several campuses where orthodox behaviorism was predominant (Mahoney, 1985a). The range of public reactions to the emergence of cognitive theories also illustrates the intensity of the controversy. Wolpe (1978) has maintained that the cognitive revolution is anachronistic in that "behavior therapy has always been cognitive." He cites his own use of mental imagery and internal events in his therapy as evidence for this argument, but he fails to acknowledge the difference between stimulus-response and cognitive models of mediation. In contrast, Skinner (1974, 1984) claims that behaviorism has never been (and ought never be) cognitive. He is opposed to the inclusion of cognition in the study of human experience and views it as a major departure from behaviorism and, hence, what he considers appropriate science.

Nevertheless, cognition and cognitive theories became increasingly popular within traditional behavioral research. Mahoney and Arnkoff (1978) summarized the development of cognitive therapies and concurrent research during this time. Three themes became apparent in cognitive therapies: behavioral self-control, covert conditioning, and cognitive learning. Behavioral self-control methods included such procedures as stimulus control, self-monitoring, self-reward, and self-punishment. Research on self-control generated many questions that continue to fuel investigations in areas ranging from health psychology to corporate management. For present purposes, it is worth noting that self-control procedures seem to have progressed from external and environmental techniques toward symbolic, cognitive activities. The first generation of these techniques were termed "covert conditioning." They are generally associated with Lloyd Homme (1965) and Joseph Cautela (1966, 1967), who essentially applied behavioral methods to what they considered to be covert stimuli and responses. The empirical evidence and clinical warrant for these covert conditioning approaches have been meager, however, and their use is now infrequent in clinical behavior therapy.

Cognitive learning therapies were the third major theme to emerge during the "cognitive movement" in the sixties. They may be further divided into cognitive restructuring, coping skills, and problem-solving approaches. The cognitive learning therapies were distinguished by their simultaneous endorsement of cognitive processes and their respect for the functional promise of experimentally developed, behavioral procedures (Mahoney & Arnkoff, 1978). One of the most widely known of the cognitive restructuring therapies is rational-emotive therapy (RET), pioneered by Albert Ellis (1962). With his assumption that irrational (and therefore maladaptive) thoughts are the cause of most emotional disturbance, Ellis was one of the leaders in popularizing cognitively focused techniques. RET has become one of the most commonly used cognitive approaches, and Ellis (1977) has asserted that its empirical support is "immense." There is still considerable controversy, however, about the processes and factors that account for its therapeutic effects as well as the magnitude and consistency of such effects (Mahoney, 1977; Rogers & Craighead, 1977; Mahoney & Arnkoff, 1978). It is clear that RET is now in the process of being reappraised and differentiated by its own adherents (Dryden, 1984; Ellis, 1985; Wessler, 1984).

Cognitive Therapy was developed by Beck (1970) and represents another important cognitive learning approach. Beck studied cognitive processes in clinical populations and found that there were several types of ideation patterns that were common to various disorders. Cognitive Therapy, like the other cognitive restructuring approaches, was designed to help the client identify maladaptive cognitions, recognize their adverse impact, and replace them with more adaptive thought patterns. Beck's therapeutic approach has also grown significantly over the last decade and currently constitutes a major representative of the cognitive therapies. Likewise, Beck's conceptualizations and therapy have continued to develop toward some of the directions outlined in the second part of this article.

Therapies focusing on coping and problem-solving skills comprised the next major developments in cognitive approaches. Coping-skills techniques attempt to help clients develop skills to facilitate their adaptation in stressful situations. Clinical applications have included the treatment of phobias and unassertiveness, and research has indicated that these methods are at least moderately effective (Mahoney & Arnkoff, 1978). They overlap to some extent with the problem-solving therapies. D'Zurilla and Goldfried (1971) noted the need for clinical exploration of problem solving and suggested that ineffectual problem solving was linked to emotional disturbance. Clinical approaches addressing this issue included the early efforts of Spivack and his associates, and problem-solving methods have continued to develop as a form of cognitive learning therapies (D'Zurilla, 1987). Training in personal problem solving has been shown to be effective in various applications and has been included in more integrated treatment packages.

Research on the cognitive learning therapies as a whole suggests that their pursuit was warranted and heuristic. Their theoretical and practical yield has been encouraging. While there is an impressive amount of empirical evidence corroborating their promise, however, much of the extant research is methodologically limited, and conclusions about change processes have been correspondingly constrained. New methodologies and therapies have begun emerging, however, and increasing emphasis is being placed on basic principles and processes of human learning. Before we move on to these more recent developments, however, it is important to acknowledge the value of the historical context briefly reviewed in this section. RET and Cognitive Therapy, for example, will continue to develop and to offer their contributions to our understanding and facilitation of human learning. Above and beyond their continuing and future contributions, however, they deserve credit for their pioneering precedents in the evolving alliance between the Cognitive and clinical sciences.

Current Cognitive Therapies

The final chapter in this brief introductory review of the cognitive revolution will bring us to the full range of present-day approaches. As noted earlier, the cognitive therapies are continuing to undergo dramatic changes and salient differentiations. These changes may, in part, reflect the growing popularity and application of cognitive approaches. In his 1982 survey of American clinical and counseling psychologists, for example, Smith (1982) found that 12.1% viewed themselves as cognitive (as compared with 14.7%, psychodynamic; 12.6%, humanistic; 6.8%, behavioral; and 41.2%, eclectic). Of the noneclectic respondents in that survey, almost 21 percent were cognitive in orientation.

Another sign of the growth and differentiation of cognitive approaches comes from analyses of the numbers of distinguishable cognitive thera-

Table 7.1 Current Cognitive Therapies

1 *Personal Construct Therapy* (Kelly, 1955)
2 *Logotherapy* (Frankl, 1959)
3 *Rational-Emotive Therapy (Ellis,* 1962)
4 *Cognitive Therapy* (Beck, 1970, 1976)
5 *Multimodal Therapy* (Lazarus, 1971, 1976)
6 *Problem-Solving Therapies* (D'Zurilla & Goldfried, 1971; Spivack & Shure, 1974; D'Zurilla, 1987)
7 *Rational Behavior Training* (Goodman & Maultsby, 1974; Maultsby, 1984)
8 *Cognitive-Behavior Modification* (Meichenbaum, 1977)
9 *Rational-Stage-Directed Therapy (Tosi* & Eshbugh, 1980)
10 *Motor-Evolutionary Psychotherapy* (Burrell, 1983)
11 *Integrated Cognitive Behavior Therapy* (Wessler, 1984)
12 *Cognitive Developmental Therapy* (Mahoney, 1980, 1985b, in press)
13 *Constructivistic Cognitive Therapy* (Guidano, 1984, in press; Guidano & Liotti, 1983, 1985)
14 *Lay Epistemic Therapy* (Kruglanski & Jaffe, 1983)
15 *Piagetian Therapy* (Leva, 1984; Rosen, 1985; Weiner, 1975)
16 *Cognitive-Experiential Therapy* (Weiner, 1985)
17 *Neo-Cognitive Psychotherapy* (Suarez, 1985)

pies at various points in time. In 1970, for example, there were only four distinct cognitive therapies—Kelly's (1955) personal construct approach, Ellis's (1962) rational-emotive therapy, Beck's (1963, 1970) Cognitive Therapy, and Frankl's (1959) logotherapy (which has been recently incorporated by both cognitive and humanistic groups—cf. Frankl, 1985). At the time of this writing, however, there are at least 13 additional cognitive perspectives that claim to be distinct approaches (Table 7.1). Although three of these new therapies (Tosi, Maultsby, & Wessler) represent differentiations of RET, the remainder represent divergent (and yet, in some cases, convergent) approaches to cognition and psychotherapy.

In the remainder of this article we will focus on some of the patterns and themes that appear to run through many of these newer approaches. Our intent is neither to compare and contrast individual therapies nor to dwell on technical particulars. Rather, our emphasis will be placed on recent developments in the cognitive, developmental, and systems sciences and their possible implications for therapeutic interventions.

RECENT DEVELOPMENTS IN THE COGNITIVE SCIENCES

During the emergence of the cognitive approaches, a "revolution within a revolution" was occurring as cognitive theorists began to diverge in their conceptualizations of cognitive processes. This divergence, it seems, has touched upon some basic assumptions about the nature of reality (ontology), theories of knowledge (epistemology), and theories of causation. In a more elaborate discussion of these issues, it has been argued that they force a reappraisal of such classic philosophical controversies as realism versus idealism and rationalism versus empiricism (Mahoney, 1987, in press). Briefly, naive realism assumes a single, stable, external reality that is accurately perceived by the organism's sensory receptors. Traditionally, realism has drawn a sharp distinction between internal and external realms and has portrayed the brain as a reactive organ whose primary function is to register and retain accurate "copies" of the external world.

In a somewhat parallel fashion, rationalism has argued that thought is superior to sensation in determining experience and validating knowledge. Rationalism also emphasizes a distinct boundary between mental and physical processes and defends the primacy of the higher cerebral functions over lower-brain and bodily processes.

Constructivism and Motor Metatheories

The historical tradition of constructivism, and its relatively new expression in what are called "motor metatheories," represents a significant challenge to realism and rationalism. Constructivism has its roots in the eighteenth- and nineteenth-century writings of Immanuel Kant, Giambattista Vico, and Hans Vaihinger. It was, in fact, the Kantian scholar Vaihinger (1911/1924) who formatively influenced the thinking of Alfred Adler and, to a lesser extent, George Kelly. Adler and Kelly are probably the best-known clinical constructivists, and it was Kelly's work that inspired some of the foundational assertions of Beck's Cognitive Therapy. Wilhelm Wundt, Franz Brentano, Frederick Bartlett, and Jean Piaget have been among the most influential nonclinical constructivists.

In essence, constructivism asserts that humans actively—and, indeed, proactively—construct and construe the realities to which they respond. From this perspective, knowledge consists of meaning-making processes by which the organism orders or organizes its experiences. Knowing is thus a much more phenomenal and complex process than has been suggested by traditional realist and rationalist theories (Guidano & Liotti,

1985; Weimer, 1977; Mahoney, 1985b). Contemporary proponents of constructivism challenge the idea that reality is fundamentally external and stable and argue that human thought is not meaningfully separable from human feeling and action (Guidano, 1984, in press; Hayek, 1952, 1978, 1982; Joyce Moniz, 1985; Mahoney, 1985b, 1987, in press; Mancuso & Adams-Webber, 1982; Neimeyer, 1985; Varela, 1979; Von Foerster, 1984; Watzlawick, 1984; Weimer, 1977, 1982).

Motor metatheories of mind are a recent expression of constructivism in cognitive psychology (Weimer, 1977). Motor metatheories may be contrasted with traditional sensory models of cognitive and perceptual processes. Sensory metatheories portray the mind as a passive receptor of incoming information collected from the external world via the senses. The products of the sensory systems constitute the basic building blocks of perception and thought, and memory is portrayed as the "storage" of accurate copies of reality. In contrast to sensory metatheories, motor metatheories add the concept of "feedforward mechanisms" to those of cybernetic feedback. The central tenet of motor metatheories is their assertion of a functional isomorphism between sensation and action (as well as knowledge and behavior):

> What the motor metatheory asserts is that there is no sharp separation between sensory and motor components of the nervous system which can be made on functional grounds and that the mental or cognitive realm is intrinsically motoric, like all the nervous system. The mind is intrinsically a motor system, and the sensory order by which we are acquainted with external objects as well as ourselves . . . is a product of what are, correctly interpreted, constructive motor skills (Weimer, 1977, p. 272).

By eliminating the distinction between input and output, motor metatheories challenge much of contemporary psychology on two fronts:

1. The adherence to linear models of causality and simple "technified" strategies of intervention (Mahoney, 1986), and
2. The questionable assumption that experience can be compartmentalized into cognitive, affective, and behavioral components, and that adjustment can be facilitated by addressing the "appropriate target" (Mahoney, 1984b, in press).

The growing interest in constructivism and motor theories may thus signal the decline of "billiard-ball determinism" in psychology (Mahoney, 1984a).

Developmental and Systems Approaches

In addition to constructivism and motor metatheories, the recent acceleration and growing visibility of developmental and systems approaches reflect significant changes in modern conceptualizations of human adaptation and experience. Developmental models address psychological growth throughout the lifespan and emphasize basic processes of change. Interest in change processes is clearly increasing in the clinical sciences and has begun to compete with the longstanding preoccupation with outcome alone (Howard & Orlinsky, 1972; Mahoney, 1980, 1985b; Orlinsky & Howard, 1975; Prochaska, 1984; Rice & Greenberg, 1984). Likewise, systems approaches have begun to focus more directly on processes and on the dynamic (versus static) equilibrations evident in spontaneously self-organizing complex phenomena (Bateson, 1972, 1979; Brent, 1984; Cook, 1980; Hayek, 1964, 1978; Land, 1973; Laszlo, 1983; Pattee, 1973; Weimer, 1982, in press). Systems theories represent a movement away from reductionism and linear models of causality and toward an acknowledgment of complexity, reciprocal interdependence, and development over time. The fields of evolutionary epistemology and autopoiesis have likewise evidenced convergence on these themes.

Evolutionary Epistemology

Evolutionary epistemology is the study of knowing systems and their development. Despite its obvious relevance to psychology and psychotherapy, interest in evolutionary epistemology on the part of psychologists is relatively recent (Campbell, 1974, 1975). Among other things, current theory and research in this field suggest the following:

1. Life forms on this planet have evolved via the complex interplay of variation and selection processes (both genetically and behaviorally).
2. Human evolution reflects a relatively recent encephalization (increase of brain to body mass).
3. The human internuncial neuron (which comprises over 98% of all neocortical nerves) evolved out of an undifferentiated sensory-motor unit.
4. Biological knowing processes rely on basic contrasts and comparisons that result in the viable self-organization of experience.
5. "Higher" knowing systems are comprised of progressively more complex, interdependent "systems of systems."

6. The evolutionary differentiation of the human nervous system has resulted in four structurally separate but interdependent brains (the reptilian complex, the limbic system, and the right and left hemispheres of the neocortex).
7. "Neoteny," or the slowing of developmental rates, may represent the key to human plasticity and help explain the primary significance of emotional attachment (relationships) in human development.

Primary sources for these generalizations include Campbell (1974), Dobzhansky (1962), Gould (1977, 1980), Jantsch (1980, 1981), Jerison (1973, 1976), Land (1973), MacLean (1973), Mahoney (in press), Passingham (1982), Reynolds (1981), Washburn & Moore (1980), and Wilson (1980). Needless to say, such work in evolutionary epistemology complements constructivism and motor metatheories in its emphasis on the viability, rather than validity, of cognitive representations, and in its acknowledgment of a complex, dynamic reciprocity between organism and environment.

Autopoiesis

Autopoiesis refers to self-organizing or self-developing processes in complex, open systems. It has become an increasingly popular topic in biology, chemistry, and physics following Ilya Prigogine's 1977 Nobel prize. Prigogine demonstrated that Newton's Second Law of Thermodynamics-i.e., that mass and energy tend toward a static state of equilibrium-is a special case that applies only to closed systems. Open, self-organizing systems (e.g., life, social systems, etc.) actively transform their basic structures and functioning as an adaptive response to environmental pressures (Prigogine, 1980; Prigogine & Stengers, 1984). Disorder and disequilibrium may be seen as "natural" phenomena that elicit a transformation to more viable, higher-order organization and are thus vital to development (Brent, 1978, 1984; Dell, 1982; Jantsch, 1980, 1981; Maturana, 1975; Maturana & Varela, 1980; Varela, 1979; Zeleny, 1980).

This structural and functional transformation, or "order through fluctuation," exemplifies the oscillatory, opponent-process nature of almost all developmental processes (Mahoney, 1985b, in press). Piaget addresses this in his famous theory of equilibration, which illustrates the operation of what Bateson (1972, 1979) has termed first-and second-order cognitive processes. "Assimilation" is the first-order process by which experience is integrated into existing structures, or schemata, that constrain the range and quality of information available to the system (Piaget, 1970, 1981).

"Accommodation" occurs when the existing schemata are unable to reconcile and equilibrate environmental fluctuations, causing the system to reorganize into a higher-order, more complex structure. Progressive development involves a second-order shift to a more complex structural organization, while regressive development (or "entrenchment") reflects attempts to salvage and retain obsolete cognitive schemata.

Social Learning and Attachment Theories

Congruent with one of the themes noted earlier under "Evolutionary Epistemology," social learning and attachment theories emphasize the importance of an individual's early and ongoing social interactions in his or her learning and development. Bandura's (1969) book *Principles of Behavior Modification* has been credited with instigating the cognitive-behavioral revolution (Mahoney & Arnkoff, 1978). His later theory of self-efficacy posits the powerful influence of one's beliefs and expectations regarding personal capabilities on actual performance. Bandura's contributions in such areas as self-regulation, vicarious learning, cognitive representation, and causal reciprocity have been significantly influential in the continuing development of the cognitive-clinical alliance (Bandura, 1976, 1977, 1985, 1986).

Bowlby's attachment theory also emphasizes the interdependence of social interaction and cognitive development (Bowlby, 1969, 1973, 1979, 1980, 1985). The quality of interaction between the primary caretaker and the child formatively shapes the child's meaning structures and self-perceptions. Thus, the attachment process is the primary organizing construct by which a person's self-concept is integrated (Guidano & Liotti, 1985). While early attachment relationships are most important, according to Bowlby, emotional attachments and separations affect emotional adjustment throughout the lifespan. Bowlby's theory in particular and the developmental sciences in general have become increasingly influential in current cognitive theories and therapies (Belsky & Nezworski, in press: Guidano, 1984, in press: Guidano & Liotti, 1983, 1985; Liotti, 1984; Mahoney, 1981, in press).

PRACTICAL DIFFERENCES BETWEEN RATIONALIST AND CONSTRUCTIVIST COGNITIVE THERAPIES

As may be apparent from the preceding discussion, cognitive therapies emanating from rationalist and constructivist traditions exhibit substantial practical differences. For the sake of brevity, the major differences are listed in Table 7.2. To begin with, the focus of intervention in rationalist

Table 7.2 Practical Differences between Rationalist and Constructivist Cognitive Therapies

Issue/Theme	Rationalist View	Constructivist View
Intervention emphases	a. Ahistorical b. Problem-focused c. Control-focused d. Teleological	a. Historical b. Process-focused c. Development-focused d. Teleonomic
Conceptualization of Problems	Problems are dysfunctions, deficits, or their emotional correlates; they should be controlled, eliminated, or redressed.	Problems are discrepancies between environmental stressors and current capacities; they reflect limits in abilities and should not be mistaken for their abstract ordering processes.
Conceptualization of Emotion	Emotion, especially when intense and negative, is the problem; irrational thinking is the cause.	Emotions are primitive, powerful ways of knowing: affective experience and exploration should be encouraged.
Resistance	Resistance reflects lack of motivation, ambivalence, or avoidance. Resistance is an impediment to therapeutic change and must be "overcome."	Resistance reflects self-protective processes that guard systemic integrity and protect against rapid "core" change. Resistance should be worked *with* rather than *against*.
Insight	Insight into irrational beliefs is necessary and (almost) sufficient for therapeutic change.	Insight may help to transform personal meanings and facilitate change, but emotional and behavioral enactments are also important.
Therapeutic relationship	The therapeutic relationship entails technical instruction and guidance.	The therapeutic relation ship provides a safe, caring, and intense context in which the client can explore and develop relationships with self and world.
Relapse and regression	Relapse and regression reflect failures in maintenance and generalization that should be avoided and minimized.	Relapse and regression reflect limits in current capacity and/or cycles in psychological development; they involve important learning opportunities.

cognitive therapy is on the control of present problems or symptomatology. Constructivists, on the other hand, tend to focus more on historical and developmental processes. Another way of thinking about this "problem-versus-process" emphasis is to recognize that rationalist therapy is usually "teleological," whereas constructivist therapy is "teleonomic." Teleology refers to a direction determined by an explicit, external goal or destination (such as symptom reduction). Teleonomy, however, refers to a direction without an explicit or external destination (evolution and personality development are two examples). While rationalists tend to guide the direction of therapy according to presenting problems, constructivists are less externally directive and allow the self-organizing processes of the individual to influence the course of counseling.

Another difference is apparent in the ways problems are conceptualized. Rationalists often view problems as deficits or dysfunctions manifested by negative affect and/or symptoms that should be controlled or eliminated. The constructivist perspective—which tends to be more developmental in emphasis—views problems as episodes of disorder that reflect discrepancies between environmental challenges and the individual's present capacities. Sudden changes in demands are reflected in acute disorders, and long-term disturbances involve ineffective, habitual, and often self-perpetuating patterns of dysfunction. Where rationalist therapists tend to conceptualize problems as perceptual or conceptual mistakes (e.g., irrational beliefs), constructivists are more likely to view problems as reflections of formerly adaptive strategies that present the individual with valuable opportunities to explore his or her developmental history and tacit views of self and world.

Rationalists generally assume that "as you think, so shall you feel," and thus, that emotional distress is the manifestation of irrational beliefs or dysfunctional thought processes. Moreover, rationalist therapists tend to be less comfortable with emotional intensity and are inclined to view "negative" emotions (e.g., anxiety, anger, and depression) as things to be controlled or eliminated. Constructivists, on the other hand, conceptualize emotions as primitive and powerful knowing processes that integrate experience at deep levels of psychological structure (Guidano, in press; Mahoney, in press; Weimer, in press). From such a perspective, episodes of intense emotionality may reflect strong epistemic expressions as well as potential cycles of autopoietic development. Constructivists take a parallel view of the phenomenon of resistance.

While rationalist therapists tend to deny the reality of resistance or view it as something to be "overcome," constructivist counselors emphasize the self-protective nature of the phenomenon. In their opinion, resistance is an adaptive process that protects core psychological structures from changing too quickly. Hence, resistance serves integrity-protecting and pacing functions and thus should be worked "with," not "against" (Bugental & Bugental, 1984; Mahoney, in press).

The role of insight in personal change has long been a controversial topic, and not only within cognitive therapies. Psychoanalysis has traditionally emphasized the importance of insight, and rationalist cognitive approaches have also instructed clients to examine their thoughts, emotions, and actions. The primary differences between these two groups has been in the nature of the insights they encourage and in what can or should be done with them. The constructivist perspective on insight is that it is a form of "metacognition"—that is, a higher-order form of knowing (Flavell, 1979; Guidano, in press; Mahoney, 1985b, in press). While constructivist therapists also emphasize insight as a means of facilitating changes in personal meanings and experiential processes, insight is not seen as a primary or sufficient strategy for change. What is important to constructivists is the integration of metacognitions, or insights, with emotional and behavioral processes. Constructivists also acknowledge contexts when insight is counterproductive, and they hesitate to place undue importance on explicit self-awareness.

The therapeutic relationship is also viewed differently by rationalist and constructivist cognitive therapies. Rationalists grant relatively little importance to the therapeutic relationship. For them, counseling consists of instruction and guidance in the development of "thinking skills," and techniques are thought to be more powerful than the helping relationship per se. Drawing on their developmental leanings, however, constructivist therapists view the counseling relationship as providing a safe context within which the client may explore interactions with self and world (Bowlby, 1979; Guidano & Liotti, 1983, 1985; Guidano, in press; Mahoney, 1986, in press). Constructivists thus concur with psychoanalytic and neoanalytic acknowledgments of the significance of the ongoing processes and dynamics of the therapeutic relationship. It is in intense emotional relationships that one's psychological structures are most likely to be developed and altered (Mahoney, in press).

The final difference between rationalist and constructivist therapies lies in their reactions to relapse and regression. For the former, relapse and regression constitute failures in generalization and maintenance. The counselor therefore urges the client to avoid them and—when they occur—may interpret them as motivational deficits or improper applications of "the lessons learned" during therapy. For the constructivist, relapse and regression are viewed as recurrences of "older," less viable adaptation patterns that are never completely eliminated. Hence, such phenomena are natural and virtually unavoidable aspects of development (Mahoney, in press; Marlatt & Gordon, 1985). Periods of regression are seen as fluctuations within an overall process that may also include episodes of accelerated progressive development. Needless to say, the constructivist conceptualization of relapse and regression reflects a vastly different approach to counseling than that traditionally espoused by rationalist cognitive therapies.

CONCLUSIONS

We have presented a brief history of the cognitive revolution and an outline of features characterizing emergent cognitive therapies. In doing so, we have argued that psychology is undergoing a significant shift in its conceptualization of human knowing processes and that there has been extensive differentiation within the cognitive perspectives. The recent amplifications of constructivism via motor metatheories of mind have challenged the traditions of realism, rationalism, and sensory metatheories. Attachment theory, social learning theory, autopoeisis, and evolutionary epistemology have also made important contributions to the constructivist-developmental movement, which represents a distinct divergence from rationalistic cognitive therapies. In conclusion, we reiterate that the cognitive therapies—both rationalist and constructivist—reflect progressive developments toward the refinement of theory and practice in our profession. It seems clear that emergent research directions signal a deepening appreciation for the complexities of human development and its facilitation.

REFERENCES

Bandura, A. (1969). *Principles of behavior modification.* New York: Holt, Rinehart & Winston.

Bandura, A. (1976). Social learning perspective on behavior change. In A. Burton (Ed.), *What makes behavior change possible?* (pp. 34–57). New York: Brunner/ Mazel.

Bandura, A. (1977). Self-efficacy: Toward a unifying theory of behavior change. *Psychological Review, 84,* 191–215.

Bandura, A. (1978). The self system in reciprocal determinism. *American Psychologist, 33,* 344–358.

Bandura, A. (1985). Model of causality in social learning theory. In M. J. Mahoney & A. Freeman (Eds.), *Cognition and psychotherapy* (pp. 81–99). New York: Plenum.

Bandura, A. (1986). *Social foundations of thought and action: A social cognitive theory.* Englewood Cliffs, NJ: Prentice-Hall.

Bateson, G. (1972). *Steps to an ecology of mind.* New York: Ballantine.

Bateson, G. (1979). *Mind and nature: A necessary unity.* New York: Ballantine.

Beck, A. T. (1963). Thinking and depression, 1. Idiosyncratic content and cognitive distortion. *Archives of General Psychiatry, 9,* 324–333.

Beck, A. T. (1970). Cognitive therapy: Nature and relation to behavior therapy. *Behavior Therapy, 1,* 184–200.

Beck, A. T. (1976). *Cognitive therapy and the emotional disorders.* New York: International Universities Press.

Belsky, J., & Nezworski, M. T. (Eds.). (in press). *Clinical implications of attachment.* Hillsdale, NJ: Erlbaum.

Bowlby, J. (1969). *Attachment and loss. Vol. 1. Attachment.* New York: Basic Books.

Bowlby, J. (1973). *Attachment and loss. Vol. 11. Separation: Anxiety and anger.* New York: Basic Books.

Bowlby, J. (1979). *The making and breaking of affectional bonds.* London: Tavistock.

Bowlby, J. (1980). *Attachment and loss. Vol. III. Loss: Sadness and depression.* London: Hogarth Press.

Bowlby, J. (1985). The role of childhood experience in cognitive disturbance. In M. J. Mahoney & A. Freeman (Eds.), *Cognition and psychotherapy* (pp. 181–199). New York: Plenum.

Brent, S. B. (1978). Prigogine's model for self-organization in nonequilibrium systems: Its relevance for developmental psychology. *Human Development, 21,* 374–387.

Brent, S. B. (1984). *Psychological and social structures.* Hillsdale, NJ: Erlbaum.

Bugental, J. F. T., & Bugental, E. K. (1984). A fate worse than death: The fear of changing. *Psychotherapy, 21,* 543–549.

Burrell, M. J. (1983). *Psychotherapy from a motor-evolutionary perspective: Implications from cognitive psychology and epistemology.* Unpublished doctoral dissertation, the Pennsylvania State University, University Park, PA.

Campbell, D. T. (1974). Evolutionary epistemology. In P. A. Schlipp (Ed.), *The philosophy of Karl Popper, Vol. 14, 1 & 11* (pp. 413–463). LaSalle, IL: Open Court Publishing.

Campbell, D. T. (1975). On the conflicts between biological and social evolution and between psychology and moral tradition. *American Psychologist, 30,* 1103–1126.

Cautela, J. R. (1966). Treatment of compulsive behavior by covert sensitization. *Psychological Record, 76,* 33–41.

Cautela, J. R. (1967). Covert sensitization. *Psychological Reports, 20,* 459–468.

Cook, N. D. (1980). *Stability and flexibility: An analysis of natural systems,* New York: Pergamon.

Dell, P. F. (1982). Beyond homeostasis: Toward a concept of coherence. *Family Process, 21,* 21–41.

Dobzhansky, T. (1962). *Mankind evolving: The evolution of the human species.* New Haven, CT: Yale University Press.

Dryden, W. (1984). Rational-emotive therapy and cognitive therapy: A critical comparison. In M. A. Reda & M. J. Mahoney (Eds.), *Cognitive psychotherapies: Re-*

cent developments in theory, research and practice (pp. 81–99). Cambridge, MA: Ballinger.

D'Zurilla, T. J. (1987). Problem-solving therapy. In K. S. Dobson (Ed.), *Handbook of cognitive-behavioral therapies.* New York: Guilford.

D'Zurilla, T. J., & Goldfried, M. R. (1971). Problem solving and behavior modification. *Journal of Abnormal Psychology, 78,* 107–126.

Ellis, A. (1962). *Reason and emotion in psychotherapy.* New York: Stuart.

Ellis, A. (1977). Rational-emotive therapy, Research data that supports the clinical and personality hypotheses of RET and other modes of cognitive-behavior therapy. *The Counseling Psychologist, 7,* 2–42.

Ellis, A. (1985). Expanding the ABC's of rational-emotive therapy. In M. J. Mahoney & A. Freeman (Eds.), *Cognition and psychotherapy* (pp. 313–323). New York: Plenum.

Flavell, J. H. (1979). Metacognition and cognitive monitoring: A new area of cognitive-developmental inquiry. *American Psychologist, 34,* 906–911.

Frankl, V. E. (1959). Man's search for meaning: An introduction to logotherapy. New York: Washington Square Press.

Frankl, V. E. (1985). *The unheard cry for meaning: Psychotherapy and humanism.* New York: Simon & Schuster.

Goodman, D. S., & Maultsby, M. C. (1974). *Emotional well-being through rational behavior training.* Springfield, IL: Charles C. Thomas.

Gould, S. J. (1977). *Ever since Darwin: Reflections in natural history.* New York: W. W. Norton.

Gould, S. 1. (1980). *The panda's thumb: More reflections in natural history.* New York: W. W. Norton.

Guidano, V. F. (1984). A constructivist outline of cognitive processes. In M. A. Reda & M. J. Mahoney (Eds.), *Cognitive psychotherapies: Recent developments in theory, research, and practice* (pp. 31–45). Cambridge, MA: Ballinger.

Guidano, V. F. (in press). *Selfhood processes and lifespan development.* New York: Guilford.

Guidano, V. F., & Liotti, G. (1983). *Cognitive processes and emotional disorders.* New York: Guilford.

Guidano, V. F., & Liotti, G. (1985). A constructivistic foundation for cognitive therapy. In M. J. Mahoney & A. Freeman (Eds.), *Cognition and psychotherapy* (pp. 101–142). New York: Plenum.

Hayek, F. A. (1952). *The sensory order.* Chicago, IL: University of Chicago Press.

Hayek, F. A. (1964). The theory of complex phenomena. In M. Bunge (Ed.), *The critical approach to science and philosophy: Essays in honor of K. R. Popper* (pp. 332–349). New York: Free Press,

Hayek, F. A. (1978). *New studies in philosophy, politics, economics, and the history of ideas.* Chicago, IL: University of Chicago Press.

Hayek, F. A. (1982). The sensory order after 25 years. In W. B. Weimer & D. S. Palermo (Eds.), *Cognition and the symbolic processes* (Vol. 2) (pp. 287–293). Hillsdale, NJ: Erlbaum.

Homme, L. E. (1965). Perspectives in psychology: XXIV. Control of coverants, the operants of the mind. *Psychological Record, 15,* 501–511.

Howard, K. L., & Orlinsky, D. E. (1972). Psychotherapeutic process. *Annual Review of Psychology, 23,* 615–668.

Jantsch, E. (1980). *The self-organizing universe: Scientific and human implications of the emerging paradigm of evolution.* New York: Pergamon.

Jantsch, E. (Ed.). (1981). *The evolutionary vision: Toward a unifying paradigm of physical, biological, and sociocultural evolution.* Boulder, CO: Westview Press.

Jerison, H. (1973). *Evolution of the brain and intelligence.* New York: Wiley.

Jerison, H. (1976). Paleoneurology and the evolution of mind. *Scientific American, 234,* 90–101.

Joyce Moniz, L. (1985). Epistemological therapy and constructivism. In M. J. Mahoney & A. Freeman (Eds.), *Cognition and psychotherapy* (pp. 143–179). New York: Plenum.

Kelly, G. A. (1955). *The psychology of personal constructs.* New York: Norton.

Kruglanski, A. W., & Jaffe, Y. (1983). The lay epistemic model in cognitive therapy. In M. Rosenbaum, C. M. Franks, & Y. Jaffe (Eds.), *Perspectives on behavior therapy in the eighties* (pp. 217–233). New York: Springer.

Land, G. T. L. (1973). *Grow or die: The unifying principle of transformation.* New York: Dell.

Laszlo, E. (1983). *Systems science and world order: Selected studies.* New York: Pergamon.

Lazarus, A. A. (1971). *Behavior therapy and beyond.* New York: McGraw-Hill.

Lazarus, A. A. (1976). *Multimodal behavior therapy.* New York: Springer.

Ledwidge, B. (1978). Cognitive behavior modification: A step in the wrong direction? *Psychological Bulletin, 85,* 353–375.

Leva, L. M. (1984). Cognitive behavioral therapy in the light of Piagetian theory. In M. A. Reda & M. J. Mahoney (Eds.), *Cognitive psychotherapies: Recent developments in theory, research, and practice* (pp. 233–250). Cambridge, MA: Ballinger.

Liotti, G. (1984). Cognitive therapy, attachment theory, and psychiatric nosology: A clinical and theoretical inquiry into their interdependence. In M. A. Reda & M. J. Mahoney (Eds.), *Cognitive psychotherapies: Recent developments in theory, research, and practice* (pp. 211–232). Cambridge, MA: Ballinger.

MacLean, P. D. (1973). *A triune concept of the brain and behavior.* Toronto: University of Toronto Press.

Mahoney, M. J. (1974). *Cognition and behavior modification.* Cambridge, MA: Ballinger.

Mahoney, M. J. (1977). Reflections on the cognitive-learning trend in psychotherapy. *American Psychologist, 35,* 5–13.

Mahoney, M. J. (1980). Psychotherapy and the structure of personal revolutions. In M. J. Mahoney (Ed.), *Psychotherapy process: Current issues and future directions* (pp. 157–180). New York: Plenum.

Mahoney, M. J. (1981). La importancia de los procesos evolutivos para la psicoterapia. *Analysis y modification de conducta, 7,* 155–170.

Mahoney, M. J. (1984a). Psychoanalysis and behaviorism: The yin and yang of determinism. In H. Arkowitz & S. Messer (Eds.), *Psychoanalytic and behavior therapy: Is integration possible?* (pp. 303–325). New York: Plenum.

Mahoney, M. J. (1984b). Integrating cognition, affect, and action: A comment. *Cognitive therapy and research, 8,* 585–589.

Mahoney, M. J. (1985a, November). *Reflections on the cognitive revolution.* Paper presented at the meeting of the Association for the Advancement of Behavior Therapy, Houston, TX.

Mahoney, M. J. (1985b). Psychotherapy and human change processes. In M. J. Mahoney & A. Freeman (Eds.), *Cognition and psychotherapy* (pp. 3–48). New York: Plenum.

Mahoney, M. J. (1986). The tyranny of technique. *Counseling and values, 30,* 169–174.

Mahoney, M. J. (1987). The cognitive sciences and psychotherapy. In K. S. Dobson (Ed.), *Handbook of cognitive-behavioral therapies.* New York: Guilford.

Mahoney, M. J. (in press). *Human change processes: Notes on the facilitation of personal development.* New York: Basic Books.

Mahoney, M. J., & Arnkoff, D. B. (1978). Cognitive and self-control therapies. In S. L. Garfield & A. E. Bergin (Eds.), *Handbook of psychotherapy and behavior change* (pp. 689–722). New York: Wiley.

Mancuso, J. C., & Adams-Webber, J. R. (Eds.) (1982). *The construing person.* New York: Praeger.

Marlatt, G. A., & Gordon, J. R. (Eds.) (1985). *Relapse prevention: Maintenance strategies in the treatment of addictive behaviors.* New York: Guilford.

Maturana, H. R. (1975). The organization of the living: A theory of the living organization. *International Journal of Man-Machine Studies, 7,* 313–332.

Maturana, H. R., & Varela, F. G. (1980). *Autopoiesis and cognition: The realization of the living.* Boston, MA: Reidel.

Maultsby, M. C. (1984). *Rational behavior therapy.* Englewood Cliffs, NJ: Prentice-Hall.

Meichenbaum, D. (1977). *Cognitive behavior modification.* New York: Plenum.

Neimeyer, R. A. (1985). Personal constructs in clinical practice. In P. C. Kendall (Ed.), *Advances in cognitive-behavioral research and therapy* (Vol. 2) (pp. 275–339). New York: Academic Press.

Orlinsky, D. E., & Howard, K. 1. (1975). *Varieties of psychotherapeutic experience.* New York: Teachers College Press.

Passingham, R. (1982). *The human primate.* San Francisco: W. H. Freeman.

Pattee, H. H. (Ed.) (1973). *Hierarchy theory: The challenge of complex systems.* New York: George Braziller.

Piaget, J. (1970). *Psychology and epistemology: Towards a theory of knowledge.* New York: Viking.

Piaget, J. (1981). *Intelligence and affectivity: Their relationship during child development.* Palo Alto, CA: Annual Reviews.

Prigogine, 1. (1980). *From being to becoming: Time and complexity in the physical sciences.* San Francisco: W. H. Freeman.

Prigogine, I., & Stengers, I. (1984). *Order out of chaos: Man's new dialogue with nature.* New York: Bantam.

Prochaska, J. 0. (1984). *Systems of psychotherapy: A transtheoretical analysis.* Homewood, IL: Dorsey Press.

Reynolds, P. C. (1981). *On the evolution of human behavior: The argument from animals to man.* Berkeley: University of California Press.

Rice, L. N., & Greenberg, L. S. (Eds.). (1984). *Patterns of change.* New York: Guilford.

Rogers, T., & Craighead, W. E. (1977). Physiological responses to self-statements: The effects of statement valence and discrepancy. *Cognitive Therapy and Research, 1,* 99–119.

Rosen, H. (1985). *Piagetian dimensions of clinical relevance.* New York: Columbia University Press.

Rotter, J. B. (1954). *Social learning and clinical psychology.* Englewood Cliffs, NJ: Prentice-Hall.

Skinner, B. F. (1971). *Beyond freedom and dignity.* New York: Knopf.

Skinner, B. F. (1974). *About behaviorism.* New York: Knopf.

Skinner, B. F. (1984). The shame of American education. *American Psychologist, 39,* 947–954.

Smith, D. (1982). Trends in counseling and psychotherapy. *American Psychologist, 37,* 802–809.

Spivack, G., & Shure, M. B. (1974). *Social adjustment of young children: A cognitive approach to solving real-life problems.* San Francisco: Jossey-Bass.

Suarez, E. M. (1985). *Neo-cognitive psychotherapy.* Manuscript in preparation, Advanced Human Studies Institute, Coral Gables, FL.

Tosi, D. J., & Eshbaugh, D. M. (1980). Rational stage-directed therapy and crisis intervention. In R. Herink (Ed.), *The psychotherapy handbook* (pp. 550–553). New York: New American Library.

Vaihinger, H. (1911/1924). *The philosophy of "as if."* London: Rutledge & Kegan Paul.

Varela, F. J. (1979). *Principles of biological autonomy.* New York: Elsevier North Holland.

Von Foerster, H. (1984). On constructing a reality. In P. Watzlawick (Ed.), *The invented reality* (pp. 41–61). New York: W. W. Norton.

Washburn, S. L., & Moore, R. (1980). *Ape into human: A study of human evolution.* Boston, MA: Little, Brown.

Watzlawick, P. (Ed.). (1984). *The invented reality: Contributions to constructivism.* New York: W. W. Norton.

Weimer, W. B. (1977). A conceptual framework for cognitive psychology: Motor theories of the mind. In R. Shaw & J. Bransford (Eds.), *Perceiving, acting, and knowing* (pp. 267–311). Hillsdale, NJ: Erlbaum.

Weimer, W. B. (1982). Hayek's approach to the problems of complex phenomena: An introduction to the theoretical psychology of the sensory order. In W. B. Weimer & D. S. Palermo (Eds.), *Cognition and the symbolic processes* (Vol. 2) (pp. 267–311). Hillsdale, NJ: Erlbaum.

Weimer, W. B. (in press). Spontaneously ordered complex phenomena and the unity of the moral sciences. In G. Radnitzky (Ed.), *Unity of the sciences.* New York: Paragon House.

Weimer, M. L. (1975). *The cognitive unconscious: A Piagetian approach to psychotherapy.* Davis, CA: International Psychological Press.

Weimer, M. L. (1985). *Cognitive-experiential therapy: An integrative ego psychotherapy.* New York: Brunner/Mazel.

Wessler, R. L. (1984). Alternative conceptions of rational-emotive therapy: Toward a philosophically neutral psychotherapy. In M. A. Reda & M. J. Mahoney (Eds.)., *The cognitive psychotherapies: Recent developments in theory, research, and practice* (pp. 65–79). Cambridge, MA: Ballinger.

Wilson, P. J. (1980). *Man: The promising primate.* New Haven, CT: Yale University Press.

Wolpe, J. (1976). Behavior therapy and its malcontents-II. Multimodal eclecticism, cognitive exclusivism and "exposure" empiricism. *Journal of Behavior Therapy and Experimental Psychiatry, 7,* 109–116.

Wolpe, J. (1978). Cognition and causation in human behavior and its therapy. *American Psychologist, 33,* 437–446.

Zeleny, M. Ed.). (1980). *Autopoiesis, dissipative structures, and spontaneous social orders.* Washington, DC: American Association for the Advancement of Science.

CHAPTER 8

Cognitive Therapy: The Repair of Memory

Karen Fleming, Rebecca Heikkinen, and
E. Thomas Dowd

Schools of psychotherapy historically differentiate themselves according to their attention to two basic organizing constructs—conscious and unconscious memory. Cognitive psychologists distinguish the same concepts as explicit and implicit memory. In this presentation we update and apply current cognitive constructs to this historical dichotomy. We focus on research that suggests that this dichotomy is a false one. In fact, the dissociations observed between people who show evidence of learning without remembering and those who recall or recognize past events may be accounted for by one memory framework (Jacoby, 1983). Memory for specific prior episodes appears to underlie both memory expressions. This contrasts with views that attribute unconscious expressions of memory to abstract representations.

We discuss the view that the conscious experience of memory is a feeling of transfer (much like sadness or anger), plus an attribution of pastness (Jacoby, Kelley & Dywan, 1989). We also discuss research that shows how, without our awareness, very mundane experiences impact our conscious experience of memory in experimental situations. Cognitive psychologists describe three variables that manipulate memory: attention, context, and the number of times an event is recalled. The variables which constrain our experience of memory in an experimental situation also manipulate a client's experience of memory in therapy. We illustrate these variables with a case study.

We suggest that the subjective experience of memory is a significant object of change in therapy. We draw parallels between experimental situations and therapeutic work which manipulate these variables to change clients' memories. Based on the experimental literature, we suggest that it may be fruitful for therapists to consider the following: (1) "Conscious and unconscious memory" may be different memory expressions which depend on the goal of a person's current task, (2) The availability of either memory expression depends on what one attended to at the time of the episode, and to the context, or the internal and external cues, available at the time of recall, (3) Memory change occurs when a past episode is recalled because during the recall an interaction takes place between the current situation and the past episode, and (4) Finally, when clients repeatedly recall a past episode they experience greater confidence that their memory is accurate, and this occurs independently of objective accuracy for the past event.

Distinctions between Implicit and Explicit Memory

We express memory in two different ways. First, we use memory to reminisce and recollect. Second, we use memory as a basis for perceiving, to make judgments, and to solve problems. These expressions of memory also differ with respect to conscious awareness. The trademark of reminiscence is conscious memory, while behavior without awareness for past experience characterizes our ability to identify, to organize what we see and hear, and to solve problems.

Jacoby et al. (1989) and Polyani (1958) distinguish between the use of memory as an object and memory as a tool. When a person focuses on the past, memory is used as an object. For example, at a high school reunion when someone brings up a specific event, we focus on pastness and thereby use memory as an object. Alternately, when the task is problem solving, we use memory as a tool. Apparently, most of us type without conscious knowledge of the keyboard; we evidence this when we must pantomime the typing process in order to recall the keys (Jacoby, Kelley, & Dywan, 1989).

Polyani (1958) provides a clear example of this distinction. Polyani, who is multilingual, sat reading a letter at the table. When he finished he handed the letter to his son who spoke only one language. Polyani suddenly realized he did not know in what language the letter was written. He had to look back at the letter to find out. The language worked as a tool for him when the goal was to read the letter, and he read without awareness of language. In contrast, he had to make the language the object of his focus to determine whether his son could read the letter.

These two uses of memory are evident in the different task demands of objective and projective personality tests. For example, when deciding whether a statement on the MMPI is either true or false, the test taker either recalls a specific example of an experience similar to the statement, and, therefore, marks the statement "true"; or he or she cannot recall a similar experience and, therefore, marks the statement "false." In contrast, the Rorschach asks a subject to tell the examiner what the inkblot looks like to the subject. Persons taking the test usually identify and label the inkblot, but remain unaware of the source of their ability to organize what they see.

Cognitive psychologists call these different memory modes *explicit* and *implicit memory.* One demonstrates explicit memory during tasks which require conscious or intentional recall of past experience. Explicit memory tasks require that the subject make their memory the focus; memory is used as an object. Implicit memory, on the other hand, shows the effects of a past experience on performance but requires no recollection of those experiences. During implicit memory tasks the subjects use their past experience to, for example, identify a word flashed on a screen, or to solve a problem. Schacter (1987) points out that the term *implicit memory* also resembles the more familiar psychological construct: unconscious memory (e.g., Freud & Breuer, 1966) or unaware memory (e.g., Jacoby & Witherspoon, 1982). However, these expressions include so many misleading psychological meanings and implications that many researchers prefer the terms *explicit* and *implicit memory* (e.g., Jacoby, Keley, & Dywan, 1989; Schacter, 1987; Jacoby, 1984, 1983).

Different research tasks are used to reveal each memory form. The tests most commonly used in implicit memory research are called repetition-priming tasks, and they measure whether exposure to a stimulus facilitates its processing when the same stimulus is encountered at a later time. Word completion tasks provide an example of a repetition priming task (e.g., Graf, Mandler, & Haden, 1982; Tulving, Schacter, & Stark, 1982: Warrington & Weiskrantz, 1974). Subjects are given a brief exposure to a list of words. Later subjects are given either a word stem (e.g., car___ for carpet) or a word fragment (e.g., _ss_ss__ for assassin) and told to complete the stem or fragment with the first word that fits. Subjects demonstrate priming or implicit memory when they show an enhanced tendency to complete the stem or word fragments with words from the study list. (See Schacter (1987) for a review of other tests used in priming research.) Explicit tests of memory typically ask the subject to recall items studied on an earlier list (free recall), or to answer whether or not the items on a new list were presented as study items (recognition test).

Modern research on memory reveals sharp dissociations between explicit and implicit memory. First, research demonstrates that amnesics show profound deficits in explicit memory, yet they show evidence of retention in priming experiments. (See Morris and Kopelman (1986) for a review of similar memory deficits in patients with Alzheimer-type dementia.) Graf, Squire, and Mandler (1984) compared amnesic and normal subjects' memory for a list of words. After studying the word list, subjects were given a test of explicit memory; they were asked to recall the words. Then they were given an implicit memory test: They were shown the first three letters of a word they had studied and told to make an English word out of it. Results showed that both amnesics and normal subjects performed at better than chance level on the test for implicit memory. That is, both groups demonstrated memory for the word list. However, the amnesic group did much worse than normal subjects on the test of free recall. So, although amnesics preserved memory for the word list, they could not gain access to their memories.

Second, dissociations also occur between explicit and implicit memory among normal people. Jacoby (1983) instructed subjects to learn a word list in one of three study contexts: Subjects either read a word such as *hot* alone (no context condition); read the word with its antonym *hot-cold* (the context condition); or were given the antonym and told to generate its opposite *cold-???* (the generate condition). The explicit test asked subjects to recognize the old words. The implicit test involved asking subjects to read the word (perceptual identification task) after a short presentation of the word (40 milliseconds). The results from the two tests varied according to the study condition. Performance on the explicit test (recall) was best in the generate condition. In contrast, performance on implicit perceptual identification was best in the no context condition and got worse in both the context and the generate conditions. Jacoby (1983) argues that explicit memory relies on the amount of elaboration or conceptual processing while implicit memory relies on data-driven processes. That is, when presented with a word to identify in the implicit test, subjects depend on having seen the word, the perceptual characteristics of the word, in order to identify it.

Theories

Three explanatory systems are postulated to account for many performance differences on tests of explicit and implicit memory, and for dissociations observed in amnesic patients. These approaches are referred to
as activation, multiple memory system, and processing accounts. We focus on the processing accounts because they describe a person's subjective experience of memory and provide ways to influence that experience.
We believe the constraints on memory that are present in experimental
situations exist in therapy. We rely heavily on Schacter (1987) for the
following summary of these views.

Activation

First, activation views assume that implicit memory tests automatically
activate abstract representations, or knowledge structures (Schacter, 1987).
This activation operates independently of elaborative processing. So, during implicit memory tests, these representations come to mind without
elaborative processing that would include information about the time or
place of the recent episode. Knowledge structures just "pop into mind"
without features specific to the event (Schacter, 1987). During explicit
memory tasks these structures presumably include information that indicates an item occurred in a recent episode.

Multiple Memory System

The proponents of multiple memory systems focus on the different content of underlying memory systems. A declarative (Squire & Cohen, 1984)
or episodic (Tulving, 1972, 1983) memory system supports conscious
recollection, or memories we can declare (Schacter, 1987). The episodic
memory system, then, is thought to be based on recent events and is
responsible for performance on explicit memory tests. By contrast, semantic memory is responsible for the implicit expression of memory, for
example, when a person perceives a word or solves a problem (Anderson,
1990). During these tasks subjects make use of more general, pre-existing
knowledge.

Process Views

Unlike activation views and the multiple memory system approach, processing views assume that both explicit and implicit expressions of mem-

ory rely on recent experience (Schacter, 1987). Both implicit and explicit memories develop to a greater degree when a strong correspondence exists between the specific details of the event and the details of the current situation (Jacoby & Kelley, 1987). Differences between implicit and explicit memory depend on the interactions between the information encoded and the demands of implicit and explicit tests (Schacter, 1987)

Therefore, the distinction between two types of encoding processes—conceptually driven processes and data-driven processes (Jacoby, 1983, 1984)—is important to a process view. Conceptually driven processes include encoding activities initiated by the subject (Schacter, 1987). Examples of conceptually driven processes are generating, elaborating, organizing, and reconstructing. Data-driven processes rely on the information present in the test material, for example, the visual information provided by the presentation of a word with no other context. Jacoby (1983) makes the point that both explicit and implicit tests may have data-driven and conceptually driven components. However, explicit memory tests usually tap conceptually driven processes, while implicit memory tests usually rely on data-driven processes.

Performance dissociations between implicit and explicit tests are attributed to the different retrieval demands for conceptually driven and data-driven processes found in either implicit (e.g., perceptual identification) or explicit (e.g., recall or recollection) tests (Schacter, 1987). Let's refer again to Jacoby (1983). This experiment was cited above to show dissociation between implicit and explicit tests of memory found in normal subjects. Jacoby manipulated *context* in order to examine the interaction between conceptually driven and data-driven processing. In the first phase of this experiment, Jacoby (1983) placed subjects in one of three conditions. A word was either (1) read out of context, (2) read in the context of a predictor word, or (3) generated from an antonym.

These conditions differ according to the extent to which the subject depends on the visual stimulus read during the first phase of the experiment. In the first condition the subject depends exclusively on what is seen (data-driven processing) for later identification. These conditions also vary according to the extent the subject conceptually processes the stimulus. In the generate condition conceptually driven processing is maximal. The subject never sees the word and instead generates meaning from the cue word. An intermediate condition between data-driven and conceptually driven processes exists when subjects read the word in the context of a predictor word.

In the second phase subjects were given either a test of recognition or perceptual identification. In the perceptual identification test, old and new words flashed on a computer screen for approximately 35 milliseconds. Subjects reported each word aloud, guessing when necessary. The recognition memory test consisted of the same words as the perceptual identification test, however, subjects saw these words as a typed sheet. Subjects circled words they had read or generated in the first phase of the experiment.

Most important to the process view is the interaction between the results of the perceptual identification test and the results of the recognition test. Other views of memory (activation and multiple memory views) assume that perception taps a general knowledge, or an abstract representation that preserves less information about the initial event than does the memory that underlies recognition for a specific event (Jacoby, 1983). These views predict that this abstract representation should not vary with the type of process used to encode the word. In contrast, results showed that a greater degree of data-driven processing of a word, such as reading the word, helped later perceptual identification of the word. Recognition memory decreased in the no-context condition. Consistent with other studies in the memory literature (e.g., Jacoby, 1978; Slamecka & Graf, 1978), when the word had been conceptually processed, i.e., when the subject generated a word from a visual cue, better recognition memory resulted while perceptual identification decreased. Therefore, tests of implicit and explicit memory both rely on the specific prior episode.

In this experiment subjects learned different types of information. They learned a word, a word and a cue, or a cue and a self-generated word. When the experimenter measured perceptual identification in the implicit memory test, the subject performed best when the original exposure was a visual presentation. When the experimenter measured ease of generating context in the explicit memory test, the subject performed better when the prior event consisted of generating the context.

Summary

To summarize, in contrast to activation and multiple memory systems views, the process view suggests that a single memory framework explains the performance on both implicit and explicit tests of memory. Memory is either facilitated or diminished by the match between the information processed at the time of the prior event and the current demand for that type of information as a basis for remembering; both implicit and explicit memory, then, depend on the prior event. In the next section we point out a difficulty with the process view of memory: it fails to account for one's experience of either awareness or unawareness on tests of explicit and implicit memory. We review Jacoby, Kelley, and Dywan's (1989) solution.

The Experience of Conscious and Unconscious

Process views generally fail to account for either the conscious experience of remembering, or for the experience of using past learning to affect the present without awareness of source (Schacter, 1987). How might the process view account for these different uses of memory? Can the process views provide an explanation for the different experiences of conscious awareness when we use our memory as an object to reminisce, and when we use our memory as a tool to perceive or to solve a problem?

In a very intriguing proposal, Jacoby, Kelley, and Dywan (1989) explain the experience of awareness in tests of explicit memory and the experience of being unaware of our source of knowledge during tests of implicit memory. These researchers insist that in order to understand memory we must understand people's subjective experience of memory. They describe conscious memory as an attribution of pastness based on a feeling of familiarity. Their ideas are based on Schacter and Singer's (1962) theory of emotion which states that an experience of nonspecific arousal will be attributed to a particular cause. Jacoby, Kelley, and Dywan (1989) argue that when the goal is to remember the past, the feeling of familiarity is not located in a memory representation. Rather, internal aspects of one's performance serve as feedback that one remembers. These are transfer effects, or cues. Ebbinghaus (1885) referred to these effects as "savings." These effects may include fluency, ability to generate an argument, ability to generate supporting details such as sensory, spacial and temporal details, and ease of recall. Transfer effects (or feelings of familiarity), according to Jacoby, Kelley, and Dywan (1989), occur at any activity level, e.g., perceptual, conceptual, and motor. We experience transfer effects when we read a word more fluently, develop a series of ideas readily, or more skillfully ride a bicycle after previous experience with either the word, those particular ideas, or with the bicycle (Jacoby, Kelley, & Dywan, 1989). However, what is most important about this explanation, is that conscious recollection is separate from assessing familiarity. Conscious recollection, in addition to assessing familiarity or noticing a transfer effect, requires an attribution of pastness.

People attribute the effects of transfer to both accurate and inaccurate sources. Whether a person correctly attributes these transfer effects to their source depends on several factors. First, attribution to a source is correct to the extent that the transfer effects are specific, rather than general, to the details of the previous occurrence. For example, one might correctly recall a specific trip to the dentist to the extent that one generates details of the procedures the dentist performed, or the specific conversation with the hygienist about her son's plans for the summer. In contrast, leafing through a magazine, or signing insurance forms, describes activities that are common to a dentist's office visit.

Second, other factors can mimic the effects of prior events. It is possible, for example, to imagine vivid details when one is attempting to remember an event, so that even specific details do not insure "correct" remembering (Jacoby, Kelley, & Dywan, 1989). Third, an actual transfer effect can be misattributed to other sources (Jacoby, Kelley, & Dywan, 1989). Examples of past experience attributed to other sources include cryptomnesia or unconscious plagiarism (Jacoby, Kelley, & Dywan, 1989). A famous case of cryptomnesia implicated Helen Keller (Jacoby, Kelley, & Dywan, 1989; Bowers & Hilgard, 1986). When she was 11 years old, Helen Keller published a story which readers found very similar to a story published earlier by another author. Although she denied plagiarism, a friend later recalled telling Helen the story three years earlier.

The "mere exposure effect" also illustrates the principle that actual transfer effects can be misattributed to other sources (Jacoby, Kelley, & Dywan, 1989; Jacoby, 1984; Mandler, Nakamura, & Van Zandt, 1987; Seamon, Brody, & Kauff, 1983). In separate experiments, subjects either saw geometric shapes or heard melodies. The prior exposure influenced subjects' preference for geometric shapes and for melodies. Later, subjects were asked, "Which do you prefer?" When giving a reason for their preference subjects stated that the geometric shape had good form, or the melody was particularly pleasing. Subjects attributed the more fluent processing of old items to their preference rather than to prior exposure. Subjects' judgment was based on their past experience, however, the situation directed subjects to use their memory as a tool rather than to remember the past. The result was that subjects misattributed the source of their judgments to present rather than past causes.

Evidently, a major factor influencing the attribution process is the subject's goal (Jacoby, Kelley, & Dywan, 1989). When the goal is remembering, fluency is attributed to past experience.

A goal directs the processing and influences the attribution of effects on performance to a particular source. Remembering can be seen as setting successively more exacting goals designed to limit irrelevant sources of effects on performance and so allow more accurate attribution of familiarity. A failure to elaborate on the cues provided at the time of test restricts the opportunity for transfer to be experienced on various levels (Jacoby, Kelley, & Dywan, 1989, p. 399).

The reader might try to remember the food eaten one week ago at his or her evening meal. The process typically illustrates this succession of goals (e.g., "What day was that?" "What did I do that day?" "Where did I eat?" "Whom did I eat with?" "What did I eat?"). In the extreme, we observe a crippling inability to form and pursue the goal of remembering among amnesics; without this ability one has little occasion for the subjective experience of remembering (Jacoby, Kelley, & Dywan, 1989; Stuss Benson, 1986).

When the goal is something other than remembering, i.e., to write a story, solve a problem, or make a judgment, people may show evidence of learning without the subjective experience of remembering. We say *may* evidence learning without remembering because, clearly, people at times remember the source of their experience when their attention is directed toward another task (Jacoby, Kelley, & Dywan, 1989). Clients who work intrapersonal conflict in a Gestalt two-chair technique often recognize the source of the "top dog's" voice. The voice is an authority figure, often a parent.

Summary

Jacoby, Kelley, & Dywan (1989) propose that the conscious experience of remembering, similar to an emotion includes (1) a feeling of transfer, or fluency (much like sadness or anger), and (2) an attribution of pastness. The subjective experience of remembering looms large because people rely on remembering to experience a continuity with their past, to act and to make decisions in the present, and to plan their future (Jacoby, Kelley, & Dywan, 1989). People also demonstrate, in their performances, the ability to express memory for prior experience without the subjective experience of remembering that prior experience. In this case, the effects of transfer are either unacknowledged or attributed to something other than one's own efforts. Whether the goal of a task is to use memory as an object to remember, or to use memory as a tool to solve a problem, to judge aesthetics, or to write a paper, the subjective experience of memory is impacted by three constraining variables. In the next sections we review research describing these variables and we apply these constraints to the therapy process.

CONSTRAINING VARIABLES

What is most exciting about the process view of memory is the ability to specify variables that manipulate the subjective experience of memory. As stated above, the goal of the task directs the attribution process. The goal determines whether one uses a memory as an object of reflection and therefore attributes fluency to pastness, or whether one uses memory for something other than remembering, to solve a problem, to judge or to perceive. During either expression of memory three broad classes of variables appear to constrain the cues provided and limit the elaboration of those cues at the time of retrieval. These are *context, attention,* and the *number of times an episode is recalled.*

Context

Context includes aspects of the environment (e.g., Smith, Glenberg, & Bjork, 1978), one's internal context, for example, one's mood (Bower, Monteiro, & Gilligan, 1978) or drug state (e.g., Overton, 1978; Weingartner, 1978), and the semantic context (e.g., Warren, 1970; Warren & Warren, 1970) which includes the modality of the available cues. Godden and Baddeley (1975) dramatized the manipulation of context by having divers learn a list of words either on the shore or 20 feet under water. They then recalled the list in either the same or a different environment. Subjects showed better memory for items recalled in the same context in which they were studied.

In addition to the above evidence that, in similar contexts, objective measures of memory improve, context manipulates the subjective experience of memory. Context in Jacoby's (1983, 1984) experiments constrained the type of processing at the time of encoding by manipulating the type of cues available. In that experiment subjects either generated their own association to the target word (conceptually driven process) , or processed the visual presentation of the word (data-driven process). Conceptually driven processes rely on internal cues that originate from the subject; for example, a person may generate emotion, elaborate meaning, or organize information. At the other extreme, during data-driven processing he or she may rely completely on presented material or environmental context, either visual, auditory, etc. Both types of processing depend, in part, on the cues available in the situation. Therefore, expressions of memory, either memory used as an object to remember or as a tool to solve a problem, etc., are enhanced or diminished according to the similarity between the processing that took place during the prior event and the demand for a similar processing in the current task.

In this view, transfer effects or feelings of familiarity will depend on the type of information available and how that information is processed. For example, we often notice clients who when angry or sad spontaneously remember past events during which they felt the same emotion.

Attention

In order for any information to affect the subjective experience of memory, the information must be noticed in order to be processed. Divided attention tasks prevent people from elaboration of the cues available, and, therefore, they experience more restricted transfer effects. We expect people whose attention is divided to have less awareness for the source of their memory.

Whether attention is singularly focused or divided impacts the subjective experience of memory. The attention required to recognize an event and specify its source differs from the attention needed for an event to have an effect (Jacoby & Kelley, 1987). In divided attention tasks subjects cannot use conscious recollection to recognize items but can still assess familiarity of the item (Jacoby & Kelley, 1987; Jacoby, Woloshyn, & Kelley, 1989). Jacoby, Kelley, and Dywan (1989) conclude that "divided attention at the time of test prevents people from checking the bases for their first impressions, a form of monitoring" (p. 408). Further, people vary in the degree to which they engage in monitoring activity. Jacoby, Kelley and Dywan (1989) use the example of an elderly person who fails to check why a story comes to mind and therefore becomes repetitive.

Milton Erickson (1980) often manipulated the clients' ability to monitor or to focus on their memory process as an object. He often confused and distracted the client's attention so he or she could not check why something came to mind. He frequently divided a client's attention between the use of memory as a tool and memory as an object. For example, Rossi (1981) described a case in which a child abuser was age-regressed to a time when he felt the tenderness of holding a puppy. The goal of the regression included the association of two variables: childhood experience and tenderness. The induction was as follows:

> Your conscious mind may realize the experience of tenderness (memory used as an object) while your unconscious mind relives that childhood experience (memory used as a tool) from which it came. Or perhaps your conscious mind will be aware of that childhood experience (memory as object), while your unconscious mind generates the feeling of tenderness (memory as tool). (From a sound recording by Ernest Rossi, 1981.)

Number of Times an Event is Recalled

The number of times an event is recalled influences one's subjective memory of an event and influences one's objective accuracy. In one study, subjects viewed line drawings and attempted daily recall for a week (Jacoby, Kelley, & Dywan, 1989; Dywan, 1984). They rated their confidence for each recall. As the week progressed a greater number of correct responses resulted as well as a greater proportion of false negative and false positive answers. In other words, many correct items received a low confidence rating while many false items received higher confidence levels. Even items correctly identified were not remembered with the original details. For example, one subject accused the experimenter of changing a slide which showed a touring bicycle. The subject stated that the original slide showed a racing bicycle similar to his own rather than a touring bicycle, which was why he had remembered it. In a later study researchers varied the number of times the event was recalled (Dywan, Segalowitz, & Otis, as cited in Jacoby, Kelley, & Dywan, 1989). Results showed that each time an item was generated it gained familiarity but decreased in accuracy as measured by a recognition test. Recognition was best for those subjects who were never given the opportunity to recall the drawings. Indeed, accuracy was lowered one-third with even one recall attempt.

In this experiment, in addition to the subjective experience of increased familiarity with each recall, subjects tended to elaborate as a result of an interaction between incoming information and past experience. Subjects also tended to draw inferences based on those elaborations. For example, the subject who remembered the racing bicycle elaborated his memory of the original slide to resemble his own bicycle. Then he inferred that the elaborated memory was accurate because the elaborated memory was familiar.

APPLICATIONS TO COGNITIVE PSYCHOTHERAPY

Kenneth Bowers (1987) remarks that although experimental psychologists currently display "unprecedented appreciation" for unconscious influences (and, we would add, for consciousness), their language and their observation base are often unrecognizable to the clinician (Cheesman & Merikle, 1986; Jacoby & Witherspoon, 1982; Marcel, 1983; Schacter, 1987). More recent experimental work (Jacoby, Kelley, & Dywan, 1989; Jacoby, 1984, 1983) shifts the observation base to the subjective experience of memory and introduces a vocabulary more familiar to clinicians. Certainly specifying a few broad variables risks simplifying the complex relationships that exist in the therapeutic relationship. Perhaps, however, a useful bridge may be built between the experimental and the clinical literatures.

Conscious and unconscious experience, according to this view, both involve a feeling of familiarity, while the subjective experience of conscious remembering requires an attribution of pastness to that feeling. One's subjective experience of memory is primarily directed by the goal of a task. When the goal is remembering, one often correctly attributes the source of familiarity to the past. When the goal is something other than remembering, one frequently attributes the experience of familiarity or fluency to some aspect of the current situation. To illustrate, often a paper flows better upon second reading (Jacoby, Kelley, & Dywan, 1989). The reader attributes his or her fluent reading to the paper rather than to past experience. Therapeutic activities evidence these same goals. Clients perform tasks whose goals consist of: (1) remembering or (2) using memory to make a decision, to solve a problem, to experiment, to enact, or to evaluate.

Attention, context and the number of times an episode is recalled or contacted manipulate the subjective experience of memory in the recent experimental literature. Variables which constrain memory processes in experimental situations are readily observed in therapy and may similarly constrain memory processes in therapy.

Context

Context manipulates a client's subjective experience of memory. Context constrains the type of information available to the client during a therapy episode and the way that information is processed. The interaction of the client and therapist determines whether the client uses more conceptually driven processes (e.g., client may elaborate meaning, reorganize information, generate emotion, or reconstruct events) which emanate primarily from the client, or collaborative processes which derive from the input of both client and therapist in an egalitarian style, or data-driven processes (e.g., specific instructions, interpretations and directives from the therapist) in which the client relies more on the therapist for structure, direction, and input. Rogerian, psychodynamic and reframing techniques influence the client to conceptually process information, while relaxation techniques, Gestalt exercises, body therapies, and behavior modification techniques may promote more data-driven client processes.

The implication of this difference in approach is that each technique encourages the client to process different levels of information whether the therapeutic goal is to use memory as a tool or as an object. When the goal is to use memory as a tool, a given technique influences clients to process information in a manner that brings a specific level of past experience to bear on the current situation. For example, Gestalt exercises and body therapies evoke sensory experience, while Rogerian, psychodynamic and reframing techniques may evoke meaning. When the goal is to use memory as an object, the client may be asked to notice how aspects of the present situation are similar to past experience, or, conversely, how a past situation is similar to the present experience. Again, clients in each type of therapy technique have processed different information.

Although schools of therapy have in the past ignored the context of therapy, recent theories of psychotherapy emphasize its importance. Ivey (1986) emphasizes that therapists provide environments for their clients. He describes four therapeutic environmental styles and specifies their relationship to the client's ability to process information at a particular developmental stage. At each stage he suggests therapies which have special strengths for coping with the client's development. Wheeler (1991), a Gestalt therapist, takes a new look at context when he insists that "the structural features of the personal ground" or "the conditions of figure formation" (p. 118) must be considered as much as figure formation itself.

Attention

In addition to the therapeutic context, attention constrains the client's subjective experience of memory. First, attention whether focused on the body of past experiences or on current experience, as we have said, manipulates one's expression of memory, and consequently one's subjective experience of memory in both experimental and therapeutic situations. The client's focus of attention influences his or her ability to monitor the source of familiarity.

Second, we said earlier that the attention required to remember something is different than that required to have an effect (Jacoby & Kelley, 1987). Attention controls the type of information processed and consequently the level of transfer possible. For example, a client who hears a message in therapy but is distracted by another task may later experience transfer based on auditory perception only, i.e., the limited attention constrains the information processed and other contextual cues are not elaborated. Transfer is experienced at the level of auditory memory, but not at other levels, e.g., the source of the message, or the surrounding environment. After a divided attention task the client may be unable to distinguish the source of the message due to this lack of contextual information linking the message to a person or place. The client could misattribute the source to him or herself. This could benefit a client who exhibits reactance (Dowd, Milne, & Wise, 1991) when he or she attempts to fully attend to the same message from an outside source.

Hypnotic effects appear related to focused attention. These techniques may change the quality of the items generated during retrieval which makes them more effortless, vivid, and detailed, more like a remembered event (Jacoby, Kelley, & Dywan, 1989). The same repeated recall paradigm was used again to examine the effects of hypnosis on memory performance and on the subjective experience of remembering (Dywan & Bowers, 1983). Subjects again examined pictures and tried to recall them once a day for a week. On the eighth day subjects were led to believe that they should recall more items. One-half of the subjects were hypnotized while the other half were given motivating instructions for recall.

Results showed the highly hypnotizable subjects in the hypnosis condition compared to nonhypnotized subjects were most affected. Although their objective memory was not improved, the subjective experience of memory was enhanced. They believed more of the images generated were remembered items and they were more confident of the recalled images than subjects who were not hypnotized.

Number of Times Recalled

Jacoby, Kelley, and Dywan (1989; Dywan, 1984) indicate that the number of times an event is recalled manipulates the memory for that event. In the repeated recall paradigm described earlier, an increase in the number of times an event was recalled increased subjects' confidence in their memory and their subjective experience of familiarity. With repeated recall, even false items received high confidence ratings. In therapy the clinician often designs a "corrective experience" (Goldfried, 1980) which is then "processed" or recalled several times. The implication is that with repeated recall the "corrective experience" gains familiarity.

In addition, each recall provided the opportunity for subjects to elaborate and to draw inferences based on those elaborations. This suggests one reason for the well documented success of most therapies: Each therapy provides, at minimum, a forum in which to recall a troublesome memory. Clients can then elaborate on that memory based on current information. Similarly, these results may explain why some clients experience improvement after arranging the initial appointment.

Research by Dywan, Segalowitz and Otis (as cited in Jacoby, Kelley, & Dywan, 1989) showed that the most accurate memories were recalled the least. The fact that subjects experienced frequently recalled material as more familiar but less accurate implies that an unconscious interaction occurred between current events and past experience. In contrast to subjects who daily recalled items, some subjects did not recall items until the last day, in effect the use of those memories was experimentally avoided. Clinically, we notice that avoided material, when finally recalled or "triggered," is particularly unmodulated by current circumstances and sometimes quite vivid, e.g., intrusive flashbacks experienced in post-traumatic stress. Process views predict that these memories may closely match the original event but may require repeated recall in order to be integrated in the current situation.

In sum, process views of memory point toward an integrated understanding of client response patterns that are constrained by various therapeutic techniques. If a single memory framework underlies both conscious and unconscious memory processes, perhaps seemingly discrepant interventions can be viewed within a single memory framework.

An example of how these three variables might play out can be seen in the following case description. In therapy we use these constraining variables by altering the therapeutic context, the amount of focused attention, and the number of times we ask a client to recall something in accord with our goal for the particular memory. This case illustrates therapy work with a three-year-old client who was evaluated for sexual abuse. The initial interview took place in the intake worker's office and was done by the sex abuse evaluator. In preparation for this interview, the parent told the child that she should tell the interviewer about the "bad things Uncle Jack did to you." The sex abuse evaluator used anatomically correct dolls in an attempt to elicit information about the alleged abuse. Upon undressing the dolls, the child became extremely anxious and refused to answer any questions. Since the child could reveal no specific information during this interview, the evaluator assigned her to a therapist who continued the evaluation in the context of therapy.

In preparation for the first therapy session, the therapist told the child that she could play with toys and talk to the therapist about anything that was on her mind. During the first several sessions, the therapist purposefully avoided any reference to the abuse or to the alleged perpetrator in order to establish rapport. Eventually, the therapist brought the dolls into the room. When the child viewed the dolls she stated, "Those are Susan's dolls." "They go in Susan's room." "I don't have to talk about scarey things here." Presumably the child's arousal, or the transfer effect, connected with the dolls was tied to information about the context of the initial assessment session, presence of a particular interviewer, and the content of a particular room.

This same child was unwilling to attend to the therapist reading a book describing appropriate versus inappropriate types of touching. She defensively distanced herself by engaging in dollhouse play and by singing when the therapist introduced the book. Her mother reported that despite her divided attention, the child absorbed some of the information presented. The child would "teach" her dolls about some of these concepts when playing. When her mother praised her for learning so much in therapy, the girl stated that it was not from therapy; she just "knew it." The fact that her attention had been divided while the therapist read her the story caused her to misattribute the source of the information.

Finally, the number of times something is recalled influences the memory of that event. In this instance, as in all cases of sexual abuse, this becomes extremely important if the goal is to obtain uncontaminated information of the abuse. The more times a child is asked to repeat the story of his or her abuse, the more difficult it is for the child to separate reality from subjective memory. In this particular case, the child repeated the details of the abuse to many people before her mother sought evaluation from experts. Unfortunately, it became very difficult to clarify what the child actually experienced as well as the changes in her subjective experience of that memory produced by frequent recall. Obviously the therapy goal becomes important when determining whether this change in what is experienced as subjective memory is helpful. When the goal is to clarify the reality of the abuse, keeping the memory as "pure" as possible is vital. Not asking the child to remember prior to the evaluation would be important. When the goal is to help the child cope with the abuse, the goal may be to change the memory in some way; perhaps allowing the child to be more in control of what happens to her body. In this instance, the memory would be recalled frequently, with changes being experienced with each recall.

Conclusions

In this presentation we have outlined current cognitive constructs of conscious and unconscious memory. The current focus on the *subjective experience of memory* represents a significant shift from an objective to a subjective base of observation. From this base researchers and clinicians may derive a common vocabulary and research variables. Clinicians who base treatment goals or outcome expectations in research on subjective experience will likely derive explanations for a number of clinical interventions across therapy schools.

We discussed the view that the conscious experience of memory is (1) a feeling of transfer (much like sadness or anger), and (2) an attribution of pastness. We emphasized that both conscious and unconscious memory experiences, although they may be different from objective reality, are an important basis of behavior. We utilize the clients' conscious experience of remembering when we strive to establish learning experiences for clients that they can then attribute to their own efforts. This view indicates that the attribution to one's own past efforts is a second necessary step. Without this conscious attribution a client cannot identify with his or her past, and cannot use the past episode for conscious planning toward the future. It is frequently the subjective experience of remembering one's own personal resources and skills that gives one the impetus to act.

In addition to the conscious experience of remembering, we discussed research which emphasized how we flexibly use our memory for tasks that require no awareness for the memory source. We discussed misattributions of past experience, and research that showed how very ordinary events can affect memory in judgment tasks. This underlines the need for therapists to be aware of their influence on the nuances of attention, context, and the repetition of client theme.

Finally, this research evidence supports a single memory framework that preserves information for specific prior events rather than abstract concepts or representations. Some researchers further suggest that concept formation may use particular instances of the concept rather than an abstracted representation that includes all instances of the concept (Jacoby, 1983; Brooks, 1978; Medin & Schaffer, 1978). Recent theories of psychotherapy focus on personal meaning as the object of change in therapy (Mahoney, 1991). Meaning, however, by the views in this paper, is only one type of information affected by therapy. The subjective experience of memory may qualify as a more significant object of change in therapy and a viable outcome in therapy research.

ACKNOWLEDGMENT

An earlier version of this article was presented at the annual meeting of the Society for the Exploration of Psychotherapy Integration, London, England, July, 1991.

REFERENCES

Anderson, J. R. (1990). *Cognitive psychology and its implications* (3rd ed.) New York: W.H. Freeman and Company.

Bower, G. H., Monteiro, K. P., & Gilligan, S. G. (1978). Emotional mood as a context for learning and recall. *Journal of Verbal Learning and Verbal Behavior, 17,* 573–587.

Bowers, K. S. (1987). Revisioning the unconscious. *Canadian Psychology, 28*(2), 93–104.

Bowers, K. S., & Hilgard, E. (1986). Some complexities in understanding memory. In H. M. Pettianti (Ed.), *Hypnosis and memory* (pp. 3–18). New York: Guilford Press.

Brooks, L. R. (1978) Nonanalytic concept formation and memory for instances. In E. Rosch & B. Lloyd (Eds.), *Cognition and categorization.* Hillsdale, NJ: Erlbaum.

Cheesman, J., & Merikle, P. M. (1986). Word recognition and consciousness. In D. Besner, T. G. Waller, & G. E. Mackinnon (Eds.), *Reading research: Advances in theory and practice.* (Vol. 5, pp. 311–352). New York: Academic Press.

Dowd, E. T., Milne, C. R., & Wise, S. L. (1991). The Therapeutic Reactance Scale: Development and reliability. *Journal of Counseling and Development, 69,* 541–546.

Dywan, J. (June, 1984). *Hypermnesia and accuracy in recall.* Paper presented at the forty-fifth annual convention of the Canadian Psychological Association, Ottawa.

Dywan, J., & Bowers, K. (1983). The use of hypnosis to enhance recall. *Science, 222,* 184–185.

Ebbinghaus, H. (1885). *Memory: A contribution to experimental psychology* (translated by H. A. Ruger & C. E. Bussenues, 1913). New York: Teachers College, Columbia University.

Erickson, M. H. (1980). The confusion technique in hypnosis. In E. L. Rossi (Ed.), *The nature of hypnosis and suggestion: The collected papers of Milton H. Erickson on hypnosis* (Vol. I, pp. 258–291). New York: Irvington Publishers, Inc.

Freud, S., & Breuer, J. (1966). *Studies on hysteria* (translated by J. Strachey). New York: Avon Books.

Godden, D. R., & Baddeley, A. D. (1975). Context-dependent memory in two natural environments: On land and under water. *British Journal of Psychology, 66,* 325–331.

Goldfried, M. R. (1980). Toward the delineation of therapeutic change principles. *American Psychologist, 35,* 991–999.

Graf, P., Mandler, G., & Haden, P. (1982). Simulating amnesic symptoms in normal subjects. *Journal of Experimental Psychology: Learning, Memory, and Cognition, 13,* 45–53.

Graf, P., Squire, L. R. , & Mandler, G. (1984). The information that amnesic patients do not forget. *Journal of Experimental Psychology: Learning, Memory, and Cognition, 10,* 164–178.

Ivey, A. (1986). *Developmental therapy.* San Francisco, CA.: Jossey-Bass Publishers.

Jacoby, L. L. (1978) . On interpreting the effects of repetition: Solving a problem versus remembering a solution. *Journal of Verbal Learning and Verbal Behavior, 17,* 649–667.

Jacoby, L. L. (1983). Remembering the data: Analyzing interactive processes in reading. *Journal of Verbal Learning and Verbal Behavior, 22,* 485–508.

Jacoby, L. L. (1984). Incidental versus intentional retrieval: Remembering and awareness as separate issues. In L. R. Squire & N. Butters (Eds.), *Neuropsychology of memory* (pp. 145–146). New York: Guilford Press.

Jacoby, L. L., & Kelley, C. M. (1987). Unconscious influences of memory for a prior event. *Personality and Social Psychology Bulletin, 13,* 314–336.

Jacoby, L. L., Kelley, C. M., & Dywan, J. (1989). Memory attributions. In H. L. Roediger & F. I. M. Craik (Eds.), *Varieties of memory and consciousness* (pp. 391–422). Hillsdale, NJ: Erlbaum.

Jacoby, L. L., & Witherspoon, D. (1982). Remembering without awareness. *Canadian Journal of Psychology, 36,* 300–324.

Jacoby, L. L., Woloshyn, V., & Kelley, C. (1989). Becoming famous without being recognized: Unconscious influences in memory produced by dividing attention. *Journal of Experimental Psychology General, 118*(2), 115–125.

Mahoney, M. J. (1991). *Human change processes: The scientific foundations of psychotherapy.* New York: Basic Books, Inc.

Mandler, G., Nakamura, Y., & Van Zandt, B. J. S. (1987). Nonspecific effects of exposure on stimuli that cannot be recognized. *Journal of Experimental Psychology: Learning, Memory, and Cognition, 13,* 646–648.

Marcel, A. J. (1983). Conscious and unconscious perception: An approach to the relations between phenomenal experience and perceptual processes. *Cognitive Psychology, 15,* 238–300.

Medin, D. L., & Schaffer, M. M. (1978). Context theory of classification learning. *Psychological Review, 85,* 207–238.

Morris, R. G., & Kopelman, M. D. (1986). The memory deficits in Alzheimer-type dementia: A review. *The Quarterly Journal of Experimental Psychology, 38A,* 575–602.

Overton, D. A. (1978). Major theories of state dependent learning. In D. Ho, D. Richards, & D. Chutes (Eds.), *Drug discrimination and state-dependent learning* (pp. 283–318). New York: Academic Press.

Polanyi, M. (1958). *Personal knowledge: Towards a postcritical philosophy.* Chicago: University of Chicago Press.

Rossi, E. (1981). *Seminar on approaches to hypnosis and psychotherapy.* Sound recording from the International Congress on Ericksonian Approaches to Hypnosis and Psychotherapy. Phoenix, AZ: Milton H. Erickson Foundation.

Schacter, D. L. (1987). Implicit memory: History and current status. *Journal of Experimental Psychology: Learning, Memory, and Cognition, 13,* 501–518.

Schacter, S., & Singer, J. (1962). Cognitive, social, and physiological determinants of emotional states. *Psychological Review, 69,* 379–399.

Seamon, J. G., Brody, N., & Kauff, D. M. (1983). Affective discrimination of stimuli that are not recognized: Effects of shadowing, masking, and cerebral laterality. *Journal of Experimental Psychology: Learning, Memory, and Cognition, 12,* 171–181.

Slamecka, N. J., & Graf, P. (1978). The generation effect: Delineation of a phenomenon. *Journal of Experimental Psychology: Human Learning and Memory, 4,* 592–604.

Smith, S. M., Glenberg, A., & Bjork, R. A. (1978). Environmental context and human memory. *Memory Cognition, 6,* 342–353.

Squire, L. R., & Cohen, N. J. (1984). Human memory and amnesia, In J. McGaugh, G. Lynch, & N. Weinberger (Eds.), *Proceedings of the conference on neurobiology of learning and memory* (pp. 3–64). New York: Guilford Press.

Stuss, D. T., & Benson, D. F. (1986). *The frontal lobes.* New York: Raven Press.

Tulving, E. (1972). Episodic and semantic memory. In E. Tulving & W. Donaldson (Eds.), *Organization of memory* (pp. 381–403). New York: Academic Press.

Tulving, E. (1983). *Elements of episodic memory.* Oxford: The Clarendon Press.

Tulving, E., Schacter, D. L., & Stark, H. A. (1982). Priming effects in word-fragment completion are independent of recognition memory. *Journal of Experimental Psychology: Learning, Memory, and Cognition, 8,* 336–342.

Warren, R. M. (1970). Perceptual restorations of missing speech sounds. *Science, 167,* 392–393.

Warren, R. M., & Warren, R. P. (1970). Auditory illusions and confusions. *Scientific American, 223,* 30–36.

Warrington, E. K., & Weiskrantz, L. (1974). The effects of prior learning on subsequent retention in amnesic patients. *Neuropsychologia, 12,* 419–428.

Weingartner, H. (1978). Human state dependent learning. In D. Ho, D. Richards, & D. Chutes (Eds.), *Drug discrimination and state-dependent learning* (pp. 361–382). New York: Academic Press.

Wheeler, G. (1991). *Gestalt reconsidered: A new approach to contact and resistance.* New York: Gardener Press, Inc.

CHAPTER 9

An Investment Model of Depressive Resistance

Robert L. Leahy

In this chapter, a functional utility model of depressive resistance is advanced, drawing upon modern portfolio theory of how individuals decide to allocate resources. According to this microeconomic model, depressed individuals believe they have few present and future resources, and low utility of gain in a market that is volatile and downward sloping. Depression is viewed as a strategy to avoid further loss, resulting in active attempts to resist change as evidenced in motivated negative cognition. Depressives take a risk-averse strategy to minimize loss, utilizing high stop-loss criteria and rejecting optimism as a high-exposure position. Unlike optimistic individuals, who believe that there are many replications over a long duration to obtain gain, depressives have low-diversification, high-information demands, and utilize hedging, waiting, hiding and other tactics to minimize risk.

Cognitive models of depression have focused on information processing biases (Beck, Rush, Shaw, & Emery, 1979), negative explanatory style (Abramson, Seligman, & Teasdale, 1978), the perception of noncontingency (Seligman, 1975), deficits in self-regulation and self-control (Rehm, 1990), and excessive self-focus (Carver & Scheier, 1981; Nolen-Hoecksema, 1987). Although these cognitive models have proven to be useful in developing therapeutic interventions and programmatic research, these models do not directly address a central issue of depression—specifically, the process of decision making and the motivation to change.

Characteristic of depression are the apparent low motivation, low energy, indecisiveness, and self-criticism that constitute a core of resistance to change. Beck's schematic model is useful in identifying the negative triad as a resistant barrier to change—namely, the depressive's negative view of self, experience, and the future undermines his motivation to modify his behavior. The proposed model extends the schematic processing model. I propose that the schematic processing model does not sufficiently explain active resistance to change as seen in chronic and refractory depressions. The theoretical model proposed here adapts the schematic model as the foundation for a decision-making model based on individual differences in the perception of utility.

The model proposed here is an investment model of decision making drawn from modern portfolio theory. According to this model, individuals make decisions about how to allocate their resources based on their estimate of present and future resources available, tolerance for risk, and probability and value of gains and losses. In the present chapter I will argue that depressed individuals resist change and hesitate in making decisions because of their specific portfolio theories. I will elaborate this model by examining the depressive paradox, information search biases in decision making, depressive evaluations of losses, ambivalence about gains, and protection against risk.

DEPRESSIVE PARADOXES

A commonplace observation in the animal and human literature is that organisms are motivated to pursue rewards and avoid punishments. The opportunity to achieve an increase in rewards should increase the probability of behavior. Yet a cursory observation of the depressed patient suggests that he will often pass on the opportunity to engage in positive behavior and, indeed, may commit his time to apparently self-punitive behaviors such as self-criticism or depressive rumination. Should we conclude from this that depressives are the exception to the law of effect—that is, unlike pigeons, rats, and nondepressed humans, they do not pursue rewarding behavior, but rather pursue a masochistic goal? Indeed, a similar observation led Freud (1917) to conclude that depression was anger turned inward—or, simply, a form of psychological masochism resulting from an overly repressive superego.

Another observation that appears, at first glance, to defy general learning theory principles is that depressed people, who are in a higher state of deprivation, are in fact less motivated than nondepressed people to engage in positives. All students of operant conditioning know that it is useful to deprive the organism (usually, of food) in order to increase the strength and frequency of responding. Yet depressed individuals appear to defy this law of deprivation—their response level is lower than that of nondepressed people.

I will argue that an explanation of these apparent paradoxes is that decisions to respond are based on expectancies of future outcomes. Past reinforcement (or extinction) histories may be important, but the cognitive mediation of depression determines how the information about past history is utilized in making future predictions about outcomes. I will argue that depressives develop strategies to avoid loss that inhibit them in taking the "risk" necessary to change. Indeed, depression may be viewed as a risk-management strategy.

MAXIMIZATION AND MINIMIZATION

The depressive paradox can be clarified if we consider the assumptions guiding optimistic and pessimistic decision makers. Consider Mr. Jones, who is thinking about an investment and who believes that he has substantial assets and substantial future earning potential. He is presented with the option of investing $8,000 with a moderate probability of making a 50% return on his investment. He also believes that, even if he does not make 50%, he has a good probability of making some profit and a very low probability of losing his entire investment. Jones enjoys the things that he buys with his wealth and he enjoys playing the game of investments. Given the offer of this investment, he reasons that he has substantial resources to absorb the unlikely losses that might occur. He takes the investment.

In contrast to our optimistic, risk-taking Mr. Jones, unfortunate Mr. Smith believes he is down to his last $100. He is offered an investment of $80, with a possibility of gaining $40 (a 50% return on his investment). Mr. Smith believes that he has little likelihood of gaining employment and he believes that he has bills coming due next week. Moreover, he attributes his dire financial straits to foolish investments that recently headed south. Mr. Smith is a "nervous Nellie" and passes on this opportunity to invest.

These two investors—optimistic Jones and pessimistic Smith—operate from what they believe are rational considerations given the information and goals that they attempt to pursue. The optimist pursues a maximization strategy—that is, a growth strategy—because he is willing to take risks. The pessimist—our "depressed" Mr. Smith—believes that his minimization strategy is rational, since his goal is to avoid further losses. The depressive paradox describes the pessimistic, but apparently rational, Mr. Smith. Perhaps Mr. Smith is incorrect (or correct) about his evaluation of his current and future resources, perhaps he is unduly negative of his chances of gaining, but there is an internal logic that tells him that he cannot absorb any further losses. His "self-protective" strategy instructs him to avoid change unless there is close to certainty of gaining.

In the pages to follow, I will outline the elements of a depressive style of decision-making. I refer to this as an investment model since decision makers are often in the position of determining how they will allocate resources for the purpose of achieving gains or protecting against loss. Modern portfolio theories are useful in providing us with the concepts necessary to describe the investment strategies of optimistic and pessimistic players. First, I will indicate how negative schemas are formed and maintained at a structurally primitive level. Second, I will indicate how these schemas "inform" decision making in depression by constraining information search and retrieval. Third, and most important for the investment model, I will indicate how depression is not simply a distortion or bias in thinking, but rather a strategy of adaptation.

SCHEMATIC BIASES AND DEVELOPMENTAL REGRESSION

Beck (Beck, 1976; Beck et al., 1979; Leahy & Beck, 1988) has proposed that depression is characterized by negative schemas about self and others which are activated during the depression and become predominant in the processing of information. These schemas often are formed during early childhood and may be characterized by the qualities of preoperational thinking, such as egocentrism, centration, magical thinking, moral realism, rigidity, and dichotomization (Leahy, 1995, 1996; in press). Because of the primitive structural qualities of early maladaptive schemas, many depressives (especially chronically depressed individuals) have difficulty treating their thinking as an object of thought. The ability to identify and test negative thoughts, especially deeply embedded assumptions and schemas, requires abilities of *metacogniton*—for example, the ability to decenter from the self and treat one's thoughts and feelings as objects of thoughts or potential rather than necessary realities. Developmental social-cognitive research indicates that very young children are unable to engage in this metacognitive process (Leahy, 1985; Selman, 1980). Indeed, similar to the preoperational child, the depressive experiences his negative thoughts as if they were reality and his emotions as if they were the only way one could feel. For the structurally regressed schema, there appears to be no alternative and no escape from the present construction of reality.

Given the predominance of early maladaptive schemas, depressives are overinclusive of negatives and underinclusive of positives. Schemata are self-sustaining information systems that reconfirm themselves through selective attention, recall, and recognition of information consistent with the schema. Because these schemata are often formed at a preoperational level of intelligence, the individual has difficulty decentering or distancing himself from his perspective, and has difficulty recognizing how his actions and choices have confirmed the schema. Of course, the task of cognitive therapy is to suggest "alternative realities," but the depressive is often captured by his own construction of reality.

Schema theory suggests several reasons why negative schemata are maintained: (1) schemas are structurally limited, lacking the ability to decenter—that is, lacking metacognitive self-reflection; (2) schemas are selective information-processing systems which are self-fulfilling or self-verifying; (3) schemas are not directly challenged because of compensations and avoidance; and (4) schemas are reconfirmed by negative life events. Although these structural and strategic factors are important in maintaining negativity, they do not sufficiently explain active efforts of resistance to change. For example, how would schema theory explain why patients would actively defend a negative schema, responding with anger and further rigidity when negativity is challenged? The proposed model of resistance extends schema theory to include what I refer to as motivated negative cognition—that is, cognitive (and behavioral) tactics and strategies that are used to maintain and defend a negative schema. I will attempt to demonstrate that depressives often believe that abandoning a negative schema exposes them to further loss.

Because of a long history of reconfirming the negative schema, recurrent depressive episodes and dysthymia are often characterized by resistance to change. The therapist often finds that the patient generates apparently ad hoc, seemingly irrational, reasons not to change, justifying his procrastination and refusal to take risks. Although one can recognize the power of the schema for information processing, it is not altogether obvious from schema theory why the patient should resist modification of negative thinking. Guidano and Liotti (1983) have suggested that these early maladaptive schemas are "guarded" by a "protective belt" of defensive maneuvers, although it is not clear why one would want to guard a negative belief. I will propose that the "protective belt" may be understood as an attempt to guard against further loss (a view consistent with Guidano and Liotti), and that the patient adapts a strategy of investment and pessimism that he believes protects him from devastation. To advance this position, I have drawn on neoclassical microeconomic models of investment strategies.

STRATEGIC PESSIMISM

The argument advanced in this article is that depressed individuals often resist change because they believe that they cannot absorb the costs of further losses. Their pessimism is a consequence of the experience of recent negative life events and underlying negative schemata, which direct their attention to negatives rather than positives. The proposed model is consistent with Beck's cognitive model (that is, negative schemata are assumed), Abramson, Seligman and Teasdale's attribution model (1978) (that is, explanatory styles result in low self-esteem), and life-event and social-skills models, such as Lewinsohn's (Lewinsohn & Gotlib, 1995), that is, life events constitute losses and low skills reflect estimation of personal resources. Many depressed individuals have some reason for thinking negatively, but their negative schemata and negative explanatory style further exacerbate this negativity.

Evolutionary psychiatry suggests that what appear to be maladaptive modes of response have, indeed, had evolutionary value (Wenegrat, 1990). For example, innate fears of heights, strangers, the dark, or animals may confer a self-protective function against real danger in primitive environments (Bowlby, 1968; Marks, 1987). Similarly, one can argue that depression and pessimism are sometimes adaptive (perhaps in "small doses"). For example, it might be useful to give up in the face of failure, to question your ability when events turn out badly so that you can correct yourself, or even to adapt a submissive posture in a group (Gardner, 1982; Price & Sloman, 1987). Indeed, excessive optimism, as evidenced in mania, can be exceptionally destructive (Leahy & Beck, 1988). Depressive pessimism is not always a distortion in thinking, but rather a bias: Sometimes the worst actually happens and it is wise to be prepared for it.

The investment model takes these cognitive-behavioral models a step further. I will argue that many depressed people assess their current and future resources as negative and view the world as a poor source of rewards, most of which are viewed as uncontrollable and unpredictable. *Given this negative triad of self, experience, and future, the depressive attempts to protect against further losses.* He adapts pessimism as a strategy which, be believes, will help him conserve his meager resources and will protect him against losses which he believes will be devastating. As a consequence, he takes an ambivalent position regarding hope, since hope may lead him to "foolhardy" exposure to greater losses. *The depressive guards against hope in order to protect himself from loss.* Contrary to the psychodynamic model that suggests that depression is anger turned inward or a form of masochism, the investment model proposes that depressives are so undermined by negatives that they direct most decision making to avoid further negatives. They are exquisitely risk averse as a strategy to avoid losses which they believe will devastate them.

PORTFOLIO THEORIES

The application of microeconomic concepts to mundane decision making has been advanced by Nobel prize laureate Gary Becker and his colleagues. Decision makers calculate costs and benefits, utilizing rational models, in making marital choices, criminal behavior, discrimination, and religious preference (Becker, 1976; Tomassi & Ierulli, 1995). Similarly, operant conditioning models have been compared to neoclassical models of economic decision (Schwartz, 1978). The investment model proposed here argues that individuals maintain strategies as to how they should invest their resources. A portfolio represents a variety of investment tools in finance theory (e.g., stocks, bonds, cash) and, as applied here, a portfolio represents a variety of behaviors—similar to a "behavioral repertoire" or "hierarchy of responses."

Individual portfolio theories represent the investor's understanding of his current and future resources, the perception of market variation or volatility, the investment goal (growth, conservative self-protection, or income generation), the functional utility of gains ("How much will this gain be valued?"), the opportunity to replicate investments ("Is this a single opportunity or will I be able to play many hands?"), the duration of investing, and the tolerance for risk (Bodie, Kane, & Marcus, 1996). For a variety of reasons that will become clearer in the subsequent sections of this article, depressed and nondepressed individuals hold different portfolio theories. These are depicted in Table 9.1.

Table 9.1 illustrates the phenomenological differences between pessimists and optimists. From Beck's schema theory of depression and from the model of the negative triad (Beck et al., 1979), we can see that the depressed individual may underestimate his current and future positives. His negative filter, overgeneralization, negative prediction, and discounting the positives, all result in his belief that he has few assets available and a bleak future.

Table 9.1 Portfolio Theories of Depressed and Non-depressed Individuals

Portfolio Concern	Depressed	Non-depressed
Assets available	Few	Some/Many
Future earning potential	Low	Moderate/high
Market variation	Volatile	Low/predictable
Investment goal	Minimize risk	Maximize gain
Risk-orientation	Risk averse	Risk neutral/risk lover
Functional utility of gain	Low	Moderate/high
Replications of investment	None/few	Many
Duration of investment	Short-term	Long-term
Portfolio diversification	Low	High

Because depressives are anhedonic and, therefore, derive little pleasure from rewards, and because they discount their positives, there is low functional utility of gains. He believes he has little and he has little to gain.

Losses for the depressive have added "negative utility" because they are overgeneralized, exaggerated, and personally internalized (Abramson et al., 1978; Beck et al., 1979). When the depressive loses, he adds to the loss the cost of self-criticism. Compared with the nondepressed individual who attempts to absorb the cost of loss as part of playing the game, the depressed individual magnifies the loss through his self-recrimination. As a result of this overvaluation of loss, the depressive's strategy is to minimize loss at all costs. We will now examine how depressives process information about loss and gain and the decision rules that guide their mundane investments.

LIMITED SEARCH

Depressive schematic processing does not allow the individual to engage in an exhaustive search of alternatives, information, or current resources. "Ideal" rational decision making suggests that one consider all alternatives, weigh the costs and benefits, consider all the information about the current situation, and choose the "best" alternative (Baron, 1994; Janis & Mann, 1977). However, almost all decision makers are "imperfect," since exhaustive searches of alternatives would be so time consuming that no decisions would be possible. Search rules are employed. For example, when you go to a restaurant for a quick lunch, it is unlikely that you compare the costs and benefits of every entree. Rather, you have a selective search question—for example, it might be, "Do they have a chicken salad sandwich?" Once the search question is answered affirmatively, the search is discontinued.

Depressive searches are similarly limited and they are guided by the "default question"—namely, "How can I lose?" Cost is the default. Once this is answered affirmatively, future questions about gains overshadowing losses are avoided. The search is myopic in that the focus is on the "up-front costs"—that is, the effort or risk that one incurs in order to achieve a gain. Thus, much of depressive avoidance appears to conflict with purposive behavior of seeking rewards. Because losses are overvalued, the depressive searches for reasons not to change. "Is it possible that I could lose," "Do I need more information?" or "Could I regret this action?" all enter into the inquiry, inevitably leading to affirmative conclusions and further avoidance. Waiting is often viewed as a positive alternative, since waiting provides the depressive with the perceived opportunity of gaining more information, reducing risk, and acquiring the "motivation" or desire to act. To the nondepressed individual, waiting can be viewed as a cost, since opportunities to "invest" or act are foregone. (This is why investors demand interest on their investments—they have opportunity costs of delaying the enjoyment of their capital.) As the depressive waits, searching for reasons not to change and demanding certainty in an uncertain world, opportunities are missed. Although his immediate goal in waiting was to protect against "risk," his procrastination then becomes a further focus of his self-criticism.

The limited search, or biased search, of the depressive also leads him to undervalue current and future resources. Rather than directing his search to "How much do I have already?," "How much do I have to absorb costs?," or "How much can I gain in the future?," the depressive investor myopically searches for losses that will draw down his perceived limited resources. Consequently, the costs have high negative utility and are to be avoided at all cost.

Because the schema is focused on the negative, the depressive searcher seeks to find reasons not to act. An example of this "searching for reasons not to change" is a woman who feared doing poorly at work and, therefore, generated ad hoc reasons not to look for a job. Another example was a commodity trader who feared making mistakes and who continually sought reasons why he should not take particular trades. In his case, the consequences of his trading were decreased by having him do "paper trades" (rather than actual monetary trades), giving him the opportunity to immunize himself against loss. By practicing losing and gaining on paper trades, he was able to recognize that the "payoff" in trading came with replications and duration.

LOSS ORIENTATION

Many of the cognitive distortions of depression emphasize the severity, personal implication, and generality of losses. For example, the depressive attributes loss to a personal deficit of his that is stable, losses are catastrophized, and losses are generalized to other areas of his life. The depressive is focused on "negative delta" (negative change)—either actual or anticipated. The loss orientation is magnified because the depressive has a low threshold for defining loss, he is driven by scarcity assumptions, he views loss as depleting, he has a high stop-loss criterion, and he has a short-term focus. Examples of the loss orientation are depicted in Table 9.2.

Let us examine each of the loss issues. Examples of the low threshold for defining loss include patients who view small rejections and minor inconveniences as significant personal failures of major proportions. Be-

Table 9.2 Loss Orientation in Depression

Loss Orientation	Example
Low threshold	The slightest decrease is viewed as a loss of significant proportion.
High "stop-loss" criteria	A small loss leads to termination of behavior. Consequently, the depressive gets stopped out early.
Scarcity assumptions	The world is viewed as having few opportunities for success. This is generalized to a zero-sum model of rewards for self and other.
Depletion assumptions	Losses are not simple inconveniences or temporary setbacks. They are viewed as permanently drawing down resources.
Cost-cascades	Losses are viewed as linked to an accelerating linear trend of further losses.
Temporal focus	The depressive takes a short-term focus, viewing his investments only in terms of how they will pay off or lose in the short-term.
Reversibility and revocability	Losses are viewed as irreversible and not compensated or off-set by gains. Negative investments are irrevocable-he cannot see himself as able to "pull out" easily.
Regret orientation	Losses are followed by regret that one should have known better. His hindsight bias is focused on the assumption that he should have been able to make perfect decisions with limited information.

cause the depressive views any loss as polarized to the negative extreme, he attempts to avoid further losses by "stopping out" (quitting) early. An example of the search for loss and a low threshold for defining loss is a woman who assumed that she would be rejected by men and who was hypervigilant for any signs of rejection. Immediately on seeing any sign of disinterest in the man, she would excuse herself and walk away. The therapist encouraged her not to "stop out" early and to stay in the situation longer. This dramatically improved her social interactions. Seligman's descriptions of helplessness are consistent with the low threshold for defining failure and the stop-loss orientation.

Depressives are often driven by scarcity and depletion assumptions. Because they view the world as an unlikely source of future rewards and because losses are considered depleting, the depressive attempts to avoid any failure by waiting until he is absolutely certain of success. For example, a salesman avoided making calls because he believed that there were few opportunities for success and that the economy was in the middle of a depression (which it was not). He viewed rejections as personally depleting and evidence of his incompetence. The longer he waited to make sales, the more evidence he thought he had that sales were impossible to make. He believed that he could only make sales when he was sure of a positive outcome and when he felt motivated and comfortable. His therapist assisted him in recognizing that his self-fulfilling scarcity and failure assumptions, coupled with his "energy depletion" idea, confirmed his negative view. The alternative view—"The world is a natural reinforcer for positive behavior" and "You don't need energy to act"—helped him overcome an inertia that had plagued him for several years.

Losses are viewed as the beginning of a linear trend of increasingly accelerating losses. I refer to these as "cost cascades," a concept borrowed from Becker's microeconomic model. The depressive often fears that he will step on a trapdoor of loss, dropping him into a never ending chasm of failure. Because he fears these cost cascades, he will stop out quickly. Linked to this cost-cascade theory is the depressive view that negative consequences are irreversible—they are not compensated by future (or past) gains. Furthermore, actions are viewed as irrevocable—that is, he fears that, once committed, he will be unable to pull out. This catalyzes him to stop out soon—"while he has the chance." For example, a single man feared getting involved with a woman he liked because he believed that, once involved, he would be trapped and he would be unable to be assertive and pull out if the relationship did not work out. He believed that he would be better off not dating her further lest he enter into an irreversible, irrevocable relationship. Examining his rights to be assertive—and the value to the woman if he was assertive—was helpful in assisting him in pursuing the woman. Revoking decisions helped him make decisions.

Depressive loss orientation is not only focused on long-term losses or hopelessness, but it is also overly focused on short-term costs or investments. Prudent and proactive individuals will view investments as purposive—that is, "I exercise to get into shape." For the optimist, the costs are up front—that is, he views costs as a means to an end, while the pessimist views costs as an end in themselves. Effort and risk serve the purpose of producing positive outcomes. In contrast to the purposive optimist, the depressive views losses as the entire field of experience. His temporal focus is short-term on the depletion of loss: "It's too much effort" and "I feel uncomfortable and tired" are examples of this short-term focus. The therapist may assist the patient in transcending the short time-frame by imagining how he will feel after he has exercised (or engaged in productive behavior). Losses may be reconstrued as costs with a purpose.

Finally, the depressive responds to loss with regret and self-recrimination. Ironically, he believes that he should have been able to avoid past mistakes but that he will be unable to control future mistakes. Regret and self-criticism are added costs to loss and failure, further motivating the depressive to avoid any loss by stopping out early. In short, depressives assume loss as a default function and search for reasons not to act in order to avoid further costs.

GAIN ORIENTATION

Similar to the negative orientation toward loss, the depressive takes an ambivalent attitude toward gains. Since his negative schemata predict that "reality" is basically negative, gains are viewed with skepticism. This ambivalence toward gains is reflected in the fact that the depressive has a high threshold for defining gains, gains are undervalued and viewed as having low probability, there is a demand for immediate gains, small reductions in frustration are preferred to longer-term investments ("contingency traps"), gains are viewed as out of the control of the depressive, and gains are viewed as self-correcting toward the negative norm ("gains have gravity"). These issues are illustrated in Table 9.3.

Let us keep in mind that the depressive strategy is viewed as an attempt to guard against further losses. If the depressive finds himself becoming "overly optimistic," he runs the risk, he believes, of added exposure. I will describe, later, how the depressive "manages expectations" to handle his loss and gain orientation, but here we will examine the ambivalence toward gain so characteristic of resistant depressives. Some of this resistance appears to be pri-

Table 9.3 Gain Orientation in Depression

Gain Orientation	Example
High threshold for definition	A major change is required to be considered a gain.
Low valuation	Gains are viewed as having little hedonic or personal value. They are often discounted.
Low probability	Future gains are viewed as unlikely and unpredictable.
Immediate demand	There is little ability to delay gratification. The depressive is *myopic,* getting caught in the immediate consequences of an action.
Contingency traps	Focusing on short-term frustration, the depressive will continue to avoid or engage in pointless behavior simply because it provides short-term reduction of anxiety.
Lack of control	Gains are viewed as non-contingent—out of the control of the depressive. Although he believes that he can produce losses, he does not believe that he has control over producing gains.
Gravity of gains	Since the norm is negative, gains are viewed as self-correcting toward the negatives, that is, they have gravity.

marily a consequence of negative schemata, while other aspects of the resistance are cognitive strategies to avoid greater exposure.

Because the schema is negative, there is selective focus on the negative and either lack of processing of, or discounting of, the positives. Depressives have a high threshold for defining positives—often a positive must be close to perfection to be counted as a positive, whereas the negative category is overly inclusive. This underinclusion of positives results in the difficulty in recognizing gains from reinforcement, since they are not viewed as "reinforcing" in the first place. Further, because of the anhedonia of depression, positives have low pleasure or mastery value—that is, they have low positive utility. This further undermines the reinforcing value of positives. Similarly, positives are expected to be improbable, further enhancing the low expectancy of further reinforcements. A string of positives is not generalized to a trend of future positives, since positives are not noticed, or are discounted, undervalued, compartmentalized, or viewed as nonpredictive. Given the discounting of gains, reinforcements provide little incentive.

Depressives, however, do experience positives, but often positives are defined as the reduction of a negative—namely, the reduction of frustration or anxiety. This negative reactive orientation is a result of the demand for immediate gratification. Like the starving man, the depressive seeks relief from his discomfort as quickly as possible—he acts as if he cannot afford delay of gratification. The myopia that is so common with drug and alcohol addiction (which are often comorbid with anxious depression) is the result of the short-sighted demand for discomfort reduction without consideration of long-term costs. Short-term gains are traded against longer-term costs—often because the depressive believes that he needs the gain desperately. This results in contingency traps—that is, the repetition of an ultimately self-defeating behavior simply because it produces short-term reinforcement. Examples of contingency traps are substance abuse, avoidance, and escape, without consideration of the advantage of alternatives that might ultimately enhance the depressive's condition. The depressive, trapped in a contingency, follows a rigid rule—"When frustrated, do X," where "X" refers to substance abuse, escape, or avoidance. The depressive becomes trapped in the contingent payoff, without considering or testing alternatives.

RISK MANAGEMENT

Individuals who believe that they have few resources and few opportunities of future earnings are wise to take a low-risk approach to their investments. Prudent investors, often with substantial capital reserves, are able to protect against risk by taking the long-duration approach to investment and diversifying across a variety of investments. In contrast, the depressive, driven by his sense of deprivation and desperation, takes a short-term view, seeking to reduce frustration immediately. Moreover, he perceives himself as having few resources to provide himself with diversification, further adding to his exposure for his single investment ("If I lose this, I lose everything"). Unlike the optimist who believes that he has many hands to play, the depressive views himself as having few "replications." Thus, this "hand" must be a winner.

Risk can be managed by demanding more information before investments are made—that is, the depressive can require that he wait it out before he is absolutely certain that he will show a gain. Waiting, as we have noted above, has opportunity costs, but these costs are discounted in depression because any alternative is viewed as having a low payoff anyway. He does not view himself as sacrificing attractive opportunities and he offsets this by focusing on how he can minimize devastating losses by waiting.

Another strategy for the depressive in risk management is to reject hope whenever hope arises. This is because the pleasure that one might derive from hope is often offset by the anxiety it arouses about further exposure—especially in a market that is viewed as volatile, negative, and uncontrollable. Hope carries risk of rising expectations that will lead to disappointment. For many depressives it is disappointment, loss, or "negative delta" that is feared more than the absence of rewards. Losing something is far more aversive than never having it in the first place.

Because hope is viewed as carrying the risk of unrealistically positive expectations, the depressive often argues that there are good reasons not to hope. For example, a research assistant for a company became angry with the therapist when the therapist argued that she (the patient) might have the ability to take on more challenging work. Although the patient had been criticizing herself for her lack of progress in the company, the idea of raising her expectations precipitated considerable anxiety: "What if I get my confidence up and then fail? Everyone will notice. I'll be far more visible." In her case, hopelessness was a strategy to avoid further risk—that is, more public exposure.

The rejection of hope underlies depressive attempts to aggressively lower expectations in oneself and in others. By lowering expectations of his performance, the depressive guards against disappointment. An alternative is to raise standards so excessively that almost no one would achieve the standard, thereby providing a "face-saving" attribution strategy: "Well, no one would achieve A+, so it means little about me. And at least I have the highest standards."

Common strategies for reducing risk involve straddling and hedging. For example, the depressive, fearing that his efforts will not work out, may bet against himself by minimizing his effort (minimizing his investment) and pulling out at the first sign of failure (straddling). This appears to be what happens in the case of helplessness—attempts at success, followed by a single failure, lead to early stopping out (quitting). The depressive who straddles, will sit on the fence, put in minimal effort, and then give up. His rationale is that this protects against further loss. For example, a husband in marital therapy, pessimistic about his marriage, put minimal effort into homework, demanding complete compliance from his wife. When he received less than perfect positive feedback from his wife, he discontinued his efforts at improving the relationship.

Hedging involves covering a potential loss in one investment with a possible insurance policy with another investment. Infidelity is an example of hedging in that the individual protects against the loss of one partner by having another readily available. For example, a woman who feared rejection by men, began pursuing an extramarital affair as soon as she got married. This was coupled with her hypervigilance that no man could be trusted. Ironically, her hypervigilance focused on her concern that her husband would find other women more appealing while she herself was pursuing other men. Her rationale was that she could protect herself against abandonment by proving to herself that she was still attractive to other men.

Another self-handicapping strategy that protects against deflation in self-esteem is to manufacture excuses or reasons why productive behavior cannot be pursued. For example, the salesman referred to earlier, would get up late during the day, focus his attention on trivial office details in his apartment, and carry out errands. He would complain about aches and pains that would become excuses for not making sales calls. He would tell the therapist that he was not yet ready to pursue sales calls, each week inventing new reasons why the calls could not be made. In fact, examining his fear of rejection revealed that he had very few rejections because he was making few calls. Indeed, the problem was not so much that he was failing when he made calls (which was his greatest fear) but rather that he almost never made calls. In fact, his goal was to avoid making calls at all costs. Thus, he would generate as many reasons as possible not to make calls. Some depressives use "not trying" as an options play: "If I don't try now, I keep open the option of trying in the future." Self-handicapping is like a smokescreen that prevents oneself and others from evaluating true ability. It protects against the risk of failure because it prevents any direct evaluation of capability. These risk management strategies are identified in Table 9.4.

Table 9.4 Risk Management Strategies in Depression

Risk Management Concerns	Example
Diversification	Low diversification: He believes that he has only a single investment—the one at hand—and, therefore, he is highly exposed to loss.
Duration	Short-term: Because he believes that he is in the game for the short-term, he is highly exposed to volatility.
Replication	Low or none: He believes that he will not have additional chances to succeed in this situation. Therefore, he must be sure that his first attempt will work.
Waiting	He believes that he needs to wait for a more opportune moment to act, and he forgoes opportunity costs because no alternative seems attractive.
Information demands	High: He requires close to certainty before he decides.
Disappointment aversion	High: He is less concerned with the ongoing lack of reinforcement than he is with the possibility of a negative *change*. He avoids *negative delta* at all costs.

ACCOUNTING PRINCIPLES IN DEPRESSION

An assumption in cognitive therapy is that the individual will examine the evidence and weigh the evidence or advantages of specific thoughts. Thaler (1985) has suggested that individuals may enter evidence into two unrelated accounts—as if their accounting principle leads them to consider these two accounts as part of separate systems. Typically most individuals will have a superordinate "account" of positives and negatives, such that negatives are offset by positives. Consider how you calculate your net income—you subtract your expenses from your income, yielding your final net income.

Depressed individuals appear to keep separate unrelated accounts—a loss account and a gain account. The loss account is not offset by the gain account, because the depressive does not consider them to be similar and because his schema directs him toward losses. For example, nondepressed people have a "self-esteem account" which includes all the positives and negatives related to their performance or qualities. One might argue that nondepressed individuals "fudge" their "returns" by exaggerating their gains and minimizing their losses (Taylor, 1989). Depressed individuals appear to have a low self-esteem account (which accumulates losses with interest) and another account, which I would label "irrelevant behavior" (which includes positive behavior which is not considered relevant to the self-esteem account). Furthermore, depressed individuals act as if they are "closing out" their positive accounts, such that positives are not carried forward into the future.

CONCLUSION

In this article I have proposed that depressive resistance is an attempt to avoid further loss. Given the negative schemata of the depressed patient, selective information processing has served to reconfirm the negative schema. Because these negative schemata are formed at a preoperational level of intelligence, metacognitive self-reflection is often absent. This limits the ability of the patient to gain distance or perspective from his negativity.

Information search is directed toward a default question—"How can I lose?"—which, when answered affirmatively, terminates further inquiry. Optimism is rejected since the depressive views his goal as prevention of loss rather than obtaining gain. Depressives have high stop-loss criteria for negatives and high criteria for defining gains.

The microeconomic utility model advanced here is applicable to other areas of psychopathology—for example, anxiety, anger, paranoia, and marital conflict. This model assists both therapist and patient in understanding resistance in a nonpejorative manner that has direct implications for interventions. The intervention strategies depend on, first, understanding the patient's portfolio theory and, second, proposing a different portfolio theory based on an optimistic view of current and future resources, duration and replication of investment, expanding the criteria for gains, modifying the overinclusion of losses, and identifying stop-loss, hedging, straddling, and other self-defeating strategies. The proposed model helps us extend other cognitive models, such as Beck's, Seligman's, and Abramson's, to the area of resistance and decisionmaking.

REFERENCES

Abramson, L. Y., Seligman, M. E. P., & Teasdale, J. (1978). Learned helplessness in humans: Critique and reformulation. *Journal of Abnormal Psychology, 87,* 49–74.

Baron, J. (1994). *Thinking and deciding.* New York: Cambridge University Press.

Beck, A. T. (1976). *Cognitive therapy and the emotional disorders.* New York: International Universities Press.

Beck, A. T., Rush, A. J., Shaw, B. F., & Emery, G. (1979). *Cognitive therapy of depression.* New York: Guilford.

Becker, G. S. (1976). *The economic approach to human behavior.* Chicago: University of Chicago Press.

Bodie, Z., Kane, A., & Marcus, A. J. (1996). *Investments.* Chicago: Irwin Publishing.

Bowlby, J. (1968). *Attachment and loss: I. Attachment.* London: Hogarth.

Bowlby, J. (1980). *Attachment and loss: III. Loss: Sadness and depression.* London: Hogarth.

Carver, C. S., & Scheier, M. F. (1981). *Attention and self-regulation: A control theory approach to human behavior.* New York: Springer.

Freud, S. (1917). Mourning and melancholia. In *Complete psychological works, Vol. 14. (Standard edition).* Translated and edited by J. Strachey. London: Hogarth Press.

Gardner, R. R. (1982). Mechanisms in manic-depressive disorder. *Archives of General Psychiatry, 39,* 1436–1441.

Guidano, V. F., & Liotti, G. (1983). *Cognitive processes and the emotional disorders.* New York: Guilford.

Janis, I. L., & Mann, L. (1977). *Decision making: A psychological analysis of conflict, choice and commitment.* New York: Free Press.

Leahy, R. L. (1985). The costs of development: Clinical Implications. In R. L. Leahy (Ed.), *The development of the self.* New York: Academic Press.

Leahy, R. L. (1991). Scripts in cognitive therapy: The systemic perspective. *Journal of Cognitive Psychotherapy, 5,* 291–304.

Leahy, R. L. (1992). Cognitive therapy on Wall Street: Schemas and scripts of invulnerability. *Journal of Cognitive Psychotherapy, 6,* 1–14.

Leahy, R. L. (1995). Cognitive development and cognitive therapy. *Journal of Cognitive Psychotherapy, ,* 173–184.

Leahy, R. L. (1996). *Cognitive therapy: Basic Principles and applications.* Northvale, NJ: Jason Aronson Publishing Company.

Leahy, R. L. (1997). Resistance and Self-Limitation. In R. L. Leahy (Ed.), *Casebook in cognitive therapy,* pp. 66–86. New York: Jason Aronson Publishing.

Leahy, R. L., & Beck, A. T. (1988). Cognitive therapy of depression and mania. In R. Cancro and R. Georgotas (Eds.), *Depression and mania,* pp. 517–537. New York: Elsevier.

Lewinsohn, P. M., & Gotlib, I. (1995). Behavioral theory and treatment of depression. In E. E. Beckham & W. R. Leber, (Eds.), *Handbook of depression,* pp. 352–375. New York: Guilford.

Lorenz, K. (1966). *On aggression.* New York: Harcourt, Brace, Jovanovich.

Marks, I. M. (1987). *Fears, phobias, and rituals: Panic, anxiety and their disorders.* Oxford: Oxford University Press.

Nolen-Hoecksema, S. (1987). Sex differences in unipolar depression: Evidence and theory. *Psychological Bulletin, 101,* 259–282.

Rehm, L. P. (1990). Cognitive and behavioral theories. In B. B. Wolman & G. Stricker (Eds.), *Depressive disorders: Facts, theories and treatment methods* (pp. 64–91). New York: Wiley.

Schwartz, B. (1978). *Psychology of learning and behavior.* New York: Norton.

Seligman, M. E. P. (1975). *Helplessness: On depression, development and death.* San Francisco: Freeman & Co.

Selman, R. L. (1980). *The growth of interpersonal understanding.* New York: Academic Press.

Sloman, L., & Price, J. S. (1987). Losing behavior (yielding subrontine) and human depression: Proximate and selective mechanisms. *Ethology and Sociobiology, 8,* 99–109.

Taylor, S. (1989). *Positive illusions: Creative self-deception and the healthy mind.* New York: Basic Books.

Thaler, R. (1985). Mental accounting and consumer choice. *Marketing Science, 4,* 199–214.

Tomassi, M., & Ierulli, K. (Eds.) (1995). *The new economics of human behavior.* Cambridge, UK: Cambridge University Press.

Wenegrat, B. (1990). *Sociobiological psychiatry: A new conceptual framework.* Lexington, MA: Lexington Books.

Wilson, E. O. (1975). *Sociobiology: A new synthesis.* Cambridge, MA: Belknap Press.

Wilson, J. Q. (1993) *The moral sense.* New York: The Free Press.

CHAPTER 10

Cognitive Psychotherapy and Postmodernism: Emerging Themes and Challenges

William J. Lyddon and Robin Weill

In this chapter we examine the mplications of postmodern thought for the theory and practice of cognitive psychotherapy in light of three postmodern influences—social constructionism, feminism, and multiculturalism. It is suggested that these influences challenge cognitive psychotherapists to (a) develop a greater appreciation for the ways in which human realities are socially negotiated, (b) provide more contextualized accounts of psychological problems, particularly with regard to the dimensions of gender, culture, and economic class, and (c) incorporate client empowerment strategies into their models of change.

Although the evolution of the cognitive perspective in psychotherapy has been characterized by significant conceptual development and differentiation, only recently have cognitive theorists and therapists begun to appreciate the way in which different cognitive psychotherapies are embodied by different philosophical and value-laden assumptions about human knowing and change (cf. Lyddon, 1992; Mahoney, 1991; Neimeyer, 1995). Mahoney (1991), for example, reminds us that

. . . our professional aspirations in the realm of human helping and our efforts to facilitate development in those we serve are inseparable from our assumptions about human change processes (pp. 16, 18).

The notion of a scientist-practitioner who is value-free, objective, and unbiased is particularly untenable by postmodern standards. From a postmodern perspective, the socially constructed nature of reality is ubiquitous and pervasive. As a result, any praxis (psychotherapeutic or otherwise) is necessarily situated in a context of socially negotiated meanings and values (McNamee & Gergen, 1992).

Rosenau (1992) describes postmodernism's emergence in the humanities and social sciences as a "radically new and different cultural movement [which] is coalescing in a broad-gauged reconceptualization of how we experience and explain the world around us" (p. 4). In contrast to modernist conceptions, postmodern thinkers eschew the notion of a reality independent of the observer, the known separate from the knower (Kvale, 1992a). Postmodern reality is fundamentally conceived as a personal and social construction of order in experience—an order that is largely negotiated through the language and forms of discourse that are unique to particular social groups (Anderson, 1990; Gergen, 1992a). As Marshall (1992) notes, crucial to understanding the postmodern perspective is

. . . the recognition that there is no 'outside' from which to 'objectively' name the present. The postmodern moment is an awareness of being-within, first a language, and second a particular historical, social, cultural framework (p. 3).

Although most contemporary inquiry in psychology continues to be tethered to a modernist worldview (Kvale, 1992a), recent developments in psychology tend to converge on postmodern conceptions of knowing and reality. For example, the emergence of the constructivist perspective in cognitive science and cognitive psychology has served to draw attention to the active role of the human mind in organizing and creating meaning—in literally inventing rather than discovering reality (Anderson, 1990; Lakoff, 1987; Lyddon, 1992; Mahoney, 1991; Teasdale & Barnard, 1993). Similarly, contemporary narrative approaches to psychological inquiry not only challenge the modernist assumption that our language about the world mirrors that world, but also underscore the role of the narrative or story as an organizing metaphor for human experience and meaning (Bruner, 1990; Howard, 1991; Meichenbaum, 1993; Russell & van den Broek, 1992; Sarbin, 1986; Terrell & Lyddon, 1996).

The purpose of this article is to explore the implications of postmodern thought for the theory and practice of cognitive psychotherapy. Toward this end, salient contrasts between modernism and postmodernism are first reviewed. The second part of this paper examines more specifically the implications of three postmodern movements for the future of cognitive psychotherapy: social constructionism, feminism, and multiculturalism.

DRAWING DISTINCTIONS: MODERNIST AND POSTMODERNIST WORLDVIEWS

Although it has been argued that the dichotomization of modern and postmodern into separate and distinct categories is itself a modernist enterprise (Kvale, 1992a), drawing distinctions between these two worldviews can nonetheless bring focus to a discussion of the implications of postmodernism for cognitive psychotherapy. The major paradigm shift (as some writers on the subject conceive it) from modernism to postmodernism has been described along a number of dimensions of contrast (cf. Kvale, 1992b; Rosenau, 1992). Among these contrasts, the differences between modern and postmodern conceptions of human knowing, reality, and the self are particularly noteworthy.

At the core of the modernist worldview is a belief in a singular, stable, and knowable reality (Gergen, 1992a; Neimeyer, 1993a). Consistent with this view of reality, modernist science tends to embrace an objectivist epistemology in which scientists—through the gradual accumulation of existing facts—are able to map the contours of the real world and discover its inherent and universal truths. By way of contrast, postmodernism questions what was once unquestionable: the assumptions about reality, knowledge, and truth that have dominated the modern era. The postmodern worldview is based on the assumption there is no single, true reality and that the "realities" that people inhabit—rather than being "given"— are instead socially constituted and thus may vary quite dramatically across cultures (or subcultures), time, and context (Neimeyer, 1993a). Furthermore, from a postmodern perspective, there is no objective datum. Instead, all "facts" incorporate theory and values which not only color what scientists purport to know but also the very questions they ask (Kuhn, 1970; Kvale, 1992a). Postmodernism is also congruent with a constructivist epistemology in the sense that belief systems—rather than being validated by their degree of correspondence or match to some universal "real" world—are instead evaluated in terms of their current viability in particular contexts (Howard, 1991). As Scarr (1985) noted:

We do not discover scientific facts; we invent them. Their usefulness to us depends both on shared perceptions of the "facts" (consensual validation) and on whether they work for various purposes, some practical and some theoretical (p. 499).

In his book, *The Postmodern Condition,* Lyotard (1984) underscored this notion exactly when he defined postmodernism as "an incredulity toward metanarratives" (p. xxiv), or grand stories which attempt to explain the world according to one overarching truth. In the postmodern worldview, universal metanarratives are instead replaced by local ones, reflecting a commitment to contextual relativism and a belief in the use-value of regional and contingent truths (Kvale, 1992a).

Another essential contrast between modern and postmodern world-views, one that is particularly relevant for psychology, involves the different ways the self is conceptualized within each framework (Kvale, 1992a). The birth of the modern subject as a distinct presence with specific attributes may be credited to Descartes, whose dictum "I think, therefore I am" served to justify the certainty of the subject's own being and set modernist philosophers on the path of reifying the thinking subject as a rational and autonomous agent (Marshall, 1992). As a result, the modern (and predominantly Western) self has been characterized as "self-contained" (Sampson, 1988), "egocentric" (Shweder & Bourne, 1982), "individualistic and rationalistic" (Hermans, Kempen, & van Loon, 1992) and "unitary and integrated" (Hoskins & Leseho, 1996)—essentially a bounded and autonomous entity that possesses a relatively coherent and consistent sense of identity across time and contexts (Cushman, 1990; 1992). From a postmodern framework, by contrast, boundedness, coherence, and consistency are both impossible and irrelevant characteristics of the self. As Gergen (1991) notes, the postmodern self is a "teeming world of provisional possibilities" (p. 139) that are enacted as performances in situated moments. Rather than viewing the self as self-contained and separate from the social world, postmodern conceptions view the self as a medium for the social world (Kvale, 1992a). In essence, postmodern conceptions replace the old Cartesian pronouncement, "I think, therefore I am" with "We communicate, therefore I am" (Gergen, 1992b). New metaphors of the self emerging from postmodern and constructivist writers and psychologists include: self as narrative and dialogical (Hermans & Hermans-Jansen, 1995; Howard, 1991; McAdams, 1993; Polkinghorne, 1991); self as self-theory (Berzonsky, 1990, 1992); self as evolving process (Guidano, 1991, 1995; Kegan, 1982; Mahoney, 1991); self as possible selves (Marcus & Nurius, 1986); and self as community (Mair, 1977) (see Hoskins & Leseho, 1996, and Cox & Lyddon, 1997). These emerging understandings of selfhood ultimately abandon the modernist belief in self as a singular, enduring essence and replace this belief with a more fluid, process view of self (or selves) as continually constructed and reconstructed in particular relationships over time. As Hart (1996) points out, from a constructivist perspective

> . . . there is no real self waiting to be discovered by the objective other (e.g., scientist or therapist) but differing versions of the self. No one perspective is more right than the other but each exists to embrace different aspects of experience. There can be more than one self, as different versions of the self may be perceived by the person or by others as the self evolves over time and across different contexts. Such versions may contain contradictory aspects, existing alongside each other as part of a double consciousness or alternative knowledges of the self (p. 45).

These postmodern changes—from objectivist to constructivist epistemology, from seeking a single truth to recognizing multiple realities, from viewing goals and outcomes as valid or invalid to evaluating them in terms of viability in contexts, and from the focus on the bounded self to a view of the self as socially constituted—are also integral features of social constructionist, feminist, and multicultural approaches in contemporary psychology and psychotherapy. It is to these postmodern movements that we now turn.

SOCIAL CONSTRUCTIONISM: PRIMACY OF THE RELATIONAL

With conceptual roots in the seminal works of Berger and Luckmann (1966) and others (cf. Danziger, 1979; Ginsberg, 1980; Goffman, 1959; Mead, 1934; Sarbin & Allen, 1968), social constructionist thinking has become a prominent epistemology in the social and behavioral sciences (Kvale, 1992b; Shotter & Gergen, 1989; Steier, 1991). Gergen (1985) identifies four assumptions of a social constructionist orientation:

1. The belief that what we know of the world is determined by the conceptual and linguistic categories we possess to define it.
2. The idea that concepts and categories by which the world is comprehended are social artifacts—products of historically situated interchanges among people.
3. The view that the degree to which a particular belief or understanding is sustained across time is not fundamentally dependent on its empirical validity, but on the vagaries of social processes.

4. The notion that descriptions and explanations of the world are of critical significance in social life, as they are integrally intertwined with the full gamut of activities in which people engage.

Social constructionists seek to transcend the conceptual limitations of traditional rationalist and empiricist theories of knowledge by suggesting that knowledge does not reside in the minds of single individuals but rather in the social processes of symbolic interaction and exchange. As Gergen (1982) contends "knowledge is not something people possess in their heads, but rather something people do together" (p. 270). Because spoken or written language is the primary medium through which the world is made intelligible, a person's verbal accounts are not viewed as the external expression of his/her internal cognitive processes, but rather as an expression of relationships among persons. Gergen and Gergen (1991) point out that a social constructionist analysis

> . . . draws attention to the manner in which conventions of language and other social processes (negotiation, persuasion, power, etc.) influence the accounts rendered of the 'objective' world. The emphasis is thus not on the individual mind but on the meanings of people as they collectively generate descriptions and explanations in language (p. 78).

From a social constructionist perspective, individual cognition is not prior to, but instead is forged out of the arena of socially shared cognition (values, beliefs, and narratives) of which the individual is part. Social constructionists invite contemporary cognitive theorists and researchers to move outward from their almost exclusive focus on the internal processes of the cognizing subject to the broader realm of shared languages. Within such a framework, the "mind" is viewed as a social construct and a person's beliefs, memories, and thoughts are understood largely as a socially constituted phenomena (Coulter, 1979, 1989; Valsiner, 1991).

An epistemic commitment to the socially negotiated nature of reality opens up the possibility for critical analyses and evaluations of status quo values, political arrangements, and power relations (Rosen, 1996). Perhaps nowhere in the areas of psychology and psychotherapy are such social constructionist critiques more salient than in feminist and emerging multicultural perspectives.

FEMINIST AND MULTICULTURAL CRITIQUES

The emergence of feminist and multicultural perspectives in psychotherapy has served to both underscore the value-laden nature of psychotherapy and raise concerns about the relevance of contemporary therapy
approaches for women, minorities, and members of other marginalized
groups. Feminist and multicultural writers have been particularly critical
of models of psychopathology and psychotherapy that (1) remove persons
and their psychological problems from relevant contextual referents (e.g.,
gender, race, ethnicity, culture, and economic status), (2) focus on the
individual as the primary source of his/her difficulties, and (3) interpret
healthy psychological adjustment only in terms of dominant cultural values (Brown & Ballou, 1992; Dutton-Douglas & Walker, 1988; Jackson,
1987; Katz, 1985; Ponterroto, Casas, Suzuki, & Alexander, 1995; Sue &
Zane, 1987).

Feminist thought has been a critical voice in psychotherapy since the
1970s, providing a forum for examining the way in which psychotherapy
theories, diagnoses, goals, and methods are situated in and influenced by
androcentric values and unequal power relations (Brown & Ballou, 1992;
Enns, 1993). Congruent with social constructionist thinking, feminists
point out that gender is not something that resides in the person, but
rather is a social construct that is constituted through interactional processes (Goldberger, 1996). As Riger (1992) succinctly notes, people "do"
rather than "have" gender. Because from a feminist standpoint gender is
both a cause and a consequence of women's experience in male-centered
societies, feminist therapists ask gendered questions about women's psychological adjustments in such contexts. For example, feminist reappraisals of anxiety disorders (Fodor, 1992), depression and affective disorders
(Hamilton & Jensvold, 1992), and trauma (Root, 1992) have described
not only the unique way that these problems are manifested in women's
lives, but also how these problems are inevitably connected to women's
experience of oppression, discrimination, and/or a relative lack of actual
or perceived power. Although it is important to note that some feminists
argue for the existence of essential differences between the genders (Mednick, 1991), those with a more postmodern perspective direct their inquiry to understanding and questioning societal prescriptions for gendered
behaviors and identity. It is this latter form of social critique that constitutes the crux of feminist approaches to therapy. As a result, feminist
therapists often help clients examine and renegotiate various gendered

beliefs, meanings, and power relations (Brown & Brodsky, 1992; Hare-Mustin & Maracek, 1990).

Paralleling contemporary feminist reappraisals of psychotherapy, multiculturalism has emerged as another critical voice in the postmodern world. Although a separate examination of feminist and multicultural critiques of psychotherapy could appear contrived because of the shared purposes of making explicit sociocultural origins and prescriptions for behavior, it is important to note that the interests of ethnic minorities are not always served by feminist writers and researchers. For example, Espin and Gawalek (1992) note that much feminist psychology (cf. Jordan & Surrey, 1986; Miller, 1986) generalizes the psychological characteristics of white, middle-class women to all women. A multicultural perspective insists that the female experience is not a monolithic one. Rather, women of color experience different cultural influences and constraints on behavior. Indeed, a social constructionist perspective necessitates such an emphasis on pluralism (Enns, 1993).

Referred to as the "fourth force" in counseling and psychotherapy by some writers in the field (Pedersen, 1991), the multicultural perspective (1) draws attention to the values associated with many contemporary approaches to psychotherapy and (2) underscores the idea that some of these values may be antithetical to the beliefs and values of many racial and ethnic minority clients (Atkinson, Morton, & Sue, 1989; Espin & Gawalek, 1992; Ponterro, Casas, Suzuki, & Alexander, 1995). Fundamental to multicultural thinking is the idea that different social and cultural groups develop different ways of construing and organizing the world, or worldviews (Hoare, 1991; Ibrahim, 1991). Furthermore, from a multicultural perspective, no particular worldview is necessarily more "right" or "correct" than any other, multicultural scholars suggest that psychotherapists should (1) be aware of their own worldviews, (2) understand and respect the different worldviews of their clients, and (3) be careful to avoid defining successful psychotherapy outcomes exclusively in terms of client conformity to therapist worldviews and values (Ibrahim, 1991; Ivey, 1993; Pedersen, 1991). As a result, multicultural writers encourage psychotherapists to acknowledge and respect cultural differences including differences in child rearing, patterns of social interaction, dependence in relationships, and spirituality.

In addition to highlighting the value-laden nature of psychotherapy, feminist and multicultural critiques also converge on the idea that some psychological problems have their origins in the social and economic inequities that separate and marginalize certain people from others. For example, because women and minorities disproportionately comprise lower economic and political positions in Western societies, they experience adverse consequences (cf. Brodsky, 1982; Jackman & Jackman, 1983; Sue & Sue, 1990; Walker, 1989). As a result, feminist and multicultural writers emphasize the role of power relations within society and how persons are affected by imbalances in power along various systems of change. In particular, they argue that the influences of discrimination, oppression, and poverty must be considered when attempting to understand many of the psychological problems faced by women, minorities, and other marginalized groups (Atkinson, Morton, & Sue, 1989).

IMPLICATIONS FOR COGNITIVE PSYCHOTHERAPY

Postmodernism and its related social constructionist, feminist, and multicultural expressions present a number of challenges for the field of cognitive psychotherapy. In particular, postmodernist understandings challenge contemporary cognitive therapists to develop a greater appreciation for (a) the ways in which human realities are personally and socially constructed, (b) the gendered and cultural dimensions of clients' experiences and beliefs, and (c) the role of empowerment strategies with clients. A discussion of each of these issues follows.

The Social Construction of Human Realities

Contemporary forms and facets of cognitive therapy predominately reflect commitments to rationalist and/or empiricist epistemologies. As Neimeyer (1993a) has recently noted, cognitive theorists such as Ellis and Beck tend to envision the well-adjusted person as either a paragon of rationality who interprets the world in a manner consistent with authorized axioms of rational thought or an objective scientist who consistently makes accurate inferences about him/herself and the world. In either case, a modernist correspondence theory of truth is endorsed. That is, both conceptualizations measure the validity of clients' beliefs in terms of the degree to which such beliefs "match" or correspond to therapist-defined standards of rationality and/or objectivity. Central to postmodernism, however, is the notion that no universal and/or stable categories of knowledge exist independent of the humans who invent them. Because human realities consist of socially negotiated meanings (Gergen, 1982, 1994), definitions of rationality and reality reflect a particular social consensus rather than some privileged view of the way things really are. Postmodernism's influence on contemporary thinking in cognitive therapy is exemplified by the emergence of the constructivist psychotherapies (cf. Guidano, 1991; Mahoney, 1991; Neimeyer, 1993a). As Neimeyer (1993a) notes

> ". . . constructivist therapies are united in their rejection of a correspondence theory of truth and its corollary assumption that any beliefs that fail to correspond to objective reality are, by definition, dysfunctional. Instead, they hold that the viability of any given construction is a function of its consequences for the individual or group that provisionally adopts it . . . as well as its overall coherence with the larger system of personally or socially held beliefs into which it is incorporated" (p. 222).

By rejecting a correspondence theory of truth, constructivists challenge contemporary cognitive therapists to move away from evaluating client beliefs by a standard of comparison that posits an objective reality. Such a view coincides with Mahoney's (1988) contention that "The key issue in therapy is the pragmatic utility, rather than the bedrock validity, of the client's system of understanding" (p. 5).

Situating of Client Problems

As previously noted, modernist conceptions tend to view the self as a bounded and contained entity, largely separate from the social world. Paralleling this view, modernist theories of psychotherapy tend to situate psychological problems within the interior of each self-contained individual (Cushman, 1992; Prilleltensky, 1990; Sampson, 1981). As Cushman (1992) argues

> ". . . the common thread uniting all . . . psychological theories is the concept of the psychotherapist as the doctor of the *interior*. . . . Psychotherapists shape, maintain, and heal the realm of the private that the modern era has located within each self-contained individual" (p. 22).

Contemporary forms of cognitive psychotherapy tend to emulate the modernist emphasis on the psychological interior. Central to many conceptions of cognitive psychotherapy is the assumption that psychological problems are largely a function of the adequacy (rationality or accuracy) of persons' beliefs and cognitions. The general implication is that emotional and behavioral problems (e.g., depression and anxiety) reflect the operation of a cognitive deficit or vulnerability that resides within the client. As a result, the primary therapeutic agenda is to change the client's beliefs in the direction of warranted standards of rational and/or objective thinking. From a postmodern perspective, however, not only is the viability of equating psychological adjustment with "rational" or "accurate" thought questioned on ontological grounds (cf. Mahoney, 1991; Neimeyer, 1993a), but the practice of situating psychological problems largely within the person is also seriously challenged. In the postmodern world, individual experience—including the experience of pathology—cannot be separated from social processes and contexts. Indeed, life span developmental researchers and theorists have pointed out that internal psychological dispositions account for a relatively small proportion of variance in developmental outcomes (Ford & Lerner, 1992; Steenbarger, 1991). According to these researchers, human development occurs within nested and interacting biological, cultural, historical, and social contexts, and developmental outcomes—rather than being a function of internal dispositions and intrapsychic structures—instead reflect the relative goodness of fit between persons and their multiple contexts (Steenbarger, 1993). Consistent with this view, multicultural therapists emphasize that it is the lack of fit between the minority client and the dominant culture—and not a deficit internal to the client—that is often the source of presenting problems (Ramirez, 1991; Steenbarger, 1993). In summary, rather than placing the focus for change predominantly on the client and the way he/she thinks about the world, postmodern conceptions encourage cognitive therapists to situate clients and their problems in the broader contexts of their lives. Two particularly significant contextual variables are those of gender and culture.

Gender and Cultural Considerations

By focusing on the "rationality" and/or "objectivity" of clients' internal thought processes, cognitive therapies in the modern era have minimized the contextual influences of gender, culture, ethnicity, race, and socioeconomic class on the development of persons' beliefs, values, and worldviews. In their critique of cognitive-behavioral therapies, Kantrowitz and Ballou (1992) make this point exactly when they boldly state:

> "There is nothing in the theory which enhances sensitivity to gender, race, and class issues. . . . The lack of a careful consideration of gender, class, race, and ethnic factors as well as contextual information, specific antecedents, and consequences of specific beliefs and behaviors is a problem in cognitive-behavioral conceptualizations of pathology" (pp. 82–83).

Although at least a couple of exceptions to this criticism may be found in the cognitive therapy literature (cf. Davis & Padesky, 1989; Padesky &

Greenberger, 1995), a central concern from a postmodern perspective is that cognitive interventions designed to change clients' thinking in the direction of more "rational" and/or "objective" thought do not acknowledge the diversity of viable ways in which humans may construct their personal and cultural realities.

For example, Kantrowitz and Ballou (1992) suggest that the rational/ logical focus of cognitive-behavioral theory is limited because it tends to encourage conformity to a stereotypically masculine thinking style. Indeed, recent research in cognitive science has provided substantial support for the existence of two fundamental modes of processing information—analytical-rational (or propositional) and intuitive-experiential (or implicational)—which operate according to different rules and which *both* play a role in successful coping, adjustment, and change (Epstein, Pacini, Denes-Raj, & Heier, 1996; Teasdale, 1996). From a multicultural perspective Jackson (1987) points out that, in contrast to the predominately deductive and inductive cognitive styles of European Americans, African Americans tend to exhibit contextual and inferential styles which may be devalued and targeted for change by cognitive-behavioral therapists who predominately adhere to rationalist (deductive) and/or empiricist (inductive) worldviews. In a similar vein, Randall (1994) has recently described ways to modify cognitive therapy practices when working with disadvantaged African American women who may have different orientations to time and more sociocentric conceptions of personhood. Corey (1991) recommends that cognitive therapists use caution in challenging clients' beliefs until the cultural context of the beliefs are understood. For example, he points out that a "hardheaded" method of convincing clients to abandon "unduly" dependent patterns of behavior ignores the fact that many cultures (e.g., Asian) consider dependency to be a feature of mental health. Padesky and Greenberger (1995) have similarly underscored the need for cognitive therapists to develop greater cultural awareness. In particular, they suggest ways for cognitive therapists to incorporate into their treatment planning and conceptualizations the contextual influences of clients' ethnic/racial heritage, socioeconomic status, religious/spiritual affiliation, and gender/sex-role values.

In the postmodern world of multiple realities, it is difficult to maintain the traditional cognitive therapy view that satisfactory adjustment to one reality is equivalent to mental health while unsatisfactory adjustment is a form of psychological disorder. The postmodern emphasis on the relativity of realities challenges cognitive psychotherapists to become sensitive to (a) the ways in which people in different cultures have strikingly different construals of self and others and (b) how these construals may determine the very nature of human experience, including cognition, emotion, and motivation (Markus & Kitayama, 1991).

Collaboration and Empowerment

Once the cognitive therapist relinquishes the cherished modernist belief in the existence of a singular, stable, external "reality," he/she also relinquishes the role of "reality" expert and arbiter of the "correct" and "rational" ways that clients should conceptualize their lives (Anderson & Goolishian, 1992). Relinquishing the role of "reality" expert not only challenges cognitive therapists to views the client/therapist relationship in more egalitarian terms, but also fosters a view of cognitive therapy as more of a *creative* than *corrective* endeavor (Neimeyer, 1990). In other words, rather than using the traditional "changing minds" strategy (getting clients to admit that their specific thoughts are irrational or inconsistent with available evidence), cognitive therapists will be challenged to adopt a more collaborative, "guided discovery" approach that helps clients develop alternative, wider, and more flexible perspectives on problematic situations (Padesky, 1993).

Encouraging clients to take more of an active and creative role in the therapeutic relationship can also be a starting point for drawing clients' attention to issues of empowerment—that is, to the larger role of power relations in society and how persons are affected by imbalances of power along various systems of exchange (Wartenberg, 1988). This broader view of empowerment is defined by McWhirter (1991) as

> . . . the process by which people, organizations, or groups who are powerless (a) become aware of the power dynamics at work in their life context, (b) develop skills and capacities for gaining some reasonable control over their lives, (c) exercise this control without infringing on the rights of others, and (d) support the empowerment of others in their community (p. 224).

From a postmodernist perspective, it is not only important to bring attention to the societal structures that systematically undermine peoples' opportunities (such as economic structures that perpetuate sexism and racism) but also to the various configurations of social power and privilege that maintain status quo definitions of mental health and mental illness (Cushman, 1992, 1995; Prilleltensky, 1990).

Empowerment strategies are fundamentally antithetical to the *blaming the victim* construct in that they underscore the view that many client problems have their origins in social, economic, and political systems rather than in the persons who are marginalized by these systems (McWhirter, 1991, 1994). This view is consistent with the feminist therapy notion that "the personal is political" (Gilbert, 1980)—which refers to the recognition that both client and therapist operate within the context of larger social and political systems of influence. Incorporating the concept of empowerment into cognitive therapy challenges cognitive therapists to become more aware of the social, political, and economic factors that contribute to clients' psychological difficulties. In this way, cognitive therapists will be more likely to help clients examine the adverse influence of these factors on their lives rather than merely assuming that the adverse consequences of these factors are evidence of client deficiencies in thinking (Padesky & Greenberger, 1995).

CONCLUSIONS

All forms of psychotherapy are products of their historical and cultural contexts (Cushman, 1995; Fancher, 1995; Frank, 1961). Because contemporary cognitive therapies are to a large extent a product of the modern era, the vast share of cognitive approaches reflects the values and assumptions of modernism. In particular—and perhaps most saliently— many cognitive therapists tend to rely on modernist conceptions of a knowable, real world and, as a result, view psychological adjustment in terms of the degree to which clients "realistically" or "rationally" interpret that world. The postmodern and constructivist emphases in psychology and the human sciences reflect a radical reevaluation of the modernist view of reality by suggesting that human reality, or more appropriately *realities,* are social constructions—invented and interpretive frameworks of meaning. Because, from a postmodern perspective, multiple and viable realities may coexist at any point in time, any particular belief or idea is open to several possible interpretations or meanings. As a result, the postmodern (or constructivist) psychotherapist attempts to promote "the elaboration of the client's narrative without the convenience of simple criteria for determining what constitutes an acceptable story" (Neimeyer, 1993a, p. 224).

By some accounts, the "postmodern turn" in psychotherapy is well under way (cf. Mahoney, 1995; Neimeyer & Mahoney, 1995; Rosen & Kuehlwein, 1996). In our view, the field of cognitive psychotherapy— intimately connected as it is to issues of human knowing, belief, and cognition—is uniquely equipped to successfully adapt to the challenges associated with the postmodern world of multiple and conflicting belief systems. In support of this notion, Neimeyer (1993b) has recently speculated that the postmodern/constructivist influence in cognitive psychotherapy —rather than serving to demarcate clear boundaries between cognitive approaches (e.g., rationalist vs. constructivist)—may more accurately reflect emerging changes occurring *within* the cognitive psychotherapies. If this is indeed the case, cognitive psychotherapists may be well positioned to usher the larger psychotherapeutic enterprise into the postmodern world.

REFERENCES

Anderson, W. T. (1990). *Reality isn't what it used to be.* New York: Harper-Collins.

Anderson, H., & Goolishian, H. (1992). The client is the expert: A not-knowing approach to therapy. In S. McNamee & K. J. Gergen (Eds.), *Therapy as social construction* (pp. 25–39). London: Sage.

Atkinson, D. R., Morton, G., & Sue, D. W. (1989). *Counseling American minorities: A cross-cultural perspective* (3rd ed.). Dubuque, IA: Wiliam C. Brown.

Berger, P. L., & Luckmann, T. (1966). *The social construction of reality.* New York: Doubleday.

Berzonsky, M. D. (1990). Self-construction over the life-span: A process perspective on identity formation. In G. J. Neimeyer & R. A. Neimeyer (Eds.), *Advances in personal construct theory: Vol. 1,* (pp. 155–186). Greenwich, CT: JAI Press.

Berzonsky, M. D. (1992). A constructivist view of identity development: People as post-positivist self-theorists. In J. Kroger (Ed.), *Discussions on ego identity* (pp. 169–203). Hillsdale, NJ: Lawrence Erlbaum.

Brodsky, A. M. (1982). Sex, race, and class issues in psychotherapy research. In M. Parks & J. Harvey (Eds.), *Psychotherapy research and behavior change.* (pp. 123–150). Washington, DC: American Psychological Association.

Brown, L. S., & Ballou, M. (Eds.) (1992). *Personality and psychopathology: Feminist reappraisals.* New York: Guilford.

Brown, L. S., & Brodsky, A. M. (1992). The future of feminist therapy. *Psychotherapy, 29,* 51–57.

Bruner, J. (1990). *Acts of meaning.* Cambridge, MA: Harvard University Press.

Corey, G. (1991). *Theory of practice of counseling and psychotherapy.* Pacific Grove, CA: Brooks/Cole.

Coulter, J. (1979). *The social construction of the mind.* New York: Macmillan.

Coulter, J. (1989). *Mind in action.* Atlantic Highlands, NJ: Humanities Press.

Cox, L. M., & Lyddon, W. J. (1997). Constructivist conceptions of self: A discussion of emerging identity constructs. *Journal of Constructivist Psychology, 10,* 201–219.

Cushman, P. (1990). Why the self is empty: Toward a historically situated psychology. *American Psychologist, 45,* 599–611.

Cushman, P. (1992). Psychotherapy to 1992: A historically situated interpretation. In D. K. Freedheim (Ed.), *History of psychotherapy: A century of change* (pp. 21–64). Washington, DC: American Psychological Association.

Cushman, P. (1995). *Constructing the self, constructing America: A cultural history of psychotherapy.* New York: Addison-Wesley.

Danziger, K. (1979). The social origins of modern psychology. In Buss (Ed.), *Psychology in social context* (pp. 27–45). New York: Irvington.

Davis, D., & Padesky, C. (1989). Enhancing cognitive therapy with women. In A. Freeman, K. M. Simon, L. E. Beutler, & H. Arkowitz (Eds.), *Comprehensive handbook of cognitive therapy* (pp. 535–557). New York: Plenum.

Dutton-Douglas, A., & Walker, L. E. A. (Eds.) (1988). *Feminist psychotherapies: Integration of therapeutic and feminist systems.* Norwood, NJ: Ablex.

Enns, C. Z. (1993). Twenty years of feminist counseling and therapy: From naming biases to implementing multifaceted practice. *The Counseling Psychologist, 21,* 3–87.

Epstein, S., Pacini, R., Denes-Raj, V., & Heier, H. (1996). Individual differences in intuitive-experiential and analytical-rational thinking styles. *Journal of Personality and Social Psychology, 71,* 390–405.

Espin, O. M., & Gawalek, M. A. (1992). Women's diversity: Ethnicity, race, class, and gender in theories of feminist psychology. In S. Brown & M. Ballou (Eds.), *Personality and psychopathology: Feminist reappraisals.* (pp. 88–107). New York: Guilford.

Fancher, R. T. (1995). *Cultures of healing.* New York: W.H. Freeman.

Fodor, I. G. (1992). The agoraphobic syndrome: From anxiety neurosis to panic disorders. In L. S. Brown & M. Ballou (Eds.), *Personality and psychopathology: Feminist reappraisals* (pp. 177–205). New York: Guilford.

Ford, D. H., & Lerner, R. M. (1992). *Developmental systems theory: An integrative approach.* Newbury Park, CA: Sage.

Frank, J. D. (1961). *Persuasion and healing: A comparative study of psychotherapy.* New York: Schocken Books.

Gergen, K. J. (1982). *Toward transformation in social knowledge.* New York: Basic Books.

Gergen, K. J. (1985). The social constructionist movement in modern psychology. *American Psychologist, 40,* 266–275.

Gergen, K. J. (1991). *The saturated self.* New York: Basic Books.

Gergen, K. (1992a). Toward a postmodern psychology. In S. Kvale (Ed.), *Psychology and postmodernism* (pp. 17–30). New York: Sage.

Gergen, K. (1992b, November/December). The postmodern adventure. *Family Therapy Networker,* pp. 50–57.

Gergen, K. J. (1994). *Realities and relationships: Soundings in social construction.* Cambridge, MA: Harvard University Press.

Gergen, K. J., & Gergen, M. M. (1991). Toward reflective methodologies. In F. Steier (Ed.), *Research and reflextivity* (pp. 76–95). Newbury Park, CA: Sage.

Gilbert, L. (1980). Feminist therapy. In A. Brodsky & R. Hare-Mustin (Eds.), *Women and psychotherapy* (pp. 245–265). New York: Guilford.

Ginsberg, G. P. (1980). Situated action: An emerging paradigm. In L. Wheeler (Ed.), *Review of personality and social psychology* (Vol. I, pp. 295–325). Beverly Hills, CA: Sage.

Goffman, E. (1959). *The presentation of self in everyday life.* New York: Doubleday.

Goldberger, N. R. (1996). Women's construction of truth, self, authority, and power. In H. Rosen & K. T. Kuehlwein (Eds.), *Constructing realities: Meaning-making perspectives for psychotherapists* (pp. 167–193). San Francisco, CA: Jossey-Bass.

Guidano, J. F. (1991). *The self in process: Toward a post-rationalist cognitive therapy* New York: Guilford.

Guidano, V. F. (1995). A constructivist outline of human knowing processes. In M. J. Mahoney (Ed.), *Cognitive and constructive psychotherapies* (pp. 89–102). New York: Springer Publishing Co.

Hamilton, J. A., & Jensvold, M. (1992). Personality, psychopathology, and depression in women. In L. S. Brown & M. Ballou (Eds.), *Personality and psychopathology: Feminist reappraisals* (pp. 116–143). New York: Guilford.

Hare-Mustin, R. T., & Maracek, J. (1990). Gender and meaning of differences: Postmodernism and psychology. In R. T. Hare-Mustin & J. Maracek (Eds.), *Making a difference: Psychology and the construction of gender* (pp. 22–64). New Haven, CT: Yale University Press.

Hart, B. (1996). The construction of the gendered self. *Journal of Family Therapy, 18,* 43–60.

Hermans, H. J. M., & Hermans-Jansen, E. (1995). *Self-narrative: The construction of meaning in psychotherapy.* New York: Guilford.

Hermans, H. J. M., Kempen, H. J. G., & Van Loon, R. J. P. (1992). The dialogical self: Beyond individualism and rationalism. *American Psychologist, 47,* 23–33.

Hoare, C. (1991). Psychosocial identity development. *Journal of Counseling and Development, 70,* 45–53.

Hoskins, M., & Leseho, J. (1996). Changing metaphors of the self: Implications for counseling. *Journal of Counseling and Development, 74,* 243–252.

Howard, G. S. (1991). Culture tales: A narrative approach to thinking, cross-cultural psychology and psychotherapy. *American Psychologist, 46,* 187–197.

Ibrahim, F. A. (1991). Contribution of cultural worldview to generic counseling and development. *Journal of Counseling and Development, 70,* 13–19.

Ivey, A. E. (1993). *Counseling and psychotherapy: A multicultural perspective.* Needham Heights, MA: Allyn and Bacon.

Jackman, M. R., & Jackman, R. W. (1983). *Class awareness in the United States.* Berkeley: University of California Press.

Jackson, G. G. (1987). Cross-cultural counseling with Afro-Americans. In P. Pederson (Ed.), *Handbook of cross-cultural counseling and therapy* (pp. 231–237). New York: Praeger.

Jordan, J. V., & Surrey, J. L. (1986). The self-in-relation: Empathy and the mother-daughter relationship. In T. Bernay & D. W. Cantor (Eds.), *The psychology of today's woman* (pp. 81–104). Hillsdale, NJ: Analytic Press.

Katz, J. H. (1985). The sociopolitical nature of counseling. *The Counseling Psychologist, 13,* 615–624.

Kantrowitz, R. E., & Ballou, M. (1992). A feminist critique of cognitive-behavioral therapy. In S. Brown and M. Ballou (Eds.), *Personality and psychopathology: Feminist reappraisals.* (pp. 70–87). New York: Guilford.

Kegan, R. (1982). *The evolving self: Problem and process in human development.* Cambridge, MA: Harvard University Press.

Kuhn, T. S. (1970). *The structure of scientific revolutions.* Chicago: The University of Chicago Press.

Kvale, S. (1992a). Postmodern psychology: A contradiction in terms? In S. Kvale (Ed.), *Psychology and postmodernism* (pp. 31–57). London: Sage.

Kvale, S. (Ed.). (1992b). *Psychology and postmodernism.* London: Sage

Lakoff, G. (1987). *Women, fire, and dangerous things.* Chicago: University of Chicago Press.

Lyddon, W. J. (1992). Cognitive science and psychotherapy: An epistemic framework. In D. J. Stein & J. E. Young (Eds.), *Cognitive science and clinical disorders* (pp. 171–184). New York: Academic Press.

Lyotard, J. (1984). *The postmodern condition: A report on knowledge* (Trans. by G. Bennington & B. Massumi). University of Minnesota Press: Minneapolis.

Mahoney, M. J. (1988). Constructive metatheory I. Basic features and historical foundations. *International Journal of Personal Construct Psychology, 1,* 1–35.

Mahoney, M. J. (1991). *Human change processes.* New York: Basic Books.

Mahoney, M. J. (1995). The cognitive and constructive psychotherapies: Contexts and challenges. In M. J. Mahoney (Ed.), *Cognitive and constructive psychotherapies* (pp. 195–208). New York & Washington, DC: Springer Publishing Co. and the American Psychological Association.

Mair, M. (1977). The community of self. In D. Bannister (Ed.), *New perspectives in personal construct theory* (pp. 125–149). London: Academic Press.

Markus, H. R., & Kitayama, S. (1991). Culture and the self: Implications for cognition, emotion, and motivation. *Psychological Review, 98,* 224–253.

Markus, H., & Nurius, P. (1986). Possible selves. *American Psychologist, 41,* 954–969.

Marshall, B. K. (1992). *Teaching the postmodern.* Routledge: New York.

McAdams, D. P. (1993). *The stories we live by: Personal myths and the making of the self.* New York: William Morrow and Company.

McNamee, S., & Gergen, K. J. (Eds.). (1992). *Therapy as social construction.* London: Sage.

McWhirter, E. H. (1991). Empowerment in counseling. *Journal of Counseling and Development, 69,* 222–227.

McWhirter, E. H. (1994). *Counseling for empowerment.* Alexandria, VA: American Counseling Association.

Mead, G. H. (1934). *Mind, self, and society.* Chicago: University of Chicago Press.

Mednick, M. T. (1991). Currents and futures in American feminist psychology. *Psychology of Women Quarterly, 15,* 611–621.

Meichenbaum, D. (1993). Changing conceptions of cognitive behavior modification retrospect and prospect. *Journal of Consulting and Clinical Psychology, 61,* 202–204.

Miller, J. B. (1986). *Toward a new psychology of women* (2nd ed.). Boston: Beacon Press.

Neimeyer, R. A. (1990). Personal construct psychotherapy. In J. K. Zeig & W. M. Munion (Eds.), *What is psychotherapy?* (pp. 159–164). San Francisco: Jossey-Bass.

Neimeyer, R. A. (1993a). An appraisal of constructivist psychotherapies. *Journal of Consulting and Clinical Psychology, 61,* 221–234.

Neimeyer, R. A. (1993b). Constructivism and the cognitive psychotherapies: Some conceptual and strategic contrasts. *Journal of Cognitive Psychotherapy: An International Quarterly, 7,* 159–171.

Neimeyer, R. A. (1995). Constructivist psychotherapies: Features, foundations, and future directions. In R. A. Neimeyer & M. J. Mahoney (Eds.), *Constructivism in psychotherapy* (pp. 11–38). Washington, DC: American Psychological Association.

Neimeyer, R. A., & Mahoney, M. J (Eds.). (1995). *Constructivism in psychotherapy.* Washington, DC: American Psychological Association.

Padesky, C. A. (1993, September 24). *Socratic questioning: Changing minds or guiding discovery?* Keynote address delivered at the European Congress of Behavioural and Cognitive Therapies, London.

Padesky, C. A., & Greenberger, D. (1995). *Clinician's guide to mind over mood.* New York: Guilford.

Pedersen, P. B. (1991). Multiculturalism as a generic approach to counseling. *Journal of Counseling and Development, 70,* 6–12.

Polkinghorne, D. E. (1991). Narrative and self-concept. *Journal of Narrative and Life History, 1,* 135–154.

Ponterroto, J. G., Casas, M. J., Suzuki, L. A., & Alexander, C. M. (Eds.) (1995). *Handbook of multicultural counseling.* Thousand Oaks, CA: Sage.

Prilleltensky, I. (1990). Psychology and the status quo. *American Psychologist, 44,* 795–802.

Ramirez, M. (1991). *Psychotherapy and counseling with minorities: A cognitive approach to individual and cultural differences.* New York: Pergamon.

Randall, E. J. (1994). Cultural relativism in cognitive therapy with disadvantaged African American women. *Journal of Cognitive Psychotherapy: An International Quarterly, 8,* 195–207.

Riger, S. (1992). Epistemological debates, feminist voices: Science, social values, and the study of women. *American Psychologist, 47,* 730–740.

Root, M. P. P. (1992). Reconstructing the impact of trauma on personality. In S. Brown & M. Ballou (Eds.), *Personality and psychopathology: Feminist reappraisals* (pp. 229–265). New York: Guilford.

Rosen, H. (1996). Meaning-making narratives: Foundations for constructivist and social constructionist psychotherapies. In H. Rosen and K. T. Kuehlwein (Eds.), *Constructing realities: Meaning-making perspectives for psychotherapists* (pp. 3–51). San Francisco: Jossey-Bass.

Rosen, H., & Kuehlwein, K. T. (1996). *Constructing realities: Meaning-making perspectives for psychotherapists.* San Francisco: Jossey-Bass.

Rosenau, P. M. (1992). *Post-modernism and the social sciences: Insights, inroads, and intrusions.* Princeton, NJ: Princeton University Press.

Rosenau, P. M. (1992). *Post-modernism and the social sciences: Insights, inroads, and intrusions.* Princeton, NJ: Princeton University Press.

Russell, R. L., & van den Broek (1992). Changing narrative schemas in psychotherapy. *Psychotherapy, 29,* 344–354.

Sampson, E. E. (1981). Cognitive psychology as ideology. *American Psychologist, 36,* 30–743.

Sampson, E. E. (1988). The debate on individualism: Indigenous psychologies of the individual and their role in personal and societal functioning. *American Psychologist, 43,* 15–22.

Sarbin, T. R. (Ed.). (1986). *Narrative psychology: The storied nature of human conduct.* New York: Praeger.

Sarbin, T. R., & Allen, V. L. (1968). Role Theory. In G. Lindzey and E. Aronson (Eds.), *Handbook of social psychology* (Vol. I, pp. 488–567). Reading, MA: Addison-Wesley.

Scarr, S. (1985). Constructing psychology: Making facts and fables for our time. *American Psychologist, 40,* 499–512.

Shotter, J., & Gergen, K. J. (Eds.). (1989). *Texts of identity.* Newbury Park, CA: Sage.

Shweder, R. A., & Bourne, E. (1982). Does the concept of the person vary cross-culturally? In A. J. Marsella & G. White (Eds.), *Cultural concepts of mental health and therapy* (pp. 97–137). Boston: Reidel.

Steenbarger, B. N. (1991). All the world is not a stage: Emerging contextualist perspectives in counseling and development. *Journal of Counseling and Development, 70,* 288–296.

Steenbarger, B. N. (1993). A multicontextual model of counseling: Bridging brevity and diversity. *Journal of Counseling and Development, 72,* 8–14.

Steier, F. (Ed.). (1991). *Research and reflexivity.* Newbury Park, CA: Sage

Sue, D. W., & Sue, D. (1990). *Counseling the culturally different: Theory and practice.* New York: Wiley.

Sue, S., & Zane, N. (1987). The role of culture and cultural techniques in psychotherapy: A critique and reformulation. *American Psychologist, 42,* 37–45.

Teasdale, J. D. (1996). Clinically relevant theory: Integrating clinical insight with cognitive science. In Paul M. Salkovskis (Ed.), *Frontiers of cognitive therapy* (pp. 26–47). New York: Guilford.

Teasdale, J. D., & Barnard, P. J. (1993). *Affect, cognition, and change: Re-modeling depressive thought.* Hove, England: Lawrence Erlbaum.

Terrell, C. J., & Lyddon, W. J. (1996). Narrative and psychotherapy. *Journal of Constructivist Psychology, 9,* 27–44.

Valsiner, J. (1991). Construction of the mental: From the 'cognitive revolution' to the study of development. *Theory & Psychology, 1,* 477–494.

Walker, L. E. A. (1989). Psychology and the violence against women. *American Psychologist, 44,* 695–702.

Wartenberg, T. E. (1988). The concept of power in feminist theory. *Praxis International, 8,* 301–316.

PART II

Applications

CHAPTER 11

Empirically Supported Treatment for Panic Disorder: Research, Theory, and Application of Cognitive Behavioral Therapy

William C. Sanderson and Simon A. Rego

Panic disorder (PD) (with and without agoraphobia) is a debilitating condition with an estimated lifetime prevalence of 1.5% (American Psychiatric Association, 1994). Approximately twice as many women as men suffer from PD. Although PD typically first appears between late adolescence and early adulthood, it can also begin in childhood and in later life. Though data on the course of PD are lacking, retrospective patient accounts indicate that PD appears to be a chronic condition that waxes and wanes in severity. Unfortunately, the chronicity of the disorder may be due, in part, to the lack of appropriate treatment.

As defined in the *Diagnostic and Statistical Manual of Mental Disorders* (DSM-IV) (American Psychiatric Association, 1994) the essential feature of PD is recurrent, unexpected panic attacks. A panic attack is defined as a discrete period of intense fear or discomfort that develops abruptly and reaches a peak within ten minutes and is accompanied by at least four of the following thirteen somatic and cognitive symptoms: shortness of breath, dizziness, palpitations, trembling, sweating, feeling of choking, nausea or abdominal distress, depersonalization, paresthesias (numbness/tingling), flushes or chills, chest pain, fear of dying, fear of going crazy or of doing something uncontrolled. To warrant the diagnosis of PD in accordance with the *DSM-IV,* the individual must experience at least two unexpected panic attacks followed by at least 1 month of concern about having another panic attack. The frequency of attacks varies widely and ranges from several attacks daily to only a handful of attacks per year.

Although community estimates suggest that approximately one half of individuals who experience PD also develop agoraphobia, the prevalence of agoraphobia is much higher in clinical samples. In fact, the vast majority of PD patients seeking treatment present with agoraphobia. The *DSM-IV* defines agoraphobia as the experience of anxiety in situations in which escape might be difficult or where help may not be immediately available in the event of the occurrence of a panic attack. Common agoraphobic places and situations include airplanes, buses, trains, elevators, being alone, and being in a crowd of people, among others. As a result of the anxiety experienced in these situations, individuals often develop phobic avoidance resulting in a constricted lifestyle. The severity of agoraphobia may range from relatively mild (e.g., traveling unaccompanied when necessary but typically avoiding traveling alone) to quite severe (e.g., being unable to leave home alone).

THE COGNITIVE MODEL OF PANIC DISORDER

The cognitive model of PD proposes that panic attacks occur when individuals perceive certain somatic sensations as considerably more dangerous than they truly are and interpret them to mean that they are about to experience sudden, imminent disaster (Clark, 1986). For example, individuals may develop a panic attack if they misinterpret heart palpitations as a signal of impending heart attack or jittery, shaky feelings as an indication that they will lose control or go crazy.

Clark (1986) believes that these "catastrophic misinterpretations" may arise not only from fear but also from a variety of other emotions such as anger or from other stimuli (e.g., caffeine, exercise). The vicious cycle culminating in a panic attack develops when a stimulus perceived as threatening creates feelings of apprehension. If the somatic sensations that accompany this state of apprehension are catastrophically misinterpreted, the individual experiences a further increase in apprehension, elevated somatic sensations, and so on, until a full-blown panic attack occurs.

PD patients themselves report having thoughts of imminent danger during their panic attacks (e.g., heart attacks, insanity) *and* report that these thoughts typically occur after they notice specific bodily sensations which provides convincing support for the cognitive model of panic. Other evidence in support of Clark's (1986) hypothesis is the finding that laboratory-provoked attacks may lead to similar physiological sensations in PD patients and normal controls, but only PD patients who catastrophically misinterpret these sensations will go on to develop panic attacks (cf. Sanderson & Wetzler, 1990). Furthermore, only patients who develop panic attacks in the laboratory following the administration of a panicogenic substance report fears of going crazy or losing self-control. Additional support for Clark's cognitive model comes from studies demonstrating that panic attacks can be alleviated with cognitive techniques, such as cognitive restructuring, which attempt to challenge and substitute catastrophic misinterpretations with rational thoughts.

EMPIRICALLY SUPPORTED TREATMENT COMPONENTS

The following psychological interventions have been shown to be effective, either alone or in a "package" of treatment strategies, for PD in controlled research studies (for a review of empirically supported psychological treatments, see Woody & Sanderson, 1998).

Psychoeducation

By the time PD patients consult with a mental health professional, they typically have been to many different doctors without receiving a clear diagnosis and explanation of PD. In the absence of such information, these patients often imagine that they are going to die, go crazy, or lose control. In almost all cases, they suspect that the doctor has overlooked some life-threatening physical condition that would account for their symptomatology. Therefore, the psychoeducation phase consists of a didactic presentation about PD, within the framework of the cognitive behavioral model of panic (see Barlow & Craske, 1989).

During the initial sessions, anxiety, panic, and agoraphobia are defined. Each symptom is identified as a feature of PD and shown to be harmless. Common myths about the danger of panic attacks (e.g., that panic attacks are a sign of an undetected brain tumor, that palpitations cause heart attacks, that hyperventilation leads to fainting) are debunked. The development of the disorder is understood as a psychological response to stress, and avoidance behavior and anticipatory anxiety are viewed as ways to ward off a recurrence of the panic attacks.

Written materials such as pamphlets and books are valuable educational tools because they may be reread whenever the patient desires. We recommend several excellent self-help books or Web sites that offer simple, supportive information about PD (e.g., Barlow & Craske, 1989; Burns, 1989; Wilson, 1987; National institute of Mental Health [NIMH] (2001). In addition, we encourage patients to join the Anxiety Disorders Association of America (6000 Executive Blvd., Rockville, MD 20852; www.adaa.org). For a nominal fee, patients receive a bimonthly newsletter providing self-help tips and educational information (e.g., latest research findings) and have access to many other valuable resources. In this way, psychoeducation becomes an ongoing venture for the patient and not just one component of the therapy.

Cognitive Restructuring

The cognitive restructuring component of cognitive behavioral therapy (CBT) derives from Beck's seminal work on how faulty information-processing may underlie anxiety and related dysfunctional behaviors (Beck & Emery, 1985). Therapeutic change is achieved as these faulty cognitions (i.e., thoughts, beliefs, and assumptions) are identified and then subjected to rigorous reality-testing.

The first step is to help the patient identify how certain cognitions accentuate or provoke panic. This is done by examining in retrospect the thoughts, beliefs, and assumptions elicited during a typical panic or anxiety episode. The first and most recent panic attacks are vividly remembered, and a detailed discussion of those two experiences is a useful place to begin this examination. Through a series of questions, the therapist tries to determine the patient's idiosyncratic panic sequence and to uncover unrealistic catastrophic thoughts. Under such questioning, the validity of these cognitions are implicitly and explicitly challenged.

A typical panic sequence follows this line:

1. I was sitting in a meeting at work.
2. I noticed my heart began to beat faster (physical symptom).
3. I assumed these palpitations were the early signs of a panic attack, and that I would lose control and start to yell. Everyone would think I was crazy! (catastrophic thought).
4. I became even more anxious, worried about losing control, and started to perspire profusely (escalation of physical symptom).

5. I excused myself from the meeting (escape and avoidance).

6. I felt depressed and discouraged because I couldn't even handle an innocuous work meeting (hopelessness).

This description of a typical panic sequence reveals the PD patient's interior monologue. In therapy, it is necessary to make these private thoughts explicit because most patients are unaware of their own thinking. For the most part, people process information automatically and stimuli are interpreted rapidly. There is also a tendency to deny catastrophic ways of thinking because these beliefs seem so incredible once the panic attack has subsided. The therapeutic setting should promote the patient's sense of comfort and acceptance in order to facilitate disclosure. In addition, we recommend that patients self-monitor their cognitions *during* episodes of panic. A written numbered format may be used, as in the earlier example of a typical sequence. After several sessions of reviewing these panic-related cognitions, a clear panic sequence emerges, and patients begin to appreciate the role cognitions play.

Once the patient becomes aware of the importance of their cognitions in eliciting and fueling their panic attacks, they are in a position to reevaluate the validity of these cognitions and ultimately to challenge them. In particular, catastrophic misinterpretations of panic-related somatic cues are targeted (Clark, 1986). But other common misinterpretations include the overestimation of the consequences of panic (e.g., public humiliation, losing one's job, interpersonal rejection).

We use a "thought record" to quickly identify the patient's thoughts, examine their validity, and challenge the patient to respond with more rational thoughts (cf. Sanderson & McGinn, 1997). The patient is provided with a list of 10 cognition distortions, misinterpretations, or types of illogic as defined by Burns (1989). By identifying distortions, the patient is able to correct the illogical conclusion by substituting a more rational response. It is important to note that cognitive restructuring is not "positive thinking," but instead is a focus on teaching people to think realistically (i.e., to weigh the evidence).

The final phase of cognitive restructuring is to "de-catastrophize" the situation with the patient, especially when dealing with agoraphobic avoidance. This is easily accomplished through a series of questions: What if your worst fears came true? Would it really be as bad as you imagine? Consider a patient who believes she will have a panic attack on a plane, causing her to scream wildly and try to escape. In fact, if her worst fears were realized and she did have a panic attack, the most likely outcome would be a feeling of great discomfort, not screaming, attempts to escape, and embarrassment. De-catastrophizing greatly reduces the patient's need to avoid panic-related situations.

Respiratory Control

Respiratory control helps the patient regain a sense of control over the somatic features of panic and anxiety. Patients are taught a method of breathing that increases relaxation and prevents hyperventilation (Clark et al., 1985). Hyperventilation initiates a cascade of somatic symptoms such as dizziness, chest pain, breathlessness, and parasthesias, which culminate in panic. These symptoms instill a frightening sense that one's body is out of control.

Under stress and anxiety, respiration rate often increases, characterized by the use of chest muscles and short, shallow breaths. To combat this tendency, the patient is taught diaphragmatic breathing (breathing that involves in and out movement of the abdomen, not the chest) at a regular rate (approximately 12 breaths per minute). This exercise is then practiced outside of the session in many different situations. The patients learn to control their breathing quickly, and come to recognize that this is an effective strategy which they can rely on in panic-provoking situations.

Relaxation Training

Relaxation training is a progressive muscle exercise that is also intended to help the patient gain a greater sense of control over their body. It is practiced daily as a way to identify and decrease tension that might otherwise escalate into a full-blown panic attack. The basic technique involves tensing and relaxing muscles to achieve a more serene state. Specific step-by-step details regarding this exercise may be found in an excellent text by Barlow and Cerny (1988).

Visualization

In therapy, discussion of anxiety-provoking situations and experiences is all too often devoid of the vivid images, associations, and emotion necessary to foster real change. Visualization is meant to enhance this dialogue. When patients close their eyes and imagine such situations, they are often flooded with anxiety. By confronting such anxiety-provoking situations in the mind's eye, patients learn how to cope before having to confront those situations for real.

The therapist helps the patient to visualize the situation in as much detail as possible. As the patient describes the image, the therapist asks relevant questions about the associated thoughts and feelings. This is meant to elaborate the image, but it is also a useful assessment (reporting on cognitions and emotions in an imagined situation in the present is usually more accurate than recalling cognitions and emotions in a real situation from the past). In time, the patient is asked to visualize effective coping techniques and responses. In this way, visualization serves as an inoculation—if patients can handle small amounts of manufactured anxiety, they will be better prepared to handle anxiety in a natural setting.

Exposure

Exposure is the final component of CBT in which the patient confronts anxiety-and panic-provoking stimuli. These phobic stimuli may be external situations or internal sensations (i.e., interoceptive desensitization). By repeatedly facing their anxiety in a structured situation, the patient learns to develop appropriate coping mechanisms and becomes further inoculated.

Based on the patient's individualized hierarchy of feared situations, he is exposed to each of these situations in a progressive, systematic fashion, where the therapist guides the patient to use coping skills when confronting anxiety-provoking situations. Similarly, interoceptive exposure is based on the patient's individualized hierarchy of feared internal sensations (e.g., dizziness, palpitations). Exposure to these sensations may be achieved using idiosyncratic methods, such as overbreathing, spinning, and physical exertion (e.g., ride an excercycle for 2 minutes).

The use of a hierarchy of least feared to most feared stimuli allows the therapy to progress and build on past accomplishments. The patient first learns to cope with mildly anxiety-provoking situations and later faces the more difficult situations. Facing anxiety within a supportive therapeutic setting helps the patient to utilize newly developed coping skills. The patient learns to tolerate anxiety without the need to escape. This lesson is passed on from one anxiety-provoking situation to the next.

As always, practice between sessions is expected and essential for rapid progress. We encourage patients to confront phobic stimuli at least three times during the week between sessions. First, the patient completes the exposure exercise with the assistance of the therapist, such as inducing heart palpitations by walking up and down stairs for 3 minutes, and later practicing the exercise at home. Patients' self-confidence soars as they realize that the therapist has confidence in their ability to handle this formerly anxiety-provoking experience on their own.

REVIEW OF EMPIRICAL SUPPORT OF CBT FOR PD

A significant amount of research exists supporting the efficacy of CBT for PD. The results of several major studies, nearly all of which can be classified as type 1, will be reviewed in this section. A summary of these results can be found in Table 11.1.

Beck, Sokol, Clark, Berchick, and Wright (1992) examined short-term and long-term effects of a focused (12-week) cognitive therapy (CT) for panic disorder.[1] The authors also used an 8-week brief supportive psychotherapy (BST) group[2] as a comparison group. Using clinician ratings and patient self-ratings, the authors found that focused CT accomplished *significantly greater reductions* in both panic symptoms and general anxiety after only 8 weeks of treatment. Both groups experienced a significant decline in their depression scores over the first 8 weeks of treatment. At the 8–week point, 71% of the CT group were panic-free, compared to 25% of the BST group. After 12 weeks, 94% of the CT group were panic-free. At a 1-year follow-up, 87% of the CT group remained panic-free and continued to have significantly lower scores[3] on all of the assessment measures used in the study (e.g., BDI, BAI, Specific Fear Inventory). The authors concluded that panic attacks are particularly sensitive to cognitive (or cognitive-behavioral) interventions and that because of the relatively low rate of relapse and absence of side effects, CT offers a promising, nonpharmacological alternative for the treatment of PD.

Black, Wesner, Bowers, and Gabel (1993) used a placebo-controlled, double-blind design to compare fluvoxamine, CT[4], and placebo in the treatment of PD. Using both completer and endpoint analyses, the fluvoxamine group showed significantly greater improvement than both the CT and placebo groups on the Clinical Anxiety Scale (CAS) and Clinical Global Impression (CGI) ratings by week 8.[5] When using an endpoint analysis, both the fluvoxamine and the CT group showed a greater reduction than the placebo group in the mean panic-attack severity score at weeks 4 and 8. When using completer analysis, however, only fluvoxamine was superior to placebo. In addition, significantly more subjects in the fluvoxamine group achieved panic-free status—and this finding was apparent after only 4 weeks of treatment. While the CT subjects also showed some improvement (see the following), they were not statistically better off than the placebo subjects.

Support found for use of CT for panic disorder includes the fact that the frequency of spontaneous and situational panic attacks decreased in 93% of subjects treated with CT, with 53% of subjects achieving panic-free status by week 8. Subjects treated with CT also showed significant

Table 11.1 Review of Empirical Support of CBT for PD

Study	CBT Components	Efficacy of CT	Comments
Beck, Sokol, Clark, Berchick, & Wright (1992)	Cognitive strategies	At 8 weeks: 71% of the CT subjects were panic-free. At 1 year (follow-up) 87% of the CT subjects were panic free.	The focused CT group achieved significantly greater reductions in panic symptoms and general anxiety after 8 weeks of treatment than did a group receiving a brief supportive psychotherapy.
Black, Wesner, Bowers, & Gabel (1993)	Reproducing symptoms using various procedures, correcting misattributions, breathing exercises, positive affirmation statements, refocusing techniques; application of techniques in vivo	At 4 weeks: 40% of the CT subjects were rated moderately improved or better, and 25% of the CT subjects were free of panic. At 8 weeks: the frequency of spontaneous and situational panic-attacks decreased in 93% of subjects given CT, with 53% of the CT subjects being panic free.	Fluvoxamine was found to be superior to CT on many variables and produced improvement earlier than CT. The CT group showed improvement, but this did not differ significantly from a placebo group for most comparisons.
Clark, Salkovskis, Hackmann, Middleton, Anastasiades, & Gelder (1994)	Cognitive procedures: identifying and challenging misinterpretations, substituting more realistic interpretations,	At 3 months: 90% of the CT subjects were panic-free and 80% reached high end-state functioning.	At 3 months: CT was superior to AR and imipramine; AR and imipramine were not significantly different from each other; CT

Table 11.1 (*Continued*)

Study	CBT Components	Efficacy of CT	Comments
Clark et al. (*continued*)	Behavioral procedures: Inducing feared sensations, stopping safety behaviors	At 6 months: 75% of the CT subjects were panic-free, and 65% reached high end-state functioning. At 15 months: 85% of the CT subjects were panic-free, and 70% reached high end-state functioning.	produced a significantly greater number of subjects who were panic-free and had reached high end-state functioning than AR or imipramine; there were no significant differences between any of the groups on the BDI. At 6 months: There were no significant differences between CT and imipramine, and both were superior to AR; CT and imipramine did not differ in number of subjects who were panic-free or had reached high end-state functioning; CT and imipramine were both superior to AR on the BDI. At 15 months: CT was again superior to AR and imipramine, with AR and imipramine not differing from each other; CT was superior to AR on number of subjects who were panic-free and

Table 11.1 (*Continued*)

Study	CBT Components	Efficacy of CT	Comments
Clark et al. (*continued*)			had reached high end-state functioning, but was not significantly different from imipramine.
Côté, Gauthier, Laberge, Cormier, & Plamondon (1994)	(1) Presentation of treatment rationale and information about PD rationale and information about PD (2) Training in anxiety-management techniques, progressive muscle relaxation, distraction strategies, and coping self-statements (3) Cognitive therapy (4) Exposure to internal anxiety cues and panic symptoms (5) Exposure to external anxiety cues	At posttreatment: 82% in the reduced therapist group and 90% in the therapist directed group were panic-free.

At 6 months: 91% in the reduced therapist group and 90% in the therapist-directed group were panic-free.

At 12 months: 91% in the reduced therapist and 100% in the therapist-directed group were panic-free. | This study lends support to the assertion that PD can be successfully treated with CBT, using either reduced therapist contact or a therapist-directed approach.

Both procedures can have long-lasting effects. |
| Craske, Brown and Barlow (1991) | The AR condition involved training in progressive muscle relaxation, followed by its application to items from an | At 6 months (excluding dropouts): 22% of the AR, 71% of the IE+C, and 83% of the combination groups achieved | |

Table 11.1 (*Continued*)

Study	CBT Components	Efficacy of CT	Comments
Craske et al. (*continued*)	individualized hierarchy of anxiety-producing situations.	panic-free status and high end-state functioning.	Panic attacks were more effectively controlled by interoceptive exposure and cognitive restructuring treatments than by relaxation training.
	The IE+C condition consisted of identification and challenging of anxiety-provoking thoughts, breathing retraining, and the application of cognitive and breathing skills to a hierarchy of anxiety-provoking items.	At 6 months (including dropouts): 14% of the AR, 62.5% of the IE+C, and 50% of the combination groups achieved panic-free and high end-state functioning	
		At 24 months (excluding dropouts): 56% of the AR, 87% of the IE+C, and 60% of the combination groups were panic-free and 44%, 53% and 50% of the AR, IE+C, and combination groups, respectively, reached high end-state functioning.	
		At 24 months (including dropouts): 36% of the AR, 81% of the IE+C, and 43% of the combination groups were panic-	

Table 11.1 (*Continued*)

Study	CBT Components	Efficacy of CT	Comments
Craske et al. (*continued*)		free and 29%, 50% and 36% of the AR, IE+C, and combination groups, respectively, reached high end-state functioning.	
Craske, Maidenberg, & Bystritsky (1991)	4 sessions of CBT: (1) Education about the nature of anxiety and panic, the physiology underlying panic attack symptoms, and the principles of cognitive restructuring (2) Continuation of cognitive restructuring and the introduction of breathing retraining (3) Continuation of cognitive restructuring and the introduction of interoceptive exposure (4) Review of the concepts and skills learned in the first three sessions	At post treatment: 53% of the CBT subjects reported no panic attacks, and 38% of the CBT subjects achieved clinically significant change.	Cognitive-behavioral therapy led to significant reductions in worry about the recurrence of panic and in the overall rating of phobic distress. Nondirective supportive therapy did not produce any significant effects.

Table 11.1 (*Continued*)

Study	CBT Components	Efficacy of CT	Comments
Klosko, Barlow, Tassinari, & Cerny (1990)	Rationale and education about panic disorder, with an emphasis on exposure to interoceptive cues; cognitive approaches, progressive muscle relaxation training, and respiration training	At post (for completers): 87% of the CBT subjects were free of panic attacks.	CBT was significantly more effective than both placebo and wait-list conditions on most measures. Alprazolam did not differ significantly from either the CBT or placebo conditions. Alprazolam may work more quickly than CBT, but may also interfere with the effects of CBT treatment.
Öst, Westling, & Hellström (1993)	AR: description and analysis, various forms of relaxation training, and a review Exposure: gradual training in phobic situations (included an introduction and analysis, instructions for coping with panic during exposure, and a summary session)	Clinically significant improvement was fulfilled by 87% of the AR, 80% of the E, and 60% of the CT subjects at the end of treatment and by 85% of the AR, 69% of the E, and 67% of the CT subjects at follow-up.	All three treatments yielded significant improvements that were maintained at follow-up. Between-group differences were observed on only two measures, with both favoring AR over CT.

Table 11.1 (*Continued*)

Study	CBT Components	Efficacy of CT	Comments
Öst et al. (*continued*)	CT: rationale and analysis, developing positive self-instructions and cognitive coping procedures, attribution training, cognitive restructuring of images and attitudes, and a summary		
Shear, Pilkonis, Cloitre, & Leon (1994)	An explanation of an ethological model of panic.	At post: 66% of the CBT subjects were free of panic for 2 weeks, but 10% of the CBT subjects had experienced four or more panic episodes.	Posttreatment and 6-month follow-up assessments revealed a good response to both treatments.
	Breathing retraining, progressive muscle relaxation, identification of cognitive errors, exposure to interoceptive cues, exposure to agoraphobic situations.	At 6 months 75% of the CBT subjects were panic-free.	A high rate of panic remission and significant improvement in associated symptoms was observed for subjects in each treatment group.
			The results raise questions about the specificity of CBT.
Telch, Lucas, Schmidt, Hanna, Jaimez, & Lucas (1993)	(1) Education and corrective information about panic (2) Cognitive therapy techniques aimed at helping to identify, monitor, and alter faulty	At posttreatment: the mean recovery rate was 81% for the CBT subjects versus 30.5% for untreated controls.	CBT is a viable alternative to pharmacotherapy in the treatment of PD.

Table 11.1 *(Continued)*

Study	CBT Components	Efficacy of CT	Comments
	appraisals of threat that contribute to panic occurrence (3) Training in slow diaphragmatic breathing (4) Interoceptive exposure exercises designed to reduce the fear of somatic sensations	Using a more stringent "composite" criteria, 64% of the treated group and 9% of the untreated group evidenced recovery at posttreatment. At 6 months: there was a 79% "mean" recovery rate and a 63% "composite" recovery rate in the treated group.	This study used a more stringent, normative approach which conceptualized recovery as the extent to which subjects attained normal functioning on three clinically relevant dimensions (panic attacks, anxiety, and agoraphobic avoidance). The authors argued that although the more stringent criteria would provide a more conservative estimate of recovery, it would be a more ecologically valid index of recovery.

improvement on several other measures (e.g., CGI and mean weekly panic-attack severity score) at weeks 4 and 8 when compared with the placebo group. Recall, however, that in this study CT was not found to be superior to fluvoxamine on *any* measures, while fluvoxamine was found to be superior to CT on *several* measures. Black et al. (1993) do note that with regard to the efficacy of CT, their findings are in contrast to those of Sokol et al. (1989) and Klosko, Barlow, Tassinari and Cerny (1990). They also acknowledge that their study did not examine relapse or assess for symptoms occurring at the discontinuation of fluvoxamine, and they failed to measure long-term effects. Finally, the authors note that the CT was only provided for 8 weeks (instead of the more typical 12 weeks), which may have had an impact on the efficacy of the treatment.

Clark et al. (1994) compared CT, applied relaxation (AR) and imipramine in the treatment of PD. Subjects in the CT or AR groups received up to 12 sessions in the first 3 months, followed by up to 3 booster sessions in the next 3 months. Subjects in the imipramine group received a similar number of sessions[6] during the first 3 months after which they were maintained at maximum dose for the next 3 months, and then gradually withdrawn from their medication.[7]

Though all three treatments were effective compared to a wait-list, several differences emerged. For example, at 3 months CT was superior to AR and imipramine on most measures, while AR and imipramine were not significantly different from each other. In addition, the proportion of subjects who were panic-free and had achieved high end-state functioning was significantly greater in the CT group than in the AR and imipramine groups. At 6 months the CT and imipramine treatments produced equivalent results on a number of measures (e.g., the number of subjects reaching panic-free status or high end-state functioning), and *both* were superior to AR on several measures (e.g., ACQ, BDI). Between the 6- and 15-month assessments, however, a number of imipramine subjects deteriorated and relapsed[8] as a result, by 15 months CT was again superior to both AR and imipramine (but on fewer measures than at 3 months). At this point, the imipramine and AR groups again were not significantly different from each other. Though CT was superior to AR based on the proportion of subjects achieving panic-free status and high end-state functioning, it was not significantly different than imipramine. It should be noted, however, that imipramine subjects were more likely to relapse and therefore receive additional treatment.

It is interesting to note that Clark et al. (1994) found preliminary evidence for the notion that sustained improvement at the end of treatment is dependent on cognitive change having occurred during the course of treatment. According to the authors, this finding suggests that clinicians should aim not only for panic-free status, but also for a marked cognitive change in the patient. There was a related finding that cognitive measures (e.g., BSQ, ACQ) taken at the end of treatment were significant predictors of outcome at follow-up.

Côté, Gauthier, Laberge, Cormier, and Plamondon (1994) examined reduced therapist contact in the cognitive behavioral treatment of PD. Participants in this study were assigned to 17 weeks of therapist-directed or reduced contact treatment.[9] In the reduced contact group, the treatment was self-administered over 17 weeks with the help of a treatment manual and limited therapist contact[10] at a clinic. Interestingly, *both* treatment procedures produced significant and comparable improvements on *all* of the outcome measures. There was a significant reduction in frequency of panic attacks from pre- to posttreatment, with no significant changes beyond the posttreatment period. There were significant improvements in apprehension of panic attacks from pre- to posttreatment, from posttreatment to 6 months, and from posttreatment to 12-month follow-up. At posttreatment, 90% of subjects in the therapist-directed group and 82% of subjects in the reduced therapist contact group were panic-free. At 6-month follow-up, 90% of subjects in the therapist-directed group and 91% of subjects in the reduced therapist contact group were panic-free. At 12-month follow-up, 100% of subjects in the therapist-directed group and 91% of subjects in the reduced therapist contact group were panic-free.

Significant improvements were also found for both groups on a measure of mobility and agoraphobic cognitions, on a measure of fear of bodily sensations, and on three measures of perceived self-efficacy: perceived self-efficacy to control a panic attack (1) with bodily symptoms, (2) with specific agoraphobic cognitions, and (3) in specific situations. Treatment credibility and expectancies were high in both conditions, and no significant differences were found between the groups. Although there were no significant therapist effects found, reduced therapist contact was significantly more efficient[11] than therapist-directed treatment in reducing the frequency of panic attacks (from pre- to posttreatment, from pretreatment to 6-month follow-up, and from pretreatment to 12-month follow-up). Therefore, Côté et al. (1994) concluded that their findings support the notion that panic disorder can be successfully treated with CBT, using either reduced therapist contact or a therapist-directed approach, and that both procedures can have long-lasting effects.[12] In this case, the therapeutic effects for both treatments were clinically[13] as well as statistically significant. At posttreatment follow-ups, the percentage of panic-free subjects ranged from 82% to 100%, with half of the subjects who were not panic-free after treatment having had only one panic attack during the follow-up assessment period (which was longer than normal in this study).

Craske, Brown, and Barlow (1991) conducted a 2-year follow-up study on the behavioral treatment of PD. Participants were assigned to 15 weekly sessions of applied progressive muscle relaxation (AR), interoceptive exposure plus cognitive restructuring (IE+C), the combination of both AR and IE+C, or a wait list.[14]

Subjects in the AR condition showed a deterioration at six months but the IE+C and combined treatment subjects maintained their treatment gains. In addition, a significantly greater percentage of subjects treated in the IE+C (71%) and combined treatment (83%) conditions were panic-free at the 6-month follow-up relative to AR subjects (22%). This same pattern was also observed when examining the distribution of subjects achieving high end-state functioning.[15] All of the treatment groups maintained their gains at the 24–month follow-up. In addition, the proportion of subjects reporting zero panic attacks was equally distributed across the three treatment conditions (56% of AR, 87% of IE+C, and 60% of the combined treatment subjects). Similarly, the percentage of subjects reaching high end-state functioning was 44%, 53%, 50% for the AR, IE+C, and the combined treatment groups, respectively (which were nonsignificant differences).

Craske et al. (1991) note, however, that a different pattern emerged when dropouts were included.[16] With dropouts included, 36% of the AR subjects, 81% of the IE+C subjects, and 43% of the combined treatment[17] subjects reported zero panic attacks (which was significant). However, no significant differences emerged when dropouts were included in the calculation of the proportion of subjects reaching high end-state functioning. Therefore, based on these results, the authors concluded that panic attacks are controlled more effectively by interoceptive exposure plus cognitive restructuring than by relaxation training. They also found that the therapeutic effects of short-term CBT were maintained for up to 2 years following treatment completion, particularly for subjects receiving IE+C treatment. Finally, the authors noted that while IE+C subjects tended to maintain their posttreatment status, AR subjects tended to deteriorate (and also had high attrition rates).

Craske, Maidenberg, and Bystritsky (1991) compared brief forms of cognitive-behavioral therapy and nondirective supportive treatment (NST) for PD. Participants received four 60–90 minute sessions of either CBT or NST.[18] Though CBT subjects reported less worry at posttreatment than pretreatment, the worry ratings did not change over time for the NST subjects. The number of agoraphobic situations avoided (as rated by the interviewer) did not change over time or differ between groups. In addition, anxiety sensitivity scores were not reduced significantly over time and did not differ between the groups.

At posttreatment, 53% of CBT subjects reported they did not experience panic attacks, compared to 23% of NST subjects (which was a nonsignificant difference). In addition, the daily ratings of anxiety, depression, and worry about panic did not differ over time or between the two groups. Finally, 38% of the subjects treated with CBT had clinically significant[19] results, as compared to 8% of those treated with NST (which "approached" significance). Craske et al. (1991) noted that although 4 weeks of CBT was somewhat effective, it was considerably less effective than what is typically achieved in 12 to 16 weeks of treatment. They also pointed out that NST did not produce *any* significant effects in this study.

Klosko et al. (1990) compared alprazolam with behavior therapy (BT) in the treatment of PD. The BT group received 15 sessions using a detailed CBT manual, which included a rationale and education component, an emphasis on exposure to interoceptive cues, cognitive approaches, progressive relaxation training, and respiration training. At posttreatment, the alprazolam and BT treatment groups were significantly more improved than a wait-list group on measures of panic frequency and intensity. Also of note was the fact that approximately half of those who completed the study achieved high end-state functioning.[20] In addition, the BT group was significantly more improved than the wait-list (both including and without dropouts) on measures of panic and general anxiety. For the alprazolam group, 63% of subjects were panic-free before the taper withdrawal, meaning that slightly fewer alprazolam subjects were experiencing panic attacks in comparison with posttreatment. Of those who still were experiencing panic, however, the attacks were more frequent and more severe in comparison with posttreatment. Therefore, the authors concluded that CBT was an effective treatment for PD. More than 85% of subjects receiving CBT achieved panic-free status for 2 weeks at the end of treatment, which was significantly better than the wait-list and placebo groups. Although this result was not significantly better than the alprazolam group, the alprazolam group itself did not differ from the CBT or the placebo groups.

Öst, Westling, and Hellström (1993) compared applied relaxation (AR), exposure in vivo (E), and CT in the treatment of PD. This study's design allowed the researchers to compare the effects of three different behavioral methods, each of which was focused on a different anxiety component[21] when delivered within the context of self-exposure instructions.

The treatment was comprised of 12 hour-long sessions, delivered weekly. Each treatment program was followed by a maintenance program that ran for 6 months posttreatment (with the therapist having a total of 90 to 120 minutes of phone contact with each patient).

On agoraphobic self-report measures, all three groups improved to approximately the same extent, and all maintained their improvements up to the follow-up assessment. On psychopathology self-report measures, all three groups showed improvement on other phobias, as well as state and trait anxiety and depression, and all three maintained their improvements up to the follow-up assessment. On behavioral test measures conducted at posttreatment, the AR group completed a significantly higher mean number of situations on the individualized behavior test (BAT) than the CT group, while the E group did not differ significantly from either of these groups on this measure. At follow-up the AR maintained its improvement, and the E and CT groups showed further improvements. Results regarding the self-rating of anxiety showed that, on average, subjects managed situation number 3 at pretreatment, situation number 11 at posttreatment, and situation number 12 at follow-up.

On cognitive measures conducted at posttreatment, subjects in all three groups reduced their frequency of negative, self-defeating statements to a large extent, but made only minor changes to their positive and neutral self-statements. Using a ratio of positive self-statements/(positive + negative self-statements), the researchers found that at pretreatment both the AR and E groups had a state of mind (SOM) characterized by negative dialogue, while the CT group had an SOM in the negative monologue range. At posttreatment, the AR group had changed to an SOM of positive monologue, while the E and CT groups were in the positive dialogue range. Finally, the E group remained in the positive dialogue range at the follow-up, the AR group changed to positive dialogue range, and the CT group changed to an internal dialogue of conflict.

Öst et al. (1993) also assessed the degree of clinically significant improvement[22] achieved by the patients. Using the percentage of situations completed in the BAT, criterion was fulfilled by 87% of the AR subjects, 80% of the E subjects, and 60% of the CT subjects at posttreatment, and by 85%, 79%, and 67% of the AR, E, and CT subjects, respectively, at follow-up.[23] There were no relapses at follow-up. Using a score on the Agoraphobia Scale, criterion was fulfilled by 53% of the AR subjects, 47% of the E subjects, and 60% of CT subjects at posttreatment. At follow-up the percentages were 46%, 50%, and 47% for the AR, E, and CT groups respectively (these differences were nonsignificant). Therefore, the researchers concluded that all three treatments yielded significant improvements on all types of measures (i.e., not just self-report, but also on behavioral and cognitive measures, as well as measures of general anxiety and depression). In addition, these effects were maintained at 1-year follow-up. As only a few significant differences were found between the groups, the researchers concluded that the three different methods do about equally well in the treatment of agoraphobic subjects.

Shear, Pilkonis, Cloitre, and Leon (1994) compared CBT with a man-ualized nonprescriptive treatment (NPT) for PD. Subjects were divided into two groups, with each group receiving three sessions of panic-related information[24] followed by 12 sessions of either NPT or a CBT package.[25] The results indicated that 66% of the CBT group and 78% of the NPT group were free of panic for 2 weeks at posttreatment. Of the CBT subjects, however, 10% had experienced four or more panic attacks in the 2 weeks posttreatment versus 0% of the NPT subjects. At 6 months, 75% of subjects in the CBT group and 68% of subjects in the NPT group were free of panic. Both treatments had significant pre-post and pre-follow-up differences on each measure of PD symptoms. No significant differences were found between the groups before treatment, after treatment, or at 6-month follow-up. Therefore, the researchers concluded that CBT and NPT were equivalent in almost every way, and that both treatments were pow-erful in achieving relief of panic symptoms. It is important to note, how-ever, that although the treatment gains were maintained at 6 months for both groups, the CBT subjects showed further improvement in panic symptoms, while the NPT subjects showed a slight decline. NPT sub-jects, however, showed further improvement on several secondary symp-toms in which CBT subjects showed either no or minimal improvement. As a result, the researchers suggested that CBT is *not* necessary to achieve relief of panic disorder symptoms. They also did not find support for the hypothesis that breaking the link between bodily sensations and fear is necessary for panic remission (as predicted by the cognitive model). The researchers suggest that NPT may be the best treatment for subjects with a high need for interpersonal control.

Telch et al. (1993) examined cognitive-behavioral *group* treatment (CBGT) for PD. Subjects were matched for panic severity and then ran-domly assigned to either a treatment or delay group. The treatment took place in small groups of 4 to 6 subjects. The subjects received twelve 90-minute sessions, delivered over an 8-week period. The delay group was measured at weeks 0 and 9, and then offered the experimental treatment. CBT[26] included four major components: education, cognitive therapy tech-niques, training in methods of slow diaphragmatic breathing, and intero-ceptive exposure.[27]

Results at posttreatment indicated that subjects receiving the group CBT treatment displayed marked improvement on *all* major indices of treatment outcome. In addition, treated subjects scored significantly less pathological than untreated controls on all measures, even after controlling for between-group differences at baseline. It should also be noted that though treated subjects achieved highly significant improvement on *all* measures, untreated subjects failed to show significant improvement on *any* measure.

Using clinical significance of treatment gains,[28] it was found that the mean recovery at posttreatment was 81% for the CBT group and 31% for the untreated controls. Using a more stringent "composite" recovery criterion, 64% of treated group and 9% of the untreated group displayed recovery on the three selected measures at posttreatment. Although recovery estimates at a 6–month follow-up were essentially identical to those at posttreatment,[29] two subjects did appear to have relapsed. Therefore, Telch et al. (1993) concluded that this study demonstrated the efficacy of group administered CBT for PD. A complete resolution of panic attacks was observed in more than 85% of the treated cases compared to only 30% for delayed treatment controls. Using a more stringent, normative conceptualization of recovery (which would be more conservative, but also more ecologically valid), between 63% and 80% of the treatment group displayed full recovery, which the authors point out is comparable to results achieved in well-controlled drug trials. Yet, in contrast to the substantial *relapse* observed in drug treatment trials, the recovery estimates at 6-month posttreatment using CBGT were essentially *identical* to those observed at the 8-week posttreatment assessment.

APPLICATION OF CBT FOR PANIC DISORDER: A CASE STUDY

R.L. is a 40-year-old White male who presented with a primary complaint of panic attacks and agoraphobia. He was never married and lives alone in New York City, where he was born. He reported a relatively unremarkable childhood, although he recalled being an "anxious kid" as far back as he could remember. R.L. is a high school graduate and was employed by a bank. He experienced his first panic attack 17 years ago while traveling after his graduation from college. Vacationing in Miami, he experienced several panic attacks and continuous anxiety. He began to fear that he would "go crazy and end up in a psychiatric hospital" from the anxiety, and he quickly returned home. The attacks began to occur more frequently, and R.L. developed moderate agoraphobia (e.g., avoiding trains, elevators, crowded places, traveling beyond a 20-mile radius, social situations). R.L. had received two prior unsuccessful treatments for PD: a 2-year course of traditional psychotherapy 10 years earlier, and more recently a 6-week trial of Paxil. He terminated both treatments and because he believed they were not helping decided he had to accept and live with PD. However, approximately 2 months prior to seeking the current treatment, R.L. watched a television show on PD that discussed new medications and cognitive behavioral treatment. This seemed different from what he had received in the past, and he decided to initiate treatment, receiving a referral to one of us from the Anxiety Disorders Association of America.

Assessment

Following a clinical interview, R.L. was assigned the diagnosis of PD with moderate agoraphobia in accordance with *DSM-IV* criteria. The anxiety symptoms were systematically assessed using the following measures to assess the full range of symptoms (panic, generalized anxiety, depression, phobia, functional impairment): Panic Attack Diary (Barlow & Cerny, 1988), Individualized Fear and Avoidance Hierarchy (Barlow, 1988), Beck Anxiety Inventory (BAI) (Beck, Epstein, & Brown, 1988); Beck Depression Inventory (BDI) (Beck, Steer, & Garbin, 1988); and Sheehan Disability Scale (Leon, Shear, Portera, & Klerman, 1992).

Treatment Implementation

During the second session, I (W.C.S) discussed the diagnostic formulation with R.L., and reviewed relevant problems. I also discussed the treatment components (as described earlier) that would be used and provided a rationale for each. Cognitive behavioral treatment was initiated and during the next session R.L. was given an education about anxiety, PD, and agoraphobia. Surprisingly, despite his substantial history of treatment, he was never formally diagnosed with PD or provided with any information about it, and therefore often feared that he had something worse (e.g., schizophrenia, heart disease). In addition, because of the stigma attached to emotional disorders, he felt it necessary to hide the fact that he had PD, which ultimately led to his living a somewhat isolated lifestyle, not allowing him to develop intimate relationships. The message that PD is a relatively common, well-researched condition that is treatable, and not a precursor to schizophrenia or heart disease, was quite reassuring to him. To bolster the psychoeducation phase, I recommended he read *Don't Panic* (1987) by Reid Wilson and *The Feeling Good Hand-*

book (1990) by David Burns. Both are cognitive-behavior-oriented self-help books that contain a significant amount of information about panic, phobia, and anxiety. Although we are not proponents of self-help books as alternatives to treatment, we do believe they can be effective adjuncts to therapy: They reinforce the information covered within the session, assisting in compliance with exercises outside of sessions; and they provide more extensive information than may be allowed within the therapy session. For example, a detailed explanation of the physiology of anxiety and the biological basis of symptoms may be easier to understand by reading than by hearing an oral explanation in session). R.L. obtained both books early in treatment and found them to be useful adjuncts to the psychotherapy sessions, especially when I would point out relevant chapters corresponding to information covered within the therapy session.

In the next several sessions, R.L. learned strategies to help him reduce his physical arousal (e.g., muscle tension, palpitations, insomnia), including *progressive muscle relaxation* and *deep breathing exercises.* He was instructed to begin using these procedures when he noticed an increase in anxiety as a way to calm his system. To facilitate his utilizing the progressive muscle relaxation at home, we taped the relaxation exercise in session so that he would have my instructions. Deep breathing exercises are intended to facilitate slow, diaphragmatic breathing (10–12 breaths/minute) and decrease the likelihood of hyperventilation that frequently occurs in panic patients during anxiety episodes, which may be responsible for many of the most uncomfortable sensations (e.g., suffocation). Once R.L. was able to master the techniques to lower arousal, we focused on *cognitive restructuring.* With the assistance of the therapist, R.L. learned to identify his catastrophic thoughts. In his case, most of these involved ideas and images that he would go crazy and end up in a psychiatric hospital or have a heart attack during a panic attack. As a result, he often avoided situations where escape was difficult, as he believed that if he was stuck in a situation and experienced a panic attack, it would lead to one of these consequences. We began challenging his catastrophic thoughts in session and generated more realistic thoughts to replace the anxiety provoking ones. In addition, R.L. started using the information he had received about PD to challenge these catastrophic thoughts. In fact, he was able to recall several situations where he was unable to escape and yet realized that the anxiety always passed (e.g., a time he was stuck on a subway train). R.L. noticed that in conjunction with his relaxation exercises, challenging his catastrophic thoughts with more realistic ones resulted in decreasing anxiety and circumventing the panic attacks that were occurring at home.

Although R.L. did not intend to address his agoraphobic avoidance when he entered treatment because he believed his "life was over," the fact that he was able remediate the panic attacks at home led him to reconsider his initial posture. I explained the rationale of *exposure therapy,* used in conjunction with relaxation exercises and cognitive restructuring, and attempted to motivate R.L. in this direction by pointing out that there were many things he wanted to do, such as travel to Florida. I consulted with his physician at this point to explain the process of exposure therapy and determine if there were any medical contraindications. The physician attested that R.L. was extremely healthy and that he had no medical problems and was able to exercise. As a result of R.L.'s longstanding health concerns related to panic (i.e., fear of heart disease), he adopted a lifestyle that resulted in healthier behaviors (eating low-fat food, keeping his weight down, regular exercise). Thus, the next several sessions involved systematic exposure to feared agoraphobic situations (e.g., using express subway trains and buses, going into elevators, going on trips of increasing difficulty and distance: Atlantic City, Philadelphia, and Boston, with the ultimate goal of going to Miami). For the most part, exposure was patient-generated. However, on a few occasions, especially early on in the exposure phase, I accompanied R.L. into an elevator, with his agreement, to facilitate his coping responses in vivo. As is typical, I started with low items on the hierarchy so that the patient could not "fail" (e.g., items that the patient reported avoiding when possible but was able to do if necessary), in order to strengthen coping skills for those times when the anxiety is more overwhelming, as well as to demonstrate the effectiveness of repeatedly facing a situation within a short period of time. This strategy, as is usual, was effective, and repeated exposure to low then high level anxiety-provoking situations resulted in habituation. As a result, there was a significant decrease of agoraphobia and elimination of panic attacks.

Following approximately 20 sessions during which I implemented the psychological interventions spelled out in Barlow and Cerny (1988), R.L. had made substantial progress, as confirmed by readministering the assessment battery described. By this point, R.L. was no longer experiencing panic attacks and was able to travel (e.g., trips to Atlantic City) and to attend social functions. Clearly, there was a substantial increase in the quality of R.L.'s life as a result of the treatment of his PD. Treatment was maintained for 7 additional months on a once a month basis following the acute phase of treatment to facilitate his movement through the entire fear and avoidance hierarchy and continue to address residual generalized anxiety. Once he reached the endpoint, treatment was terminated.

NOTES

1. An extension of Sokol, Beck, Greenberg, Wright, and Berchick (1989).

2. Based on Carl Rogers' nondirective therapy.

3. Compared to their pretreatment scores.

4. The CT was based on the treatment manual of Clark and Salkovskis (1986), but modified from a 12-week format to an 8-week format.

5. At week 8, 90% of fluvoxamine subjects showed at least moderate improvement, compared to 50% of CT subjects and 39% of placebo subjects.

6. The CT and AR sessions were 1 hour long, however, while the imipramine sessions were 25 minutes long.

7. During medication withdrawal subjects were seen occasionally to monitor for withdrawal symptoms.

8. Recall that medications were withdrawn at 6 months.

9. All subjects received the CBT for PD adapted from Barlow and Cerny (1988), Beck (1988) and Clark and Salkovskis (1989).

10. Therapist contact was 7 irregularly scheduled meetings at the clinic (75 min average) and 8 brief, irregularly scheduled telephone consultations (11 min average).

11. Percentage of improvement on each panic attack variable divided by the total therapist contact time.

12. In terms of apprehension of panic attacks, therapist-directed treatment may lead to a more rapid decrease in fear of panic attacks than a reduced therapist contact procedure.

13. To meet the status of "clinically improved," subjects had to be panic free for 6 weeks and for the whole period to have had none or only some slight apprehension of panic attacks; not to have engaged in any avoidance behavior whatsoever, to have been only slightly frightened by sensations associated with autonomic arousal; and never or rarely to have thought of the negative consequences of experiencing anxiety.

14. Treatment manuals were used for each of the active conditions.

15. High end-state functioning was defined as achieving a rating of clinical severity less than or equal to 2 (i.e., mild) and zero panic attacks in the past month.

16. It was assumed that dropouts were continuing to panic.

17. Interestingly, this may suggest that adding relaxation to IE+C procedures may have a detrimental effect (i.e., dilution).

18. Both treatments were manualized. The CBT was a condensed version of exposure-cognitive treatment by Barlow et al. (1989), while the NST was modeled on nonprescriptive therapy by Shear et al. (1994).

19. Clinical significance was defined as the number of subjects who, after completion of therapy, (a) declined to enter the medication trial because they no longer wanted treatment and/or (b) did not meet the criteria for PD and were therefore not eligible for the medication trial.

20. High end-state functioning was defined by achieving a rating of less than 4 (non-clinical severity) on the ADIS-R.

21. Exposure in vivo (which focuses on avoidance behaviors), AR (which focuses on physiological reactions), and cognitive treatment (which focuses on negative cognitions).

22. Using the method described by Jacobson, Follette, and Revenstorf (1984).

23. These differences at posttreatment and follow-up were nonsignificant.

24. To ensure credibility of control treatment necessary for meaningful comparisons. However, as this is typical in CBT, it may have confounded the results.

25. While a manual was used for each condition, it should be noted that when treatment adherence was checked, the CBT group received a rating of only 4.5 (out of 8).

26. Derived from PCT by Craske and Barlow (1990).

27. The protocol was, of course, modified to allow for group administration. In addition, two of the components (education and interoceptive exposure) were expanded in an attempt to increase the potency of treatment.

28. Measured in two ways in this study: (1) as an average across the five major clinical outcome dimensions of the disorder; and (2) as a proportion of subjects who attained scores in the normal range on all three of the following measures: panic attacks, anxiety, and avoidance.

29. Suggesting a general trend for maintenance of improvement.

REFERENCES

American Psychiatric Association. (1994). *Diagnostic and statistical manual (4th ed. rev.).* Washington, DC: American Psychiatric Press.

Barlow, D. H. (1988). *Anxiety and its disorders.* New York: Guilford Press.

Barlow, D. H., & Cerny, J. (1988). *Psychological treatment of panic.* New York: Guilford Press.

Barlow, D. H., & Craske, M. G. (1989). *Mastery of your anxiety and panic.* Albany, NY: Graywind.

Beck, A. T. (1988). Cognitive approaches to panic disorder: Theory and therapy. In S. Rachman & J. D. Maser (Eds.), *Panic: Psychological perspectives* (pp. 91–109). Hillsdale, NJ: Lawrence Erlbaum Associates, Inc.

Beck, A. T., & Emery, G. (1985). *Anxiety disorders and phobias: A cognitive perspective.* New York: Basic Books.

Beck, A. T., Epstein, N., & Brown, G. (1988). An inventory for measuring clinical anxiety. *Journal of Consulting and Clinical Psychology, 56,* 893–897.

Beck, A. T., Sokol, L., Clark, D. A., Berchick, R., & Wright, F. (1992). A crossover study of focused cognitive therapy for panic disorder. *American Journal of Psychiatry, 149,* 778–783.

Beck, A. T., Steer, R. A., & Garbin, M. G. (1988). Psychometric properties of the Beck depression inventory: Twenty-five years later. *Clinical Psychology Review, 8,* 77–100.

Black, D. W., Wesner, R., Bowers, W., & Gabel, J. (1993). A comparison of fluvoxamine, cognitive therapy, and placebo in the treatment of panic disorder. *Archives of General Psychiatry, 50,* 44–50.

Burns, D. D. (1989). *The feeling good handbook: Using the new mood therapy in everyday life.* New York: Morrow.

Clark, D. M. (1986). A cognitive approach to panic. *Behaviour Research and Therapy, 24,* 461–471.

Clark, D. M., Salkovskis, P. M., Hackmann, A., Middleton, H., Anastasiades, P., & Gelder, M. (1994). A comparison of cognitive therapy, applied relaxation, and imipramine in the treatment of panic disorder. *British Journal of Psychiatry, 164,* 759–769.

Côté, G., Gauthier, J. G., Laberge, B., Cormier, H. J., & Plamondon, J. (1994). Reduced therapist contact in the cognitive behavioral treatment of panic disorder. *Behavior Therapy, 25,* 123–145.

Craske, M. G., Brown, T. A., & Barlow, D. H. (1991). Behavioral treatment of panic disorder: A two-year follow-up. *Behavior Therapy, 22,* 289–304.

Craske, M. G., Maidenberg, E., & Bystritsky, A. (1991). Brief cognitive-behavioral versus nondirective therapy for panic disorder. *Journal of Behavior Therapy and Experimental Psychiatry, 26,* 113–120.

Jacobson, N. S., Follette, W. C., & Revenstorf, D. (1984). Psychotherapy outcome research: Methods for reporting variability and evaluating clinical significance. *Behavior Therapy, 15,* 336–352.

Klosko, J. S., Barlow, D. H., Tassinari, R., & Cerny, J. A. (1990). A comparison of alprazolam and behavior therapy in treatment of panic disorder. *Journal of Consulting and Clinical Psychology, 58*(1), 77–84.

Leon, A. C., Shear, M. K., Portera, L., & Klerman, G. L. (1992). Assessing impairment in patients with panic disorder: The Sheehan disability scale. *Social Psychiatry and Psychiatric Epidemiology, 27,* 78–82.

National Institute of Mental Health (9-13-2001). Understanding Panic Disorder [brochure]. Available Internet: http://www.nimh.nih.gov/anxiety/upd.cfm

Öst, L. G., Westling, B. E., & Hellström, K. (1993). Applied relaxation, exposure in vivo and cognitive methods in the treatment of panic disorder with agoraphobia. *Behavior Research and Therapy, 31,* 383–394.

Salkovskis, P. M., & Clark, D. M. (1991). Cognitive therapy for panic attacks. *Journal of Cognitive Psychotherapy, 5,* 215–216.

Sanderson, W. C., & McGinn, L. K. (1997). Psychological treatment of anxiety disorder patients with comorbidity. In S. Wetzler & W. C. Sanderson (Eds.), *Treatment strategies for patients with psychiatric comorbidity.* New York: Wiley.

Sanderson, W. C., & Wetzler, S. (1990). Five percent carbon dioxide challenge: Valid analogue and marker of panic disorder? *Biological Psychiatry, 27,* 689–701.

Shear, M. K., Pilkonis, P. A., Cloitre, M., & Leon, A. C. (1994). Cognitive behavioral treatment compared with nonprescriptive treatment of panic disorder. *Archives of General Psychiatry, 51,* 395–401.

Sokol, L., Beck, A. T., Greenberg, R. L., Wright, P. D., & Berchick, R. (1989). Cognitive therapy of panic disorder: A nonpharmacological alternative. *Journal of Nervous and Mental Disease, 177,* 711–716.

Telch, M. J., Lucas, J. A., Schmidt, N. B., Hanna, H. H., Jaimez, T. L., & Lucas, R. A. (1993). Group cognitive behavioral treatment of panic disorder. *Behavior Research and Therapy, 31,* 279–287.

Wilson, R. R. (1987). *Don't panic: Taking control of anxiety attacks.* New York: Harper & Row.

Woody, S. R., & Sanderson, W. C. (1998). Manuals for empirically supported treatments: 1998 update from the task force on psychological interventions. *The Clinical Psychologist, 51*(1), 17–21.

CHAPTER 12

Cognitive Factors in Panic Attacks: Symptom Probability and Sensitivity

Anke Ehlers

Psychological models of panic disorder propose that panic attacks result from the patient's fear response to certain body sensations. In the present study, we assessed three aspects of the fear of body sensations: subjective symptom probability, symptom sensitivity, and perceived coping ability (Symptom Probability and Cost Questionnaire, SPCQ). Respondents were 110 patients with panic disorder (88 with current panic attacks, 22 in remission), 81 infrequent panickers, 37 patients with other anxiety disorders. They and 61 normal controls without a history of psychiatric disorders answered the SPCQ for three groups of bodily sensations: general anxiety, panic, and nonanxiety control symptoms. Significant group differences were found for the anxiety and panic scales and for control symptom probability. With the exception of panic symptom sensitivity in the patient control group, all anxiety groups differed from normal control subjects on the anxiety and panic scales.

Overall, group differences in anxiety and panic symptom appraisal could not be accounted for by differences in trait anxiety or depression scores. Even when these variables were controlled for by analysis of covariance, panic disorder patients and infrequent panickers differed significantly from normal controls. Panic patients endorsed a higher probability of anxiety and panic symptoms and a higher sensitivity and lower coping ability for panic symptoms than infrequent panickers, as well as higher anxiety and panic symptom probabilities and sensitivities than patients with other anxiety disorders. Subjects with infrequent panic attacks gave similar ratings on the anxiety symptom scales as patients with other anxiety disorders, but had higher probability and sensitivity scores for panic symptoms. The present study provides evidence that a fear of bodily sensations associated with anxiety is a prominent characteristic of patients with panic disorder, but that this fear is also found to a lesser degree among infrequent panickers and patients with other anxiety disorders.

Panic attacks are discrete episodes of apprehension or fear accompanied by a variety of symptoms such as palpitations, dyspnea, sweating, or dizziness (American Psychiatric Association, 1987). There is agreement among current psychological models that panic attacks result from the patient's maladaptive response to internal stimuli, most commonly bodily sensations (Barlow, 1986; Beck, 1988; Clark, 1986; Ehlers, Margraf, & Roth, 1988; Foa, 1988; Rapee, 1987; van den Hout, 1988). Evidence supporting this psychological perspective of panic is rapidly accumulating (for a review see Ehlers et al., 1988).

Current psychological models of panic are related to the older concept that patients with agoraphobia and anxiety neurosis suffer from "fear of fear" (Evans, 1972; Fenichel, 1945; Frankl, 1975; Goldstein & Chambless, 1978). Especially relevant to the study of panic disorder is the idea that patients are afraid of certain bodily sensations associated with anxiety. Questionnaire studies have demonstrated that panic patients show a bias in the interpretation of bodily cues in that, compared to normal or clinical control groups, these patients report more fear of bodily sensations and tend to interpret these changes as indicators of an immediate impending danger (Chambless, Caputo, Bright, & Gallagher, 1984; Chambless & Gracely, 1989; Clark et al., 1988; Foa, 1988; McNally & Foa, 1987; McNally & Lorenz, 1987; Reiss, Peterson, Gursky, & McNally, 1986; van den Hout, van der Molen, Griez, & Lousberg, 1987). Interview studies concur that catastrophic misinterpretations of bodily sensations occur during panic attacks (Beck, Laude, & Bohnert, 1974; Hibbert, 1984; Ottaviani & Beck, 1987; Rachman, Levitt, & Lopatka, 1987; Rapee, 1985; Zucker et al., 1989) and that bodily symptoms usually precede the experience of panic (Hibbert, 1984; Ley, 1985; Ottaviani & Beck, 1987; Zucker et al., 1989).

Reiss and McNally (1985) have argued that two components of the fear of fear can be distinguished: anxiety expectancy and anxiety sensitivity. Together with the expectation that certain external stimuli are associated with danger (danger expectancy), these two components of fear of fear determine the individual's total degree of avoidance motivation.

In panic disorder, danger expectancy concerning external stimuli only seems to play a minor role. Bodily sensations are seen as the primary trigger of panic attacks. In the present study, we therefore decided to distinguish different aspects of the appraisal of bodily sensations, similar to the components of the fear of fear proposed by Reiss and McNally (1985) and to the distinction between the subjective probability and cost of events by McNally and Foa (1987). Panic patients might overrespond to benign physiological changes because of their expectation that unpleasant symptoms are likely to occur (symptom probability), that these symptoms are dangerous (symptom sensitivity), or that these symptoms are hard to cope with (coping ability).

We assessed the appraisal of anxiety and nonanxiety control symptoms of panic disorder patients on these dimensions. We included panic patients in remission and infrequent panickers in our research design to explore the stability of symptom appraisal over the course of the disorder. Furthermore, we included a control group with other anxiety disorders to study specificity for subjects with panic attacks.

METHOD

Subjects

Four groups of subjects were compared in the present study: patients with panic disorder (PAT), subjects with infrequent panic attacks (INFR), patients with other anxiety disorders without a history of panic attacks (PATC), and normal control subjects without a history of psychiatric disorders or panic attacks (NORM). The majority of subjects was recruited to participate in a psychophysiological laboratory study. Diagnoses were assessed with the Structured Clinical Interview for *DSM-III-R* diagnoses (SCID-P) (Spitzer & Williams, 1986 [German translation of Ehlers & Margraf, unpublished] see Margraf & Ehlers, 1988). The remaining subjects had contacted the author for treatment referrals, or information about panic attacks, or about the psychophysiological study and did not participate in the laboratory assessment. Their diagnoses were assessed by telephone interviews following *DSM-III-R* criteria. However, no full SCID was given. Prior to data analysis we checked whether the two recruitment procedures yielded different subject samples. Because the respective subsamples in each group who were either given the full SCID or just the telephone interview did not differ with respect to their anxiety, depression, avoidance behavior, or scores on the Symptom Probability and Cost Questionnaire described further on, they were collapsed in order to reduce the number of statistical comparisons performed in this study.

Panic disorder patients (PAT, $N = 110$) had a lifetime diagnosis of panic disorder. The majority of these patients ($N = 88$) met DSM-III-R criteria for current panic disorder. Also participating in the laboratory study were 41 patients with current panic attacks (31 women, 10 men). Their ages ranged from 18 to 54 years with a mean of 31.5 years. They reported an average number of 6.9 panic attacks during the 3 weeks prior to answering the questionnaire (standard deviation 8.9). An additional 47 patients with current panic disorder (34 women, 13 men) were recruited for the questionnaire study. Their ages ranged from 19 to 57 years with a mean of 35.5 years. They reported having experienced an average of 5.9 (+/- 6.6) panic attacks during the past 3 weeks. Another 22 patients (5 men, 17 women) had a diagnosis of panic disorder according to *DSM-III-R* criteria but had not had a panic attack during the 6 months prior to their participation (panic disorder in remission). Their ages ranged from 23 to 61 years with a mean of 35.7.

Infrequent panickers (INFR, $N = 81$) reported having experienced at least one panic attack meeting *DSM-III-R* criteria during their lifetime. Of these subjects 49 (35 women, 14 men) were recruited for the laboratory study. Another 32 infrequent panickers (23 women, 9 men) only participated in the questionnaire study. These subjects reported panic attacks in the Panic Attack Questionnaire (PAQ) (Norton, Dorward, and Cox, 1986 [German translation, Margraf & Ehlers, unpublished] see Margraf & Ehlers, 1988). Because a previous study had shown that the PAQ yields a substantial proportion of false positives (Margraf & Ehlers, 1988), additional telephone interviews were conducted to ensure that the subjects' panic attacks met *DSM-III-R* criteria. Ages in the combined infrequentpanic group ranged from 18 to 78 years.

The group of *patients with other anxiety disorders* (PATC, N = 37) comprised 27 patients (22 women, 5 men) with *DSM-III-R* diagnoses of simple phobias participating in the laboratory study and 10 patients (6 women, 4 men) with social phobias or generalized anxiety disorder recruited for the questionnaire study. Ages in the combined group ranged from 19 to 61 years. In line with the hierarchy of anxiety disorders in *DSM-III-R* (American Psychiatric Association, 1987), patients were only assigned to this group if they had never met *DSM-III-R* criteria for panic attacks.

The *normal control subjects* (NORM, $N = 61$; 44 women, 17 men) were free of any history of psychiatric disorders and had never experi-

Table 12.1 Subjects

	Age	Anxiety (STAI)	Depression (BDI)	Avoidance (MI) Accomp	Alone
Panic Groups					
Panic disorder (PAT)	34.0	52.2	15.9	1.94	2.64
(N = 110; 82 F, 28 M)	(9.6)	(10.3)	(8.4)	(0.92)	(1.13)
Infrequent panic	33.6	46.7	11.4	1.38	1.71
(INFR)	(14.0)	(9.1)	(7.8)	(0.50)	(0.68)
(N = 81; 58 F, 23 M)					
Control Groups					
Patients with other	34.1	45.9	10.4	1.42	1.66
anxiety disorders	(11.2)	(10.8)	(7.7)	(0.50)	(0.58)
(PATC)					
(N = 37; 28 F, 9 M)					
Normal controls	34.3	34.5	2.6	1.08	1.22
(NORM)	(10.0)	(7.0)	(3.2)	(0.14)	(0.27)
(N = 61; 44 F, 17 M)					

Note. Means (standard deviations) are presented.

enced a panic attack as determined by the SCID. Their ages ranged from 20 to 52 years.

Further information about the subject groups is shown in Table 12.1. Means and standard deviations are given for the subjects' ages, trait anxiety scores (STAT/T, German version of the State-Trait-Anxiety-Inventory) (Laux, Glanzmann, Schaffner, & Spielberger, 1981), Beck Depression Inventory scores (BDI) (Kammer, 1983 [German version]), and Mobility Inventory scores (Chambless, Caputo, Jasin, Gracely, & Williams, 1985 [German translation, Ehlers & Margraf, unpublished]). The groups differed significantly on all of the measures except age (STAI: F (3,284) = 46.02; BDI: F (3,284) = 42.82; MI-accompanied: F (3,277) = 24.93i MI-alone: F (3,279) = 44.89; all p's < .0001). Panic disorder patients had significantly higher trait anxiety, depression and avoidance scores than all the other groups (all p's < .05). Infrequent panickers and patients with other anxiety disorders reported higher anxiety, depression, and avoidance than normal controls (all p's < .05; results based on Newman-Keuls tests as described by Winer, 1970).

Procedure

Subjects were sent a package of questionnaires including the STAI, BDI, MI, and the Symptom Probability and Cost Questionnaire described in the next section. They were instructed to answer the questionnaires at home without asking other people for input. They either brought the completed questionnaires to the laboratory assessment or mailed them to the author. Subjects were paid DM 10 (approximately U.S. $6) for answering the questionnaires.

Symptom Probability and Cost Questionnaire (SPCQ)

The Symptom Probability and Cost Questionnaire (SPCQ) was designed to assess three aspects of symptom appraisal: symptom probability, symptom sensitivity, and perceived coping ability. Three groups of symptoms were included:

(a) *Anxiety symptoms* as defined by the Autonomic Perception Questionnaire (APQ; Mandler, Mandler, & Uviller, 1958; German version by Nikula, 1985); 15 items. Examples: My muscles are tense; my heart is beating faster; I begin to sweat; my face is hot.

(b) Additional physical *panic symptoms* not covered in the original APQ; 8 items. Examples: I feel dizzy; I feel faint; I have nausea; parts of my body tingle.

(c) *Control symptoms* generally not associated with anxiety; 5 items. Examples: I feel itchy; my eyes are burning; I have toothache.

In the *Symptom Probability* scale, subjects are asked to rate how likely it is for them to experience each symptom. The 11–point Lickert scale ranges from 0 (very unlikely) to 10 (labeled "very likely"). In the *Symptom Sensitivity* scale, subjects are asked to rate how bad it is for them to experience each symptom, ranging from not at all bad (0) to very bad (10). In the *Coping Ability* scale, subjects are asked to rate how well they can cope with each symptom on a scale from 0 (very poorly) to 10 (very well).

The first two scales are similar to the ratings used in the Subjective Probability and Cost Questionnaires by McNally & Foa (1987). Although the dimensions measured by the SPCQ also bear similarities with the distinction between anxiety expectancy and anxiety probability, they were not designed to be directly transformed into Reiss and McNally's (1985) dimensions. The symptom probability scales correspond to the concept of anxiety expectancy, but no situational context is described in the SPCQ because panic attacks may occur in many different situations. While the focus of the Anxiety Sensitivity Index (ASI) (Reiss et al., 1986) is to measure the belief that the experience of anxiety has undesirable consequences in addition to the immediate unpleasantness of the anxiety sensation, our symptom sensitivity scales include the unpleasantness of symptoms.

RESULTS

The significance levels given in this paper are two-tailed. If not mentioned otherwise, the results meet at least the 5% level of significance.

The overall return rate for subjects recruited for the psychophysiological assessment was 91% (subjects that failed to come to the laboratory session are included in this calculation). For subjects who just participated in the questionnaire study, the return rate was 89%.

Figures 12.1, 12.2, and 12.3 show the subjects' ratings of symptom probability, sensitivity, and coping ability for the three groups of symptoms, respectively. High scores reflect that symptoms are rated as highly probable, very bad, and easy to cope with.

In a multivariate analysis of variance (MANOVA), we compared the nine different questionnaire scores of the four subject groups. We found a significant effect of the group factor (Wilks' Λ, F (27,786.26) = 8.00, p < .001). Table 12.2 summarizes the results of univariate ANOVAs and Newman-Keuls tests for each of the nine variables. The groups differed on all aspects of their appraisal of anxiety and panic symptoms. For control symptoms, the only difference was found for symptom probability.

In the evaluation of general anxiety symptoms, panic disorder patients (PAT) reported a higher subjective probability and sensitivity than all other groups. Similarly, they reported a higher probability, sensitivity, and lower coping ability for panic symptoms than the other groups. Subjects with infrequent panic attacks (INFR) found anxiety and panic symptoms more likely, more negative, and harder to cope with than normal controls. The patient control group (PATC) gave ratings similar to infrequent panickers on the anxiety and control symptom scales. However, they found panic symptoms less probable and less negative than infrequent panickers and did not differ from normal controls on the panic sensitivity scale.

Patients with panic disorder not only differed from the other anxiety groups in the SPCQ measures, but also had higher STAI and BDI scores. Therefore, the question arises whether the group differences on the SPCQ might be due to differences in anxiety or depression. To approach this question, Pearson correlations were calculated. Table 12.3 shows the cor-

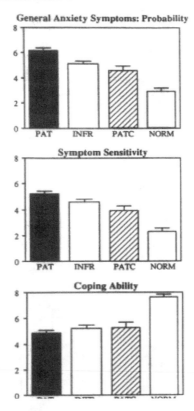

Figure 12.1 Results of the General Anxiety Scales (means and standard error) of the Symptom Probability and Cost Questionnaire (SPCQ). All scales used ratings from 0 to 10. High scores reflect a high symptom probability, symptom sensitivity, and a high coping ability. The panic groups are subjects with panic disorder (PAT) and subjects with infrequent panic attacks (INFR). The control groups are patients with other anxiety disorders (PATC) and normal controls (NORM).

relations of the STAI and BDI with the anxiety and panic scales of the SPCQ based on the combined sample of anxiety patients ($N = 228$). Overall, correlations were significant, but moderate. The low correlations cannot be due to a low reliability of the SPCQ scales since Cronbach's alphas were high (0.88, 0.88, and 0.88 for the three general anxiety scales; 0.83, 0.85, and 0.84 for the three panic scales; and 0.73, 0.79, 0.87 for the control symptom scales, respectively). Similarly, SPCQ scores showed low correlations with panic frequency in the panic patient group (PAT)

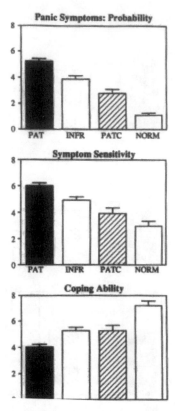

Figure 12.2 Results of the Panic Symptom Scales (Means and Standard error) of the Symptom Probability and Cost Questionnaire (SPCQ). All scales used ratings from 0 to 10. High scores reflect a high symptom probability, symptom sensitivity, and a high coping ability. The panic groups are subjects with panic disorder (PAT) and subjects with infrequent panic attacks (INFR). The control groups are patients with other anxiety disorders (PATC) and normal controls (NORM).

(panic symptom probability: $r = .23$, $p < .01$; control symptom probability $r = .25$, $p < .01$; coping abilityanxiety symptoms: $r = -.26$, $p < .01$; coping ability-panic symptoms: $r = -.21$, $p < .05$; all other correlations nonsignificant).

The MI-alone score is also included in Table 12.3 because of Reiss and McNally's (1985) hypothesis that avoidance motivation depends on anxiety expectancy and sensitivity. Panic probability and sensitivity scores correlated significantly higher with the MI-alone than with STAI scores ($p < .001$).

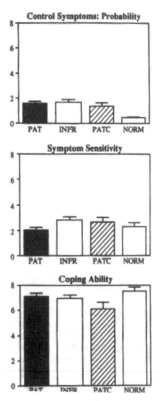

Figure 12.3 Results of the Control Symptom Scales (means and standard error) of the Symptom Probability and Cost Questionnaire (SPCQ). All scales used ratings from 0 to 10. High scores reflect a high symptom probability, symptom sensitivity, and a high coping ability. The panic groups are subjects with panic disorder (PAT) and subjects with infrequent panic attacks (INFR). The control groups are patients with other anxiety disorders (PATC) and normal controls (NORM).

To assess further whether the group differences on the SPCQ between the different anxiety groups were independent of differences in anxiety and depression, multivariate ANCOVAs were calculated using the STAI and BDI scores as covariates. The multivariate group comparisons were still highly significant (Wilks' Λ: F (27, 780.42) = 4.64, $p < .001$ for covariate STAI score; Wilks' Λ: F (27, 780.42) = 4.58, $p < .001$ for covariate BDI score). Significant univariate group effects were found for all general anxiety and panic symptom scales (all p's <.001), but not for the control symptom probability scale. As shown in Tables 12.4 and 12.5,

Table 12.2 Results of the ANOVAs and Newman-Keuls Tests

F/ANOVA	Significant Group Differences

General Anxiety
Symptoms

Probability	38.28****	PAT > INFR, PATC > NORM
Sensitivity	29.88****	PAT > INFR, PATC > NORM
Coping ability	24.89****	PAT, INFR, PATC < NORM

Additional Panic
Symptoms

Probability	57.37****	PAT > INFR > PATC > NORM
Sensitivity	22.51****	PAT > INFR > PATC, NORM
Coping ability	24.54****	PAT < INFR, PATC < NORM

Non-Anxiety Control
Symptoms

Probability	6.96***	PAT, INFR, PATC > NORM
Sensitivity	$1.86^{n.s.}$	
Coping ability	$2.21^{n.s.}$	

ANOVAs: **** $p < .0001$; *** $p < .001$; n. s.—nonsignificant.
Newman-Keuls Tests: > significantly greater ($p < .05$ or smaller).
PAT = Patients with panic disorder.
INFR = Subjects with infrequent panic attacks.
PATC = Patients with other anxiety disorders.
NORM = Normal control subjects.

Table 12.3 Correlations for the Combined Anxiety Groups (N = 228)

	STAI	BDI	MI-Alone
General Anxiety			
Symptoms			
Probability	.31	.34	.37
Sensitivity	.28	.36	.46
Coping ability	−.33	−.39	−.32
Additional Panic			
Symptoms			
Probability	.34	.44	.55
Sensitivity	.23	.29	.47
Coping ability	−.34	−.38	−.39

Note. All correlations are significant at $p < .0001$.

Table 12.4 Results of ANCOVAS—Covariate Trait Anxiety (STAI)

	PAT vs.			INFR vs.		PATC vs.
	INFR	PATC	NORM	PATC	NORM	NORM
All SPCQ scales (multivariate)	***	***	***	(*)	***	*
General Anxiety Symptoms						
Probability	**	***	***	n.s.	***	*
Sensitivity	n.s.	*	***	n.s.	***	*
Coping ability	n.s.	n.s.	***	n.s.	***	*
Additional Panic Symptoms						
Probability	**	***	***	**	***	**
Sensitivity	*	***	***	*	***	n.s.
Coping ability	**	(*)	***	n.s.	**	*

$***p < .001; **p < .01; *p < .05; (*)p < .10.$

Table 12.5 Results of ANCOVAS—Covariate Trait Anxiety (BDI)

		PAT vs.		INFR vs.		PATC vs.
	INFR	PATC	NORM	PATC	NORM	NORM
All SPCQ scales (multivariate)	***	***	***	(*)	***	n.s.
General Anxiety Symptoms						
Probability	*	**	***	n.s.	***	*
Sensitivity	n.s.	*	***	n.s.	***	n.s.
Coping ability	n.s.	n.s.	***	n.s.	***	**
Additional Panic Symptoms						
Probability	*	***	***	**	***	*
Sensitivity	(*)	***	***	*	***	n.s.
Coping ability	*	n.s.	***	n.s.	**	*

$***p < .001; **p < .01; *p < .05; (*)p < .10.$

further ANCOVAs showed that panic disorder patients and infrequent panickers differed from normal controls on all anxiety and panic scales even when trait anxiety and depression was controlled for (all p's <.01). In contrast, the difference between patients with other anxiety disorders and normal controls on the SPCQ scales did not reach significance when the BDI score was used as the covariate (F (9.86) = 1,63, p = .12).

ANCOVAs controlling for trait anxiety yielded the same results as the ANOVAs for the comparison of the PATC and NORM groups. The differences between panic disorder patients and patients with other anxiety disorders on the panic and anxiety scales remained significant with the exception of coping ability ratings. Panic patients differed from infrequent panickers on the anxiety symptom probability scale and on all panic scales (panic symptom sensitivity: $p < .054$).

To study the question of whether symptom appraisal varies over the course of panic disorder, the SPCQ scores of the 88 patients with current panic attacks were compared with those of 22 patients who had not had panic attacks during the past 6 months. The overall MANOVA showed a significant difference between the groups (Wilks' Λ F (9.96) = 2.15, $p <$ .05). Significant univariate differences were found for the control symptom probability scale and all panic and anxiety symptom scales (all p's < .05) with the exception of a trend for anxiety symptom probability ($p <$ .10). Panic disorder patients in remission had similar scores on the SPCQ as infrequent panickers (MANOVA: Wilks' Λ F (9.89) = 1.82, $p < .08$; no univariate differences on panic or anxiety scales).

Further exploratory data analyses were performed comparing ratings of specific clusters of symptoms between the groups. For cardiac and respiratory symptoms as well as dizziness or faintness, the same differences between the anxiety groups were found as for panic symptoms in general (all p's < .05). In contrast, the anxiety groups did not differ in their appraisal of gastrointestinal symptoms.

DISCUSSION

Subjects with panic attacks and other anxiety disorders found both anxiety and nonanxiety symptoms more probable than subjects without a history of psychiatric disorders. However, their elevated ratings of the subjective cost of symptoms (high symptom sensitivity and low coping ability) were specific to anxiety symptoms. This lends support to the idea of specific "fear of fear symptoms" in anxiety disorders. Anxiety patients do not seem to be indiscriminately oversensitive to any bodily symptom.

Patients with panic disorder reported a higher probability and sensitivity for panic symptoms than subjects with infrequent panic attacks or patients with other anxiety disorders. A similar pattern of results was found for general anxiety symptoms. Are these group differences due to differences in the severity of the disorders? A large proportion of our patient control group consisted of simple phobics who are generally considered to be less disabled than patients with panic disorder. The same applies by definition to infrequent panickers. The subject's reported trait anxiety, depression, and avoidance behavior clearly underlines such differences in symptom severity.

However, the results showed that group differences on the SPCQ can only to a small degree be accounted for by differences in trait anxiety or depression. Multivariate ANCOVAs, using anxiety or depression scores as covariates, still showed significant differences between the groups. Patients with panic disorder and infrequent panickers differed clearly from normal controls on all anxiety and panic symptom scales. Patients with panic disorder reported the greatest fear of panic symptoms independent of their high anxiety and depression levels. From our correlational data, however, we cannot draw conclusions on the causal relationship between the severity of panic attacks and SPCQ scores. The experience of severe panic attacks may lead to a higher fear of anxiety symptoms, or a high fear of anxiety symptoms may lead to more frequent or more severe panic attacks.

In this context, the relatively high scores of infrequent panickers on the SPCQ are interesting to note because the majority of this group comprised nonclinical subjects who had never sought treatment for anxiety problems. This group allows the study of factors associated with panic attacks, independent of factors associated with being a patient. Infrequent panickers differed highly significantly from normal controls and gave even higher probability and sensitivity ratings for panic symptoms than patients with other anxiety disorders. Compared to panic disorder patients, infrequent panickers gave more similar ratings on *sensitivity* scales, whereas patients with other anxiety disorders gave more similar *coping ability* ratings when differences in anxiety and depression levels were controlled for by analyses of covariance. Again, our correlational design does not allow causal interpretations. The pattern of our results is consistent with the idea that symptom sensitivity may be a predisposing factor in the development of panic disorder, although longitudinal studies are needed to test whether the negative appraisal of anxiety and panic symptoms develops prior or secondary to having panic attacks. Our results are in line with previous findings that infrequent panickers differ from controls without panic attacks on similar dimensions as panic attack patients (Margraf & Ehlers, 1988; Norton et al., 1986).

Patients with anxiety disorders other than panic attacks (PATC) had elevated ratings on the SPCQ compared to normal controls, except for panic sensitivity. When depression levels were covaried out, the difference in anxiety symptom sensitivity failed to reach significance. The results on the probability and coping ability scales are in keeping with the suggestion of Reiss, McNally and collaborators that fear of fear is not limited to agoraphobia and panic disorder (Reiss, 1987; Reiss & McNally, 1985; Reiss et al., 1986), but can be seen as a dimension on which patients with all anxiety disorders differ from the normal population. In this context it is interesting to note that another recent study in our laboratory did not find differences between depressed patients (*DSM-III-R* diagnoses of Major Depressive Episodes or Dysthymic Disorder) and normal controls on the panic scales of the SPCQ (Margraf, Frank, & Freitag, in preparation). Data from Chambless and Gracely (1989) are also in line with the relevance of a fear of anxiety symptoms to all anxiety disorders. Patients with generalized anxiety disorder, obsessive-compulsive disorder, or social phobia showed higher scores on the Body Sensations Questionnaire than normal controls. In our patient control sample, it was not possible to distinguish between the various other anxiety disorders because of a small sample size. The sample size may also have been partially responsible for the lack a multivariate difference between the patient and normal control groups in the ANCOVA with depression scores.

Compared to subjects with panic attacks, the most prominent differences of the patient control group were found on the panic symptom scales, as could be expected. The question arises whether the group differences found in our study may be an artifact due to a possible difference in item interpretation. If panickers systematically thought of more severe symptoms than patient or normal controls, this could explain their higher sensitivity ratings. This criticism would apply to all fear-of-fear questionnaires. However, we do not think that our results are invalidated by this possibility. First, subjects with panic attacks do not always experience dramatic bodily sensations because the average panic attack is of only moderate severity (Margraf et al., 1987). In addition, most phobics experience panic attacks when exposed to their phobic stimulus and thus experience similarly severe bodily symptoms. Second, the interpretation is not plausible for the difference between infrequent panickers and patients with other anxiety disorders. Many infrequent panickers participating in our study had only had very few attacks and—in contrast to the anxiety patient—were not disabled by an anxiety problem. Finally, even if the panickers' increased perceived symptom probability and sensitivity is secondary to having experienced severe panic symptoms from time to time, this cognitive bias could still be involved in the maintenance of the disorder.

Interpreting the group differences, we have to bear in mind that there is a large comorbidity among the anxiety disorders or precursors of these disorders. This may obscure differences that would be evident in "pure" samples. Of the simple phobics tested in our laboratory 67% reported panic attacks on the PAQ but did not meet the full *DSM-III-R* criteria according to the SCID (e.g., because their attacks were triggered by the phobic stimulus). Similarly, 50% of the infrequent panickers and 51% of the patients with current panic disorder reported at least borderline simple or social phobias in the SCID (e.g., they were not disabled by their phobia). The large overlap among the anxiety disorders makes issues of specificity difficult to investigate. However, lack of specificity does not mean that our results are irrelevant, because they provide valuable descriptive information about the subject groups and may be more generalizable to clinical populations than results on samples selected for having just one disorder.

Only moderate correlations were found between STAI scores or panic frequency and symptom appraisal in the SPCQ. This result is in line with the moderate correlations between measures of anxiety and fear of fear reported by Chambless et al. (1984), Chambless and Gracely (1989), McNally and Lorenz (1987), and Reiss et al. (1986). Reiss et al. argued that their Anxiety Sensitivity Index (ASI) measures something different from conventional anxiety scales and adds important information to the explanation to clinical fears besides anxiety levels. In their study, the ASI explained variance of the Fear Survey Schedule (FSS-II) not explained by the Taylor Manifest Anxiety Scale (TMAS). Similarly, Chambless and Gracely (1989) reported that the Body Sensations Questionnaire (BSQ) and the Agoraphobic Cognitions Questionnaire (ACQ) predicted agoraphobic avoidance (MI) even when trait anxcty was partialed out. In the present study, we found the same pattern of results: Probability and sensitivity ratings of panic symptoms correlated significantly higher with agoraphobic avoidance behavior (MI-alone) than trait anxiety did. As could be expected from the often postulated role of panic attacks in the development of agoraphobia (e.g., Goldstein & Chambless, 1978; Klein, 1980), this difference was only found for panic symptoms, not for other anxiety symptoms.

CONCLUSION

Our study provides further evidence that subjects with panic attacks and with other anxiety disorders show a fear of body sensations associated with anxiety. They consider these symptoms as probable, very unpleasant or dangerous, and hard to cope with. This fear of body sensations is particularly pronounced in patients with panic attacks but is also present to a lesser degree in subjects with infrequent panic attacks and patients with other anxiety disorders. The negative appraisal of anxiety symptoms seems to be an important dimension characteristic of anxiety patients in addition to their elevated anxiety level.

ACKNOWLEDGMENT

Preparation of this paper was supported by the German Research Foundation (Grants Eh 97/1–1, 1–2, and 1–3).

REFERENCES

American Psychiatric Association. (1987). *Diagnostic and statistical manual of mental disorders* 3rd ed. rev. Washington, DC: Author.

Barlow, D. H. (1986). A psychological model of panic. In. B. F. Shaw, F. Cashman, Z. V. Segal, & T. M. Vallis (Eds.), *Anxiety disorders: Theory, diagnosis, and treatment* (pp. 93–114). New York: Plenum Press.

Beck, A. T. (1988). Cognitive approaches to panic disorder: Theory and therapy. In S. Rachman, & J. D. Maser (Eds.), *Panic: Psychological perspectives* (pp. 91–110). Hillsdale, NJ: Erlbaum.

Beck, A. T., Laude, R., & Bohnert, M. (1974). Ideational components of anxiety neurosis. *Archives of General Psychiatry, 31,* 319–325.

Chambless, D. L., Caputo, G. C., Bright, P., & Gallagher, R. (1984). Assessment of fear of fear in agoraphobics: The body sensations questionnaire and the agoraphobic cognitions questionnaire. Journal of Consulting and Clinical Psychology, 52, 1090 1097.

Chambless, D. L., Caputo, G. C., Jasin, S. E., Gracely, E. J., & Williams, C. (1985). The mobility inventory for agoraphobia. *Behaviour Research and Therapy, 23,* 35–44.

Chambless, D. L., & Gracely, E. J. (1989). Fear of fear and the anxiety disorders. *Cognitive Therapy and Research, 13,* 9–20.

Clark, D. M. (1986). A cognitive approach to panic. *Behaviour Research and Therapy, 24,* 461–470.

Clark, D. M., Salkovskis, P. M., Gelder, M., Koehler, K., Martin, M., Anastasiades, P., Heckman, A., Middleton, H., & Jeavonne, A. (1988). Test of a cognitive theory of panic. In I. Hand & H. U. Wittchen (Eds.), Panic *and phobias 2 (pp. 149–158)*. Berlin: Springer.

Ehlers, A., Margraf, J., & Roth, W. T. (1988). Selective information processing, interoception, and panic attacks. In I. Hand & H. U. Wittchen (Eds.), *Panic and phobias 2* (pp. 129–148). Berlin: Springer.

Evans, I. M. (1972). A conditioning model of a common neurotic pattern—Fear of fear. *Psychotherapy: Theory, Research, and Practice, 9,* 238–241.

Fenichel, O. (1945). *Psychoanalytic therapy of the neuroses.* New York: Norton.

Foa, E. B. (1988). What cognitions differentiate panic disorders from other anxiety disorders? In I. Hand & H. U. Wittchen (Eds.), *Panic and phobias, 2* (pp. 159–166). Berlin: Springer.

Prankl, V. E. (1975). Paradoxical intention and dereflection. *Psychotherapy, 12,* 226–237.

Goldstein, A. J., & Chambless, D. L. (1978). A reanalysis of agoraphobia. *Behaviour Therapy, 9,* 47–59.

Hibbert, G. A. (1984). Ideational components of anxiety. *British Journal of Psychiatry, 144,* 618–624.

Kammer, D. (1983). Eine Untersuchung derpsychometrischen Eigenschaften des deutschen Beck-Depressionsinventars (BDI). *Diagnostica, 29,* 48–60.

Klein, D. F. (1980). Anxiety reconceptualized. *Comprehensive Psychiatry, 21,* 411–427.

Ley, R. (1985). Agoraphobia, the panic attacks and the hyperventilation syndrome. *Behaviour Research and Therapy, 23,* 79–81.

Laux, L., Glanzmann, P., Schaffner, P., & Spielberger, C. D. (1981). *Das State-Trait Angstinventar.* Weinheim, Germany: Beltz.

Mandler, G., Mandler, J. M., & Uviller, E. T. (1985). Autonomic feedback: The perception of autonomic activity. *Journal of Abnormal and Social Psychology, 56,* 367–373.

Margraf, J., & Ehlers, A. (1988). Panic attacks in non-clinical subjects. In I. Hand & H. U. Witichen (Eds.), *Panic and phobias 2* (pp. 103–116). Berlin: Springer.

Margraf, J., Frank, B., & Freitag, M. (in preparation). *Learning history and symptom appraisal in psychosomatic patients.*

Margraf, J., Taylor, C. B., Ehlers, A., Roth, W. T., & Agras, W. S. (1987). Panic attacks in the natural environment. *Journal of Nervous and Mental Disease, 175,* 558–565.

McNally, R. J., & Foa, E. B. (1987). Cognition and agoraphobia: Bias in the interpretation of threat. *Cognitive Therapy and Research, 11,* 567–581.

McNally, R. J., & Lorenz, M. (1987). Anxiety sensitivity in agoraphobics. *Journal of Behavior Therapy and Experimental Psychiatry, 18,* 3–11.

Nikula, R. (1985). Viszerozeption undphysiologische Prozesse beim emotionalen Erleben: Ein Vergleich. *Unpublished doctoral dissertation,* University of Bochum, Germany.

Norton, G. R., Dorward, J., & Cox, B. J. (1986). Factors associated with panic attacks in nonclinical subjects. *Behavior Therapy, 17,* 239–252.

Ottavani, R., & Beck, A. T. (1987). Cognitive aspects of panic disorder. *Journal of Anxiety Disorders, 1,* 15–28.

Rachman, S., Levitt, K., & Lopatka, C. (1987). Panic: The links between cognitions and bodily symptoms—I. *Behaviour Research and Therapy, 2S,* 411–423.

Rapee, R. M. (1985). Distinction between panic disorder and generalized anxiety disorder: Clinical presentation. *Australian and New Zealand Journal of Psychiatry, 19,* 227–232.

Rapee, R. M. (1987). The psychological treatment of panic attacks: Theoretical conceptualization and review of evidence. *Clinical Psychology Review, 7,* 427–438.

Reiss, S. (1987). Theoretical perspectives on fear of anxiety. *Clinical Psychology Review, 7,* 585–596.

Reiss, S., & McNally, R. J. (1985). Expectancy model of fear. In S. Reiss & R. R. Bootzin (Eds.), *Theoretical issues in behavior therapy* (pp. 107–121). New York: Academic Press.

Reiss, S., Peterson, R. A., Gursky, D. M., & McNally, R. J. (1986). Anxiety sensitivity, anxiety frequency, and the prediction of fearfulness. *Behavior Research and Therapy, 24,* 1–8.

Spitzer, R. L., & Williams, J. B. (1986). Structured Clinical Interview for DSM-III-R patient version. (SCID-P). New York: Biometrics Research Department, New York State Psychiatric Institute.

van den Hout, M. A. (1988). The explanation of experimental panic. In S. Rachman & J. Maser (Eds.), *Panic: Psychological perspectives* (pp. 237–258). Hillsdale, NJ: Erlbaum.

van den Hout, M. A., van der Molen, M., Griez, E., & Lousberg, H. (1987). Specificity of interoceptive fears to panic disorders. *Journal of Psychopathology and Behavioral Assessment, 9,* 99–106.

Winer, B. J. (1970). *Statistical principles in experimental design.* London: McGraw-Hill.

Zucker, D., Taylor, C. B., Brouillard, M., Ehlers. A., Margraf, J., Telch, M. J., Roth, W. T., & Agras, W. S. (1989). Cognitive aspects of panic attacks: Content, course, and relationship to laboratory stressors. *British Journal of Psychiatry, 155,* 86–91.

CHAPTER 13

The Consequences of Panic

Stanley Rachman

The most common behavioral consequence of panic is the emergency of avoidance behavior. If this behavior becomes excessive it can be disabling. It is postulated that the major determinant of panic-related avoidance behavior is the person's present prediction of the probability of experiencing a panic in specified circumstances. Other factors, such as the expected aversiveness of the panic and the availability of safety signals, also contribute to the avoidance. The cognitive consequences of panic include the following: Episodes of panic are followed by increases in the prediction of future panics and in expected fear, but with little or no increase in reported fear. Unexpected panics contribute most to these changes, and expected panics are followed by little or no change in predictions or reports of panic or of fear. Disconfirmed predictions of panic are followed by reductions in fear, and with sufficient repetitions by reductions in predictions of panic.

The experience of panic usually is distressing, and the consequences tend to be disabling. The brevity of a panic, usually lasting approximately 20 minutes (Taylor et al., 1986), can be overshadowed by the disability that appears to arise from the distress of the panic. The most common major disability is compressed and fearful avoidance behavior. A broad analysis of the consequences of panic has been set out elsewhere, and the present emphasis is on the cognitive and behavioral consequences (see Rachman, 1988, 1990).

One product of that analysis was the conclusion that "avoidance be-havior develops or strengthens if a person predicts that there is a high probability of experiencing a panic" (Rachman, 1990). The relationship between panic and avoidance is an interesting example of the complex and imperfectly understood relationship between fear and avoidance (Gray, 1971; Rachman, 1976, 1978; Seligman & Johnston, 1973). Early evi-dence of a strong relationship between predicted fear and subsequent avoidance was described in an experiment carried out on phobic patients by Rachman and Lopatka (1986), and new findings add support to that observation.

PREDICTION OF PANIC AND AVOIDANCE

In light of this new information, it will be argued that in patients with panic disorder, the main determinant of (agoraphobic) avoidance behavior is their present prediction of the probability that they will experience a panic in a specifiable set of circumstances. They do not engage in avoid-ance simply because of past panics; rather, it is hypothesized, *that they avoid because of their current prediction that they are likely to panic in a particular place during a particular period of time.* The greater the specificity of the prediction, especially as to time and place, the stronger and clearer the connection between the person's estimate of the probabil-ity of a panic and the associated avoidance behavior. The frequency of past panics is only weakly related to avoidance behavior (see, for exam-ple, Craske, Rachman, & Tallman, 1986; Craske, Sanderson, & Barlow, 1987; Telch, Brouilard, & Telch, 1988). Past panics have an indirect effect on avoidance behavior by virtue of their influence on the present predictions. Part of this article will deal with the connection between past panics and present predictions, and it will tackle the question of the determinants of present predictions.

Telch et al. (1988) recently reported important results that bear on the hypothesis that the main determinant of avoidance is the present predic-tion of panic. They compared 35 panic disorder patients who had minimal or no phobic avoidance with 40 patients whose panic disorder was asso-ciated with severe agoraphobia. The two groups were highly similar on the measures of panic frequency but differed considerably in the extent to which they anticipated future panics.

In a regression analysis incorporating 19 predictor variables, anticipat-ed panic emerged as the most significant predictor of avoidance. Telch et al. concluded from this and other analyses that patients with panic disor-der and agoraphobia "exaggerate the likelihood of a panic occurrence, engage in more catastrophic thinking about the consequences of panic occurrence, and report less confidence in their personal resources to manage panic" ($p < .000$). The patients' judgments of the probability of panic accounted for almost 80% of the variance in avoidance ratings. Recognizing some weaknesses in the design of their study, Telch et al. recommend that a prospective investigation be undertaken. The study by Warren, Zgourides, and Jones (1988) also has limitations, but the results of their multiple regression analyses of slightly different data produced remarkably similar results to those of Telch and his colleagues. "Subjective probability (of experiencing a panic) emerged as a particularly potent predictor of avoidance" ($p < .000$). This finding was found not to depend on the patient's diagnostic subgrouping.

Craske et al. (1987) analyzed data from 75 panic disorder patients and found a high correlation between fear and avoidance. However, the frequency of the panics was weakly related to avoidance. They made the interesting suggestion that "panickers who avoid extensively may prevent the occurrence of panic attacks that are *expected* to occur . . . but continue to experience" some unexpected panics (p. 159).

Exceptions

Before proceeding, some exceptions must be noted. Panics are not always followed by avoidance, and avoidance is not always preceded by panic (Rachman, 1982, 1989). A significant minority of agoraphobic patients report the development of avoidance behavior after events in which there was no panic (e.g., after a bereavement; see Thorpe & Burns, 1983). Additionally, there is a small group of patients who continue to show normal approach behavior despite having experienced some panics (Uhde et al., 1985). There is also a significant minority of people in the community who experience panic but remain free of apparent psychological problems, such as agoraphobia (e.g., Craske et al., 1986; Norton, Harrison, Hauch, & Rhodes, 1986; and others).

The plausible belief that there is a crucial connection between panic experiences and the subsequent development of avoidance behavior comes from reports given by patients ("That is how it started," "I avoid because I might panic"). Moreover, their reports are consistent with the temporal relations between the panic experience and the emergence of avoidance behavior in many cases. The avoidance begins to emerge shortly after the initial panics. However, the clinical reports are retrospective and should be treated with reserve, particularly as people try to make sense of their experiences by imposing on them a plausible interpretation (e.g., Alloy &

Tabachnik, 1984). The information given to the clinician may be a mixture of fact and interpretation.

If a patient's present prediction of probable panic is the main determinant of the avoidance behavior, how can we account for the stated exceptions? Presumably the people and the patients who experience one or more panics but do not engage in avoidance rate the chances of future panics as low (e.g., the people in the community samples); or they rate the expected aversiveness as low or have developed adequate coping skills or safety signals. The acceptability of this explanation needs to be investigated, and it may prove convenient to do so in the context of testing some of the therapeutic implications of the hypothesis (contained herein).

Similar views about the important connection between anticipatory anxiety and avoidance behavior have been expressed by proponents of expectancy theory (Kirsch, 1985; Reiss & McNally, 1985) and by Craske and Barlow (1989) in their dimensional analysis of panic and avoidance. Craske and Barlow include "heightened anticipation of the probability of a panic" as one of five factors that maintain behavioral avoidance ($p <$ .000). The hypothesis advanced here places greatest emphasis on present predictions of probable panic, but it is not incompatible with the more ambitious explanations set out by Kirsch, Reiss, and McNally (1985) and by Craske and Barlow (1989). My emphasis on the primacy of the present predictions of panic appears to be justified by the available information and is deliberately simplified in the service of clarity. The contribution of other determinants (safety signals, cost, etc.) is less substantial but not dispensable.

Other Determinants

Although the main determinant of the avoidance behavior is the person's prediction of the probability of experiencing a panic, Telch et al. (1988) and Warren et al. (1988), among others, have argued that the aversiveness of the predicted panic (the "cost") also contributes in a minor way. Craske and Barlow (1989) draw attention to the role of social demands, and it has been suggested that the person's ability to cope with a panic (Telch et al., 1988) and the occurrence of irrational thinking (Warren et al., 1988) also make small contributions. I have argued elsewhere for the importance of safety signals in generating and maintaining avoidance and will not go into that aspect of avoidance behavior at present (Rachman, 1984, 1989), except to remark that the presence or likely availability of safety signals can reduce the person's estimation of the probability of panicking or reduce the aversiveness of the panic experience. (Recognition of the operation of safety signals arises from the occurrence or persistence of avoidance behavior even in the absence or decline of fear. See Gray, 1971; Rachman, 1978, 1984).

The Overprediction of Fear

Addressing the question of the determination of present predictions of panic, why is the avoidance behavior so extreme, pervasive, and persistent? In short, because there is a strong tendency to exaggerate the probability of experiencing a panic. (Most of the information on the overprediction of fear was collected in laboratory studies, using a match-mismatch procedure [see Rachman, 1988, 1989].) Fearful people have a strong tendency to overestimate how frightened they will be when they encounter a fear-evoking object or situation. The overprediction of fear is common among people who are disturbed by excessive fear and includes patients suffering from panic disorder (Rachman & Bichard, 1988). Recent evidence also suggests that this tendency might be part of a more general phenomenon in which we are inclined to overestimate the probability or subjective impact of aversive events of various types, including pain (Rachman & Lopatka, 1986; Arntz & van den Hout, 1988).

The evidence on overprediction can be summarized: Fearful subjects tend to overpredict how much fear they will experience. Their predictions of fear tend to decrease after they have made an overprediction and to increase after they have underpredicted. After a correct prediction, the subsequent prediction remains unaltered. The *reports* of fear tend to decrease with repeated exposures to the fearful stimulus, regardless of the accuracy of the predictions. With practice, people can learn to predict their fear with increasing accuracy.

These patterns of prediction and their consequences now have been found in research on panic. Predictions of panic tend to decrease after an overestimation and tend to increase after an underestimation. Predictions of panic tend to remain unchanged after a person has made a correct prediction of panic or a correct prediction of no-panic. It is the erroneous predictions of panic, whether they are overestimations or underestimations, that are followed by changes. The underprediction of panic, equivalent to an unexpected panic, is particularly disruptive (Rachman & Bichard, 1988). The laboratory findings suggest that people who experience many panics tend to develop some degree of tolerance of these experiences, particularly if they learn to predict with accuracy when a panic is likely to occur. Expected panics may continue to be distressing but are unlikely to be particularly disruptive or to produce major changes

in prediction or behavior. For these reasons, Rachman (1988) has speculated that the first one or two panics (presumably the least expected)
might be the most damaging. It appears that the connection between past
panics and present predictions is based on the match-mismatch pattern of
past predictions (Rachman, 1988, 1989). Furthermore, the person's predictions are likely to become increasingly accurate with practice.

The overprediction of fear may be functional and may serve to prevent
distress insofar as the predictions promote avoidance of the fear-evoking
situations. If this is so, however, the prevention of fear (and of panic) is
achieved at some cost, because the avoidance behavior can become excessive and severely restrict the person's mobility. If that happens, the avoidance
behavior serves to reduce the opportunities for disconfirmation.

The persistence of overpredictions of fear raises a problem. Given that
repeated overpredictions tend to be followed eventually by reductions in
predicted and reported fear, they should show a natural decay. There are
three overlapping answers to the question of why they are nevertheless
persistent. First, most overpredictions probably do undergo natural decay.
Second, it requires only a single underpredicted fear experience, as in an
unexpected panic, to steeply increase the likelihood and degree of subsequent overpredictions. Third, the initial decline of predicted fear that
follows a single occurrence of overprediction tends to be slight. Large
decreases in overprediction begin to take place after repeated disconfirmations of the overprediction.

The effect of repeated disconfirmations of cognitive expectations was
considered by Seligman (1988) in his critique of cognitive theories of
panic. "A person who has had a panic disorder for a decade may have had
about 1,000 panic attacks. In each one, on the cognitive account, he
misinterpreted his racing heart as meaning that he was about to have a
heart attack, and this was disconfirmed. Under the laws of disconfirmation that I know, he received ample evidence that his belief was false, and
he should have given it up" (p. 326).

One possible answer to the mystery introduced by Seligman requires
acceptance of the views expressed by Levitt and Lopatka (1987) on the
changing content of panic cognitions. They suggested that even if the
initial cognitions are expectations of catastrophe (Clark, 1986), such as
an impending heart attack, the predominant expectation of patients with
panic disorder is that they will experience further panics. This prediction
is confirmed from time to time, hence it persists. The avoidance behavior
that flows from the predictions of a probable panic also persists. The
catastrophic cognitions are not confirmed, and therefore are replaced by
more accurate predictions—"I will panic."

There may be no lasting mystery here; catastrophic cognitions that are disconfirmed do extinguish. The cognitions that persist ("I will panic") are the ones that receive intermittent confirmation.

Predictions About Predictions

This analysis of the relations between prediction, panic, and avoidance can be used to extract four counterintuitive deductions. After predicted panics, there should be little change in the prediction of future panics. Also, when a person predicts that he or she will not have a panic in a particular situation at a particular time, and this prediction is confirmed, no changes in prediction will follow.

This gives rise to a third counterintuitive possibility: Early in treatment, exposure treatments carried out on patients' "good days" will produce little or no change. If the person feels secure and estimates a low probability of panicking on this particular day, then a failure to panic will be confirmatory. Little will change. On good days, however, there is a risk of experiencing a damaging underprediction, at least in the early stages of treatment. In the later stages of treatment, of course, there will be an increasing number of good days as the fear and expectations decline. These repeated confirmations of no-panic are cumulatively helpful. A fourth counterintuition is that in the early stages of treatment panic patients will benefit most from the treatment sessions that are carried out on their "bad days," when there is a greater opportunity for disconfirmation of fearful expectations. They feel apprehensive and predict that there is a high probability of having a panic. This fearful prediction is likely to be disconfirmed and if it is will lead to a slight decrement in the following prediction of panic. If the prediction of panic is confirmed, however, little change can be expected. Most change, and cumulative contributions to change, will take place after treatment sessions on patients' bad days, rather than sessions on good days.

The Links Between Bodily Sensations and Cognitions

The cognitive theory that panics "result from the catastrophic misinterpretation of bodily symptoms" (Clark, 1988, p. 73) entails a causal link between bodily sensations and fearful cognitions. Our research on the relationship between the prediction of panic and avoidance behavior provided an opportunity for searching out such links (Rachman, Levitt, & Lopatka, 1987). In the course of a number of experimental investigations of the induction of panic by psychological methods (see Rachman, 1988;

Rachman & Levitt, 1985), we compared the bodily sensations and cognitions reported by subjects and patients on panic trial episodes and no-panic trial episodes.

As deduced from cognitive theory, panic episodes were indeed accompanied by many more bodily symptoms and fearful cognitions than were the no-panic episodes. Several understandable links between sensations and cognitions emerged. In their analysis of the (few) differences between expected and unexpected naturally occurring panics, Street, Craske, and Barlow (1989) collected incidental information on the correlations between cognitions and sensations. A direct comparison with the findings of the experiment reported by Rachman et al. (1987) is not possible because the lists of cognitions and sensations used by the two groups are not identical, but the overall patterns of correlation have some common features, notably the high correlation between the sensation of faintness and the cognition of passing out (0.86 in the Rachman study, 0.83 in the Street study).

The links between *combinations* of bodily sensations and cognitions in our research were even clearer than the links between single sensations and single cognitions (Rachman, 1988). For example, when claustrophobic subjects reported bodily symptoms of dizziness, choking, and shortness of breath in association with the cognition of "suffocation," a panic was almost always recorded. Among panic disorder patients, the combination of palpitations, dizziness, and shortness of breath accompanied by the cognition of "passing out" usually was associated with a panic. As expected, the links observed in the panic disorder patients were different from the links observed among claustrophobic subjects. Although the observed links were meaningful, it must be said that they were fewer than might have been expected, and a number of panics were reported by patients even in the absence of an associated fearful cognition. For technical reasons, it is premature to draw any conclusions from these so-called noncognitive panics, but if the finding is replicated in a dependable way, it will limit the explanatory stretch of the cognitive theory.

Having established that more bodily sensations and fearful cognitions are reported on panic trials than on no-panic trials and that understandable links can be demonstrated between the sensations and the cognitions, we next attempted to synthesize the panic experience. Claustrophobic subjects were instructed to notice and concentrate on the relevant bodily sensations (i.e., those on the *DSM-III-R* list) during their periods in the small enclosed space that was used as our test chamber. In this experiment, we obtained some slight suggestion that when the subjects concentrated on their bodily sensations the probability of a panic was increased.

However, the instructions to concentrate on bodily sensations proved to be too weak to produce a significant increase in the attention paid to the bodily sensations.

The results of our second attempt to synthesize panic production produce an unexpected outcome.

We improved the instruction to the subjects and gave them repeated reminders through a prerecorded taped message that they kept with them throughout their time in the test chamber. The improved method certainly increased the percentage of time they spent concentrating on their bodily sensations (and in the case of the control subjects, their concentration on the neutral mental task that was given to them), but the outcome of the experiment was a surprise nevertheless. We found that those subjects who successfully concentrated on the designated task (bodily sensations in the experimental group and a neutral mental task in the control group) reported less fear and fewer panics than did the subjects who failed to improve their concentration on these tasks while in the test chamber. It appears that successful concentration on a task, even a task that we thought would increase the opportunities for panic episodes, serves to inhibit the occurrence of panics. This conclusion is consistent with the stress that Beck and Emery (1985) place on distraction tactics in controlling fear and panic.

CONCLUSIONS

Returning to a question at the opening of this chapter, the present prediction of the probability of experiencing a panic in specifiable circumstances is determined to a considerable extent by the accuracy of the previous predictions. Coming after a series of repeated disconfirmations of expected panics, the current prediction of the probability of panic will be comparatively low. However, the present prediction of the probability of panicking will be increased if the previous prediction was a significant underprediction. The prediction of the probability of future panics will be increased by unexpected panics and remain unchanged by a history of accurate predictions. No systematic research has yet been directed at the genesis of the first set of predictions of panic, and presumably a close link will be found between the initial experience of panic and the development of subsequent predictive accuracy or inaccuracy. However, it should not be assumed that people will predict a probability of panicking only if they have actually experienced a panic; it is possible for people to anticipate that they will have a panic even if they have never experienced one. Another important subject for research is the relationship between panic occurrence and the absence of avoidance. On the present analysis, avoidance behavior will fail to emerge after a panic if the person predicts that there is a low probability of repeat panics or that an expected panic has a low predicted "cost," or if strong safety signals are available. The predicted cost will almost certainly be related to the person's estimation of his self-efficacy and his skills for dealing with the expected event. In sum, a strong and precise link between panic and agoraphobic avoidance behavior will not be observed if the person predicts a low possibility of recurrences or attaches a low cost to the experience.

If the present hypothesis gains support and it can be shown that the major determinant of agoraphobic avoidance behavior is the predicted possibility of a panic occurring in specific and specifiable circumstances, some practical implications will follow.

Any method that succeeds in reducing a person's predicted probability of panic should be followed by a reduction in avoidance; the currently most powerful method for reducing avoidance—exposure exercises—presumably acts on the person's current predictions. It follows, however, that any method that successfully reduces the person's prediction of future panic, whether it includes exposure exercises or not, should produce a degree of success in reducing the avoidance behavior. (This deduction is easily compatible with a cognitive explanation of panic and its reductions.) A second approach would be to minimize the predicted costs or aversiveness of the panic episodes. If the person predicts it highly likely that he or she will have a panic in specifiable circumstances, but no longer feels that the panic episode will be unduly aversive, then avoidance behavior will diminish. Third, if the person acquires coping skills that serve to reduce the predicted aversiveness of a panic episode, then that too should serve to reduce the avoidance behavior. Safety signals would have the same effect.

The behavioral consequences of panic often take the form of avoidance behavior, but there are exceptions. Avoidance can develop after nonpanic experiences; panics are reported by patients who do not display avoidance; and panics are reported by nonpatient samples who do not display avoidance behavior. Panic and avoidance frequently are connected, but panics can occur without avoidance emerging, and avoidance can occur without panics.

The cognitive consequences of panic include the following. Subject to possible moderation by safety signals, panics are followed by increases in predictions of future panics. Panics are followed by increases in expected fear, but little or no increase in reported fear. They are also followed by expectations of reduced safety. Unexpected panics contribute most to these changes in prediction. Expected panics have little effect on reports or expectations of fear and safety. Disconfirmed expectations of panic are followed by reductions in fear. Subjects correctly predict roughly one in three laboratory panics, but show a high rate of overprediction.

The psychophysiological consequences of panic have yet to be analyzed, but four postulates can be formulated.

1. Unpredicted panics are likely to be followed by increases in tonic level of arousal.
2. Unpredicted panics are likely to be followed by the development of conditioned psychophysiological reactions.
3. The consequences of predicted panics will be different and show little or no sign of these changes.
4. Repeated experiences of predicted/unpredicted no-panics will be followed by reduced levels of tonic arousal and the extinction of any conditioned psychophysiological reactions (Rachman, 1988).

Some patients report that they are left exhausted and incapable for as long as 24 hours after a panic episode. Beck (1988) states that during the height of an episode, the person's cognitive ability is impaired and he may find it difficult to access corrective information (see also Teasdale, 1988). Other cognitive and perceptual consequences of panic include a possible state-dependent loss of skill knowledge (Eich, 1980) and an unadaptively narrow focusing of attention as described in the four studies by Baddeley (1972).

Research on the consequences of panic should expand to include experimental analyses of psychophysiological as well as behavioral and cognitive changes. The hypothesis that present predictions of probable panic are the main determinant of panic-related avoidance must be subjected to rigorous testing.

REFERENCES

Alloy, L., & Tabachnik, N. (1984). Assessment of covariation by humans and animals: The joint influence of prior expectations and current situational information. *Psychological Review, 91,* 112–149.

Arntz, A., & van den Hout, M. (1988). Generalizability of the match/mismatch model of fear. *Behaviour Research and Therapy, 26,* 207–224.

Baddeley, A. (1972). Selective attention and performance in dangerous environments. *British Journal of Psychology, 36,* 537–546.

Beck, A. T. (1988). Cognitive approaches to panic disorder: Theory and therapy. In: S. Rachman & J. D. Maser (Eds.), *Panic: Psychological perspectives* (pp. 91–109). Hillsdale, NJ: Lawrence Erlbaum Associates, Inc.

Beck, A. T., & Emery, G. (1985). *Anxiety disorders and phobias—A cognitive perspective.* New York: Basic Books.

Clark, D. (1986). A cognitive approach to panic. *Behaviour Research and Therapy, 24,* 461.

Clark, D. (1988). A cognitive model of panic attacks. In S. Rachman & J. Maser (Eds.), *Panic: Psychological perspective* (pp. 71–90). Hillsdale, NJ: Erlbaum.

Craske, M., & Barlow, D. (1989). A review of the relationship between panic and avoidance. *Clinical Psychological Review, 8,* 667–685.

Carske, M., Rachman, S., & Tallman, K. (1986). Mobility, cognitions and panic. *Journal of Psychopathology, 8,* 199–210.

Craske, M., Sanderson, W., & Barlow, D. (1987). The relationships among panic, fear and avoidance. *Journal of Anxiety Disorders, 1,* 153–160.

Eich, E. (1980). The cue-dependent nature of state-dependent retrieval. *Memory and Cognition, 8,* 157–173.

Gray, J. (1971). *Psychology of fear and stress.* London: Weidenfeld.

Kirsch, I. (1985). Response expectancy as a determinant of experience and behavior. *American Psychologist, 42,* 1189–1202.

Levitt, K., & Lopatka, C. (1987). *The development of panic cognitions.* Unpublished manuscript.

Norton, G., Harrison, B., Hauch, J., & Rhodes, L. (1985). Characteristics of people with infrequent panic attacks. *Journal of Abnormal psychology, 94,* 216–221.

Rachman, S. (1976). The passing of the two-stage theory of fear and avoidance. *Behaviour Research and Therapy, 14,* 125–131.

Rachman, S. J. (1978). *Fear and courage.* San Francisco, CA: W. H. Freeman.

Rachman, S. (1982). Fear and courage: Some military aspects. *Journal of the Royal Army Medical Corps, 128,* 100–104.

Rachman, S. (1984). Agoraphobia—A safety-signal perspective. *Behaviour Research and Therapy, 22,* 59–70.

Rachman, S. (1988). Panics and their consequences. In S. Rachman & J. Maser (Eds.), *Panics: Psychological perspectives.* Hillsdale, NJ: Erlbaum.

Rachman, S. (1989). *Fear and courage* (2nd ed.). New York: W. H. Freeman.

Rachman, S. J. (1990). *Fear and courage* (3rd ed.). San Francisco, CA: W. H. Freeman.

Rachman, S., & Bichard, S. (1988). The overprediction of fear. *Clinical Psychology Review, 8,* 303–312.

Rachman, S., & Levitt, K. (1985). Panics and their consequences. *Behaviour Research and Therapy, 23,* 585–600.

Rachman, S., Levitt, K., & Lopatka, C. (1987). I. Panics: The links between bodily symptoms and cognitions. *Behaviour Research and Therapy, 25,* 411–423.

Rachman, S., & Lopatka, C. (1986). Match and mismatch in the prediction of fear. *Behaviour Research and Therapy, 24,* 387–393.

Reiss, S., & McNally, R. (1985). The expectancy model of fear. In S. Reiss & R. Bootzin (Eds.), *Theoretical issues in behavior therapy* (pp. 46–72). New York: Academic Press.

Seligman, M., & Johnston, J. (1973). A cognitive theory of avoidance learning. In J. McGuigan & B. Lumsden (Eds.), *Contemporary approaches to conditioning and learning.* New York: Wiley.

Seligman, M. E. P. (1988). Competing theories of panic. In: S. Rachman & J. D. Maser (Eds.), *Panic: Psychological perspectives* (pp. 321–329). Hillsdale, NJ: Lawrence Erlbaum Associates, Inc.

Street, L., Craske, M., & Barlow, D. (1989). Sensations, cognitions and cues associated with expected and unexpected panic attack. *Behaviour Research and Therapy, 27,* 189–198.

Taylor, C., Sheikh, J., Agres, S., Roth, W., Margraf, J., Ehlers, A., Maddock, R., & Gossard, D. (1986). Ambulatory heart rate changes in patients with panic attacks. *American Journal of Psychiatry, 143,* 478–482.

Teasdale, J. (1988). Cognitive models and treatments for panic. In S. Rachman & J. Maser (Eds.), *Panic: Psychological perspectives.* Hillsdale, NJ: Erlbaum.

Telch, M., Broulard, M., & Telch, C. (1988). Role of cognitive appraisal in panic-related avoidance. *Behaviour Research and Therapy, 27,* 373–382.

Thorpe, G., & Burns, L. (1983). *The agoraphobic syndrome.* Chichester, England: Wiley.

Uhde, T., Boulenger, J. P., Roy-Byrne, P., Geraci, M., Vittone, B., & Post, R. (1985). Longitudinal course of panic disorder: Clinical and biological considerations. *Progression in Neuro-Psychopharmacology and Biological Psychiatry, 9*(1), 39–51.

Warren, R., Zgourides, G., & Jones, A. (1988). Cognitive bias and irrational belief as predictors of avoidance. *Behaviour Research and Therapy, 27,* 181–188.

CHAPTER 14

A New Cognitive Treatment for Social Phobia: A Single-Case Study

Anthony Bates and David M. Clark

We have outlined a recent cognitive model of social phobia which pays particular attention to the maintenance of the disorder. Within this model self-focused attention, safety behaviors, and selective retrieval strategies interact to prevent social phobics from disconfirming their negative beliefs about the way they appear to others. The model suggests specific clinical interventions which target each of the maintaining factors and which also address key interpersonal assumptions particular to this disorder. The successful 12–session cognitive application of this model to a 30-year-old woman with a 13–year history of the problem is described.

Social phobia is a common and disabling anxiety disorder (Chapman, Mannuzza, & Fyer, 1995). Its defining feature is a marked and persistent fear of social or performance situations due to the individual's belief that they will act in a way that will be embarrassing or humiliating. Typically, feared situations are avoided whenever possible and otherwise endured with considerable discomfort. For some individuals only a small number of specific performance situations (such as writing in public or speaking to an audience) are feared. Others fear a wide range of performance and social interaction situations. In either instance, social phobia is only diagnosed if the fears interfere significantly with the individual's daily routine, occupational, or social functioning. The average age of onset for this problem is during the sufferer's mid-teens, although on average, people generally do not seek professional help until they are about 30 years old (Rapee, 1995). Secondary problems of depression, alcohol abuse, low self-esteem, and social isolation inevitably develop when this problem is left untreated. Controlled trials have shown that existing psychological treatments are effective but there is room for improvement since only about 40% of treated patients fully recover, i.e., achieve "high end-state function" (Mattick & Peters, 1988).

A new cognitive formulation of social phobia (Clark & Wells, 1995) proposes that there are several critical variables which serve to maintain and intensify the problem of social anxiety. When phobics enter threatening social situations, critical *assumptions* are activated regarding the likelihood that they will fail to perform adequately in some aspect of their interpersonal behavior and thereby incur the ridicule of others. Their *focus of attention* rapidly shifts to physiological and cognitive symptoms of their uneasiness. They then use the interoceptive information produced by self-monitoring to construct a *negative image of themselves* as they imagine they must appear to others. Fearful that they will do something wrong and be exposed as inadequate in some way, they resort to specific *safety behaviors*. These behaviors refer to what an individual does to prevent a specific feared outcome from occurring, e.g., covering one's face to prevent others noticing that they are blushing, breaking eye contact to ensure that others won't notice they look tense. Paradoxically these maneuvers serve to draw attention to one's anxiety, increase self-consciousness, and reinforce the individuals' negative image of themselves as a social object.

The interaction of self-focused attention and safety behaviors results in individuals becoming trapped in a closed system in which most of the evidence for their fears is self-generated and disconfirmatory evidence is ignored. These variables interact with, and reinforce, one another in the manner outlined in Figure 14.1. Finally, it is hypothesized in this model that before and after social encounters, social phobics selectively retrieve, and dwell on, negative information which appears to confirm their fears of being socially inadequate.

The treatment approach which Clark, Wells, and colleagues have developed from the above formulation combines a series of cognitive and behavioral interventions which systematically address each of these key variables. This report represents a preliminary account of the successful application of this approach to the treatment of a case of severe social phobia.

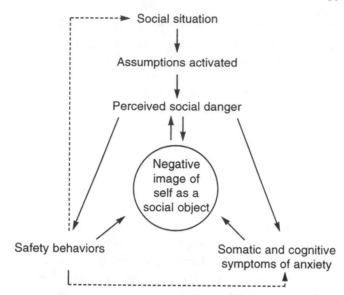

Figure 14.1 A Cognitive Model of Social Phobia (Adapted from Clark and Wells, 1995).

DESCRIPTION OF THE CLIENT

The client, "Lynn," was a 29-year-old woman, separated, with two young children, and a 13–year history of social phobia. She described how she was experiencing severe panic attacks in an ever-increasing number of social situations. These had severely restricted her life and frustrated any hope of pursuing a career. On presentation she was depressed, demoralized, and had become increasingly isolated in her life.

In contrast to her clinical presentation, she remembered being outgoing and confident as a child. She was somewhat shy in her mid-teens but this did not cause her undue distress. However, she recalled that she was 17 when she "crossed over from shyness to panic" in social situations:

> When I was seventeen we moved to a new house and I started a new school. After 3 or 4 days the teacher asked me to read something. I'd never had a problem with this before. I took a deep breath and started off fine. Halfway through reading the passage I suddenly became totally aware that everybody was listening to me, looking at me, that the focus of attention was *completely on me*. I couldn't continue reading. I panicked. I started to feel incredibly anxious, my voice broke up, my breathing went funny. It was a really humiliating experience, really embarrassing. I felt frightened

because I didn't know what was happening. The next time I went to read I thought I would be OK, but the same thing happened.

In the years that followed, Lynn's panic in public was triggered by an ever-increasing range of events. For example, she started at a university and at a tutorial, when she was asked to describe her favorite poem, a panic attack occurred. She found it increasingly difficult to attend classes and eventually left the university for a job she anticipated would not expose her to stressful social situations, i.e., a telephone switchboard operator. For a while she coped with this role, but then she became worried about how her voice sounded on the phone and when certain individuals were around she would "seize up" and be unable to speak.

At this stage of her life she still felt too embarrassed to seek help, and did everything to conceal this problem from friends. She felt the problem was "stupid," and imagined that if she told anyone, their response would be ridicule or criticism. However, when her anxiety attacks began to impact on her relationships with her closest and most trusted friends, she consulted a therapist. Her symptoms at this stage included consistent episodes of sweating, choking, inability to make eye contact, and blushing, in all types of social situations.

ASSESSMENT MEASURES

Standardized measures of anxiety (*BAI:* Beck, Epstein, Brown, & Steer, 1988), depression (*BDI:* Beck, Rush, Shaw, & Emery, 1979), and fear of negative evaluation (*FNE:* Watson & Friend, 1969) were employed to measure mood and general assumptions pertinent to social phobia. More specific measures of those variables considered critical in the cognitive model were also completed weekly by the client to evaluate progress and assess the impact of specific interventions and behavioral assignments. The Social Cognition Questionnaire (*SCQ:* Wells, Stopa, & Clark, 1993) is a 22–item inventory of common cognitions which can preoccupy phobic individuals in social situations, e.g., "I am going red," "People will think I'm boring," "I will babble or talk funny." Items are rated separately along two dimensions: how *frequently* each thought occurred in the past week (rated on a 0–4 scale) and the degree to which the client *believed,* on a 0–100% scale, each thought when it did occur. The Social Behavior Questionnaire (*SBQ:* Clark, Wells, Hackmann, Butler, & Fennell, 1994a) is a 28–item questionnaire which assesses the degree to which clients employ safety behaviors, e.g., "avoid asking questions," "rehearse sentences in your mind." Each item on the SBQ is rated on a 0–3 scale according to how frequently an individual employed a safety strategy (never, sometimes, often, always).

Finally, the Social Summary Questionnaire (*SSQ:* Clark, Wells, Hackmann, Butler, & Fennell, 1994b) is a 5–item inventory which measures level of anticipatory anxiety prior to social encounters, degree of self-focused attention in social situations, and the degree to which subjects engage in postmortem self-critiques following these situations.

CASE CONCEPTUALIZATION

From the earliest moments of therapy a shared conceptualization of her problem was developed with Lynn, and self-monitoring of her anxiety episodes between sessions was used to identify the key components of her social phobia. Recent episodes of anxiety were reviewed to highlight key variables, and self-report inventories were completed by her on a weekly basis.

Table 14.1 illustrates some of the typical symptoms and safety behaviors that characterized Lynn's social anxiety, based on her own monitor-

Table 14.1 Typical Social Situations and Reactions That Characterized Lynn's Social Phobia

Trigger Situations	Perceived Physical Symptoms	Negative Thoughts	Safety Behaviors
Meeting friend of one of my friends in a bar	Heart races rapidly	"Oh my god this is awful"	Break eye contact, hunch shoulders
Sitting down talking to male friend face to face	Blushing	"I'm going to have a major panic attack"	Cover face
Somebody watching me intently doing something	Shaky voice	"How can I stop this person from seeing what a basket case I am"	Smile a lot/talk a lot
Meeting someone I feel I might be attracted to sexually	Hot flushes	"If this guy thinks I'm sexually attracted to him, he'll think I'm a slut"	Curl up and make myself as insignificant as possible

ing of difficult situations she experienced between sessions 1 and 3. Through a process of guided discovery, Lynn was able to identify the manner in which her thoughts, feelings, and behaviors in these situations interacted and reinforced one another.

A common theme in Lynn's accounts of her anxiety experiences was that of being in a situation where there was potential for sexual attraction or sexual demands from another. She had grown up with a father who had berated her for appearing sexual and she was constantly alert to the danger of other people noticing signs of sexual attraction/sexual arousal in her behavior. Being in the company of a man triggered anxiety reactions which were mediated by cognitions such as "This guy will see I'm sexually attracted to him and think I'm a slut." At other times she reported first becoming aware of unpleasant physical sensations, which were accompanied by cognitions such as "Oh my god, I'm going to panic . . . this guy will see I'm a complete nutcase." Somatic sensations included shortness of breath, hot flushes, and a racing heart.

To cope with these crises, Lynn adopted certain safety behaviors, e.g., breaking eye contact, leaning away from the other person, hiding her hands between her knees and partially covering her face. She believed these maneuvers would reduce the chance her anxiety or her sexual interest would be detected.

The net effect of the above reactions was to shift Lynn's focus of attention entirely onto herself, and intensify the negative image she formed of herself as a social object, i.e., as someone who appeared "weird." She pictured herself as someone who "sounded stupid," and as someone who "looked nervous and shaky." She believed that she would be perceived immediately by others to be ill at ease, and therefore be an object of ridicule. This self-focused attention also prevented her from picking up positive cues from social companions. Following these interactions she engaged in "postmortem" evaluations, where she recalled her distorted impressions of others' behavior and further reinforced her negative appraisal of her social presentation.

TREATMENT

Treatment of Lynn's difficulties was based on Clark and Wells's (1995) cognitive model and the clinical interventions suggested by this model (Butler & Wells, 1995; Clark, 1997; Clark & Wells, 1995; Wells, 1997). Through self-monitoring of her thoughts, sensations, and safety behaviors in socially threatening situations a formulation of her disorder was evolved collaboratively with her (Fig. 14.2).

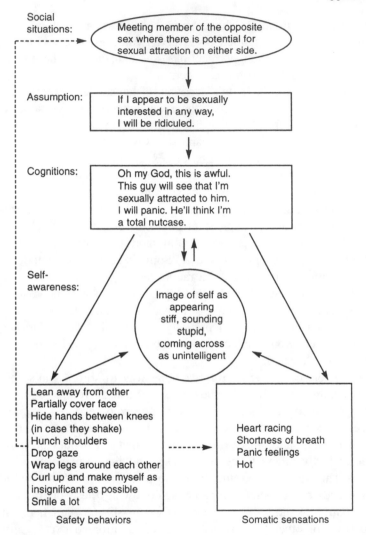

Figure 14.2 A Cognitive Behavioral Formulation of Lynn's Social Anxiety.

Figure 14.2 illustrates the structure of Lynn's anxiety response to a typical socially threatening situation, i.e., where she thought that someone would think she was sexually attracted to them, or that the other person was being attracted to her and pursuing a relationship with her. Treatment combined a series of cognitive and behavioral interventions designed to change her appraisal of herself in social situations, and to shift her attention to others so that she could process positive feedback cues. Homework involved her gradual letting go of safety behaviors in social situations outside of sessions, and risking behaviors which she previously believed would be unacceptable. Key interventions were as follows:

Constructing a More Realistic Image of Self in Social Interactions

While Lynn accepted the formulation of her disorder outlined in Figure 14.2, and while she could see how her use of safety behaviors in particular was self-defeating, she remained concerned about the way she thought she came across in threatening social situations. In social situations a vivid picture of herself as "stiff, stupid, and unintelligent" was activated quite spontaneously and completely dominated her field of awareness. To enable her to see how distorted her self-image was on these occasions, a video-feedback experiment was devised.

The first step in this experiment involved having Lynn write out her most common safety behaviors and practice using them in role-play with the therapist. Moving to another chair in the therapist's office she would practice "dropping" these behaviors and repeating the role-play. When she was clear about these two conditions we proceeded to the next stage of the experiment. A "stooge" (a young attractive male psychiatric registrar who was completely unaware of the purpose of this experiment) was invited to sit with her in the video room and engage her in a normal conversation. For the first five minutes Lynn engaged in conversation with this stranger and according to a prearranged plan employed her usual safety behaviors. This interaction was filmed and at the end of this sequence the stooge was asked to step outside for a few minutes. Lynn then rated the following on a 0 to 10 scale:

- How anxious did she feel during the conversation?
- How anxious did she feel she came across to the registrar?
- What was she attending to in the situation?
- What was her image of herself?
- What general impression did she feel she made on the registrar?

Having written down this self-rating Lynn invited the stooge to rejoin her and her therapist who then asked him the same questions. While Lynn had estimated her felt anxiety to be 6, and her visible anxiety at 6, she was surprised to get feedback to the effect that she was rated at only 3 on this scale by the registrar. Furthermore she had impressed him not so much as being anxious as "unfriendly," or perhaps "bored." This particular feedback came as a visible shock to Lynn, since it conflicted radically with her image of herself as outgoing and friendly, albeit anxious. In subsequent discussions, the therapist and Lynn were able to identify what had made her appear unfriendly and bored to the registrar were in fact her safety behaviors (leaning away from him, dropping her gaze).

Following this feedback phase Lynn continued to converse with the stooge for another five minutes, while deliberately dropping her safety behaviors. Her ratings for how anxious she *felt,* and how anxious she *appeared* to the stooge during this phase of the experiment were both 7. She believed her anxiety would be more apparent to him when she didn't deliberately try to cover it up. The feedback she received, however, was that she seemed even less anxious now to the stooge, and that she impressed him as being much more friendly and interested.

Lynn rated her attention as being completely self-focused during the exercise, and she was unable to describe objectively how the stooge had behaved during their conversation. When she received the stooge's feedback she realized her social image of herself, which had been that of a "nervous wreck," was entirely based on how she was feeling. While this feedback was surprising and encouraging for Lynn, the major shift in her social anxiety occurred a week later when she watched the complete video footage of this experiment with the therapist.

Homework was assigned in the intervening week which involved Lynn writing out her predictions about what she would see when she watched herself on video during her next session. Among the items she included were additional concerns about her voice sounding "stupid," her demeanor looking "uneasy," and her anxiety being very obvious to her, even if the stooge had failed to notice it. All of these predictions were written down and rated. At the next session she watched the video and rated herself in respect to each of her fears. The discrepancy between the video image and the much more negative self-image she had of herself was striking and made a very strong impact on her. Even those moments where she appeared slightly awkward or uneasy were not nearly as obvious in Lynn's own judgment as she had predicted. Furthermore she saw that many of her apparent social difficulties were merely the observable effects of her safety behaviors and she saw how these disappeared in the second part of the experiment when she "dropped" these behaviors. In the week following (between the fourth and fifth sessions), her scores on the Social Cognition Questionnaire belief scale showed a dramatic drop (see Fig. 14.3).

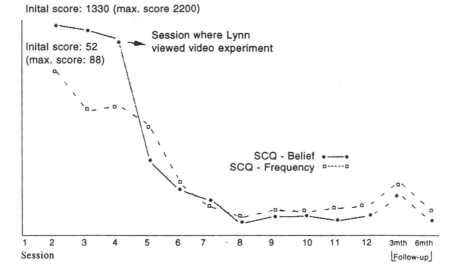

Figure 14.3 Changes in Social Cognition Questionnaire Scales Over the Course of Treatment.

Her homework assignment following the session where she watched the video was to write out for herself what she had observed, and draw out the possible implications of this for her image of herself in social situations, e.g., "how I feel is no indication of how I come across to others."

Testing Predictions About Negative Evaluations by Others

Having deconstructed Lynn's compelling negative image of herself, the focus of therapy moved to helping Lynn construct an alternative image of herself in social situations by focusing on the situation rather than her subjective sensations, risking new behaviors, and paying careful attention to others' reactions. Given that one of her central fears concerned the dreaded possibility that some eligible male might become aware she was attracted to him sexually and ridicule her for this, we devised the following experiment, scripted by Lynn herself, to allow her to test this prediction.

Another naive confederate—a 28-year-old male research psychologist—was invited to engage her in conversation. At a particular point in their conversation, Lynn, having dropped her safety behaviors, asked him whether he was currently in a relationship. He confirmed that he was, and she quite spontaneously commented, "what a pity." This was a major risk for her as it clearly suggested she found him attractive. However, she discovered that taking this risk made her feel more relaxed, while her partner was overcome with blushing. He said later he had not felt so much anxious as flattered and slightly embarrassed. Lynn followed up this experiment with other social risks, which she recorded, and found that contrary to her fears she was becoming more comfortable in situations where she allowed herself to be a little spontaneous with others. She commented that the effect of these experiments was to make her pay more attention to the response of others rather than be absorbed in her own fantasy of how she was coming across.

Modifying Dysfunctional Assumptions

An assumption which led Lynn to interpret many social situations in a threatening way concerned her right as a woman to present herself in a sexual way. While the earlier part of treatment had focused on her overt appraisals and symptomatology, the latter part of treatment began to focus on modifying many of the abusive messages she had received as a young teenager regarding her sexuality. This shift in the focus of therapy was prompted by a spontaneous eruption of anger which occurred at the beginning of the seventh session.

Lynn presented at this session in a very agitated state and began to recount the words her father had used toward her when she emerged out of puberty with a positive regard for her appearance, and a natural concern to make herself attractive to boys. She presented a list of words her father had used in response to these changes. Terms such as "slut," "whore," "dumb blonde," "stupid bitch," "cheap," "brainless" were among the many words he had fired at her daily. She experienced intense affect in recalling these abuses, and became very upset as she realized how she had been "set up" to experience incredible confusion and shame about her sexuality in adulthood. She also realized how angry she felt generally toward men, and admitted to having had a series of lesbian relationships which she now interpreted as one expression of this anger. By asking questions such as "Looking back on that time, what was the worst thing about this for you?" it was possible to direct Lynn to express and process her feelings about what had been said to her, and clearly identify the negative assumption she had concluded as a result.

Lynn's core interpersonal schema gradually became crystallized in the following way: "If people see me as I really am, they will see I'm bad and reject me." Over the remaining sessions she addressed many key childhood experiences that underpinned this belief:

I had always held the belief that I was intrinsically "bad" and I was fearful of revealing my "true" self to others believing that they would shun me if they saw how bad I really was. Having someone independent listen and validate me as a useful person, entitled to her opinions, helped my recovery enormously. I learned by degrees to be more "real" with people, and through continued exposure I realized that nothing catastrophic actually happened. Over time, my confidence blossomed to the point now where I don't really care what other people think about me. I am happy with myself and I take care of myself in lots of ways I never considered important before.

Writing a Personal 'Blueprint' for Recovery

At the tenth session Lynn was invited to write a comprehensive account of the therapy experiences which had been critically important in helping her overcome her social phobia. Specific questions were suggested to help her complete this exercise and maximize its effectiveness:

- What is it that keeps your social anxiety going?
- What were your main negative automatic thoughts in social situations, and how do you now answer these?
- What evidence do you have that these thoughts are not true?
- What is the best way to deal with social anxiety in the future?

The purpose of the blueprint was to help Lynn consolidate her understanding of what she had learned about her condition, and to make explicit the alternative ways of thinking she had evolved regarding her self-image and other people's expectations of her. The final session involved a review of this material, and a relapse rehearsal exercise where the therapist confronted her with familiar negative thoughts that were likely to occur when she became socially anxious. Formal treatment was then terminated and follow-up sessions were scheduled.

Outcome

Table 14.2 summarizes Lynn's scores on the inventories described above, before and after treatment and at three- and six–month follow-up visits. Substantial reductions in symptomatology are evident on all measures, and these gains are maintained or improved upon at six–month follow-ups. Of particular interest was the reduction in Lynn's scores on the FNE, a measure which is generally considered difficult to change (Taylor, Woody, McClean, & Koch, 1997). At pretreatment Lynn had the maximum pos-

Table 14.2 Changes Over the Course of Treatment and Follow-Up to Key Aspects of Lynn's Social Phobia

Measure	Pre	Post	3–month Follow-up	6–month Follow-up
Fear of Negative Evaluation – *FNE* (0–30)	30	9	15	8
Social Summary Questionnaire – *SSQ* (0–40)	3	6	15	11
Social Cognition *SCQ* – Frequency (0–88)	52	10	24	14
Social Cognition *SCQ* – Belief (0–2200)	1330	160	320	120
Social Behavior Questionnaire – *SBQ* (0–84)	49	24	23	19
Beck Anxiety Inventory – *BAI* (0–63)	31	8	13	6
Beck Depression Questionnaire – *BDI* (0–63)	21	9	25	6

sible FNE score (30). At posttreatment, her score (9) was in the normal range and below the general population mean.

Figure 14.3 summarizes changes in her scores on each of the two central measures of negative social cognitions employed. These reflect a definite reduction in negative cognitions and suggest she was far less persuaded by these cognitions at termination and follow-up. Two features of her score profiles deserve comment. On the one hand it is interesting to observe that the most significant drop in her SCQ—Belief scores occurred between sessions 4 and 5, which coincided with her watching the video of herself in the original video experiment, and being struck with the discrepancy between her predicted and actual response to seeing herself cope with a socially threatening situation. This is consistent with the cognitive conceptualization of this disorder which views the patients' distorted image of themselves as a social object as a pivotal factor in maintaining the disorder.

Another feature of these score profiles is the slight lapse in her mood at the three–month follow-up. This coincided with Lynn's returning from a week's holiday with her mother. For the first time she realized how critical her mother was. Most days she criticized her two grandchildren for their appearance, the noise they created, and the "mess" they made of the house. What was striking for Lynn was the frequency with which her mother made comments to the effect of "What will the neighbors think?" Lynn's preoccupation with making the right impression became even more understandable to her from this perspective, but she also became briefly depressed as she acknowledged how little support her mother had been to her throughout her childhood.

CONCLUSION

A cognitive model of social phobia was applied to the treatment of a woman with a 13–year history of panic in social situations. These attacks had severely restricted her social life and created secondary problems of demoralization and low self-esteem. The success of this approach was attributed by the patient herself to the realization that her image of herself as a social object was grossly distorted. This image had been based exclusively on self-focused attention to negative interoceptive cues rather than on any objective social feedback. Through in-session experimentation she discovered the benefits of letting go her safety and focused outwardly on others' reactions. Through regular homework practice she gradually constructed a new image of herself in social situations and disconfirmed long-standing assumptions regarding what was acceptable social behavior. This represents an encouraging preliminary report for this new treatment approach. Further research is required to validate the treatment and a controlled trial is under way.

REFERENCES

American Psychiatric Association (1994). *Diagnostic and Statistical Manual of Mental Disorders, 4th. Edition–DSM-IV.* Washington, DC: Author.

Beck, A. T., Epstein, N., Brown, G., & Steer, R. A. (1988). An inventory for measuring clinical anxiety: Psychometric properties. *Journal of Consulting and Clinical Psychology, 56,* 893–897.

Beck, A. T., Rush, A. J., Shaw, B. F., & Emery, G. (1979). *Cognitive therapy of depression.* New York: Guilford Press.

Butler, G., & Wells, A. (1995). Cognitive-behavioral treatments: Clinical applications. In R. G. Heimberg, M. R. Liebowitz, D. A. Hope, & F. R. Schneier (Eds.), *Social phobia: Diagnosis, assessment, and treatment* (pp. 310–333). New York: Guilford.

Chapman, T. F., Mannuzza, S., & Fyer, A. J. (1995). Epidemiology and family studies of social phobia. In R. G. Heimberg, M. R. Liebowitz, D. A. Hope, & F. R. Schneier (Eds.), *Social phobia: Diagnosis, assessment, and treatment* (pp. 21–40). New York: Guilford.

Clark, D. M., Wells, A., Hackman, A., Butler, G., & Fennell, M. J. U. (1994a). *Social Behavior Questionnaire.* Unpublished. Department of Psychiatry, University of Oxford, Warneford Hospital, Oxford, England.

Clark, D. M., Wells, A., Hackmann, A., Butler, G., & Fennell, M. J. U. (1994b). *Social Summary Questionnaire.* Unpublished. Department of Psychiatry, University of Oxford, Warneford Hospital, Oxford, England.

Clark, D. M., & Wells, A. (1995). A cognitive model of social phobia. In R. G. Heimberg, M. R. Liebowitz, D. A. Hope, & F. R. Schneier (Eds.), *Social phobia: Diagnosis, assessment, and treatment* (pp. 69–93). New York: Guilford.

Clark, D. M. (1997). Panic disorder and social phobia. In D. M. Clark & C. G. Fairburn (Eds.), *Science and the practice of cognitive behavior therapy.* Oxford: Oxford University Press.

Marks, I. M., & Gelder, M. G. (1996). Different ages of onset of different phobias. *American Journal of Psychiatry, 11,* 757–769.

Mattick, R. P., & Peters, L. (1988). Treatment of severe social phobia: Effects of guided exposure with and without cognitive restructuring. *Journal of Consulting and Clinical Psychology, 56,* 251–260.

Rapee, R. M. (1995). Descriptive psychopathology of social phobia. In R. G. Heimberg, M. R. Liebowitz, D. A. Hope, & F. R. Schneier (Eds.), *Social phobia: Diagnosis, assessment, and treatment* (pp. 41–66). New York: Guilford.

Taylor, S., Woody, S., McLean, P. D., & Koch, W. J. (1997). Sensitivity of outcome measures for treatments of generalized social phobia. *Psychological Assessment, 4,* 181–191.

Watson, D., & Friend, R. (1969). Measurement of social evaluation anxiety. *Journal of consulting and clinical psychology, 33,* 448–457.

Wells, A. (1997). *Cognitive therapy of anxiety disorders.* Chichester: Wiley.

Wells, A., Stopa, L., & Clark, D. M. (1993). *Social cognition questionnaire.* Unpublished. Department of Psychiatry, University of Oxford, Warneford Hospital, Oxford, England.

World Health Organization. (1992). *The ICD-10 classification of mental and behavioral disorders: Clinical descriptors and diagnostic guidelines.* World Health Organization: Geneva.

CHAPTER 15

Cognitive Therapy for Generalized Anxiety Disorder: Significance of Comorbid Personality Disorders

William C. Sanderson, Aaron T. Beck, and Lata K. McGinn

Thirty-two patients diagnosed with generalized anxiety disorder were treated with cognitive therapy. Patients attended weekly one-hour sessions and there was no predetermined duration of treatment. Prior to treatment, each patient was evaluated for a comorbid personality disorder (PD) using the Structured Clinical Interview for the DSM-III-R Personality Disorders (SCID-II). Patients completed the Beck Anxiety Inventory (BAI) and Beck Depression Inventory (BDI) at the intake evaluation and at their final session. Sixteen of the 32 patients were diagnosed with a comorbid PD at the intake evaluation. A total of 22 patients completed a minimum course of cognitive therapy, which was defined as six sessions. Overall, there was a significant reduction of BAI and BDI scores for patients with and without a PD. There was no significant difference between the two groups. However, patients with a comorbid PD were more likely to drop out of treatment. Seven of the ten dropouts had a comorbid PD as compared to only nine out of the 22 completers.

Compared with the substantial progress made in the cognitive behavioral treatment of many of the anxiety disorders (e.g., panic disorders, social phobia), generalized anxiety disorder (GAD) has received surprisingly little attention, especially in view of data from the Epidemiological Catchment Area survey demonstrating that GAD is a common disorder, with a one-year prevalence rate of 3.8% (Blazer, Hughes, George, Swartz, & Boyer, 1991). The lack of treatment studies with GAD patients may be due in part to the fact that GAD was not officially recognized as a primary diagnostic category until the appearance of the DSM-III-Revised (American Psychiatric Association, 1987; Sanderson & Barlow, 1990). In the DSM-III (American Psychiatric Association, 1980), GAD was a residual diagnostic category, only to be diagnosed when the patient did not meet the criteria for any other anxiety or affective disorder. This may have prohibited the notion that GAD is an independent disorder requiring treatment, resulting in the lack of treatment studies.

To date, many of the studies evaluating cognitive behavioral treatments of *chronic anxiety* have been conducted with anxious volunteer subjects rather than carefully diagnosed patients presenting for treatment (cf. Brown, Hertz, & Barlow, 1992). More recently, several studies have demonstrated the efficacy of various cognitive behavioral approaches among patients appropriately diagnosed with GAD (e.g., Barlow, Rapee, & Brown, 1992; Blowers, Cobb, & Mathews, 1987; Borkovec & Mathews, 1988; Butler, Fennell, Robson, & Gelder, 1991).

Over the past several years there has been an increasing interest in the clinical significance of personality disorders (PDs) in patients with anxiety disorders. Much of the renewed interest in this area is due to research demonstrating that comorbid PDs are prevalent among patients with anxiety disorders (cf. Brooks, Baltazar, & Munjack, 1989; Sanderson, Wetzler, Beck, & Betz, in press) which may predict a poor response to psychological and pharmacological treatment (Noyes, Reich et al., 1990; Green & Curtis, 1988; Reich & Green, 1991; Turner, 1987). Although nearly 50% of patients with GAD have a comorbid PD (Sanderson, Wetzler, Beck, & Betz, 1994; Sanderson, Friedman, Wetzler, Kaplan, M., & Asnis, 1992), to date no study has examined the impact of comorbid PDs on the treatment of GAD. Therefore, the present study examined the impact of PD on the treatment outcome of 32 GAD patients receiving cognitive therapy.

METHOD

Thirty-two patients diagnosed with GAD (17 females, 15 males, mean age = 35.4 years, *SD* = 10.6) served as subjects in this study. Axis I and

Axis II diagnoses were determined during a comprehensive intake evaluation and were based upon the administration of the Structured Clinical Interview for the DSM-III-R (SCID). The Axis I (SCID-P; Spitzer, Williams, Gibbon, & First, 1990a) and Axis II (SCID-II; Spitzer, Williams, Gibbon, & First, 1990b) versions were administered. Patients were treated with cognitive therapy (as described by Beck & Emery, 1985) by postdoctoral psychologists at the Center for Cognitive Therapy, University of Pennsylvania. Patients attended weekly one-hour sessions and there was *no* predetermined duration of treatment. All patients completed the Beck Anxiety Inventory (BAI; Beck, Epstein, & Brown, 1988) and Beck Depression Inventory (BDI; Beck, Steer, & Garbin, 1988) at the intake evaluation and at the final session. The BAI is a measure of general anxiety (somatic and psychological symptoms), which is the most relevant feature of GAD. Since patients with GAD often present with depressive symptomatology (Riskind et al., 1991), the BDI is a relevant outcome measure as well.

RESULTS

Sixteen of the 32 (50%) patients were diagnosed with a comorbid PD at the intake evaluation (avoidant [5], dependent [4], PD not otherwise specified [4], obsessive-compulsive [1], histrionic [1], paranoid [1]). This rate is consistent with that found in several other independent samples using the same assessment procedure (49% in Sanderson et al., 1994; 47% in Sanderson et al., 1992).

Out of 32 patients who entered the study, 22 completed a minimum course of cognitive therapy, which we defined as six sessions (completers). The remaining ten patients were categorized as dropouts, since they did not receive an adequate trial of cognitive therapy. For completers, the mean number of cognitive therapy sessions was 14.7 ($SD =$ 10.4, range = 6–39, median = 11). Seventeen patients attended 15 sessions or less. The number of sessions attended was not related to severity of illness, as determined by intake evaluation BAI and BDI scores (Pearson correlation of BAI with number of sessions, $r = .22$, $p = .21$; BDI with number of sessions, $r = -.13$, $p = .49$).

Treatment efficacy was compared for GAD patients (completers only) with ($N = 9$) or without a PD ($N = 13$). Repeated measures analyses of variance (ANOVA) were conducted separately on BAI and BDI scores to assess treatment efficacy. As can be seen in Table 15.1, there was a significant reduction of BAI scores for patients with and without a PD (F {1,20} = 35.3, $p < .001$). There was no significant difference between the

Table 15.1 Mean (SD) Beck Anxiety Inventory and Beck Depression Inventory Scores at Pre and End of Treatment for Patients with GAD

	Intake	End of Treatment*
Beck Anxiety Inventory Score		
Patients with a Personality Disorder (n = 9)	19.7 (11.6)	8.0 (7.6)
Patients without a Personality Disorder (n = 13)	22.3 (10.5)	5.2 (3.6)
Beck Depression Inventory Score		
Patients with a Personality Disorder (n = 9)	15.9 (11.3)	5.4 (6.1)
Patients without a Personality Disorder (n = 13)	19.4 (7.3)	6.4 (5.8)

Note. *Final Session

two groups (F {1,20} = .001, p = .97), and the group by time interaction was not significant (F {1,20} = 1.3, p = .27).

There was also a significant reduction of BDI scores for patients with and without a PD (Table 15.1) (F {1,20} = 45.9, p < .001). There was no significant difference between the two groups (F {1,20} = .6, p = .44) and the group by time interaction was not significant (F {1,20} = .6, p = .46).

In an attempt to address the clinical significance of these findings, we used the following composite criterion: at least a 50% reduction and a score of 10 or less on the BAI (BDI) at the end of treatment. Eighteen of the 22 patients (82%) met this criterion on the BAI. These 18 patients comprised 12 with no comorbid PD and six with a comorbid PD (X^2 = 2.4, df = 1, p = .13). Sixteen of the 22 patients (73%) met this criterion on the BDI. These 16 patients comprised nine with no comorbid PD and seven with a comorbid PD (X^2 = 0.2, df = 1, p = .66).

Dropouts

Patients with a comorbid PD were more likely to drop out of treatment. Seven of the ten dropouts had a comorbid PD as compared with only nine out of the 22 completers (X^2 = 2.3, df = 1, p = .13).

Dropouts and completers were compared on pretreatment BAI and BDI scores. On the BAI, the mean score for dropouts was 16.5 *(SD = 5.9)* compared with 21.2 (*SD* = 10.8) for completers (*t* = 1.3, *df* = 30, *p* = .21). On the BDI, the mean score for dropouts was 15.7 *(SD* = 8.4) compared with 18.0 *(SD* = 9.1) for completers (*t* = .7, *df* = 30, *p* = .51).

DISCUSSION

Results from this study demonstrate that cognitive therapy is an effective treatment for GAD, as determined by reductions on both anxiety and depression self-rating scales. A majority of patients were treated within 15 sessions. These findings are in agreement with previous controlled studies examining the efficacy of various forms of cognitive behavior therapy for GAD (Barlow et al., 1992; Blowers et al., 1987; Borkovec & Mathews, 1988; Butler et al., 1991).

Recently, there has been an increased interest in the prevalence and clinical significance of PDs in patients with anxiety disorders. Much of the renewed interest in this area is due to research which suggests that: (1) PDs are prevalent among patients with anxiety disorders (Baer et al., 1990; Friedman, Shear, & Frances, 1987; Reich & Noyes, 1986; Sanderson et al., 1994; Sanderson et al., 1992; Turner, Beidel, & Borden, 1992); (2) The presence of a comorbid PD diagnosis may predict a poor response to psychological and pharmacological treatment of anxiety disorder patients (Noyes et al., 1990; Gren & Curtis, 1988; Turner, 1987).

To date, we are not aware of any study examining the impact of a PD on treatment outcome in GAD patients. In our study, the presence of a comorbid PD did not diminish the efficacy of treatment for those patients completing an adequate trial. However, patients with a comorbid PD accounted for a greater proportion of the dropouts. Although the results only approached statistical significance, seven of the ten dropouts had a comorbid PD as compared with only nine out of the 22 completers.

In the present study, 31% of the patients dropped out before completing a minimum course of treatment. This rate is equivalent to that found in Barlow et al. (1992) and Blowers et al. (1987). Our data suggest that the high dropout rate observed in these GAD treatment studies may be primarily accounted for by the high rate of comorbid PDs. Although Barlow et al. (1992) and Blowers et al. (1987) did not assess for the presence of a comorbid PD, it is likely that the rate of comorbid PDs in their studies is equivalent to that observed in the present study, which is consistent with other independent samples (Sanderson et al., 1994; Sanderson et al., 1992). Presumably, interpersonal difficulties common in patients with PDs impact upon the therapeutic relationship and interfere with the patient's ability to engage in a full course of therapy.

ACKNOWLEDGMENT

This paper was presented at the Annual Meeting of the Association for the Advancement of Behavior Therapy, New York City, November 1991.

REFERENCES

American Psychiatric Association. (1980). *Diagnostic and statistical manual of mental disorders* (3rd ed.). Washington, DC: Author.

American Psychiatric Association. (1987). *Diagnostic and statistical manual of mental disorders* (3rd ed. rev.), Washington, DC: Author.

Baer, L., Jenike, M., Ricciardi, J., Holland, A., Seymour, R., Minichiello, W., & Buttolph, L. (1990). Standardized assessment of personality disorders in obsessive-compulsive disorder. *Archives of General Psychiatry, 47,* 826–830.

Barlow, D. H., Rapee, R. M., & Brown, T. A. (1992). Behavioral treatment of generalized anxiety disorder. *Behavior Therapy, 23,* 551–570.

Beck, A. T., & Emery, G. (1985). *Anxiety disorders and phobias: A cognitive perspective.* New York: Basic Books.

Beck, A. T., Epstein, N., & Brown, G. (1988). An inventory for measuring clinical anxiety. *Journal of Consulting and Clinical Psychology, 56,* 893–897.

Beck, A. T., Steer, R. A., & Garbin, M. G. (1988). Psychometric properties of the Beck depression inventory: Twenty-five years later. *Clinical Psychology Review, 8,* 77–100.

Blazer, D. G., Hughes, D., George, L. K., Swartz, M., & Boyer, R. (1991). Generalized anxiety disorder. In L. N. Robins & D. A. Regier (Eds.), *Psychiatric disorders in America: The Epidemiological Catchment Area study* (pp. 180–203). New York: The Free Press.

Blowers, C., Cobb, J., & Mathews, A. (1987). Generalised anxiety: A controlled treatment study. *Behavioral Research Therapy, 25*(6), 493–502.

Borkovec, T. D., & Mathews, A. M. (1988). Treatment of nonphobic anxiety disorders: A comparison of nondirective, cognitive, and coping desensitization therapy. *Journal of Consulting and Clinical Psychology, 56*(6), 877–884.

Brooks, R. B., Baltazar, P. L., & Munjack, D. J. (1989). Co-occurrence of personality disorders with panic disorder, social phobia, and generalized anxiety disorder: A review of the literature. *Journal of Anxiety Disorders, 3,* 259–285.

Brown, T. A., Hertz, R. M., & Barlow, D. H. (1992). New developments in cognitive-behavioral treatment of anxiety disorders. In A. Tasman (Ed.), *Psychiatric Press Review of Psychiatry:* Vol. 11. (pp. 285–306). Washington, DC: American Psychiatric Association.

Butler, G., Fennell, M., Robson, J., & Gelder, M. (1991). Comparison of behavior therapy and cognitive behavior therapy in the treatment of generalised anxiety disorder. *Journal of Consulting and Clinical Psychology, 59*(1), 167–175.

Friedman, C. J., Shear, M. K., & Frances, A. (1987). DSM-III personality disorders in panic patients. *Journal of Personality Disorders, 1,* 132–135.

Green, M. A., & Curtis, G. C. (1988). Personality disorders in panic patients: response to termination of antipanic medication. *Journal of Personality Disorders, 2*(4), 303–314.

Noyes, R. J., Reich, J., Christiansen, J., Suelzer, M., Pfohl, B., & Coryell, W. A. (1990). Outcome of panic disorder. *Archives of General Psychiatry, 47,* 809–818.

Reich, J. H., & Green, A. I. (1991). Effect of personality disorders on outcome of treatment. *Journal of Nervous and Mental Disease, 179*(2), 74–82.

Reich, J. H., & Noyes, R. (1986). A comparison of DSM-III personality disorders in acutely ill panic and depressed patients. *Journal of Anxiety Disorders, 1,* 123–131.

Riskind, J. H., Moore, R., Harman, B., Hohmann, A. A., Beck, A. T., & Stewart, B. (1991). The relation of generalized anxiety disorder to depression in general and dysthymic disorder in particular. In R. M. Rapee & D. H. Barlow (Eds.), *Chronic anxiety, generalized anxiety disorder, and mixed anxiety-depression* (pp.153–171). New York: Guilford.

Sanderson, W. C., & Barlow, D. H. (1990). A description of patients diagnosed with DSM-III-R generalized anxiety disorder. *Journal of Nervous and Mental Disease, 178,* 588–591.

Sanderson, W. C., Friedman, T. A., Wetzler, S., Kaplan, M., & Asnis, G. M. (1992, November) . *Personality disorders in patients with major depression, panic disorder, and generalized anxiety disorder.* Paper presented at the annual meeting of the Association for the Advancement of Behavior Therapy, Boston, MA.

Sanderson, W. C., Wetzler, S., Beck, A. T., & Betz, F. (1994). Prevalence of personality disorders in patients with anxiety disorders. *Psychiatry Research, 51,* 167–174.

Spitzer, R. L., Williams J. B. W., Gibbon, M., & First, M. B. (1990a). *Structured Clinical Interview for DSM-III-R–Patient Edition* (SCID-P, Version 1.0). Washington, DC: American Psychiatric Press.

Spitzer, R. L., Williams J. B. W., Gibbon, M., & First, M. B. (1990b). *Structured Clinical Interview for DSM-III-R–Personality Disorders* (SCID-II, Version 1.0). Washington, DC: American Psychiatric Press.

Turner, S. M. (1987). The effects of personality disorder on the outcome of social anxiety symptom reduction. *Journal of Personality Disorders, 1,* 136–143.

Turner, S. M., Beidel, D. C., Borden, J. W., (1992). Social phobia: Axis I and II correlates. *Journal of Abnormal Psychology, 101,* 326–331.

CHAPTER 16

Imagery Rescripting: A New Treatment for Survivors of Childhood Sexual Abuse Suffering From Posttraumatic Stress

Mervin R. Smucker, Constance Dancu,
Edna B. Foa, and Jan L. Niederee

Imagery rescripting is presented as a new treatment of posttraumatic stress disorder (PTSD) for adult survivors of childhood sexual abuse. A theoretical discussion illustrates the model's consistency with schema theory and information processing models of PTSD, and suggests that the rescripting process may affect change in pathological schemas associated with interpretation of the traumatic event(s). It is proposed that this combination of imaginal exposure, mastery imagery, and cognitive restructuring goes beyond extinction models to alter recurring images of the trauma and create more adaptive schemas. Hypothesized mechanisms for PTSD symptom reduction are presented, implications for cognitive restructuring are noted, and the model's potential for facilitating personal empowerment and self-nurturance are discussed. Preliminary outcome research data are summarized that support the efficacy of imagery rescripting in significantly reducing PTSD symptomatology with this population.

Over the past decade, a growing body of literature has attested to the alarming prevalence of childhood sexual abuse and its deleterious effects on the lives of adult survivors (Briere, 1989, 1992; Finkelhor, Hotaling, Lewis, & Smith, 1989; Russell, 1986). Numerous studies have indicated that a history of childhood sexual abuse is associated with psychological difficulties in adulthood, such as increased rates of chronic depression, suicidality and self-destructive behaviors, interpersonal and sexual difficulties, chronic anxiety, and posttraumatic stress disorder. Feelings of guilt, self-blame, self-disgust, self-hatred, low self-esteem, inferiority and powerlessness, and mistrust of others are frequently cited in the clinical literature as long-term effects of sexual abuse (Bagley & Ramsay, 1986; Briere, 1989; Briere & Runtz, 1992; Browne & Finkelhor, 1986; Courtois, 1979; Elliot & Briere, 1992; Herman, 1981, 1992; Janoff-Bulman, 1985; Jehu, 1991; McCann, Sackheim, & Abrahamson, 1988; Tsai & Wagner, 1978).

A number of the above effects may be generated by cognitive distortions and maladaptive beliefs about the self and the interpersonal world that became part of the child's cognitive schemata when the trauma(s) occurred. Indeed, the pathogenic effects of negative core beliefs associated with sexual abuse have been posed as a significant component of posttrauma reactions (Jehu, Gazan, & Klassen, 1984–1985; Jehu, Klassen, & Gazan, 1985–1986). Briere (1989, 1992) has noted that the cognitive effects of negative self-evaluation, guilt, helplessness, hopelessness, and profound distrust may act as contributory factors in producing the affective and interpersonal problems which plague survivors. Jehu, Klassen, and Gazan (1985–1986) report that survivors of childhood sexual abuse often hold distorted beliefs arising from the experience which appear to contribute to disturbances such as low self-esteem, sadness, and guilt. McCann and Pearlman (1990a, 1990b) cite disruption of cognitive schemas as pathogenic factors in postabuse symptomatology, noting that such disturbance occurs in core areas of safety, trust, power, esteem, intimacy, independence, and frame of reference. Factors such as vulnerability, isolation, powerlessness, anger, betrayal, and sadness and loss have been reported by Edwards and Donaldson (1989), who utilize cognitive techniques to restructure the beliefs thought to underlie such effects (Donaldson & Gardner, 1985). Janoff-Bulman (1985) proposes that posttraumatic reactions result, in part, from the "shattering of assumptions" by the onslaught of trauma—assumptions about the benevolence and meaningfulness of the world, self-worth, and personal invulnerability.

Two cognitive processes, assimilation and accommodation, have been proposed as key factors in the interpretation of trauma (McCann, Pearlman, Sakkheim, & Abrahamson, 1988; Resick and Schnicke, 1990). As noted by Hollon and Garber (1988) and Resick and Schnicke (1990), when persons are exposed to schema-discrepant information, either assimilation or accommodation may occur. In the first instance, the information itself may be altered in order to be assimilated into already-existing schemas. In cases of incest, pathological assimilation could manifest as, "Daddy wouldn't do something like that—maybe it really wasn't so bad." At times the information may actually defy assimilation, existing instead as dissociated material which reemerges as flashbacks, nightmares, flashes of affect, or memory fragments (Horowitz, 1976).

With accommodation, however, the existing schema is altered in order to "take in" the discrepant information (Hollon & Garber, 1988). Thus, a child's schema related to self-efficacy may become disrupted to the point that a schema of powerlessness becomes dominant, trust may be replaced by mistrust, and a schema of the self as positive may be so distorted that a sense of the self as stigmatized and evil is formed.

Because childhood sexual abuse is, by definition, pathological, it is not surprising that changes in existing schemas are predominately pathogenic. Several basic themes emerge in the thinking of adult abuse survivors which suggest the influence of maladaptive schemas. The presence of degrading self-perceptions, guilt, powerlessness, helplessness, passivity, profound mistrust, and fear of intimacy may indicate that fundamental assumptions were distorted by the trauma of sexual abuse and that maladaptive schema formation occurred.

As the effects of schema disruption in sexual abuse survivors receive increasing attention in the literature, interventions designed to address this aspect of postabuse pathology are becoming more prevalent in clinical work. Cognitive-behavioral techniques such as assertiveness training, stress inoculation training, recording of automatic thoughts, examining the current validity of assumptions, and using imagery to identify core beliefs have recently been integrated into abuse-focused therapy (Blake-White & Klein, 1985; Fallon & Coffman, 1991; Jehu, Gazan, & Klassen, 1988; Jehu, Klassen, & Gazan, 1985–1986; Resick & Schnicke, 1992; Staton, 1990). This cognitive focus is well-expressed by Fallon and Coffman's contention that effective treatment with abuse survivors "must address the cognitions so deeply affected by the abuse experience."

While the restructuring of cognitive distortions and maladaptive schemas thus appears to be a critical component of therapy for childhood abuse survivors, other sequelae of trauma—most notably the clinical syndrome of posttraumatic stress disorder (PTSD)—are also part of the symptom picture. Indeed, the presence of PTSD symptomatology in abuse survivors has been well documented in clinical literature over the past decade, with widespread consensus among clinicians on the appropriateness of the diagnosis (Blake-White & Kline, 1985; Briere & Runtz, 1987; Donaldson & Gardner, 1985; Lindberg & Distad, 1985; van der Kolk, 1987). Some studies indicate that as many as 96% (Donaldson & Gardner, 1985) to 100% (Lindberg & Distad, 1985) of abuse survivors in clinical samples may meet diagnostic criteria for PTSD. It thus seems critical that treatment of this population encompass an understanding of posttraumatic stress and its deleterious effects.

PTSD AS AN EFFECT OF CHILDHOOD SEXUAL ABUSE

Diagnostic Criteria and Symptom Picture

Posttraumatic stress disorder refers to specific psychological reactions which may occur as a result of disaster, combat, interpersonal violence, or other forms of extreme psychological stress. As defined by the American Psychiatric Association's *Diagnostic and Statistical Manual of Mental Disorders,* 4th edition (DSM IV, 1994), a combination of features from four core criteria comprise the PTSD syndrome: (a) exposure to a traumatic event; (b) subsequent reexperiencing of the trauma in the form of recurrent and intrusive recollections, dreams, flashbacks, or heightened physiological reactivity; (c) emotional numbing or persistent avoidance of stimuli reminiscent of the event; and (d) symptoms of increased arousal such as hypervigilance, irritability, exaggerated startle response, and sleep disturbance.

Without exception, each of the above symptoms has been reported in the literature as a long-term effect of childhood sexual abuse (Briere, 1989). This evidence strongly suggests that PTSD is part of the clinical picture presented by adult survivors of childhood sexual abuse.

RELEVANT THEORIES OF PTSD

Information-Processing Models of PTSD

As the conceptualization of PTSD has evolved over the past several decades, information-processing models which emphasize the role of emotional networks have gained considerable support as explanations of PTSD symptomatology. Taken together, such models offer explanations for the "state dependent" nature of traumatic memories and for the reexperiencing phenomena which are the hallmark of PTSD, and provide a paradigm for understanding habituation and extinction in therapy (Chemtob et al.,

1988; Foa & Kozak, 1986; Foa, Steketee, & Olasov-Rothbaum, 1989; Lang, 1977, 1979, 1986; Rachman, 1980).

In his theory of emotional processing of fear, Rachman (1980) suggests that PTSD-like symptoms result from inadequate emotional processing of trauma and that such symptoms could be ameliorated by the facilitating of successful emotional processing. Lang (1977, 1979, 1986) proposes a model of emotional processing in which emotion is defined as a specific information structure in memory consisting of *stimuli, responses,* and the *meaning* assigned to the stimulus and response data. Lang contends that vivid response imagery is critical in accessing a fear memory and that affective involvement must be present in order for the memory unit to be altered.

Foa and Kozak (1986), who expanded Lang's theory of emotional processing, contend that the meaning associated with stimuli and responses is most critical in the development of PTSD. Foa and Kozak further assert that in order for the fear network to be modified, the fear memory—and the associated affect—must be activated. Concurrently, "corrective" information, which includes elements incompatible with those in the fear structure, must be provided to the patient and integrated into the memory. The authors conclude that the clinical application of prolonged (imaginal) exposure changes the meaning of the threat memory by facilitating physiological habituation, a process which is incongruent with the belief that anxiety decreases only through escape and avoidance.

While Foa and Kozak's (1986) model may account for a major portion of PTSD symptomatology found in adult rape victims, and its application has shown significant treatment results with that population (Foa, Olasov-Rothbaum, & Riggs, 1991), its circumscribed definition of meaning elements may need to be expanded to account for the "meanings" experienced by survivors of childhood sexual abuse with PTSD. Frequently, the meanings which victims ascribe to their childhood sexual traumas greatly exceed the relationship between perceived danger and physiological reactivity, as evidenced in other postvictimization responses which often accompany intrusive phenomena (e.g., a pervasive sense of helplessness and powerlessness, strong feelings of self-disgust, self-blame and self-denigration, and globalized distrust of others).

Need for an Expanded Information-Processing Model and Treatment Approach

The concurrent presence of PTSD symptomatology and pervasive maladaptive schemata in childhood sexual abuse survivors raises important clinical issues for conceptualization and treatment. Although a number of theories have been offered to explain posttraumatic symptoms in individuals traumatized as adults, an expanded information-processing model which addresses underlying cognitive schemata as well as intrusive aspects of the posttraumatic syndrome could significantly broaden our understanding of adult survivors of childhood sexual abuse and enhance the development of more effective treatment strategies with this "therapy-resistant" population.

If the "meanings" of childhood abuse trauma are reconceptualized to include early-acquired, ingrained schemata which influence subsequent perceptions and behavior (for one such schema-focused approach, see McCann & Pearlman, 1990b), current theories and therapies which focus on early maladaptive schemas might be readily integrated into an information-processing model similar to that proposed by Foa and Kozak (1986). Broadening the definition of "meaning propositions" to include the victim's core schematic beliefs would allow these maladaptive cognitive structures to be included as a target for intervention when the traumatic network is accessed in therapy. While variations of imaginal exposure could still be used to reduce PTSD symptomatology, schema-focused interventions could simultaneously be employed to effect changes in meaning propositions at the schema level. The goals of treatment thus would be to: (a) decrease physiological arousal, (b) decrease intrusive PTSD symptoms such as recurring flashbacks or nightmares, (c) facilitate cognitive change in the meaning of the event(s), and (d) modify maladaptive abuse-related beliefs and schemas.

According to theories of emotional processing (Foa & Kozak, 1986; Lang, 1979) and state-dependent recall (Bower, 1981), maladaptive schemas associated with childhood abuse could most readily be accessed and modified when the patient is in an emotional state similar to that which occurred during the abuse experience; that is, when the greatest number of "elements" of the experience are included in the imagery. Implementing this in treatment would essentially involve evoking the images and responses experienced by the victim, and offering alternative interpretations with the "network" accessed. It would also be useful for the therapist to have some understanding of the nature of traumatic memories, the early childhood encoding of these memories, and how they might be accessed so that "corrective" information can be effectively integrated into the memory network.

THE NATURE OF TRAUMATIC MEMORY AND IMPLICATIONS FOR THERAPY

In research with traumatized children and adults, van der Kolk and van der Hart (1989, 1991) suggest that, in contrast to narrative memory, traumatic memories lack verbal narrative and context. Second, they are state dependent (i.e., memories are reactivated when a person is exposed to a situation, or is in a somatic state, reminiscent of the one during which the original memory was stored). Third, they are encoded in the form of vivid sensations and images (regardless of the victim's age) and cannot be accessed by linguistic means alone. Fourth, traumatic memories are difficult to assimilate or integrate, which causes them to be stored differently, be dissociated from conscious awareness and voluntary control, and be unavailable for retrieval under ordinary conditions, and fifth, such memories tend to remain "fixed" in their original form and unaltered by the passage of time or subsequent experience. (Thus, traumatic flashbacks or nightmares may be reexperienced over and over without modification, change, or resolution.)

In addition to the characteristics noted above, abuse memories appear to be influenced by the age of the child when the molestation began (Staton, 1990). According to Bruner (1973), a child's earliest memories are encoded in the sensorimotor system, while visual representation becomes dominant between the ages of 2 and 7. By contrast, linguistic representation develops more slowly, and may not be fully integrated with the kinesthetic and visual modes of representation until adolescence (Bruner, 1973).

Factors specific to sexual abuse further constrain the child's ability to linguistically process the trauma. Because the abuse itself is primarily physical, it is most likely to be encoded in memory through visual or sensorimotor modalities. Moreover, the language spoken during the incident(s) is often minimal, which would lessen the probability of verbal encoding and recall (Staton, 1990).

These characteristics of trauma have profound implications for treatment of survivors. If indeed early abuse memories are encoded primarily in images, utilizing imagery in transforming their meanings would appear essential. This view is supported by Staton (1990) who asserts that without corrective imagery, abusive images may be retained no matter how much "talk" occurs. In a similar vein, Beck, Freeman, and associates (1990) conclude:

> Simply talking about a traumatic event may give intellectual insight about why the patient has a negative self-image, for instance, but it does not actually change the image. In order to modify the image, it is necessary to go back in time, as it were, and recreate the situation. When the interactions are brought to life, the misconstruction is activated—along with the affect—and cognitive restructuring can occur (p. 92).

Edwards (1989, 1990) elaborates further on the use of imagery interventions to facilitate the identification and restructuring of maladaptive cognitions, including those related to childhood sexual abuse. (See Anderson, 1980, and Beck, Emery, & Greenberg, 1985 for a review of imagery techniques in cognitive therapy.)

It appears thus from the current literature that therapeutic effectiveness with abuse survivors will be enhanced if (a) both imagery and verbal modalities are employed in recall, desensitization, and cognitive restructuring; and (b) the affect and level of arousal during initial exposure are similar to that which occurred at the time of trauma. The therapeutic approach described below was developed with these conditions in mind.

IMAGERY RESCRIPTING

Imagery rescripting is an imagery-focused treatment designed to alleviate PTSD symptomatology and alter abuse-related beliefs and schemas (e.g.,, powerlessness, victimization, inherent badness, unlovability) of survivors of childhood sexual abuse. The procedure combines *imaginal exposure* (visually recalling and reexperiencing the images/thoughts and associated affect of the traumatic event) with *imaginal rescripting* (changing the abuse imagery to produce a more favorable outcome). The aim of rescripting is to replace victimization imagery with mastery imagery, thus enabling the abuse victim to experience herself[1] responding to the abuse scene as an empowered individual no longer "frozen" in a state of helplessness. Through this imaginal psychodrama, the recurring victimization imagery is modified and the maladaptive schemas underlying abuse-related cognitions are identified, explored, and challenged. The use of imagery allows these traumagenic schemas to be addressed directly through the eyes of the traumatized child.

The treatment program consists of nine sessions ranging in length from 90 minutes to two hours each, as shown in Table 16.1. Patients are deemed appropriate if they meet criteria for PTSD and are currently experiencing intrusive images, flashbacks, or nightmares of the abuse. Prior to treatment, patients are fully informed of the affective distress which may be temporarily evoked during imagery.

The first session is devoted to information-gathering in a semistructured interview format. In the second session, the therapist presents the treatment rationale and begins the exposure and rescripting procedure. The exposure phase involves an imaginal reenactment of the traumatic event in its entirety, as experienced by the patient in recurring flashbacks or nightmares. The individual is asked to reexperience the images of the

Table 16.1 Summary Treatment Outline

Session 1: (1.5 hrs)	Information gathering (initial interview)
Session 2: (2.0 hrs)	Explain treatment rationale Reexperience in imagery the sexual abuse scene (reexperience in the present what actually happened) Develop mastery imagery: Rescript abuse scene to include coping strategies to drive out the perpetrator After completion of mastery imagery, facilitate "adult-nurturing-child" imagery
Session 3: (1.5 hrs)	Review homework Repeat abuse scene Repeat mastery scene Repeat "adult-nurturing-child" imagery Explain letter rationale and homework assignment
Session 4: (2.0 hrs)	Review homework and discuss letter Repeat abuse scene Repeat mastery scene (include any new information from the letter if appropriate) Repeat "adult-nurturing-child" imagery
Session 5: (1.5 hrs)	Review homework Repeat abuse scene Repeat mastery scene Repeat "adult-nurturing-child" imagery
Session 6: (1.5 hrs)	Review homework Repeat abuse scene Repeat mastery scene Repeat "adult-nurturing-child" imagery
Session 7: (1.5 hrs)	Review homework Adult "check in" with child Repeat "adult-nurtuing-child" imagery Assign homework
Session 8: (1.5 hrs)	Review homework Adult "check in" with child Repeat "adult-nurturing-child" imagery Discuss termination issues
Session 9: (1.5 hrs)	Review homework Adult "check in" with child Repeat "adult-nurturing-child" imagery
Follow-up:	3 months posttreatment 6 months posttreatment

abuse scene and verbalize aloud what she is experiencing, in the present tense (e.g., "He's walking toward me now.)" The therapist's role is to provide a supportive, safe environment in which the patient can visualize and verbalize the traumatic imagery while reprocessing the associated painful affect. The therapist helps the patient "stay with" the affectively charged imagery as the patient determines the level of detail included in the description. The following instructions are given to the patient:

> I'm going to ask you to recall the memories of the abuse. It is best if you close your eyes so you won't be distracted. I will ask you to recall these painful memories as vividly as possible. It is important that you describe the abuse in the present tense, as if it were happening now, right here. We will work together on this. If you start to feel too uncomfortable and want to run away and avoid it by leaving the image, I will help you to stay with it. Every so often, I'll ask you to rate your discomfort level on a scale from '0' to '100'. Please answer quickly and do not leave the image. Do you have any questions before we start?. . . . I'd like you now to close your eyes, visualize the beginning of the abuse scene, and describe what you see and feel as well as the thoughts you are having about what is happening. (Smucker, Dancu, & Foa, 1991, p. 8)

Following imaginal exposure to the abuse scene, the rescripting phase begins. During rescripting, the patient again visualizes the beginning of the abuse memory. This time, however, when the molestation begins, she develops mastery imagery by creating a new scenario in which she visualizes her "adult" self today entering the abuse scene to assist the "child." The therapist may facilitate this through such questions as: "Can you now visualize your ADULT self today entering the scene?" "Does he (the perpetrator) see you?" "How does he respond to your presence in the room?" "What would you, the ADULT, like to do at this point? . . . Can you see yourself doing that?" "And how does he (the perpetrator) respond?" "And what's happening now?"

Essentially, the role of the ADULT during rescripting is to: (a) "rescue" the CHILD and protect her from any further abuse, (b) "drive out" the perpetrator (or take the CHILD away to a safe place) so that the CHILD is no longer in the presence of the perpetrator, and (c) "nurture" the CHILD. During the initial phase of rescripting, the ADULT uses whatever means necessary to rescue the CHILD from the abuser and provide protection for her. If the ADULT is unable to visualize herself "driving out" the perpetrator, she may bring additional support people (e.g., a spouse, police officer, therapist) into the abuse scene to help her accomplish this task.

Throughout the rescripting phase, the therapist remains largely nondirective and is careful *not* to tell the patient what to do, or suggest what should be happening, or push her beyond that which she is able or willing to do. The therapist's role is thus primarily facilitative, as the patient is encouraged to decide for herself what coping strategies to use in the mastery imagery.

Following completion of the mastery imagery, the therapist fosters "adult-nurturing-child" imagery, in which the ADULT is encouraged to interact directly with the traumatized CHILD. The therapist facilitates this by asking the ADULT such questions as: "What would you the ADULT like to say to the CHILD?. . . . Can you see yourself saying that to the CHILD?" "How does the CHILD respond?" "What does the CHILD need at this point?" In many instances, the ADULT will begin to hold or hug the CHILD, reassure the CHILD that the abuse will not happen again, and promise not to abandon the CHILD.

If the ADULT has difficulty nurturing the CHILD, or blames the CHILD for the abuse and wants to abandon or hurt the CHILD, it is sometimes helpful to ask the ADULT: "How far away are you from the CHILD? . . . When you look directly into the CHILD's eyes from up close, what do you see?" "Might you be able to go up close to the CHILD and tell her how she is to blame for the abuse?" "And how does the CHILD respond?" Generally, as the ADULT moves closer to the CHILD, she becomes more affected by the CHILD's pain and finds it more difficult to continue blaming, hurting, or abandoning her.

When the therapist senses that the patient may be ready to bring the "adult-nurturing-child" imagery to a close, the therapist asks: "Is there anything more you, the ADULT, would like to do or say to the CHILD before coming out of the imagery?" Once the patient has indicated her readiness to terminate the imagery session, the therapist concludes with, "When you are ready, you may let the imagery fade away and open your eyes."

When the imagery has ended, the therapist asks the patient to rate on a 0–100 scale (a) how difficult it was to drive away the perpetrator, (b) how difficult it was for the ADULT to nurture the CHILD, and (c) how vivid the imagery was for the patient. The remainder of the session (the last 15 minutes or so) is spent processing the patient's reactions to the imagery session and discussing homework. An audiotape of the entire imagery session is given to the patient for review twice daily as a homework assignment. The patient is asked to record on a standardized homework sheet her subjective units of discomfort (SUDS) each day, prior to and after listening to the imagery tape. The patient also records in a journal any PTSD reactions (e.g., nightmares, flashbacks) she may experience during the week, and brings her journal for review at the beginning of the next session. It is important to allow the patient sufficient time to gain control over her emotions prior to leaving the session. Arrangements are also made for the patient to call the therapist between sessions if difficulties arise.

In sessions 3 through 6, the first 15 minutes are devoted to reviewing the patient's general mood, shifts in mood since last session, and homework assignment (including sharing from her journal). Next, the abuse imagery followed by the mastery imagery and the "adult-nurturing-child" imagery are carried out for approximately one hour. In the remaining 15 minutes of the session, the patient's reactions to the session are discussed and homework is assigned, which involves reviewing the audiotape of the imagery session twice daily. In all of the imagery sessions throughout treatment, the therapist records the patient's discomfort level (SUDS) every ten minutes during the abuse imagery, the mastery imagery, and the "adult-nurturing-child" imagery.

Between sessions 3 and 4 the patient is asked, as part of her homework assignment, to write a letter to the perpetrator (which she does not mail) in which she expresses her thoughts and feelings about the abuse. The rationale behind writing such a letter is explained to the patient in the following manner:

> One of the ways we have found helpful to express your feelings and thoughts is to write a letter to the perpetrator or family member. This is a coping strategy to help you digest the painful memories and current intense emotions that must be assimilated as part of your life. I am going to ask you to write a letter this week as a homework assignment. Do you have any questions? [Provide sufficient time to discuss feelings and concerns about the assignment.] In the beginning of the next session, you will have the opportunity to read your letter and discuss your feelings (Smucker, Dancu, & Foa, 1991, p. 11).

During the last three sessions, the entire focus of the imagery work is on "adult-nurturing-child" imagery. The patient no longer repeats the abuse imagery, but instead closes her eyes and uses her own imagery to "check in" with the child. The therapist facilitates the self-nurturing imagery by asking such questions as: "Where is the CHILD now?" "What is she doing?" "Is she alone?" "How is she feeling?" "What are her needs?" "Where are you, the ADULT?" "How far are you, the ADULT, from the CHILD?" "When you look directly into the CHILD'S eyes, what do you see?" "What would you like to say to the CHILD?" "How does the CHILD respond to you, the ADULT?"

For homework during this phase of treatment, the patient is asked to: (a) listen twice daily to the audiotape of the "adult-nurturing-child" imagery session, (b) "check in" each day with the CHILD on her own, followed by self-initiated "adult-nurturing-child" imagery, and (c) continue with daily entries in her journal, recording her experience with and reactions to the self-nurturing imagery.

Throughout the rescripting sessions, interactions between the ADULT and CHILD provide an opportunity for both the patient and therapist to identify, confront, and modify abuse-related cognitions and underlying schemata at a child's level of representation and understanding. The early origins of the traumagenic beliefs are clarified, and through the dialogue between the ADULT and CHILD, the patient is encouraged to construct new, more adaptive meanings.

In the last 20 minutes or so of sessions 8 and 9, the therapist and patient review progress made during treatment and prepare for termination. This includes discussion of ways to cope with future stressful situations.

Although the nine-session format is standard, it is open to adjustment according to patient need. Additionally, the patient has ready access to the therapist between sessions, and provision is made for additional therapy sessions if required.

SUMMARY

The theoretical rationale for the use of imagery rescripting in the treatment of adult survivors of childhood sexual abuse is presented and the procedure briefly described. When the technique was first developed, the primary goal was alleviation of intrusive PTSD symptoms, with cognitive change a secondary goal. Preliminary outcome data from a pilot study conducted at the Medical College of Pennsylvania and the Medical College of Wisconsin (Dancu, Foa, & Smucker, 1993) have supported the efficacy of the treatment in alleviating PTSD symptoms with this population. At posttreatment and follow-up (three months and six months), none of the subjects met criteria for PTSD. (The results of these findings will be described in more detail in a separate article.)

Analyses of patient "mastery" imagery protocols further suggested notable changes in their maladaptive abuse-related beliefs. Not only did a number of abuse survivors' statements reveal an enhanced sense of control and empowerment following mastery imagery, they also showed less self-blame and a greater capacity to assign responsibility for the abuse to the perpetrator. Also noteworthy were the changes observed during the "adult-nurturing-child" imagery. Initially, negative self-perceptions, self-hatred, worthlessness, and shame were revealed in the statements of a number of the subjects when they attempted to nurture the abused CHILD. Across the sessions, however, their perceptions of the CHILD appeared to undergo profound changes (e.g., "It wasn't her fault." "She's not evil." "She's really a strong kid." "She's so tiny, there was nothing she could have done." "She's just a beautiful kid."). Likewise, their ability to self-nurture and self-soothe appeared to be enhanced, both in and out of the imagery sessions.

Although the indicators of the above cognitive changes are subjective patient statements and excerpts of recorded sessions rather than objective test data from controlled studies, they are nonetheless encouraging. To be sure, additional outcome research is needed to empirically evaluate the efficacy of imagery rescripting, both in alleviating PTSD symptomatology and in facilitating the restructuring of core maladaptive schemas (e.g., powerlessness, inherent badness, unlovability) over a relatively short period of time. Such research is presently being undertaken by several of the authors.

NOTE

1. The feminine pronoun is used throughout the treatment protocol. This is done for the sake of clarity and because of the prevalence of women in this population.

REFERENCES

American Psychiatric Association. (1994). *Diagnostic and statistical manual of mental disorders* (4th ed.). Washington, DC: Author.

Anderson, M. P. (1980). Imaginal processes: Therapeutic applications and theoretical models. In M. J. Mahoney (Ed.), *Psychotherapy process: Current issues and future directions.* New York: Plenum Press.

Bagley, C., & Ramsay, R. (1986). Disrupted childhood and vulnerability to sexual assault. Long-term sequels with implications for counselling. *Social Work and Human Sexuality, 4,* 33–48.

Beck, A. T., Emery, G., & Greenberg, R. L. (1985). *Anxiety disorders and phobias: A cognitive perspective.* New York: Basic Books.

Beck, A. T., Freeman, A., & Associates (1990). *Cognitive therapy of personality disorders.* New York: Guilford Press.

Blake-White, J., & Kline, C. M. (1985). Treating the dissociative process in adult victims of childhood incest. *Social Casework: The Journal of Contemporary Social Work, 9,* 394–402.

Bower, G. H. (1981). Mood and memory. *American Psychologist, 36,* 129–148.

Briere, J. (1989). *Therapy for adults molested as children: Beyond survival.* New York: Springer Publishing.

Briere, J. N. (1992). *Child abuse trauma: Theory and treatment of the lasting effects.* Newbury Park, CA: Sage.

Briere, J., & Runtz, M. (1987). Post sexual abuse trauma: Data and implications for clinical practice. *Journal of Interpersonal Violence, 2,* 367–379.

Briere, J., & Runtz, M. (1992). The long-term effects of sexual abuse: A review and synthesis. In J. Briere (Ed.), *Treating victims of child sexual abuse* (pp. 3–14). San Francisco: Jossey-Bass.

Browne, A., & Finkelhor, D. (1986). Impact of child sexual abuse: A review of the research. *Psychological Bulletin, 99,* 66–77.

Bruner, J. (1973). *Beyond the information given.* New York: Norton.

Chemtob, C., Roitblat, H. L., Hamada, R. S., Carlson, J. G., & Twentyman, C. T. (1988). A cognitive action theory of posttraumatic stress disorder. *Journal of Anxiety Disorders, 2,* 253–275.

Courtois, C. A. (1979). The incest experience and its aftermath. *Victimology: An International Journal, 4,* 337–347.

Dancu, C. V., Foa, E. B., & Smucker, M. R. (1993, November). *Treatment of chronic posttraumatic stress disorder in adult survivors of incest: Cognitive/behavioral interventions.* Paper presented at the annual meeting of the Association for Advancement of Behavior Therapy, Atlanta, GA.

Donaldson, M. A., & Gardner, R. (1985). Diagnosis and treatment of traumatic stress among women after childhood incest. In C. R. Figley (Ed.), *Trauma and its wake: The study and treatment of post-traumatic stress disorder* (Vol. 1, pp. 356–377). Philadelphia, PA: Brunner/Mazel.

Edwards, D. J. A. (1989). Cognitive restructuring through guided imagery: Lessons from Gestalt therapy. In A. Freeman, K. M. Simon, L. E. Beutler, & H. Arnkowitz (Eds.), *Comprehensive handbook of cognitive therapy.* New York: Plenum Press.

Edwards, D. J. A. (1990). Cognitive therapy and the restructuring of early memories through guided imagery. *Journal of Cognitive Psychotherapy: An International Quarterly, 4,* 33–51.

Edwards, P. W., & Donaldson, M. A. (1989). Assessment of symptoms in adult survivors of incest: A factor analytic study of the responses to childhood incest questionnaire. *Child Abuse and Neglect, 13,* 101–110.

Elliott, D. M., & Briere, J. (1992). Sexual abuse trauma among professional women: Validating the trauma symptom checklist-40 (TSC-40). *Child Abuse and Neglect, 16,* 391–398.

Fallon, P., & Coffman, S. (1991). Cognitive behavioral treatment of survivors of victimization. *Psychotherapy in Private Practice, 9,* 53–64.

Finkelhor, D. (1987). The trauma of child sexual abuse: Two models. *Journal of Interpersonal Violence, 2,* 348–366.

Finkelhor, D., & Browne, A. (1985). The traumatic impact of child sexual abuse: A conceptualization. *The American Journal of Orthopsychiatry, 55,* 530–541.

Finkelhor, D., Hotaling, G., Lewis, I.A., & Smith, C. (1989). Sexual abuse and its relationship to later sexual satisfaction, marital status, religion, and attitudes. *Journal of Interpersonal Violence, 4,* 279–299.

Foa, E. B., & Kozak, M. J. (1986). Emotional processing of fear: Exposure to corrective information. *Psychological Bulletin, 99,* 20–35.

Foa, E. B., Rothbaum, B., Riggs, D. S., & Murdock, T. B. (1991). Treatment of posttraumatic stress disorder in rape victims: A comparison between cognitive-behavioral procedures and counseling. *Journal of Consulting and Clinical Psychology, 59,* 715–723.

Foa, E. B., Steketee, G., & Olasov-Rothbaum, B. (1989). Behavioral/cognitive conceptualizations of posttraumatic stress disorder. *Behavior Therapy, 20,* 155–176.

Herman, J. L. (1981). *Father-daughter incest.* Cambridge: Harvard University.

Herman, J. L. (1992). *Trauma and recovery.* New York : Basic Books.

Hollon, S. D., & Garber, J. (1988). Cognitive therapy. In L. Y. Abramson (Ed.), *Social cognition and clinical psychology: A synthesis* (pp. 204–253). New York: Guilford.

Horowitz, M. J. (1976). *Stress response syndromes.* New York: Jason Aronson.

Janoff-Bulman, R. (1985). The aftermath of victimization: Rebuilding shattered assumptions. In C.R. Figley (Ed.), *Trauma and its wake* (Vol. 1, pp. 15–35).

Jehu, D. (1991). Posttraumatic stress reactions among adults molested as children. *Sexual and Marital Therapy, 6,* 227–243.

Jehu, D., Gazan, M., & Klassen, C. (1988). *Beyond sexual abuse: Therapy with women who were childhood victims.* New York: John Wiley & Sons.

Jehu, D., Gazan, M., & Klassen, C. (1984–1985). Common therapeutic targets among women who were sexually abused. *Journal of Social Work and Human Sexuality, 3,* 25–45.

Jehu, D., Klassen, C., & Gazan, M. (1985–1986). Cognitive restructuring of distorted beliefs associated with childhood sexual abuse. *Journal of Social Work and Human Sexuality, 4,* 49–69.

Lang, P. J. (1977). Imagery in therapy: An information processing analysis of fear. *Behavior Therapy, 8,* 862–886.

Lang, P. J. (1979. A bio-informational theory of emotional imagery. *Psychophysiology, 16,* 495–512.

Lang, P. J. (1986). The cognitive psychophysiology of emotion: Fear and anxiety. In A.H. Tuma & J. D. Maser (Eds.), *Anxiety and the anxiety disorders* (pp. 130–179). Hillside, NJ: Erlbaum.

Lindberg, F. H., & Distad, M. A. (1985). Posttraumatic stress disorder in women who experienced childhood incest. *Child Abuse and Neglect, 9,* 329–334.

McCann, I. L., & Pearlman, L. A. (1990a). Constructivist self-development theory as a framework for assessing and treating victims of family violence. In S. M. Stith, M. B. Williams, & K. Rosen (Eds.), *Violence hits home: Comprehensive treatment approaches to domestic violence* (pp. 305–329). New York: Springer Publishing.

McCann, I. L., & Pearlman, L. A. (1990b). *Psychological trauma and the adult survivor: Theory, therapy, and transformation.* New York: Brunner/Mazel.

McCann, I. L., Pearlman, L. A., Sakheim, D. K., & Abrahamson, D. J. (1988). Assessment and treatment of the adult survivor of childhood sexual abuse within a schema framework. In S. Sgroi, (Ed.), *Vulnerable populations: Evaluation and treatment of sexualy abused children and adult survivors* (Vol. 1, pp.77–101). Lexington, MA: Lexington Books.

McCann, I. L., Sakheim, D. K., & Abrahamson, D. J. (1988). Trauma and victimization: A model of psychological adaptation. *The Counseling Psychologist, 16,* 531–594.

Olasov-Rothbaum, B., & Foa, E. B. (1992). Exposure therapy for rape victims with posttraumatic stress disorder. *The Behavior Therapist,* October, 219–222.

Rachman, S. (1980). Emotional processing. *Behavior Research and Therapy, 18,* 51–60.

Resick, P., & Schnicke, M. K. (1990). Treating symptoms in adult victims of sexual assault. *Journal of Interpersonal Violence, 5,* 488–506.

Resick, P., & Schnicke, M. K. (1992). Cognitive processing therapy for sexual assault victims. *Journal of Consulting and Clinical Psychology, 60,* 748–756.

Russell, D. E. H. (1986). *The secret trauma: Incest in the lives of girls and women.* New York: Basic Books.

Smucker, M. R., Dancu, C. V., & Foa, E. B. (1991). *A manual for the treatment of adult survivors of childhood sexual abuse suffering from posttraumatic stress.* Unpublished manuscript.

Staton, J. (1990). Using nonverbal methods in the treatment of sexual abuse. In S. M. Stith, M. B. Williams, & K. Rosen (Eds.), *Violence hits home: Comprehensive treatment approaches to domestic violence.* New York: Springer Publishing.

Tsai, M., & Wagner, N. (1978). Therapy groups for women sexually molested as children. *Archives of Sexual Behavior, 7,* 417–429.

van der Kolk, B. A. (1987). The psychological consequences of overwhelming life experience. In B. van der Kolk (Ed.), *Psychological trauma.* Washington, DC: American Psychiatric Press.

van der Kolk, B. A. (1989). The compulsion to repeat the trauma: Re-enactment, revictimization, and masochism. *Psychiatric Clinics of North America, 12,* 389–411.

van der Kolk, B. A., & van der Hart, O. (1989). Pierre Janet and the breakdown of adaptation in psychological trauma. *American Journal of Psychiatry, 146,* 1530–1540.

van der Kolk, B. A., & van der Hart, O. (1991). The intrusive past: The flexibility of memory and the engraving of trauma. *American Imago, 48,* 425–454.

CHAPTER 17

Hypotheticals in Cognitive Psychotherapy: Creative Questions, Novel Answers, and Therapeutic Change

Cory F. Newman

Creativity is one of those terms that is very difficult to define, yet most discerning people claim they know it when they see it. One of the hallmarks of an intriguing concept is that there are usually many ways to describe it, and this special edition on the topic of creativity in cognitive psychotherapies demonstrates this phenomenon quite well.

So what *is* creativity in cognitive therapy and why is it potentially useful to clients? Let us start with the latter part of the question. When we choose to add a creative ingredient to our methods, whether it is something specific such as personally tailored homework or a more amorphous element such as humor, we must do so because it will be advantageous for the clients. Therefore, a "good" use of creativity in therapy is not simply an expressionistic self-indulgence on the part of the therapist, nor is therapeutic creativity without form or context (Kuehlwein, 1996). Rather, it is a *clinical strategy* executed within a framework of understanding the client that has hypothesized benefits for these individuals who entrust the therapist with their psychological care. A creative technique has the power to stimulate a client's interest in the process of therapy, and perhaps aid in his or her retention of important information across sessions so that new understanding and knowledge can accumulate.

This brings us back to the first and most basic part of the question—how do we *define* the notion of creativity in general, and describe how it can manifest itself in cognitive therapy in particular? The following are some potential definitions.

1. Creativity is a process of thinking that produces new solutions to old problems. This is highly relevant to the process of cognitive therapy, whereby therapists attempt to teach their clients to think about their concerns in new, more constructive ways. A basic example is the therapist's highlighting of the client's "tunnel vision," or "all-or-none" thinking, which limits the clients' ability to change their helpless mindset. By shifting to a more *divergent* thinking strategy, such as when the clients use Socratic questions to address their problems (see Beck, 1995; Greenberger & Padesky, 1995), they are able to come up with solutions they had never considered (or had summarily dismissed) previously.

2. Creativity involves a presentation of stimuli or other information in a new *form,* so that the data are more clear and comprehensible. A prime example of this type of creativity in cognitive therapy is the use of imagery. A particular client may have trouble understanding the semantic point the therapist is trying to make until the therapist paints a mental picture of the concept. One of my favorite examples comes from the 12–step tradition for dealing with substance abuse. In purely verbal terms, the saying in question posits that recovery from substance dependence requires continual, active awareness and coping. However, the creative picture that is painted is that "Recovery is like walking up a 'downward escalator'—If you're not moving forward, you're moving backward."

3. Creativity involves "packaging" mundane information in such a way that it gives the message a more effective punch. Again, it is the *form* of the message interacting with the content that produces a synergistic effect. This benefits the client. For example, one client had trouble believing almost any positive rational response about herself and therefore seemed impervious to the data she herself had written on her Daily Thought Records in support of herself. However, the client and therapist hypothesized that the client might believe the supportive statements more if they came from a source that evoked high emotion—in this case, her deceased father. After

much preparation, the therapist and client used a relaxation induction and role-play whereby the therapist took the role of the deceased father in conveying hope and support to the client. This was a highly evocative experience for the client and produced greater positive change than any previous, purely written technique.

4. Creativity also refers to the use of novel methods when standard methods have not produced the desired results. For example, a client who was very religious did not wish to use the Daily Thoughts Records as she believed that it brought her further away from her faith in G-d to fix all things. However, she became much more receptive to this important technique when the standard method was changed to a novel method that fit the unique needs of this client. Specifically, the "Automatic Thoughts" column was changed to "Things that Satan would have me believe," while the substitute title for the "Rational Responses" heading was converted to "What the Good L-ord wants me to remember so I don't feel weak." With these creative changes, the client became receptive to making self-helpful modifications in her thinking.

Let us consider a number of additional methods for producing these positive results through creative applications of cognitive therapy. Some have been eloquently described in this volume, including: (1) narrative stories, (2) apt metaphors, (3) representational imagery, (4) elucidating analogies, (5) humor, and (6) modifications of standard techniques to make them more personally appealing and stimulating to clients and others.

Enacted with skill, these strategies give the process of change an extra nudge forward, in part because the clients now find the process more understandable, meaningful, and interesting. It is not just about "entertaining" the clients, though they may indeed be amused. Rather, the creative therapeutic strategies become a boon to the client's degree and rate of adaptive learning. This is analogous to the classroom setting, where effective teachers do not merely get their students' attention just for the sake of stimulating them— they get them to pay attention for an educational *purpose*. Such an approach has a distant historical precedent, as Plato, in *The Republic* (Grube, 1974) reflects on Socrates' assertion that learning occurs best when it is in the form of an engrossing pursuit or game, and worst when it is compulsory and rote.

"HYPOTHETICAL": THE CREATIVE USE OF 'WHAT-IF?' QUESTIONS

This paper will briefly examine the creative use of *hypotheticals* in the therapeutic dialogue. These are thinking exercises that allow clients to test the limits of their cognitive appraisal and decision-making systems, because the obstacles of the practical, corporeal world can be removed at will. This frees up the clients to consider and envision how they might think, feel, and behave in an almost limitless set of circumstances—a range of conditions that far exceeds the finite and limiting environments that real life presents. In the process, clients come to learn more about the complete nature of their reactions, as real-life obstacles—some of which the clients had previously used as excuses for maintaining the status quo—are magically removed by their imagination.

Hypotheticals have a long tradition in the legal profession, especially in the training of law students (Ashley, 1991). Law professors present hypothetical cases to students in order to test their knowledge of case law, as well as to hone their decision-making skills across a wide range of possible situations. One of the benefits of this method is that the specifics of the moot cases can be manipulated so as to produce an optimal amount of ambiguity and complexity, thus compelling students to stretch the limits of their capacity to reason and present persuasive arguments.

Similarly, students aspiring to gain entry into their college of choice are quite familiar with hypothetical questions serving as the basis for their application essays. Admissions committees are eager to know how prospective matriculants will answer questions such as, "If you could have a dinner conversation with any famous person, living or dead, who would it be, and why?" or "If you could choose to live in any time in history, and in any place on earth, when and where would you choose to be, and why?" Such hypothetical questions serve to highlight the student's thinking process, value system, and aspirations. Hypothetical essay questions also serve to educate the author as well—a bonus for the college applicant, and a vital part of the self-assessment and change process in cognitive therapy clients who answer similar questions.

In cognitive therapy, hypothetical questions can be used toward a similar goal—that is to say, to aid the clients in their appraisals of potential life decisions and choices across a wide range of situations, some plausible and some not. Therapists can use hypothetical questions to stimulate clients to draw firm conclusions about aspects of their lives that otherwise may not be amenable to easy decision-making. Using this method, clients have the advantage of considering a number of scenarios and hypothesizing how they may think, feel, and act in each situation. This can be accomplished without real-life consequences, therefore the trial-and-error decision-making process can be relatively "safe" for the clients except for the revelations that occur when clients confront the meaning of their hypothetical choices!

Similar to law professors in the classroom, cognitive therapists can shape the hypothetical questions in any way they see fit, presumably in order to help clients confront issues from perspectives that lie outside the realm of their ordinary experiences. Herein lies the "creative" aspect of the process. The therapists' task is to find novel ways to present old questions.

For example, a therapist had conceptualized his client's value system as too enamored with intellectual achievement at the expense of interpersonal warmth and camaraderie. The "old question" that was falling on the client's deaf ears was, "What are some of the advantages of paying a little more attention to your emotions and relationships?" The "new, *creative* question" involved a hypothetical choice. After determining that the client had seen the movie *Forrest Gump,* the therapist asked him the hypothetical question, "If you were forced to choose one or the other, who would you rather have been—Forrest Gump, or Jenny, his girlfriend?" The client said, "the girlfriend." The reason he gave was that Jenny had all of her intellectual faculties, whereas Forrest Gump had a cognitive disability.

However, the therapist asked the client to reconsider his choice in light of the fact that Jenny had been abused multiple times in her life, had many emotional demons, and almost committed suicide, while Gump had a loving mother, many friends, and an optimistic view of the world. The client replied, "It's fiction. It doesn't mean anything." The therapist countered by getting to the point of the exercise, which was to examine how the client would want to participate in the fictional story if it *were* true, and therefore *did* mean something. Hypothetical thought exercises, as logicians will confirm, involve "nonsituations" (Rescher, 1964). We "suppose for the sake of argument" that a particular situation exists and determine how we should proceed under such contrived circumstances.

To continue, the therapist asked the client to consider the qualities that Gump possessed that were so extraordinary and enviable. Specifically, Forrest Gump was an expert at relationships, a "relationship savant," if you will. He had close friends from all walks of life and many of his improbable successes stemmed in part from his uncanny ability to bond with others. One line from the film summed up the central theme neatly—Gump said, "I may not be a smart man, but I know what love is." This hypothetical exercise was a means by which to highlight in dramatic fashion how the client would overlook very important data in the service of his excessive focus on intellect to the exclusion of other important variables.

Turning "Negative Rhetorical Questions" into "Positive Literal Questions"

One of the most commonly heard utterances from anxious clients is the dreaded "what-if?" question. They rhetorically ask, "What if I get rejected?" or "What if I can't do it?" or "What if I fall apart and nobody is there to help me?" and other similar questions. When clients ask such questions, they are not usually looking for an answer or for alternative viewpoints. More typically, they are rhetorically implying that they would be helpless and hopeless.[1] These clients rarely if ever give equal time to the positive, literal *opposite* question, "What if I succeed?" Therein lies a fundamental cognitive bias, because an objective assessment of future outcomes requires the careful consideration of both the positive and negative possibilities.

Here is where hypothetical questions can play a creative, helpful role in therapy. Each time a client asks a negative rhetorical question (NRQ) (Ellis & Newman, 1996), the therapist requires that the client consider its symmetrical positive literal question (PLQ). The client may say, "But I *know* I will fail, and things will be bad." The therapist's response is to say, *"Hypothetically,* if you were to succeed, what would it look like, and what might the overall results be for your life, your anxiety problems, your self esteem, and so on?" A typical initial response from a client may be, "But I probably *won't* succeed, so what's the point in answering this question?" The therapist can then point out that this is yet another NRQ, which compounds the problem created by the first NRQ. The literal answer to this latter question is that by thinking about how he or she may succeed, it broadens the client's heretofore narrow views *of* potential outcomes. Arguably, to envision a positive outcome is a vital step toward enacting it.

Clients who frequently ask themselves NRQs can be quite creative themselves in terms *of* imagining all sorts *of* unfavorable future scenarios, including some that are rather bizarre. For example, a client *of* mine who taught a course on philosophy and ethics often worried that his students would one day take wanton license with the lessons learned in the class and would commit heinous acts, and it would be "all [the client's] fault." Clinically speaking, we don't call this type *of* thinking "creative," we call it "obsessional." However, *if* we ask the client to mirror this sort *of* thinking in the positive direction, it suddenly becomes a difficult cognitive-emotional exercise for the client to execute, and therefore requires creativity.

The client above, when asked what good may come *of* his teaching, finally, begrudgingly noted that it was conceivable that some *of* his students would one day lead organizations to adopt policies and practices of the highest moral standards. Although this outcome may sound a bit grandiose, it is in fact no more grandiose than saying that his class would produce students who would commit acts *of* diabolical evil as a result *of* the course's ambiguities and Socratic method. The therapist, emphasizing the fact that the client had imagined the worst-case scenarios in great detail, instructed the client to give equal time to imagining what *good* may come of his course, and to write about this in the form of narrative stories. Again, the client stated, "But this is fiction, and conjecture." Again, the therapist's response was, "No more so than the worst-case scenarios you regularly dwell on, and believe to be prophetic. Use the powers of your imagination to create *balance* between your negative and positive future images."

The reader must keep in mind that the above intervention was but one part of the treatment package. It was also necessary to conceptualize and to intervene with regard to this client's tendency toward excessive guilt—and not just with regard to his academic course—but also with regard to historical events in which the client felt he had erred and sinned. However, the use of "positive what-if?" questions (or, "PLQs") was extremely useful in getting the client to get out of his cognitive "rut," and to open up his imagination to a fuller range of possible outcomes. In other words, the client was instructed and encouraged to use his creativity in the service of counterbalancing his obsessive worries. For good measure, I recommended that the client rent the video of the movie *Grand Canyon,* which depicts the ways in which simple, low-key, apparently minor acts of thoughtfulness and awareness can lead to untold good fortune for many unsuspecting individuals.[2]

Clarifying Desires, Motives, and the Decision-Making Process

Hypothetical questions also can be used in the service of clarifying the client's desires, motives, and decision-making process. These questions, used creatively, can cut through many of the obstacles that clients perceive to be in the way of their happiness, their goals, and/or their understanding of themselves. Additionally, therapists can pose these questions in such a way that they force clients to confront the implications of their beliefs head on. At the very least, this leads to fruitful therapeutic dialogue, if not outright change, as the following example will illustrate.

One of my clients ("Edwina") bitterly decried the fact that her boyfriend of three years had just broken up with her. Through her tears,
Edwina both vilified him, and insisted that the "whole relationship had
been an entire waste, and just made everything worse." In my clinical
opinion, having heard about the ups and downs of this relationship for
many months, I believed that the picture was far more complicated, and
that both the three-year relationship and its break-up could be viewed as
a growth-enhancing experience for this client.

While taking great care to empathize with her sense of loss and loneliness, I took issue with Edwina's notion that she had just wasted three
years of her life, and that only bad things came from this relationship and
its dissolution. So I asked her the following hypothetical question, in the
form of a little, magical story:

"Edwina, bear with me while I ask you a question which may sound
very silly, but I want you to try to answer it seriously, because it could
give us some very useful information. Here it is. Someone, we'll call her
a Guide, appears before you and says, 'Edwina, I'm going to take you
back three years to the day you met your boyfriend—and she does. Suddenly you are transported back in time and you recognize that you are
about to be introduced to your boyfriend for the first time. The Guide
then tells you that you have to make a decision between two choices and
you *must* choose one or the other. The first choice is to miss out on
meeting the boyfriend, which will lead to never having known him, never
having had a love affair with him, and never experiencing any of the
things you experienced with him for three years. Your life will take a
different course. The second choice is to meet the boyfriend, and go
through *exactly* the same course of events that you have known for the
past three years down to the last detail. Once you make this choice, you
cannot go back, and you will forget that you have ever met the Guide.
You will simply live out your life as you have chosen it—either reliving
your three years with your boyfriend, or bypassing him altogether, for all
time. What is your choice, Edwina?"

Of course, there is no "right" or "wrong" answer to this question,
because it is hypothetical. However, the manner in which the client answers this question is extremely revealing, and will necessitate that she
look at her own desires, motives, and decisions more carefully than would
otherwise be allowed by her current anger and grief (not to mention the
Law of Increasing Entropy)! If she says that she would "do it all over
again" with the boyfriend, then this implies that she did indeed "get
something" out of having been in this relationship, and therefore it could
not have been an "entire waste." In fact, if she even hesitates to answer

the Guide's hypothetical question, it means that Edwina is entertaining the possibility that she may choose to go through the relationship again, which introduces the notion that she may have gotten something useful from having experienced this three-year relationship.

In fact, this is what happened. Edwina said she could not make up her mind. This ambivalence laid bare the fallacy of her angry declaration that her relationship "only made everything worse." In fact, she had gotten something out of having been with the boyfriend and had learned a great deal about herself in the process. This became a very important topic in therapy and helped mitigate her bitterness to a moderate extent because the relationship had served an important *purpose* in her life, even if it did not last "till death do us part."

On the other hand, if Edwina had said that she would choose a different course, one without the boyfriend, then it would be very important for the therapist to ask Edwina to expound on this decision with the use of further hypothetical questions. What would Edwina have done with those three years? Would she have chosen to remain unattached? What would that have looked and felt like? What kinds of things could she have accomplished? Would she have looked for a different kind of partner? How might she herself have behaved differently if she had chosen a different sort of relationship? The reason that these questions are so important is because they potentially shed light on what Edwina can do *now,* in the aftermath of the break-up, rather than simply surrender to her anger and despair.

As another illustration, one of my supervisees used a hypothetical question to confront her client on his motives for therapeutic change. The client, who had a history of extramarital affairs, said that he was "tired of all the shenanigans," and that he was "too old for all of these affairs." The therapist responded with the following hypothetical question: "Suppose you suddenly were to have more energy again, and felt much younger. Would we be having this conversation right now?" The implication was clear—the client needed to look at his motivations and desires more carefully in order to spell out how much of his attempts to change was inspired by a guilty conscience or by fatigue!

Hypotheticals as a Prompt for Problem-Solving

One of the ways that therapists assess their clients' prospects for long-term maintenance of gains is to examine the clients' hypothetical responses to predicted future situations. Therapists wonder aloud whether their clients will be able to anticipate and deal with life's "bumps in the road" in the months and years ahead. For example, can a client who is recovering from substance abuse identify potentially high-risk situations? What would he or she do in such situations? Similarly, a client who suffers from severe abandonment fears could be asked how he or she may respond to future setbacks in relationships so that the client maintains perspective, hope, and appropriate behavior. This approach may sound rather routine and straightforward, but in fact it requires some creative thinking to do effective contingency planning of this sort. Anybody can respond automatically to short-term rewards and punishments, but it takes forethought and some ingenuity to evaluate how one might respond to longer-term contingencies.

The use of hypotheticals as a prompt for advance problem-solving is demonstrated well by Selman, Brion-Meisels, & Wilkins (1996). In their residential treatment facility for troubled adolescent males, the authors incorporate an assessment and intervention procedure that asks the clients to respond to a set of hypothetical psychosocial dilemmas that are relevant and meaningful to their lives. The clients' responses shed light on how the clients view their world and their role in it, their propensity for empathy and collaboration, their decision-making process, their potential for developing good social problem-solving skills, and their beliefs about what should and should not be.

These hypotheticals jumpstart the process of teaching these clients how to navigate their psychosocial world more effectively in the future than they have in the past. This is critical if the clients are to steer clear of repeating devastating past mistakes. The therapists' creative, fictitious stories automatically raise the bar for the adolescent residents, who must use their own creative abilities to devise solutions to the presented dilemmas.

In routine outpatient practice, therapists can use this type of hypothetical exercise in order to help clients carefully consider the cognitive, affective, and behavioral responses that they would like to bring to bear on predicted future scenarios. This sort of preparation enables the client do to two seemingly oppositional but actually complementary tasks—creative brainstorming, and methodical planning. For clients who might otherwise be prone to problematic, impulsive reactions in stressful situations, the use of hypothetical problem-solving strategies is the best of both worlds. The clients get to consider a wide range of responses, to evaluate the potential pros and cons, and to rehearse their proposed approach, without being unduly pressed for time, or overwhelmed with task-interfering, high affect.

The following is just a small sampling of hypothetical questions used in this manner:

- "If you try these assertive requests with your husband at home, and he stonewalls you, what will you have to think to yourself in order to stay focused on your goals, rather than become hurt and lash back?"
- "No matter what happens at the meeting, what will you seek to gain from having been there? Who are you determined to consult with? What will you do if at first it is difficult to get an audience with the persons of your choice?"
- "When you get the results of the medical tests, what questions will you ask of the doctor? If you get good news, what will you need to do in order to prevent a new cycle of worries? If the news is more complicated, what will you do to maximize your social support, and to do all the things you need to do to take care of yourself?"

Although these seem like rather mundane questions, they involve a creative process, in that they stimulate the clients to think of *multiple* solutions to problems that may or may not branch out into heretofore unseen directions. The therapist must exercise creativity in the way he or she crafts the hypothetical question, so that the client's intellectual and affective curiosity is stimulated. This provides fertile ground for generating multiple pathways for anticipating and solving potential problems.

Hypotheticals as Explorations Into Future "Scripts"

Literature's most famous example of this approach is Shakespeare's Hamlet, as he ponders whether "To be, or not to be?" As Hamlet debates the merits of living and dying, he is using this hypothetical question as a way to chart a course for the future—will his personal script be an epitaph, or will it be to go forward in a noble attempt to find meaning and justice? This is the essence of the soliloquy and it is not altogether different from what clients are confronted with as they struggle through critical times in their lives, and in therapy.

The narrative approach that is part and parcel of constructivist methods in therapy is not simply about making sense of the past. It is also about scripting one's future, at least to the extent that this is humanly possible. Goncalves (1994) calls this the process of generating *projecting narratives* and states that this is typically a task for later in therapy. The intent is to help patients become active authors of the rest of their lives, rather than passive reactors, or a minor character in someone else's life script (Rosen, 1996). To do this requires a thoughtful, determined consideration of the directions that one could take, and hypothesizing what one would need to do in order to enact the roles that have the best chance at increasing long-term quality of life.

Hypothetical questions are a potentially important part of this exploration. They require a certain degree of imagination and creativity on both the therapist's and client's parts. For example, consider the following queries that might stimulate the client to construct a projecting narrative:

- "What would your life look like if you went through each day determined to make personal contact with the people in your life, rather than putting up your interpersonal 'wall'? What directions might your life take if you did this every day?"
- "Can you imagine how things would be different in your life if— instead of predetermining that you weren't good enough to pursue new ambitions—you simply decided to strive, and let *others* be the ones to give you feedback, based on what you actually do? If you didn't defeat yourself, would others get in your way? If not, where might you go in life?"
- "How do you think you might grow and develop as a person if— every time you made an honest but regrettable mistake—you were determined to learn from it, and not be demoralized by it? What's an example of how you might play out such a scenario? How would your moods change? How would your life be different, and better?"

The clients may point out that this is pure conjecture, but this is only partially true. Our attitudes affect outcomes. This is why we run double-blind experiments, so that our preconceived notions do not interfere with the "results." Given this phenomenon, it is arguably in our best interest to entertain specific, positive expectancies for a better life, based on a thoughtful, sensible plan. By asking hypothetical questions that guide clients toward hopeful projective narratives, we can help our clients positively to bias the naturalistic, longitudinal experiment that is their life.

CONCLUSION

Creativity in therapy is not simply a therapeutic indulgence into idle, free-form expressionism. Rather, it can be construed as the use of novel methods, within a coherent context and framework pertinent to the client's life, toward the goal of stimulating the client's attention, learning, memory, and divergent thinking. Hypothetical questions represent one category of creative methods, in that they do not require that the therapist and client remain grounded in *what is,* but instead allow for the exploration of what *could be.* This removes many of the earthly obstacles that clients often point to as reasons why they cannot make choices, plan for the future, clarify their goals, or acknowledge their desires. The strategy of hypotheticals requires that therapists use creativity to ask the questions that will be most effective in "cutting to the chase," and similarly demands creative thinking on the part of clients who must now think in a more open-ended fashion.

Although hypotheticals arguably can be categorized in numerous ways, the four classes of hypotheticals reviewed herein were:

1. Asking positive "what-if?" questions,
2. Clarifying desires, motives, and decisions under contrived conditions,
3. Prompts for advance problem-solving, and
4. Explorations into future scripts.

The most meaningful research starts with an intriguing question. Similarly, the most potent therapeutic interventions often begin with exploratory queries that pique the client's interest. Hypotheticals are but one method to stimulate this process. At their best, hypotheticals represent the therapist and client pushing the limits of their imaginations in the pursuit of new, improved possibilities in the client's life.

NOTES

1. In the classic American film *The Wizard of Oz,* the Wizard instructs Dorothy and her three motley companions to capture the broomstick of the Wicked Witch of the West. To succeed in this task would require killing the witch. The Cowardly Lion, feeling helpless and hopeless, replies, "But what if she kills us first?" Thankfully, unlike the Wizard, most therapists do not reply to such questions by yelling "Silence!"

2. In a memorable scene from *Grand Canyon,* a woman asks her doubting husband a series of PLQ's, including the query, "What if these are miracles we're experiencing, but we just don't notice them?" When the husband replies that he is getting a headache, his more hopeful but very assertive wife counters that "It is an inappropriate response to get a headache in the presence of a miracle!"

REFERENCES

Ashley, K. D. (1991). Reasoning with cases and hypotheticals in HYPO. *International Journal of Man-Machine Studies, 34*(6), 753–796.

Beck, J. S. (1995). *Cognitive Therapy: Basics and beyond.* New York: Guilford.

Ellis, T. A., & Newman, C. F. (1996). *Choosing to Live: How to defeat suicide through Cognitive Therapy.* Oakland, CA: New Harbinger Publications, Inc.

Gonçalves, O. F. (1994). Cognitive narrative psychotherapy: The hermeneutic construction of alternative meanings. *Journal of Cognitive Psychotherapy: An International Quarterly, 8*(2), 105–125.

Greenberger, D., & Padesky, C. A. (1995). *Mind over mood: Change how you feel by changing how you think.* New York: Guilford.

Grube, G. M. A. (1974). *Plato's Republic.* Indianapolis, IN: Hackett Publishing.

Kuehlwein, K. T. (1996). Interweaving themes and threads of meaning-making. In H. Rosen & K. T. Kuehlwein (Eds.), *Constructing realities: Meaning-making perspectives for psychotherapists (pp.* 491–512). San Francisco: Jossey-Bass Inc., Publishers.

Rescher, N. (1964). *Hypothetical reasoning.* Amsterdam, The Netherlands: North-Holland Publishing Co.

Rosen, H. (1996). Meaning-making narratives: Foundations for constructivist and social constructionist psychotherapies. In H. Rosen & K. T. Kuehlwein (Eds.), *Constructing realities: Meaning-making perspectives for psychotherapists* (pp. 3–51). San Francisco: Jossey-Bass Inc., Publishers.

Rosen, H., & Kuehlwein, K. T. (Eds.) (1996). *Constructing realities: Meaning-making perspectives for psychotherapists.* San Francisco: Jossey-Bass Inc., Publishers.

Selman, R. L., Brion-Meisels, S., & Wilkins, G. G. (1996). The meaning of relationship in residential treatment: A developmental perspective. In H. Rosen & K. T. Kuehlwein (Eds.), *Constructing realities: Meaning-making perspectives for psychotherapists* (pp. 455–488). San Francisco: Jossey-Bass Inc., Publishers.

CHAPTER 18

Implicit Learning, Tacit Knowledge, and Implications for Stasis and Change in Cognitive Psychotherapy

E. Thomas Dowd and Karen E. Courchaine

With the evolution of cognitive psychotherapy, there has been an increasing focus on the nature and influence of cognitive structures or schemata. These structures are out of conscious awareness and therefore can be thought of as tacit in nature. As yet, however, little has been written regarding the implications of the investigations in cognitive psychology of implicit learning and tacit memory for cognitive psychotherapy. This chapter describes the work of Arthur Reber and other cognitive psychologists on implicit learning and tacit memory and draws tentative implications for the practice of cognitive psychotherapy. Implicit learning processes have been described as robust in nature, holding evolutionary primacy over explicit learning processes, as dissociated from explicit learning, as involving different processes of learning, and as occurring through the tacit detection of covariation. Tacit knowledge precedes and is less available than explicit knowledge.

Throughout its relatively short life, cognitive psychotherapy has gradually shifted from an emphasis on conscious thoughts and images to an increasing focus on underlying cognitive schemata that operate at a tacit or unconscious level. Meichenbaum and Gilmore (1984) have cogently documented this shift. With the advent of the cognitive movement in the early 1970s, therapists first focused on "cognitive events," or thoughts and images that are conscious and identifiable. These cognitions can also be recalled at will, although sometimes not without prompting. Cognitive events have been labeled automatic thoughts (Beck, 1976), internal dialogue (Meichenbaum, 1977), or belief systems (Ellis, 1977). Primary and secondary cognitive appraisal (Coyne & Lazarus, 1980) may also involve cognitive events, at least in part.

Cognitive processes (Meichenbaum & Gilmore, 1984) are those cognitive activities that shape, process, and guide mental representations. Information processing, metacognition (thinking about one's thinking), the availability and representativeness heuristics (Tversky & Kahneman, 1977), and confirmation bias (Taylor & Crocker, 1981) are examples of cognitive processes. The cognitive model of Guidano and Liotti (1983), in which cognitive development and elaboration are seen as occurring through the repeated interaction of the individual and environment, is heavily based on cognitive processes. In their view, social reality is progressively constructed, elaborated, channeled, and differentiated by this repeated interaction. The development of personal identity (Mahoney, 1991) also heavily involves cognitive processes, as the individual develops a sense of ongoing and consistent selfhood by repeated interactions with the environment and other people.

Cognitive structures have been described by Kovacs and Beck (1978) as "relatively enduring characteristics of a person's cognitive organizations . . . organized representations of prior experience" (p. 526). As such, they have also been referred to as schemata (Taylor & Crocker, 1981) and can be thought of as an organized system of tacit rules or assumptions that are the result of repeated cognitive processing over time that in turn supports further cognitive processing. Knowledge organization, as described by Guidano and Liotti (1983), consists of cognitive structures that have been progressively elaborated and differentiated over the years and operate at a tacit or "unconscious" level. Because cognitive structures operate at a tacit processing level, they cannot generally be explicated by individuals, even with external assistance. Thus, in many ways they resemble what are commonly thought of as unconscious processes, although without the elaborate explanatory structure and metaphorical constructs characteristic of psychoanalytic thought.

Schemata can be considered as cognitive structures involving a network or organization of the meaning attached to past experiences and past reactions. Schemata tend to be self-serving and resistant to change, although there is often a gradual modification and occasional massive change over time. There are several types of schemata (Dowd & Pace, 1989). These include prototypes, frames, scripts, and self-schemata. Not only may schemata range from the highly concrete to the highly abstract, but some schemata may be embedded within other schemata and schemata may be arranged hierarchically (i.e., from peripheral to core). Core cognitive schemata are seen as being laid down at an early age (Liotti, 1989; Mahoney, 1991), as not easily accessible via language, and as being especially resistant to change. Peripheral schemata, by contrast, are seen as much more accessible and modifiable. Self-schemata (Markus, 1977), or schemata about one's self in relation to the world that have been derived from interaction with the environment, represent a particularly important class of phenomena for the practice of cognitive therapy, as they are responsible for what is known as the self-concept.

As can be seen from this discussion, cognitive psychotherapy has evolved considerably from a focus on overt self-statements to an increasing consideration of core cognitive rules and assumptions that underlie these self statements. Additionally, different variants of cognitive psychotherapy differentially address peripheral cognitive events versus core cognitive structures. What may not be so obvious from the discussion, however, is the extent to which these types of cognitive psychotherapy rely on different mechanisms of knowledge acquisition and behavior change. Initially, cognitive psychotherapy relied on models derived from various theories of learning and cognitive psychology involving explicit knowledge acquisition. However, as the focus turned toward an examination of core cognitive structures and their impact on stasis and change in cognitive psychotherapy (Dryden & Trower, 1989), theories of tacit or implicit knowledge and learning became much more relevant. We will now turn to an examination of those theories.

TACIT KNOWLEDGE AND IMPLICIT MEMORY

Schacter (1987) describes the difference between implicit and explicit memory in these terms. "Implicit memory is revealed when previous experiences facilitate performance on a task that does not require conscious or intentional recollection of those experiences; explicit memory is revealed when performance on a task requires conscious recollection of previous experiences" (p. 501).

There have been relatively few attempts to use principles derived from theories of tacit knowledge and implicit learning in conceptualizing the process of psychotherapeutic change and in developing new methods and models of change. Tataryn, Nadel, and Jacobs (1989) argued that the cognitive system is "modularized," in that it is composed of separate subsystems. In particular, they discuss the difference between "knowing that" and "knowing how." The former refers to "factual, propositional knowledge" whereas the latter refers to "implicit, dispositional knowledge." Work with amnesiac patients has demonstrated that these individuals are still capable of "learning how" even though they are seriously impaired in "learning that." Generally, however, they are unaware of learning anything new. Infantile amnesia demonstrates the same phenomenon; we are unaware of events that occurred when we were very young, even though those events may profoundly influence our subsequent lives. Tataryn and associates suggest that infantile amnesia may occur because different learning and memory systems may mature at different developmental stages.

As Tataryn and associates (1989) mention, however, such phenomena are not restricted to amnesiacs. Normal individuals, when presented with tachistoscopically displayed stimuli, show learning of which they are subsequently unaware. Dowd (1971) thoroughly reviewed the literature (up to 1971) on the effect of awareness in operant conditioning and concluded that conditioning can occur in the absence of awareness. However, it appeared to be slow and uncertain, and awareness had a substantial quickening effect on conditioning. His study showed that conditioning of counselor verbal behavior could occur without awareness of response-reinforcement contingency (and at about the same rate as awareness without conditioning), but that awareness and conditioning resulted in substantially greater learning. Thus, it appears that significant learning can occur outside of awareness, although the extent to which this takes place may be open to question.

Using the distinction between "memory as an object" (explicit memory) and "memory as a tool" (implicit memory), Fleming, Heikkinen, and Dowd (1992) discussed evidence suggesting that there are sharp dissociations between explicit and implicit memory and that there are performance differences for both amnesiacs and normals under learning conditions appropriate to each type of memory. Furthermore, explicit and implicit memory appear to derive from two types of encoding systems. Explicit memory tests usually tap conceptually driven processes, where the individual generates, elaborates, organizes, or reconstructs the material. Implicit memory tests usually tap data-driven processes, where the material is presented without context and therefore cannot be elaborated or reconstructed. Although data-driven processing increased later perceptual identification and reduced recognition, conceptually driven processing increased later recognition memory and reduced identification. Thus, differential processing may result in an interaction effect on subsequent memory. The conscious and explicit experience of remembering (memory as an object) may require an attribution of pastness. However, the use of memory as a tool may not require this attribution. Implicit memory can be thought of as part of the individual's core cognitive structure and therefore beyond awareness and recall. Events in explicit memory, however, although they may temporarily be out of awareness, can be recalled with assistance.

Fleming and associates (1992) discuss research that specified the variables that manipulate the subjective experience of memory. These are context, attention, and the number of times an episode is recalled. Memory has been shown to improve for material recalled in the same context in which it was learned, whether that context be situational, semantic, or affective. For example, clients who are angry or sad may spontaneously remember past events during which they felt the same emotion. When affective material is involved, this phenomenon is known as mood-state congruence and has been shown to be fairly robust in a variety of situations (Blaney, 1986; Haaga, 1989). Bower (1987) found evidence for the existence of mood-state congruent learning, but also reported that this effect could be replicated even if subjects were not actually happy or sad. It was sufficient for them to follow instructions to act "as if" they were. In addition, Bower (1987) reported that the mood congruent effect only seemed to appear when subjects studied lists of pleasant and unpleasant words, not when they studied lists consisting of all pleasant or all unpleasant words.

MacLeod and Mathews (1991), however, investigated the literature that examined the evidence for mood congruence in anxiety and depression and found more conflicting results. Specifically, they found that evidence for mood congruence varied according to whether the cognitive process involved was perception/attention, comprehension, or retrieval and whether anxiety or depression was the psychological problem. Where perception and attention was the cognitive process, they found consistent evidence for mood congruency effects for anxiety but not for depression. That is, anxiety was associated with an increased attention to. threat-related stimuli, but depression did not seem to be associated with an increased attention to negatively toned stimuli. Where comprehension was the cognitive process, however, they found evidence for mood congruency effects for both anxiety and depression. Depression was associated with a negative interpretation of ambiguous stimuli, and anxiety was associated with a threat interpretation of ambiguous stimuli. In the case of retrieval processes, they found mood congruency effects for depression but not for anxiety. Depression was associated with an increased ability to recall negatively toned information whereas anxiety was not associated with an increased ability to recall threat-related information. Bower (1994) has reported research from several sources indicating that when happy, individuals recall more happy events, and when sad, they recall more sad events. This phenomenon was found in a variety of contexts.

Mood congruence has been confused with a related phenomenon, state- (or mood-) dependent retention (or retrieval). The latter refers to the actual facilitation of recall and retrieval by a deliberate matching of current mood with the mood the subject was in during the initial learning. What is remembered in a certain mood depends on what was learned when in that mood previously; for example, sad memories are more likely to be recalled, and more quickly, when the individual is currently sad. This matching has been accomplished by a variety of methods: by hypnosis, by listening to affectively oriented music (continuous music technique, or CMT), or by the presentation of affectively charged statements (the Velten procedure). Regardless of the type of matching used, however, state-dependent retrieval has been said to be an unreliable phenomenon (Bower, 1987; Haaga, 1989; Mueller, Grove, & Thompson, 1991) that is, attempts to facilitate recall by matching current mood to mood at the time of original learning has not been shown to produce consistent effects. Thus, while clients may spontaneously remember past events when their mood matched their current mood, attempts to deliberately facilitate recall of past material by matching current mood to past mood (e.g., by the use of Gestalt exercises or hypnotic imagery) may not succeed. Bower (1987), however, has reported some tentative evidence that the mere contiguity between mood and a past event may not be sufficient to demonstrate mood-dependent retrieval. The individual must causally attribute the mood to the event to be remembered. Thus, individuals may use the causal association between an event and the mood at the time of original learning to recall more. Clients may demonstrate this effect when they are more able to recall unpleasant events than pleasant events when they are depressed. Pleasant events may be more easily recalled when clients are less depressed.

Recently, however, Eich (1995) has presented evidence suggesting a mood-dependent effect under certain conditions. First, the event in question should be internally generated rather than externally produced. Second, the mood should be strong and stable. Third, the individual should produce the cues required for retrieval of the target events. Under these conditions, Eich argues, mood-dependent retrieval can be demonstrated. These conditions are typically met in most clinical situations.

Divided attention may result in less elaboration of cues available and therefore less awareness for the source of the memory. Thus, a client who hears a message while distracted may process that message at an auditory level only. Hypnotherapists often use divided attention as a technique to manipulate a client's experience of memory. Jacoby, Lindsay, and Toth (1992) present evidence indicating that the result of dividing attention is to reduce the possibility of conscious recollection, leaving unconscious influences largely intact.

The number of times an event is recalled may manipulate the memory for that event. Research has indicated that repeated recall increased subjects' confidence in their memory (whether correct or not) but decreased the accuracy of that memory (Jacoby, Kelley, & Dywan, 1989). The most accurate memories were recalled the least. Thus, a major goal of therapy may be to recall highly affect-laden material repeatedly so that it can be gradually modified and thereby integrated into an individual's cognitive structure and the memory of it changed in the process. In that way, the memory of the event is reconstructed. It is a truism that memories of war stories change over time with repeated telling, generally in a self-enhancing direction. As a survivor of an airline crash said, "After the 50th time [of telling her story] you begin to heal."

IMPLICIT LEARNING

Within cognitive psychology, Arthur Reber and his colleagues, among others, have investigated for some time the conditions under which implicit learning takes place. It is to a consideration of that literature that we will now turn. Reber and his colleagues have defined implicit learning as follows: [It occurs when] "complex abstract knowledge of a structured stimulus domain is acquired, held tacitly, and used unconsciously to make accurate decisions about the well-formedness of novel items" (Reber, Allen, & Regan, 1985, p. 17). The term has also been used "to characterize the manner in which subjects came to apprehend the underlying structure of a complex stimulus environment" (Reber & Lewis, 1977, p. 333).

Although Reber and his colleagues use the term *implicit,* it is essentially equivalent to what others have referred to as tacit learning. Implicit learning has been studied by asking subjects to memorize several artificial grammar strings of letters and then testing their subsequent ability to distinguish letter strings that follow the artificial grammatical rules from those that do not. Although subjects are able to use these rules to differentiate grammatical from ungrammatical strings, they are generally unable to describe the rule. Implicit learning has been described as having several properties.

1. Implicit learning systems are considered to be robust, in that implicit learning can occur in individuals who have serious defects in overt learning capacities. As previously discussed, implicit or tacit learning can be demonstrated in amnesiac individuals that is essentially the same as that demonstrated by nonimpaired individuals, even though they show markedly different explicit learning abilities. Schacter (1987) discusses research that indicates that the memory of amnesiac individuals is much greater for implicitly learned material than for explicitly learned material. Other studies (e.g., Abrams & Reber, 1988) have shown that psychotic patients have a capacity to implicitly acquire and use artificial grammar equal to that of college students. However, this robustness was not shown for explicit learning with these patients.

2. Implicit learning systems are believed to hold evolutionary primacy over explicit learning systems (Reber, 1989a, 1989b, 1990). Evolutionary biology teaches that phylogenetically older systems show greater resistance to degradation following trauma than do younger systems. Likewise, implicit knowledge has been shown to be acquired faster than explicit knowledge (Reber, 1989a). Consciousness is thought to be an evolutionary newcomer (Reber, 1989b), leading to the conclusion that implicit, unconscious learning is phylogenetically older than explicit learning. Therefore, it is likely that much learning even today, particularly of an affective nature, may occur implicitly. It is also likely that because they are not available to consciousness, implicitly learned phenomena are much more resistant to change.

3. There may be a dissociation between implicit learning processes and explicit learning processes. Evidence in support of this hypothesis comes from several sources. As discussed earlier, there has been consistent evidence that cognitively impaired individuals do not show the same implicit memory impairment that they show for explicit memory. In addition, there are other studies (Reber, 1991) that indicate that these individuals demonstrate implicit learning, although their explicit learning is seriously impaired. There is also some evidence (Reber, 1992) indicating that very young children are capable of implicit learning, that implicit learning shows less intersubject variability than explicit learning, and that implicit learning is more independent of IQ than is explicit learning. Allen and Reber (1980) found that long-term memory for implicitly ac-

quired knowledge is greater than that for explicitly acquired knowledge, implying that the former is more deeply processed. Jacoby and associates (1992) discuss research that points to dissociations between direct and indirect tests of memory. Recently, Gabrieli, Fleischman, Keane, Reminger, and Morrell (1995) found evidence that separate memory systems in the brain may be responsible for implicit and explicit memory, leading to the conclusion that we might be able to locate centers for different cognitive functions in different parts of the brain.

4. Implicit learning processes may differ from explicit learning processes. In a series of studies, Reber (1989a) showed that explicit processing of complex material was less effective than implicit processing. Indeed, explicit instructions regarding a complex learning task either did not help or actually interfered with the learning of the material, when compared to subjects who received no explicit instructions. Reber found that actual experience with the learning task, a sort of hands-on experience, was the most useful in acquiring the knowledge base necessary for learning; as he stated, "Looking for rules will not work if you cannot find them" (Reber, 1989a, p. 223). Explicit instructions were effective in assisting learning if given early, however, as they seemed to provide a coding scheme structure that assisted subjects in learning, or cognitive parameters circumscribing the implicit learning processes subjects were engaged in (Reber, Kassin, Lewis, & Cantor 1980). But even early explicit instructions were detrimental to learning if they were incongruent with the tacit structure that was emerging from the subject's experience with the material. Therefore, implicit learning in general may be more effective than explicit learning. A combination of explicit and implicit learning may be more effective than either alone (Reber et al., 1980). Unlike explicit learning, which occurs by direct rule induction, implicit learning seems to function by the gradual induction of an underlying and abstract representation that mirrors the structure of the environment (Reber, 1989a). This learning occurs naturally and is not open to direct introspection, in that the rules behind this representation cannot generally be explicated by the individual. Reber concludes that "A considerable portion of memorial content is unconscious, and, even more important, a goodly amount of knowledge acquisition takes place in the absence of intent to earn" (Reber, 1989a, p. 230).

5. Implicit learning appears to occur through the tacit detection of covariation and as such is resistant to consciousness. Reber (1991, 1992) has argued that the principle of covariation is fundamental to learning among all species, from the lowest organism to humans. The principle of covariation essentially states that events that occur together are perceived

as related and form the basis of implicit learning. What distinguishes species higher on the phylogenetic scale from those lower is not the operation of this mechanism, but rather the ability of more neurologically complex organisms to detect more tenuous and subtle covariations (Reber, 1991, 1992). In the process, tacit rules are formed. Lewicki, Hill, and Czyzewska (1992) have discussed evidence indicating that nonconscious (i.e., implicit) acquisition of information occurs faster than conscious acquisition and that nonconscious cognition can more efficiently process relationships among variables than can conscious cognition. The principle of covariation also forms the basis of behavioral approaches to learning and therapy, where it has been termed *associational learning* (Wolpe, 1990). The difference is not in the nature of the basic processes, but rather in the tacit nature of those processes that are inherent in more structurally differentiated organisms. Furthermore, the very nature of this learning, outside of consciousness, means that such knowledge should be extremely resistant to conscious understanding and therefore to subsequent change. Indeed, Lewicki and associates (1992) discuss evidence indicating that when faced with ambiguous stimulus events, individuals often impose preexisting interpretive categories on these events, even if the categories and the events do not objectively match. This biased interpretation has been demonstrated to lead to subsequent experiences consistent with the previous interpretive encoding, thus providing for a self-perpetuation of interpretative categories (or encoding algorithms). Lewicki and associates go on to state that this self-perpetuation of previous encoding algorithms of ambiguous social stimuli may be a major reason for individual differences in reactions to the same events. Seger (1994) discusses evidence indicating that the implicit learning system is inflexible and resistant to change. From a psychotherapeutic perspective, Mahoney (1991) has noted that core cognitive events and processes are much less accessible than peripheral events or processes and therefore are more resistant to change. As any therapist or social psychologist knows, all of us are much more aware of the nature of our interpersonal interactions and behaviors than we are of our underlying motivations and emotions.

6. Tacit knowledge precedes and is less available than explicit knowledge. Reber (1989a, 1989b) has discussed research indicating that although implicit knowledge can be partially explicated by probes and assisted recall, the knowledge so explicated is more impoverished than the richer and more complex implicit knowledge. Furthermore, although subjects could verbalize some rules, implicit rule-generation was consistently ahead of the subjects' ability to explicitly describe those rules.

After examining other research, Schacter (1987) concluded that repetition priming (facilitation of the processing of a stimulus by repeated encounters with the same stimulus) illustrated a dissociation between implicit and explicit memory and that priming effects were stronger for implicit memory than for explicit. Furthermore priming effects were found to occur only for morphologically similar words, that is, words that were similar in meaning. Schacter, Church, and Bolton (1995) found a greater priming effect in a same-voice over time context than in a different-voice context for normal individuals but no differences between the two conditions for amnesiac patients. However, other studies have found certain similar effects between priming and recall.

APPLICATIONS TO COGNITIVE PSYCHOTHERAPY

Since the early 1970s, behavior therapy has been "going cognitive." What is not as obvious is that since the early 1980s cognitive (behavior) therapy has been "going implicit." That is, as already discussed, there has been an increasing focus on core cognitive structures and processes rather than on peripheral cognitive events. In the process, however, there has been a concomitant realization that these core cognitive structures and processes are largely outside the realm of overt awareness. As yet, there have been no basic research findings documenting these assumptions nor a theoretical framework within which to explain these findings. Cognitive psychotherapy has been criticized for not grounding its therapeutic techniques sufficiently in the principles of cognitive psychology. The literature on tacit knowledge and implicit learning provides an excellent framework for explaining the newer developments in cognitive psychotherapy. Some tentative implications of this literature will now be described.

1. *Theory and research on implicit learning can help us understand the resistance of core cognitive structures to therapeutic change.* Liotti (1989) has linked resistance in therapy to the preservation of the client's meaning structures and the principle of hierarchial structuralism, in which these core cognitive structures are protected from massive pressure to change. Dowd (1989) sees reactance as arising from the client's need to control self and events in life and argues that this need is particularly salient in Western culture. Mahoney (1991) sees resistance to change as a self-protective device of the client to protect his or her self-identity and argues that such protection is evolutionarily valuable. Dowd (1993a) has suggested that reactance may arise from the client's need to maintain both autonomy and identity, and that reactance may be associated with auton-

omy as a linear function and with identity as a curvilinear function. Subsequent studies, however, have found reactance to be related linearly to autonomy but not at all to identity (Seibel, Pepper, Dowd, & McCarthy, 1995).

Some of these ideas approach those found in the literature on implicit learning. Core structures of personal meaning and self-identity, via the principle of covariation, are laid down early in life and thereafter are elaborated and differentiated rather than drastically modified. Knowledge of this cognitive core is likely implicit in nature and therefore is more robust, less available, and less easily recalled than explicit knowledge. Such knowledge can be explicated somewhat with repeated processing, but the explicit knowledge gained thereby is likely to be an impoverished version of the implicit knowledge. Repetition priming suggests that stimuli previously presented are more likely to be implicitly perceived in the future and under certain circumstances (e.g., implicit memory for new associations; Schacter, 1987) explicitly recalled as well. In this regard, Amir, Rieman, and McNally (1994) found that patients diagnosed with panic disorder showed an implicit bias for panic-relevant sentences whereas normal control subjects did not. Perhaps repeated and explicit recall of problem-related stimuli may modify the implicit processing. The self-perpetuating nature of encoding algorithms (Lewicki et al., 1992) may be a major source of resistance to alternative cognitive constructions of reality. Cognitive constructs of autonomy and identity, for example, are likely tacit in nature and as such resistant to rapid change.

2. *Theory and research on implicit learning can inform cognitive psychotherapists of the process of therapeutic learning that has already occurred.* Because implicit learning may be phylogenetically older and take place faster than explicit learning, it may occur more often than we think. Indeed, it should occur in all individuals, regardless of age, level of intelligence, motivation, or other individual differences. In particular, it is likely that it is implicated strongly in the learning of highly affectively charged material, thus resulting in the oft-noted therapist observation that insight without emotion does not result in lasting change. Or, as Franz Alexander (1963) put it, a corrective emotional experience is necessary for psychological change. The involvement of older, more primitive, knowing systems may occur whenever strong affect is present and, as Jacoby and associates (1992) have discussed, past emotional memory may affect current subjective experiences.

The tacit knowledge that is implicated in core cognitive structures, such as implicit rules, underlying motivations, and primitive emotions, may be resistant to change and require repeated cognitive challenges as well as repeated and different individual-environment interactions. The latter point is especially important, because implicit learning is thought to occur slowly by the process of covariation and be resistant to change. Thus, although brief therapy may change certain peripheral behaviors and attitudes, it is unlikely to change core cognitive structures unless a covariation "ripple effect" is begun. However, Seger (1994) discusses evidence indicating that when explicit learning was pitted against conflicting implicit knowledge, the latter tended to be disregarded. Reber and associates (1980) found the most facilitative effects when explicit and implicit learning acted together. Thus, although direct explicit challenges of implicit material may be effective, a conjunction of the two wherein clients learn by doing (i.e., engaging in new behavior) may be even more effective.

The fact that neurologically advanced organisms can detect increasingly subtle covariations may not be an unmitigated blessing, however. For in the process of becoming aware of subtle covariations, they may also cognitively create nonexistent covariations, which they then reify and subsequently use to create new tacit assumptions. This may be one cause of the dysfunctional cognitions that underlie common psychological problems. Once created, these dysfunctional assumptions may become self-perpetuating encoding algorithms (Lewicki et al., 1992) and therefore be extremely resistant to change.

The number of times an event is recalled has been found to increase the confidence of the memory of that event but decrease the accuracy of the memory (Fleming et al., 1992). Although this point seems intuitively backwards, the finding has important implications for cognitive psychotherapy. Only with repeated recall of a traumatic event can the meaning and memory of that event be integrated into the client's cognitive system. In the process, the memory of the event may be changed, but the client may hold even more firmly to the revised memory. Those therapists who do crisis intervention know that the first recall of a traumatic event is likely to be especially unsettling and that part of the process of healing is the repeated evocation of that memory and its eventual integration within the existing cognitive system. As those who do crisis intervention also know, however, this is also a time when the possibility that a major change will occur is most likely. The individual's cognitive system may be significantly modified by repeated recall of the experience. If Schacter and associates (1995) are correct, however, perhaps the repeated recall should be done with the same therapist for maximum effect.

The mood-dependency memory phenomenon (Bower, 1994) suggests that depressed individuals may be more prone to recall sad times and events and may have to be prodded to recall happy times and events. However, this repeated activation of happy events might serve to reduce the depression, although as noted further on it may prove to be unreliable.

The evidence that mood-dependent retrieval is apparently a less robust phenomenon than mood congruence, however, should lead to caution in assuming that reinvoking an original mood will necessarily result in retrieval of material learned while in that mood. The conditions noted by Eich (1995) for the maximization of the likelihood of the mood-dependency effect are generally present in most clinical settings. Therefore, mood-matching techniques such as hypnotic imagery and Gestalt exercises may be used profitably but they should be used with due caution and without the expectation of immediate and major effect. However, spontaneously generated client emotion may be more reliably taken as reflecting past emotion when learning first occurred. The mood-dependent retrieval phenomenon suggests that depressed clients may be more likely to perceive negativity in events and to more easily and quickly retrieve negative memories. Likewise, acting "as if" the client felt a certain mood may assist mood-state congruent learning. Finally, as MacLeod and Mathews (1991) have indicated, the evidence is strong that there is a retrieval of negative information in depression. Perhaps the reverse may be true as well; if we assist clients in retrieving positive information, we may reduce the level of depression.

3. *Theory and research on implicit learning can assist cognitive therapists in the development of new techniques and in the modification of existing techniques.* The discussion that follows is speculative and is meant to be heuristic in generating new hypotheses and interventions. The techniques described have not yet been subjected to empirical verification.

Fleming and associates (1992) discussed the finding that memory improves for material recalled in the same context in which it was learned. The implications for the practice of cognitive psychotherapy are very interesting. Although it may not always be possible for clients to return to the scene of a traumatic memory (though it might be helpful if they did), the appropriate context may be provided via imagery in a hypnotic trance. Dowd (1992) has described the use of hypnotic imagery to enable a client to reexperience a traumatic memory and thereby integrate it into her cognitive system. Dowd (1993b) has also argued that hypnosis may be especially helpful in modifying disordered implicit cognitive schemata, because it involves a concentrated focus, imaginal and intuitive processing, and increased receptivity to influence. If Jacoby and associates (1992) are correct, dividing attention between conscious and unconscious recollection may aid in the retrieval of the latter.

Several techniques developed by Mahoney (1991) may offer possibilities for modifying implicit cognitive schemata. These include the life review project, consciousness streaming, and mirror time. Like hypnosis, these techniques, in varying forms, may alter the individual's awareness and allow access to implicitly held schemata, as well as provide the opportunity for new constructions of reality to emerge.

The life review project begins with individuals recording memories, either explicit or implicit. Explicit memories are apparent, while implicit material may be recorded as vague feelings or impressions, trace memories, or associations. Mahoney reports that "the research phase . . . is emotionally challenging: in recalling and recording their developmental histories, they frequently encounter personal memories and life episodes that are difficult to acknowledge" (p. 293). Recall of explicit and implicit associations appears to trigger difficult memories and traumatic experiences that are walked through later.

The final phase is followed by a review of the review, wherein clients are to examine their life patterns and to extrapolate personal interpretations and meaning (with the therapist's assistance). Clarke (1993) has stated that it is at this point, where a client can extract meaning from a traumatic experience, that healing can take place. The recollection of implicit memories through a technique such as the life review project, in combination with an explication of meaning, may help facilitate the healing process by the alteration of pretherapy meanings and implicitly held schemata.

Consciousness streaming (Mahoney, 1991) involves the combination of several experiential techniques (imagery and a modified version of free association) designed to bring to awareness "ongoing thoughts, sensations images, memories, and feelings" (p. 295). A sense of trust and safety is established as clients are instructed to report only those experiences they wish to share. Much like initial sessions of hypnotherapy, relaxation techniques are used at the beginning of the consciousness-streaming exercise. As memories are recalled and reported, clients are encouraged to extract their own individual meaning for the events. The implications for accessing implicit memories are clear and Mahoney reports that more than any other technique I have used, it [consciousness streaming] has facilitated the recall of experiences that were painful and formative in clients' earlier development but which had come to be denied, distorted, or 'forgotten' " (p. 296).

Consciousness streaming may enable the client to recall and reexperience affectively laden memories that had previously been inaccessible. As these memories are revealed, clients may then be able to work toward modifying existing schemata and integrating them into their cognitive structures.

Another technique specifically designed to enhance self-awareness and perhaps to provide the client and therapist with access to self-constructions or schemata is what Mahoney (1991) has referred to as mirroring. With the therapist's assistance, the client engages in powerful self-confrontation using a mirror. Clients are encouraged to engage in dialogue with themselves or other individuals significant in their lives. This technique is hypothesized to allow direct access to self-schemata and may serve as a catalyst to the exposure of traumatic memories and implicitly held assumptions. Clients who engage in mirroring have found the experience to be affectively powerful.

As stated earlier, mood-congruence of negative emotions at both the time of learning and the time of recall may aid in the recollection of memories.

The use of such techniques may facilitate the intense emotions typically associated with implicitly held material, thereby stimulating the recall of traumatic memories. It is important to note, however, that simply inducing a negative mood may not be sufficient for accessing traumatic memories. In his review article on the relationship between affect and memory Blaney (1986) has stated that this mood must be activated above a certain threshold in order to influence memory retrieval.

SUMMARY

There is considerable evidence suggesting that explicit and implicit learning proceeds in different ways and that implicit learning occurs outside of conscious awareness. However, while learning can occur both explicitly and implicitly, there is also evidence suggesting that complex material may be best learned implicitly (Reber, 1989a) and that together they are more effective than alone (Dowd,1971; Reber et al., 1980). The important issue may be the juxtaposition of the two; perhaps explicit learning should occur early, be alternated with actual experience with the learning task, and the explicit and implicit representational structures be matched. Thus, cognitive psychotherapists may wish to alternate an examination and challenge of dysfunctional cognitions with behavioral and environmental interventions, as well as imagery exercises. Successful behavior change is likely to result in eventual cognitive change, as the client reflects (with the therapist's help) on the meaning of the changed behavior or environmental manipulation (Hobbs, 1962) and thereby gradually modifies his or her cognitive structure. Indeed, the literature on implicit learning is optimistic in that it indicates that it occurs continuously in all people and needs only to be properly channeled and directed.

Much work remains to be done regarding the role that implicit memory and learning play in human psychological distress and the use of implicit change strategies in cognitive psychotherapy. Schacter (1987) has stated that an especially promising area is the role of implicit memory in such phenomena as mood states, fears and phobias, impression formation, and self-concept. Seger (1994) seems to imply that learning by doing, accompanied by explicit instruction, can aid in the conversion of implicit to explicit learning. Liotti (1985) has called attention to the similarities between unconscious information processing and the "unconscious mind," as described by Ericksonian hypnotherapists. The divided attention between the conscious and unconscious mind can be used as a way of fostering implicit processing or as distinguishing between memory as an object and memory as a tool (Fleming et al., 1992). Dowd (1993b) has argued for the use of hypnosis in accessing and modifying affective and self-knowledge schemata. Mahoney's (1991) life review project, consciousness streaming, and mirror time are also examples of techniques that may be useful in accessing implicit self-schemata. Cognitive psychotherapy would benefit richly by the development of other techniques for the modification of tacit schemata and implicit learning, based on a sound understanding of the theoretical and empirical literature.

ACKNOWLEDGMENTS

Earlier versions of this paper were presented at the 1992 World Congress on Cognitive Therapy, Toronto, and the 1992 annual meeting of the Association for Advancement of Behavior Therapy, Boston. The authors wish to thank Arthur Reber and Michael Mahoney for their comments on that version and Gordon Bower for recent consultation.

REFERENCES

Abrams, M., & Reber, A. S. (1988). Implicit learning: Robustness in the face of psychiatric disorders. *Journal of Psycholinguistic Research, 17,* 425–439.

Alexander, F. (1963). *Fundamentals of psychoanalysis.* New York: Norton.

Allen, R., & Reber, A. S. (1980). Very long term memory for tacit knowledge. *Cognition, 8,* 195–185.

Amir, N., Reimann, B. C., & McNally, R. J. (1994, November). *Implicit and explicit memory bias in panic disorder.* Paper presented at the annual meeting of the Association for Advancement of Behavior Therapy, San Diego, CA.

Beck, A. T. (1976). *Cognitive therapy and the emotional disorders.* New York International Universities Press.

Blaney, P. H. (1986). Affect and memory: A review. *Psychological Bulletin, 99,* 229–246.

Bower, G. H. (1987). Commentary on mood and memory. *Behavior Research and Therapy, 25,* 443–455.

Bower, G. H. (1994). Temporary emotional states act like multiple personalities. In R. M. Klein & B. K. Doane (Eds.), *Psychological concepts and dissociative disorders* (pp. 207–234). Hillsdale, NJ: Erlbaum.

Clarke, K. M. (1993). Meaning making in incest survivors. *Journal of Cognitive Psychotherapy, 7,* 195–204.

Coyne, J. C. I., & Lazarus, R. (1980). Cognitive style, stress perception, and coping. In I. L. Kutash, L. B. Schlesinger, & Associates (Eds.), *Handbook on stress and anxiety* (pp. 144–158). San Francisco: Jossey-Bass.

Dowd, E. T. (1971). *The effect of awareness of response-reinforcement contingency on the acquisition and extinction of operantly conditioned counselor behavior.* Unpublished doctoral dissertation, University of Minnesota, Minneapolis, MN.

Dowd, E. T. (1989). Stasis and change in cognitive psychotherapy: Client resistance and reactance as mediating variables. In W. Dryden & P. Trower (Eds.), *Cognitive psychotherapy: Stasis and change* (pp. 139–158). London: Cassell.

Dowd, E. T. (1992). Hypnotherapy. In A. Freeman & F. M. Dattilio (Eds.), *Comprehensive casebook of cognitive therapy* (pp. 277–284). New York: Plenum.

Dowd, E. T. (1993a). Motivational and personality correlates of psychological reactance and implications for cognitive therapy. *Psicologia Conductual (Behavioural Psychology), 1,* 145–156.

Dowd, E. T. (1993b). Cognitive developmental hypnotherapy. In J. W. Rhue, S. J. Lynn, & I. Kirsch (Eds.), *Handbook of clinical hypnosis* (pp. 215–232). Washington, DC: American Psychological Association.

Dowd, E. T., & Pace, T. C. (1989). The relativity of reality: Second order change in psychotherapy. In A. Freeman, K. M. Simon, L. E. Beutler, & H. Arkowitz (Eds.), *Comprehenslve handbook of cognitive therapy* (pp. 213–226). New York: Plenum.

Dryden, W., & Trower, P. (1989). *Cognitive psychotherapy: Stasis and change.* London: Cassell.

Eich, E. (1995). Searching for mood dependent memory. *Psychological Science, 6,* 67.

Ellis, A (1977). The basic clinical theory of rational-emotive therapy. In A. Ellis & R. Grieger (Eds.), *Handbook of rational-emotive therapy* (pp. 3–34). New York: Springer.

Fleming, K., Heikkinen, R., & Dowd, E. T. (1992). Cognitive therapy: The repair of memory. *Journal of Cognitive Psychotherapy, 6,* 155–173.

Gabrieli, J. D. E., Fleischman, D. A., Keane, M. M., Reminger, S. L., & Morrell, F. (1995). Double dissociation between memory systems underlying explicit and implicit memory in the human brain. *Psychological Science, 6,* 76–82.

Guidano, V. F., & Liotti, G. (1983). *Cognitive processes and emotional disorders.* New York: Guilford.

Haaga, D. A. F. (1989). Mood state-dependent retention using identical or nonidentical mood inductions at learning and recall. *British Journal of Clinical Psychology, 28,* 75–83.

Hobbs, N. (1962). Sources of gain in psychotherapy. *American Psychologist, 17,* 18–34.

Jacoby, L. L., Kelley, C. M., & Dywan, J. (1989). Memory attributions. In H. L. Roediger & F. I. M. Craik (Eds.), *Varieties of memory and consciousness* (pp. 391–422). Hillsdale, NJ: Erlbaum.

Jacoby, L. L., Lindsay, D. S., & Toth, J. P. (1992). Unconscious influences revealed. *American Psychologist, 47,* 802–809.

Kovacs, M., & Beck, A. T. (1978) Maladaptive cognitive structures and depression. *American Journal of Psychiatry, 135,* 525–533.

Lewicki, P., Hill, T., & Czyzewska, M. (1992). Nonconscious acquisition of information. *American Psychologist, 47,* 796–801.

Liotti, G. (1985). A cognitive view of the change process in Ericksonian hypnotherapy. Paper presented at the International Congress of Hypnosis and Family Therapy, Catholic University, Rome.

Liotti, G. (1989). Resistance to change in cognitive psychotherapy: Theoretical remarks from a constructivistic point of view. In W. Dryden & P. Trower (Eds.), *Cognitive psychotherapy: Stasis and change* (pp. 28–56). London: Cassell.

MacLeod, C., & Mathews, A. M. (1991). Cognitive-experimental approaches to the emotional disorders. In P. R. Martin (Ed.), *Handbook of behavior therapy and psychological science: An integrative approach* (pp. 116–150). New York: Pergamon.

Mahoney, M. J. (1991). Human change processes. New York: Basic Books.

Markus, H. (1977). Self-schemata and processing information about the self. *Journal of Personality and Social Psychology, 35,* 63–78.

Meichenbaum, D. (1977). *Cognitive behavior modification: An integrative approach.* New York: Plenum.

Meichenbaum, D., & Gilmore, J. B. (1984). The nature of unconscious processes: A cognitive behavioral perspective. In K. S. Bowers & D. Meichenbaum (Eds.), *The unconscious reconsidered* (pp. 273–298). New York: Wiley.

Mueller, J. H., Grove, T. R., & Thompson, W. B. (1991). Mood-dependent retrieval and mood awareness, *Cognition and Emotion, 5,* 331–349.

Reber, A. S. (1989a). Implicit learning and tacit knowledge. *Journal of Experimental Psychology: General, 118,* 219–235.

Reber, A. S. (1989b). More thoughts on the unconscious: Reply to Brody and to Lewicki and Hill. *Journal of Experimental Psychology: General, 118,* 242–244.

Reber, A. S. (1990). On the primacy of the implicit: Comment on Perruchet and Pacteau. Journal of Experimental Psychology: Ceneral, 119, 340–342.

Reber, A. S. (1991, April). *Personal knowledge and the cognitive unconscious.* Paper presented at the Centennial Celebration of the birth of Michael Polanyi, Kent State University, Kent, OH.

Reber, A. S. (1992). An evolutionary context for the cognitive unconscious. *Journal of Philosophical Psychology, 5,* 33–51.

Reber, A. S., Allen, R., & Regan, S. (1985). Syntactical learning and judgment, still unconscious and still abstract: Comment on Duleny, Carlson and Dewey. *Journal of Experimental Psychology: General, 114,* 17–24.

Reber, A. S., Kassin, S. M., Lewis, S., & Cantor, G. (1980). On the relationship between implicit and explicit modes in the learning of a complex rule structure. *Journal of Experimental Psychology: Human Learning and Memory, 6,* 492–502.

Reber, A. S., & Lewis, S. (1977). Implicit learning: An analysis of the form and structure of a body of tacit knowledge. *Cognition, 5,* 333–361.

Schacter, D. L. (1987). Implicit memory: History and current status. *Journal of Experimental Psychology: Learning, Memory, and Cognition, 13,* 501–518.

Schacter, D. L., Church, B., & Bolton, E. (1995). Implicit memory in amnesiac patients: Impairment of voice-specific priming. *Psychological Science, 6,* 20–25.

Seger, C. A. (1994). Implicit learning. *Psychological Bulletin, 115,* 163–196.

Seibel, C. A., Pepper, H., Dowd, E. T., & McCarthy, J. (1995, July). *Developmental antecedents of psychological reactance and implications for cognitive therapy.* Paper presented at the World Congress of Behavioural and Cognitive Therapies, Copenhagen, Denmark.

Tataryn, D. J., Nadel, L., & Jacobs, W. J. (1989). Cognitive therapy and cognitive science. In A. Freeman, K. M. Simon, L. E. Beutler, & H. Arkowitz (Eds.), *Comprehensive handbook of cognitive therapy* (pp. 85–98). New York: Plenum.

Taylor, S., & Crocker, J. (1981). Schematic bases of social information processing. In E. Higgins, C. Herman, & M. P. Zanna (Eds.), *Social cognition: The Ontario Symposium.* Hillsdale, NJ: Erlbaum.

Tversky, A., & Kahneman, D. (1977). Causal schemata in judgments under uncertainty. In M. Fishbein (Ed.), *Progress in social psychology.* Hillsdale, NJ: Erlbaum.

Wolpe, J. (1990). *The practice of behavior therapy* (4th ed.). Elmsford, NY: Pergamon.

CHAPTER 19

Stress and Stress Management: A Cognitive View

James L. Pretzer, Aaron T. Beck, and
Cory F. Newman

Recent evidence suggests that stress contributes to the development of disorders ranging from depression (Beck, Rush, Shaw, & Emery, 1979, p. 222; Hammen & deMayo, 1982; Hammen, Mayol, deMayo, & Marks, 1986; Krantz, 1985; Nezu, Nezu, Saraydarian, Kalmar, & Roman, 1986) to cancer (Sklar & Anisman, 1981) to general immunological dysfunction (Borysenko, 1984; Zegans, 1982). It is apparent, therefore, that a clear understanding of stress and methods for managing and reducing stress are needed. Despite the contributions of a number of major theorists and researchers, the current theoretical models (e.g., Klinger, 1975, 1977; Lazarus, 1975, 1977, 1982; Shontz, 1965, 1975; Wortman & Brehm, 1975) have little predictive power when applied to individual cases (Silver & Wortman, 1980). Most of these theoretical models suggest that people will respond to stress with predictable, normative response patterns, and that these responses will occur in orderly sequences of stages. However, empirical studies of reactions to stressors find extreme variability in both the responses observed and the time periods over which these responses occur (see Silver & Wortman, 1980). Overall, leading theories of stress and their corresponding approaches to stress management have been criticized for paying insufficient attention to individual differences (Lazarus & Folkman, 1984).

One of the most basic difficulties in the field has been to adequately define and operationalize the concept of stress (Mason, 1975a). Part of the problem is that the term has been used alternately to describe environmental stimuli (i.e., stress = agent outside the person), the response of the person to environmental stimuli, and the interaction between the two. This lack of consensus on the meaning of stress has resulted in considerable confusion. However, the term has immense public and professional appeal and is therefore too firmly established to be abandoned. In keeping with Mason's (1975b) persuasive recommendations, *stress* will be used in this article as a collective term to refer to situations in which environmental demands, internal demands, or the combination of the two tax or exceed the person's adaptive capacity. *Stressor* will be used to refer to the environmental and internal stimuli that require an adaptive response from a person.

Stress researchers have gradually approached a consensus on the view that stress is cognitively mediated (Forsythe & Compas, 1987; Mason, 1975a, 1975b; Singer, 1986; Zegans, 1982). The most widely known view of the role of cognition in stress has been developed by Lazarus (Lazarus, 1975, 1977, 1982; Lazarus, Averill, & Opton, 1970; Lazarus & Folkman, 1984; Lazarus & Launier, 1978). He and his colleagues emphasize the impact that a person's appraisal of situational demands and of responses for coping has on both stress and coping. In this case, stress is seen as being related to a person's perceptions of the magnitude of environmental risks (e.g., challenges, demands, threats) that must be faced, relative to perceptions of his or her personal resources for coping. If such a risk/resource ratio is believed to be high (i.e., coping responses are deemed to be relatively ineffective) or if it persists over time (i.e., coping responses have actually been insufficient), stress is increased, as are the chances for deleterious physical and psychological consequences.

Other theorists focus on additional aspects of cognition in their analyses of stress and stress management. Meichenbaum (1977) emphasizes the role of cognitive processes in stress and focuses on the role of internal dialogue and self-statements in mediating responses to potentially stressful situations. Hamilton (1980) presents a theoretical analysis of stress in which he acknowledges the importance of interpretation of stimuli but emphasizes the role of selective attention and information processing in shaping responses to stressors. Cohen (1980) highlights the importance of meaning and context in determining the amount of stress produced by intense environmental stimulation. Nezu et al. (1986) indicate that stress events per se account for only a small amount of variance in predicting physical and mental disorders, and that much of the remaining variance can be explained by the person's level of problem-solving ability. Similarly, Breslau and Davis (1986) support the notion that even chronic stressors, in and of themselves, do not reliably precipitate clinical depression without stress-exacerbating cognitive mediation.

Each of these authors examines important aspects of the cognitive processes that are involved in stress reactions; however, their limited attention to individual differences in cognitive processing limits the power of their models in anticipating the reactions of specific people to stressful situations. At the same time, they provide a fruitful starting point for the development of methods (and utilization of currently existing methods, e.g., Beck et al., 1979) for individual cognitive assessment, which may provide clinicians with the means to apply powerful, individualized stress-management therapy techniques.

BECK'S COGNITIVE ANALYSIS OF STRESS AND STRESS MANAGEMENT

Beck's detailed observation of people undergoing cognitive therapy has contributed to the development of a cognitive view of stress that emphasizes the role of thought patterns that are unique to different people (Beck, 1983, 1984). This article presents further developments of this model in the hope that attention to idiosyncratic aspects of cognition will contribute to greater success in predicting variations in reactions to stress.

Beck's general theoretical model has been used extensively with depression (Beck et al., 1979), anxiety disorders (Beck & Emery, 1985), personality disorders (Beck & Freeman, 1990), and other problems.
The definition of stress that is currently used (Mason, 1975b) allows for a great deal of overlap between stress-related problems and official *DSM III-R* diagnostic categories such as depression and anxiety disorders. Aside from suggesting that a cognitive approach could be useful with stress-related psychological disorders such as those mentioned above, this model implies that subclinical stress-related problems may be efficaciously treated as well. In this sense, a demonstrably effective therapy for depression, anxiety, and other disorders could be used for clients who present with stressful problems in living, such as family discord or difficulties at school or work, before they lead to full-blown clinical episodes. A cognitive approach to stress management would then be valuable as a preventive treatment. It would address clients' specific concerns and teach them to view and act on such concerns in a more realistic and constructive way. The resultant decrease in actual environmental demands and increase in constructive coping skills may stave off the onset of full-blown disorders.

The following section contains a set of hypotheses (and subhypotheses) that are illustrative of an idiographically oriented, cognitive model of stress. These hypotheses will later be applied to a specific case and therefore serve as guidelines for ascertaining the client's personal set of stress-enhancing cognitions.

Hypotheses

Hypothesis I (H1). A person's cognitive appraisal of a situation plays a central role in the development of stress.

Note: This premise is at the heart of cognitive therapy, yet it has been argued that persons experiencing stress-related disorders [e.g., depression] are responding essentially to real life crises, such as critical failures in social, academic, and vocational endeavors, or extreme loss in terms of personal property, physical health, or deaths of significant others (Hammen et al., 1986; Hammen & Mayol, 1982; Krantz, 1985). At the same time, these authors note that this does not imply that cognitive appraisals are unimportant or less important than information about reality. To argue either that cognitions are the sole source of stress or that real life situations are the exclusive source is to set up a false dichotomy. In actuality, each plays an important role. However, to the extent that interpretations, generalizations, and predictions play a role in stress and in the development and exacerbation of psychological disorders, they are fruitful points of intervention in their own right. This is especially true when the client's life circumstances are relatively uncontrollable (Wheaton, 1983). Even when a person's environmental situation is alterable, cognitive interventions may help the client mobilize his or her resources and act constructively, thus ameliorating the external stress-inducing situation.

Subhypothesis A. This appraisal of the situation is based only on a subset of the available information. This subset represents the information that the person expected to be most important and to which he or she therefore selectively attended (selective abstraction).

Subhypothesis B. The perceived aspects of the situation are evaluated in terms of the person's beliefs and assumptions. The initial evaluation is produced by an automatic, involuntary, nonreflective process (automatic thoughts). Subsequent reflective thoughts can produce more sophisticated evaluations (rational responding).

Subhypothesis C. Unrealistic or distorted beliefs and assumptions related to a situation may produce idiosyncratic errors in evaluating the situation. (The words "unrealistic" and "distorted" mean that the person's view of the situation is maladaptive. His or her dysfunctional evaluation of the situation hinders ascertaining and implementing problem-solving alternatives that would otherwise be apparent to an objective observer).

Hypothesis 2 (H2). The initial evaluation of the situation shapes the subsequent cognitive processing.

Subhypothesis A. When people evaluate a situation as presenting a threat, they appraise the degree and nature of threat involved and assess their resources for dealing with it. These appraisals are by and large automatic.

Subhypothesis B. If the situation is evaluated as presenting an opportunity for self-enhancement, the nature and degree of desirability of the opportunity is appraised, as is the person's capacity for taking advantage of the opportunity. These appraisals are similarly automatic.

Subhypothesis C. If the situation is evaluated as presenting both a threat and an opportunity for self-enhancement, then priority in cognitive processing is determined by the perceived magnitude and immediacy of each.

Hypothesis 3 (H3). The person's evaluation of the situation provokes congruent emotional and concomitant physiological responses.

Subhypothesis A. Specific categories of appraisals elicit specific emotional responses. For example, appraisals of danger elicit anxiety, appraisals of gain elicit joy, appraisals of loss elicit sadness, etc.

Subhypothesis B. A broad range of physiological responses occur in association with the subjective experience of emotion. These responses include, but are not limited to, secretion of adrenaline, increase in pulse rate and blood pressure, and suppression of immune responses (Selye, 1982). The psychoendocrine picture is very complex, however, and no universal or totally nonspecific responses have been conclusively demonstrated as yet.

Hypothesis 4 (H4). The behavioral response to the situation is based on the perceived risk/resources ratio, as well as the likelihood of success entailed by alternative responses.

Subhypothesis A. If the expected benefits of actively responding to the threat or opportunity do not exceed the expected costs, the person will not attempt to actively eliminate the threat or to attain the goal.

Subhypothesis B. The person will choose the method of coping that maximizes the expectancy of success while minimizing risk.

Hypothesis 5 (H5). Stress intensifies when the person is unable to eliminate the threat or to attain the goal for an extended period of time.

Subhypothesis A. This deficiency or discrepancy results in a more negative appraisal of one's own coping resources, a reduced expectancy of success, and prolonged emotional and physiological arousal. Such pro-

longed physiological arousal, expressed as a chronic increase in neuroendocrine activity, may lead to specific physiological dysfunctions (Beck,
1984). Furthermore, the person may cease attempting to actively modify
the situation.

Subhypothesis B. If the person is able to respond to the situation effectively, he or she appraises the situation more positively. This appraisal
may be a result of a shift in selective attention and the modification of
beliefs and assumptions or actual positive situational changes that the
person has created via direct action. These changes will reduce emotional
and physiological arousal and thereby reduce stress.

Hypothesis 6 (H6). Interventions that result in a revised evaluation of
(a) the situation; (b) environmental risks, costs, and benefits; (c) the person's coping resources; and (d) the probability of success, can alter the
person's level of stress.

Subhypothesis A. If a benign situation has been interpreted in a stress-
eliciting way through selective attention, cognitive distortions, and negatively biased beliefs and assumptions, interventions that will lead to a
more objective evaluation of the situation will reduce or eliminate stress.

Subhypothesis B. If a normatively stressful situation has been exaggerated through selective attention, cognitive distortions, and negatively biased beliefs and assumptions, interventions that facilitate a more objective
evaluation of the situation will reduce stress to a more manageable level.

Subhypothesis C. If negatively biased evaluations of coping resources
and methods, expected risks, costs, and benefits, and probability of success have interfered with effective responses to the situation, then interventions that lead to a more objective view will facilitate successful coping
and thereby reduce stress.

Subhypothesis D. Interventions that result in the person's acquirement
of improved cognitive and behavioral coping skills will reduce stress.

Subhypothesis E. Interventions that produce positive changes in the
situation with which the person is confronted will reduce stress to the
extent that these changes translate into a more benign appraisal of the
situation.

CLINICAL APPLICATION OF THE COGNITIVE MODEL OF STRESS MANAGEMENT

"Steve," a 50–year-old father of two, was referred by his family physician
for counseling to help him overcome the intense stress that he experienced during job interviews. During his initial telephone contact, Steve
explained to his therapist (the first author) that after 10 years of success

in middle management, he had started to find his job increasingly demanding. In spite of his familiarity with popular stress-management techniques such as relaxation, time-management strategies, improved diet and physical exercise, he found himself overwhelmed with stress and unable to respond effectively. His job performance had gradually deteriorated and he had been laid off for about 4 months before entering therapy. Steve found both unemployment and job-hunting to be quite stressful. In addition to experiencing considerable subjective distress, he experienced somatic symptoms of stress including tension headaches, indigestion, and sleep-onset insomnia, and he was having great difficulty taking active steps toward finding a new job.

Unemployment and job-hunting are normatively stressful life events. Likewise, Steve's responsibilities on previous jobs, which included tasks such as presenting his view to superiors and colleagues and defending these views against criticism, were situations that many persons would find stressful. However, Steve's implementation of nomothetic stress-management techniques (relaxation, time-management strategies, and others) proved only minimally helpful.

The cognitive view asserts that an idiographic approach can facilitate understanding of atypical responses and permit more effective and efficient interventions than nomothetic approaches to stress and stress management. The cognitive approach requires a specific, individual, and idiographic assessment to provide a basis for effective intervention. In Steve's case, an initial evaluation included (a) assessing the onset and course of his problems with stress, (b) identifying his cognitions when under stress, (c) evaluating his attempts at coping with stressful situations, and (d) appraising the relevance of his individual and family history. The following picture emerged.

Steve grew up as the oldest of two children in a small Midwestern farming community where his father owned a dry goods store. Both his parents were quiet, reserved people who never expressed anger to each other or to their children. He was popular with peers, active in athletics, and he did reasonably well in school. However, he was not achievement-oriented and was thoroughly intimidated by the harshness of the nuns at the parochial school he attended. After an uneventful tour of duty in the service and a business degree in college, he married the sister of one of his boyhood friends and started an entry-level management position in a major corporation. He found his superiors and colleagues to be hard-working, cooperative, "buttoned-down" people with whom he was very comfortable, and he distinguished himself in planning programs and developing policies.

After several years he was recruited to join another major corporation at a more responsible position with a corresponding increase in salary. Steve was initially quite enthusiastic about his new position but soon discovered that his colleagues and superiors at the new firm were much more outspoken, competitive, and aggressive than the associates at the previous job. He also found that each person was expected to present his own point of view forcefully at meetings and to openly criticize other proposals. As a result, Steve found his new job to be intimidating and highly stressful even though his new responsibilities were well within his capacity.

Steve's attempts to reduce this stress involved the following strategies: (a) avoiding interpersonal conflict and criticism whenever possible, (b) indiscriminately agree with others in order to pacify them, (c) working very hard in a desperate attempt to avoid making any mistakes that could be criticized, and (d) increasing his alcohol consumption in order to relax. Unfortunately, these attempts at stress reduction interfered with his effectiveness as a manager, and his job performance suffered. He interpreted his poor job performance as a sign of his general inadequacy and became increasingly insecure and self-critical. He attempted to cope with his insecurity, self-doubt, and lack of confidence by constantly monitoring his own behavior in the hope of preventing any mistakes and by concealing all signs of self-doubt. However, this simply resulted in heightened self-consciousness, which made minor slips seem like major errors and further intensified his stress and anxiety.

When Steve was introduced to stress-management techniques as part of his training for a new position, he found that relaxation exercises and lifestyle changes (e.g., improving his diet, getting regular exercise, and decreasing his alcohol consumption) produced some benefits but, unfortunately, did not prove sufficient for managing his stress.

Each time Steve received a negative evaluation or had his position shot down, it intensified his belief that he had to stop making mistakes. At the point when Steve was referred for therapy, he had become preoccupied with the fear that he might make mistakes during job interviews. He was convinced that any slip he made during an interview would reveal his inadequacies and prevent his getting the job. In addition, he was convinced that the best way to cope with his situation was to watch what he said during the interview very closely in order to avoid making mistakes. Furthermore, he was certain that his inadequacies would eventually result in his failing at any job he obtained. Nevertheless, he believed that there was no alternative but to get a job and then at all costs try to conceal his deficiencies.

By Steve's description, his parents did not provide good models of appropriate assertion or of effective responses to assertion or aggression. Instead, his parents' example and his experiences in parochial school conveyed the idea that it was important to avoid conflict and self-assertion and to be polite, cooperative, and considerate instead. He did well in jobs where a polite, cooperative, considerate approach was consistent with the corporate culture. He reported that his problems with stress began when he accepted a new position where a more aggressive style was the norm. According to the cognitive model, Steve's appraisal of the new corporate culture in terms of his preexisting beliefs and expectancies, rather than the aggressive corporate culture per se, initiated his stress (H1–C: Dysfunctional beliefs produce errors). His construal of the situation as presenting the threat of possibly angering others (and thereby eliciting criticism and hostility) produced anxiety and concomitant physical symptoms (H3: Evaluation provokes affective and physiological responses). Additionally, his construction resulted in focusing primarily on the potential threat presented by the situation rather than on the opportunities for success and advancement presented by the situation (H2–C: Priority in processing determined by the perceived magnitude of each).

As he evaluated his capability for coping effectively with the situation, Steve concluded that attempts at appropriate assertion would precipitate the hostility and criticism that he feared (H4–A: Person will not act if expected costs of behavior outweigh the expected benefits), while being cooperative and avoiding conflict might appease colleagues and superiors. Therefore, he took this latter course of action (H4–B: Method of coping that maximizes the expectancy of success will be chosen). Unfortunately, this strategy proved ineffective and resulted in both criticism from others and increased corporate demands for aggressive self-assertion. A purely rational analysis might suggest that Steve should have concluded that his initial strategy was ineffective and, therefore, should have tried another approach. Instead, however, his lack of success in coping with the situation resulted in a more negative appraisal of his job performance capabilities, which in turn exacerbated his emotional and physiological responses and decreased his expectancy that active coping attempts could succeed (H5–A: Coping failures, having been driven by dysfunctional appraisals, will induce further distortions, including negative appraisals of one's own coping, reduced expectancy of success, and prolonged emotional and physiological arousal).

As the situation continued to deteriorate, Steve's increasingly negative evaluation of his capabilities and of his prospects led to deepening demoralization (cf. Hammen & deMayo's [1982] use of this term to denote subclinical depression and hopelessness). Additionally, it served to fortify his conclusion that the criticism he received was due to mistakes on his part and, therefore, he should be very careful to make no mistakes. This resulted in constant vigilance for signs of disapproval on the part of others and mistakes on his part (H1–A: Person selectively attends to information expected to be most important; H2: Initial appraisals shape subsequent processing). Such self-consciousness generated additional anxiety that further interfered with his performance and prolonged his stress (H5: Coping failures, having been driven by dysfunctional appraisals, will induce further distortions and maladaptive behaviors, thereby prolonging and intensifying stress).

A vicious cycle was established in which Steve's dysfunctional appraisal of the situation produced maladaptive behaviors and an increase in magnitude and chronicity of stress, which in turn perpetuated the tendency toward dysfunctional appraisals. This cycle was well established by the time Steve was introduced to stress-management techniques. The interventions that he tried lowered his level of distress temporarily but did not provide him with the skills needed to cope effectively with the situation nor have a significant impact on his beliefs about his capacity for coping with the situation. In order to be efficacious, the interventions needed to do the following: (a) highlight his unique maladaptive views (H1–C: Dysfunctional beliefs produce errors) and his misguided corrective behaviors (H4–B: Method of coping that maximizes the expectancy of success will be chosen); (b) produce a more objective view of the situation (H6–B: Objective appraisals will reduce stress to a more manageable level) and his capacity for coping with it (H6–C: Objective appraisals will facilitate successful coping and reduce stress); and (c) result in his mastering the skills and strategies needed to cope effectively (H6–D: Acquisition of improved cognitive and behavioral coping skills will reduce stress).

When Steve was referred for therapy, an individualized treatment plan was developed on the basis of the theoretical analysis being presented. Using the approach of collaborative empiricism characteristic of cognitive therapy (Beck et al., 1979), Steve was first helped to recognize the relationship between his momentary evaluation of situations and his resulting emotions and actions. It was then possible to help him look critically at his idiosyncratic evaluations of problem situations and at the way in which he attempted to cope with these situations. This strategy counteracted the biasing effects of selective attention and resulted in his recognition that his appraisal of problem situations and his ability to cope with them were negatively distorted. Equally important, this plan facilitated his identification of alternative strategies for handling these problem situations.

The process of trying to implement these strategies brought to the fore the fears, beliefs, and skill deficits that blocked effective coping and made it possible to address them directly. In nine individual sessions over a 2-month period he was able to develop a realistic view of the risks and opportunities presented by previously stressful situations, to develop adaptive ways of coping with these circumstances, to revise problematic beliefs, and to develop a plan for preventing relapse. Most basic of all was the fact that Steve's dysphoria and anxiety diminished; he felt much better.

A follow-up appointment 4 months later showed that this improvement had been maintained. He was feeling good overall, was able to handle job interviews effectively with no more than a normative level of stress, and was a finalist for a promising job opening. Because the interventions produced lasting changes in his beliefs and in his preferred methods of coping with stress, and because these changes were reinforced by their effectiveness in handling problem situations, we would expect the improvement to persist. An idiographically based stress-management treatment was successful where nomothetically based interventions had been far less successful in meeting the client's unique therapeutic needs.

DISCUSSION

In a fairly pessimistic evaluation of contemporary stress management approaches, Lazarus and Folkman (1984) write:

> The problem with stress management programs is that, in contrast to most one-on-one clinical treatments, they are not tailored to the particular dynamics of the individual but are usually created for people in general. No attempt is made to pin down the special vulnerabilities that have gotten the individual into trouble . . . Group programs may be useful when coping failure is due to an uncomplicated lack of skill, or experience . . . What is missing, however, are concerns with the emotional factors that may underlie maladaptation and impair rational problem-solving processes, as well as the regulation of the distressing emotions. (pp. 361, 363, 364)

Although this criticism applies to many of the current approaches to stress management, recognition of the role that individual differences in cognition play in shaping response to stressors should make it possible to intervene effectively in individual therapy (cf. Kendall, 1983). Similarly, this understanding can be applied to the design of self-help and group therapies for stress management that address the person's particular needs.

Our model suggests that a number of aspects of cognition, including immediate thoughts, beliefs and assumptions, cognitive distortions, and expectancies, among others, can play a role in determining whether a given person copes successfully with a stressor or not. If it can be determined empirically which aspects of cognition are most influential, or if subgroups that share common problems can be identified, interventions could be targeted for those areas that are most likely to be problematic. This strategy could be combined with a guided discovery approach in which clients are taught self-assessment and self monitoring skills so that they can identify the aspects of their cognitions that are sources of stress. Although self-help and group therapies based on these principles cannot be tailored to the client to the same extent as in individual therapy, the lower cost and greater accessibility of these avenues makes them worth pursuing as well.

Cognitive processes play a prominent role in both idiosyncratic and normative stress reactions. It is hoped that the cognitive model of stress, which pays closer attention to individual differences in cognitive processing, will have greater predictive power than nomothetic approaches and will facilitate more effective intervention. However, if this increase in predictive power is achieved, it will not be without cost. Prediction of a person's cognitive, emotional, and behavioral responses to a stressful life event requires considerable information concerning factors such as (a) the underlying beliefs and assumptions (which typically necessitate obtaining a historical profile), (b) the characteristic cognitive distortions, (c) the expectations concerning alternative coping strategies, and (d) the repertoire of coping skills. At the same time, collection of detailed individual information proves both practical and necessary in clinical practice (Pretzer, 1990; Safran, Vallis, Segal, & Shaw, 1986).

It is in clinical practice that an idiographic approach to stress may have its clearest advantage. A striking example in support of this premise can be found in Holroyd (1979). A 34–year-old secretary was successfully treated for tension headaches via biofeedback/relaxation in the lab, but she continually experienced a recurrence of symptoms while at her place of work. This aberration was a mystery until it was discovered that the client held the belief that taking time to relax at work was a sign of laziness and would interfere with her job performance. This belief not only contributed to her tension headaches in the first place, but it also prevented her from actively using the skills she learned in biofeedback training. Inattention to the client's belief system would have rendered treatment ineffective.

The role of cognition in the stress-management techniques analyzed here is consistent with both the clinical experience of therapists at the Center for Cognitive Therapy (University of Pennsylvania, Philadelphia) and the empirical literature on stress. However, clinical observation and case examples do not provide an adequate test of a theory. An empirical assessment of the validity and predictive power of this analysis is needed.

Unfortunately, empirical tests of this model will not be easy because of the large amount of data needed on each subject and the need for the development of improved methods for assessing cognitive variables (Sundberg, 1981). In addition, the study of an idiographic approach to stress management, by its very intent, is not likely to be amenable to traditional group-design experimentation. Nevertheless, methods exist that make individual case study—and repeated trials of case studies—more rigorous (Kazdin, 1980). In this scenario, objective measures of client cognition, affect, behavior, and subjective level of stress are made on several occasions before, during, and after treatment, so that changes in these domains can be attributed more confidently to treatment or, conversely, to extraneous factors.

Another obstacle involves the use of objective measures of cognition, which (again) are usually based on group norms. In order to be useful for idiographic research, cognitive assessment self-report inventories would need to include a vast array of items that are reflective of dysfunctional beliefs and attitudes, so that individual differences in cognitive style could be teased out more readily. One such scale is the Dysfunctional Attitudes Scale (DAS; Weissman & Beck, 1978), which includes 100 commonly encountered maladaptive cognitive beliefs that may cause or exacerbate psychological dysfunction. Although these items do not address the specific external stressors to which the client applies his or her beliefs, these can be ascertained easily through direct questioning once the DAS items are scored and available for perusal by the therapist. Overall, the use of measures such as the DAS, in the context of rigorous $n = 1$ designs, may facilitate empirical tests of the cognitive model of stress and its treatment.

Judging the relative effectiveness of the cognitive therapy model to other treatment modalities is yet another thorny issue. One approach that clinicians and researchers may use is a variant on the A-B-A design. Here, a baseline period, including pretherapy and early assessment (A), is followed by a treatment period, such as cognitive therapy (B), which is followed still by a second treatment period, e.g., nomothetic stress management techniques (C). Clients presenting with stress-related problems may be randomly assigned to receive therapy in either A-B-C or A-C-B order. Although such a design complicates the issue by introducing inter-active effects of treatments B and C, it does elucidate their relative additive properties. In other words, if treatment B reliably produces a sharper increase in therapeutic gain (after treatment C had been applied) than treatment C (after treatment B had been applied), there is evidence that B is more efficacious than C. If both B-C and C-B produce therapeutic gains above and beyond B or C alone, there would be evidence that a combination of nomothetic and idiographic treatments is highly efficacious. A current example of such a successful combined approach is Kendall's (1983) Stress Inoculation Training, which involves cognitive restructuring and relaxation training among its treatment components.

Given the value that a valid and powerful model of stress and stress management would have in intervention, we hope that the complexities of individual variability do not discourage theorists and researchers from attending to idiographic as well as normative aspects of stress. When nomothetic approaches do not provide a sufficient basis for effective intervention, the added complexity of an idiographic approach is a price worth paying if it results in increased predictive power and more effective intervention.

REFERENCES

Beck, A. T. (1983). Cognitive approaches to stress reactions. In P. Lehrer & R. L. Woolfolk (Eds.), *Clinical guide to stress management.* New York Guilford Press.

Beck, A. T. (1984). Cognitive approaches to stress. In R. Woolfolk & P. Lehrer (Eds.), *Principles and practice of stress management* (pp. 255–305). New York: Guilford Press.

Beck, A. T., & Emery, G. (1985). *Anxiety disorders and phobias: A cognitive perspective.* New York: Basic Books.

Beck, A. T., & Freeman, A. (1990). *Cognitive therapy of personality disorders.* New York: Guilford Press.

Beck, A. T., Rush, A. J., Shaw, B. E, & Emery, G. (1979). *Cognitive therapy of depression.* New York: Guilford Press.

Borysenko, I. (1984). Stress, coping, and the immune system. In J. D. Matarazzo, S. M. Weiss, J. A. Herd, & N. E. Miller (Eds.), *Behavioral health: A handbook of health enhancement and disease prevention* (pp. 248–260). New York: Wiley.

Breslau, H., & Davis, G. C. (1986). Chronic stress and major depression. *Archives of General Psychiatry, 43,* 309–314.

Cohen, S. (1980). Cognitive processes as determinants of environmental stress. In I. G. Sarason & C. D. Spielberger (Eds.), *Stress and anxiety, Vol. 7.* New York: Hemisphere.

Forsythe, C. J., & Compas, B. E. (1987). Interaction of cognitive appraisals of stressful events and coping: Testing the goodness of fit hypothesis. *Cognitive Therapy and Research, 1,* 473–485.

Hamilton, V. (1980). An information processing analysis of environmental stress and life crisis. In I. G. Sarason & C. D. Spielberger (Eds.), *Stress and anxiety, Vol. 7.* New York: Hemisphere.

Hammen, C., & deMayo, R. (1982). Cognitive correlates of teacher stress and depressive symptoms: Implications for attributional models of depression.]ournal of Abnormal Psychology, 91, 96–101.

Hammen, C., & Mayol, A. (1982). Depression and cognitive characteristics of stressful life-event types. *Journal of Abnormal Psychology, 91,* 1651–74.

Hammen, C., Mayol, A., deMayo, R., & Marks, T. (1986). Initial symptom levels and the life-event—depression relationship. *Journal of Abnormal Psychology, 95,* 114–122.

Holroyd, K. A. (1979). Stress, coping, and the treatment of stress-related illness. In S. R. McNamara (Ed.), *Behavioral approaches to medicine* (pp. 191–226). New York: Plenum Press.

Kazdin, A. E. (1980). *Research design in clinical psychology.* New York: Harper & Row.

Kendall, P. C. (1983). Stressful medical procedures: Cognitive-behavioral strategies for stress management and prevention. In D. Meichenbaum & M. E. Jaremko (Eds.), *Stress reduction and prevention* (pp. 159–190). New York: Plenum Press.

Klinger, E. (1975). Consequences of commitment to and disengagement from incentives. *Psychological Review, 82,* 1–25.

Klinger, E. (1977). *Meaning and void.* Minneapolis: University of Minnesota Press.

Krantz, S. E. (1985). When depressive cognitions reflect negative realities. *Cognitive Therapy and Research, 6,* 595–610.

Lazarus, R. S. (1975). A cognitively oriented psychologist looks at biofeedback. *American Psychologist, 30,* 553–561.

Lazarus, R. S. (1977). Cognitive and coping processes in emotion. In A. Monat & R. S. Lazarus (Eds.), *Stress and coping: An anthology* (pp. 145–158). New York: Columbia University Press.

Lazarus, R. S. (1982). The psychology of stress and coping. In N. A. Milgram (Ed.), *Stress and anxiety. Vol. 8.* New York: Hemisphere Publishing.

Lazarus, R. S., Averill, J. R., & Opton, E. R., Jr. (1970). Towards a cognitive theory of emotion. In M. B. Arnold (Ed.), *Feelings and emotions* (pp. 207–232). New York: Academic Press.

Lazarus, R. S., & Folkman, S. (1984). *Stress, appraisal, and coping.* New York: Springer.

Lazarus, R. S., & Launier, R. (1978). Stress-related transactions between person and environment. In L. A. Pervin & M. Lewis (Eds.), *Perspectives in interactional psychology* (pp. 287–327). New York: Plenum Press.

Mason, J. W. (1975a). A historical view of the stress field. Part 1. *Journal of Human Stress, 1,* 6–12.

Mason, J. W. (1975b). A historical view of the stress field. Part 2. *Journal of Human Stress, 1,* 22–36.

Meichenbaum, D. (1977). *Cognitive-behavior modification: An integrative approach.* New York: Plenum Press.

Nezu, A. M., Nezu, C. M., Saraydarian, L., Kalmar, K., & Roman, G. F. (1986). Social problem-solving as a moderating variable between negative life stress and depressive symptoms. *Cognitive Therapy and Research, 10,* 489–498.

Pretzer, J. L. (1990). Clinical assessment in cognitive therapy. In A. Freeman, B. Fleming, K. Simon, & J. Pretzer (Eds.), *Clinical applications of cognitive therapy.* New York: Plenum Press.

Safran, J. D., Vallis, T. M., Segal, Z. V., & Shaw, B. F. (1986). Assessment of core cognitive process in cognitive therapy. *Cognitive Therapy and Research, 10,* 509– 526.

Selye, H. (1982). History and present status of the stress concept. In L. Goldberger & S. Breznitz (Eds.), *Handbook of stress: Theoretical and clinical aspects* (p. 116). New York: Free Press.

Shontz, F. C. (1965). *Reaction to crisis.* Volta Review, 67, 364–370.

Shontz, F. C. (1975). *The psychological aspects of physical illness and disability.* New York: Macmillan.

Silver, R. L., & Wortman, C. G. (1980). Coping with undesirable life events. In J. Garber & M. E. P. Seligman (Eds.), *Human helplessness* (pp. 279–340). New York: Academic Press.

Singer, J. E. (1986). Traditions in stress research: integrative comments. In D. C. Spielberger & I. G. Sarason (Eds.), *Stress and anxiety, Vol. 10* (pp. 25–33). New York: Hemisphere.

Sklar, L. S., & Anisman, A. (1981). Stress and cancer. *Psychological Bulletin, 89,* 369–406.

Sundberg, N. D. (1981). Historical and traditional approaches to cognitive assessment. In T. V. Merluzzi, C. R. Glass, & M. Genest (Eds.), *Cognitive assessment* (pp. 52–76). New York: Guilford Press.

Weissman, A. N., & Beck, A. T. (1978). *Development and validation of the Dysfunctional Attitudes Scale.* Paper presented at the Association for the Advancement of Behavior Therapy, Chicago, IL.

Wheaton, B. (1983). Stress, personal coping resources, and psychiatric symptoms: An investigation of interactive models. *Journal of Health and Social Behavior, 24,* 208–229.

Wortman, C. B., & Brehm, J. W. (1975). Responses to uncontrollable outcomes: An integration of reactance theory and the learned helplessness model. In L. Berkowitz (Ed.), *Advances in experimental social psychology, Vol. 8* (pp. 277–336). New York: Academic Press.

Zegans, L. S. (1982). Stress and the development of somatic disorders. In L. Goldberger & S. Breznitz (Eds.), *Handbook of stress: Theoretical and clinical aspects* (pp. 136–152). New York: Free Press.

CHAPTER 20

Dysfunctional Beliefs About Intimacy

Karen Kayser and David P. Himle

In recent times intimacy has become an essential characteristic and primary goal of marital satisfaction, and of interpersonal relations in general (Veroff, Douvan, & Kulka, 1981). Kingsbury and Minda (1988) have identified intimacy and love as the best indicators of whether or not couples plan to continue or to end their relationships. Descriptions of the general positive beliefs and behavioral characteristics of intimacy have been developed by a number of investigators. For example, Levinger and Snoek (1972) have stressed the importance of self-disclosure, interaction, and jointly held values in the relationship. Walster, Walster, and Berscheid (1978) have identified intense liking or loving, the value of exchanged resources, and "we-ness," as characteristics of intimacy. Chelune, Robison, and Kommor (1984) have stressed the ideas of trust, commitment, caring, and knowledge of the partner in their definition of intimacy.

The characteristics of intimacy have been addressed and measured in a number of questionnaires (Orlofsky, 1974; Schaefer & Olson, 1981; Miller & Lefcourt, 1982), but these measures usually assess intimate behaviors, not dysfunctional beliefs about intimacy. A number of questionnaires have assessed beliefs and expectations about marital relationships in general, but not necessarily of intimacy in particular (Eisenberg & Zingle, 1975; Epstein & Eidelson, 1981; Epstein, 1986).

Ellis (1982; 1986a; 1986b) has described a number of irrational beliefs that interfere with interpersonal relationships. Briefly summarized, these beliefs are based on romantic myths about intimate relationships which stress the dire necessity of intimacy in such relationships, and absolute "shoulds" and "musts" about its manner of expression. For example, "You must give me the intimacy I want or our relationship is worthless."

McClellan and Stieper (1977) have identified four major irrational beliefs which contribute to marital dysfunction, and which may have relevance for intimacy. They are summarized as follows: (1) an excessive demand for approval from partners, (2) expecting things to go the way each partner wanted, (3) expecting perfection in the relationship, and (4) blaming the partner when things go wrong. These beliefs may affect the development of various types of marital interaction, such as issues of control, and idealistic expectations, but are not necessarily directly related to intimacy.

Eidelson and Epstein (1982) have developed an inventory (RBI; Relationship Belief Inventory) designed to measure dysfunctional beliefs associated with marital distress. The RBI has five basic dysfunctional themes: (1) disagreement between spouses is destructive to their relationship; (2) spouses should be able to "mind read" each other needs; (3) partners cannot change their relationship once a pattern has been established; (4) one must be a perfect sexual partner; and (5) conflicts between spouses are primarily due to basic and enduring differences in needs and personalities of the two sexes. Epstein (1982) states that this set of beliefs is not exhaustive, but representative of major dysfunctional themes reported by marital therapists. While a few of the items in the inventory do address the concept of intimacy directly, many items measure other aspects of marital maladjustment.

More recently, Jack (1991) has developed a scale to measure women's beliefs about intimate relationships. Jack's "Silencing the Self Scale" contains 31 statements that reflect beliefs about oneself in intimate heterosexual relationships. These items are based on interviews with depressed women and are indicative of many social imperatives which form the traditional female role.

Some progress has been made in the assessment of maladaptive behavioral patterns and irrational beliefs about interpersonal relationships. For example, Epstein and Eidelson (1981) found a relationship between spouses' marital distress and unrealistic standards about marriage. This type of study provides the beginning of an empirical basis for the assumption that dysfunctional beliefs affect levels of marital satisfaction.

While it is true that this survey of the literature about interpersonal relationships can be useful in understanding the dynamics of intimacy, we believe that a set of dysfunctional beliefs about intimacy needs to be identified, that are less generic and more situationally specific. Therefore, it is the purpose of this article to identify and specify examples of such dysfunctional beliefs in detail, and to describe them in ways that can be useful to an assessment process.

DYSFUNCTIONAL BELIEFS ABOUT INTIMACY: SITUATIONAL SPECIFICITY

While we have defined intimacy as an emotional closeness resulting from the display of certain behaviors such as self-disclosure, emotional support, physical contact, and companionship (Kersten & Himle, 1990), it is obvious that there are a number of beliefs which may hinder the development of such intimacy, as listed above. In general, these beliefs may result in avoidance of intimacy, or in its subversion (Hatfield, 1984; Miller, 1988). Although individuals may have the behavioral repertoire for intimacy, emotional closeness can be subverted by these specific beliefs. For example, the belief that the disclosure of personal feelings always leads to rejection, may inhibit the person from engaging in self-disclosure and developing greater intimacy. It is therefore important to identify these dysfunctional beliefs as closely as possible.

Based on our clinical observation of individuals and couples seeking counseling for relationship problems, we have identified the following dysfunctional and irrational beliefs about intimacy, which may be useful to the development of a general set of beliefs related to this problem. These clients were primarily white, middle class, and of both genders, seen in private practice.

While these observations are subjective in nature, we believe that they can be the basis for further study as to their validity through experimental research. In describing them we have sought to link them to the general proposition that beliefs were considered dysfunctional when they hindered the development of a desired level of intimacy (Eidelson & Epstein, 1982), and irrational when they were unverifiable, self-defeating, and based on cognitive errors such as overgeneralization and arbitrary inference (Burns, 1980). We believe that a more concentrated analysis of dysfunctional thinking at the core level of intimacy is needed since the literature shows that it has been neglected.

The following examples are illustrative of such beliefs:

(1) "If I become close to someone, he/she will leave me." This is a typical belief among many clients who have experienced a traumatic loss, such as a parent's death, divorce, abandonment, or a series of losses involving other significant relationships when they were a child or adolescent. These clients believe that all close relationships will end in a traumatic loss, regardless of individual differences and changing environmental circumstances. The result of this belief is a distancing of partners so that painful feelings can be avoided if the relationship ends. This belief is based on a cognitive error such as "mind reading" in which assumptions are made about others and about the future, without adequate evidence. It is also based on the error of overgeneralization in which the negative consequence of expressing feelings to one partner has generalized to all possible partners.

(2) "If I have any conflict in a relationship, I can't be intimate." This belief is usually apparent when one spouse avoids conflict in the relationship. These persons believe that as long as they do not talk about the problem in a relationship, the relationship will survive. Sometimes these individuals were raised in families in which parents were always in conflict and lacked skills to reach solutions or compromises. Because they avoided or could not reach such solutions or compromises, there was increased anger and resentment and little, if any, intimacy in the family. Such individuals then attempt to avoid such conflict in their own relationships. However, the therapist and the client can challenge the accuracy of this belief by pointing out that the resolution of conflict within a relationship may actually lead to intimacy, through the process of increased self-disclosure and problem-solving procedures.

(3) "I will lose all personal control and power in relationships, if I am intimate." The mutual experience of intimacy requires a certain degree of equality in the relationship. The person who wants to remain in a dominant position may be threatened by intimacy, which may require behaviors such as the expression of fears, and anxieties that may be perceived as undesirable and weak. The rigid preferences by partners for either dominant or submissive patterns of control related to such disclosures, are seen to be the causes for many problems in relationships (Jacobson, 1989). McGill (1986) has attributed the problem men have in their intimate relationships to their perceptions that intimate self-disclosure is a loss of power in relationships and a source of increased vulnerability. However, men can adopt the alternative view that their lack of self-disclosure may actually limit their ability to act powerfully in a relationship, that self-disclosure in loving relationships empowers a man rather than

emasculates him (McGill, 1986). Because this belief may be firmly entrenched, many male clients may need to experience this empowerment before they are willing to revise this belief.

(4) "I am solely responsible for the lack of intimacy in my relationships." Many women who seek treatment have been socialized to feel that they alone must "fix" the marriage. These women have also been socialized to believe that they are the "intimacy experts" and the person solely responsible for the intimate relationship. It is this belief, combined with an unsuccessful relationship, that may contribute to the high incidence of depression and self blame among certain women (Jack, 1987). However, in therapeutic work regarding this belief, the therapist can help the women consider the mutual responsibility of both partners for the lack of intimacy in the relationship, by enabling her to choose when and where to be intimate rather than seeing the relationship as primarily her total responsibility (Jack, 1987). This change in attribution of responsibility for the problem and corresponding reduction of total responsibility for intimacy, may alleviate the pressure on her to constantly nurture the relationship (Epstein, 1982).

(5) "I must do everything my partner wants in order to be a truly intimate person and to achieve intimacy." This is a traditional belief held by many individuals is that rewarding intimate relationships involves being a "pleaser," and that assuming this role will bring the approval of others, and intimacy itself (Jack, 1987). Such individuals may also have the same expectations of their partners, and be disappointed when partners do not display the same self-sacrificing behavior. In other words, these individuals do not view pleasing behavior or self-sacrificing behavior as a choice to be made related to present circumstances, but rather a constant life style regardless of the consequences to the individual or partner. These people tend to view themselves in a dichotomous fashion, as either totally self-sacrificing or totally selfish, and view relationships as either complete submission to, or isolation from, the partner (Jack, 1987). It may be helpful for the client to develop the capacity of choice regarding when it is important to care for others, and when it is important to seek to fulfill private needs.

(6) "If I am a good father (bring home the paycheck) or a good mother and wife (put my family's needs before my own) then I will get intimacy in return." This is usually an implied contract, not explicitly discussed by partners, but assumed to be true based on gender socialization. Since this belief is based on traditional gender roles, the assumption has been made that intimacy would develop if such role behaviors were followed (Jack,

1987). Unfortunately, this is not always the case, since the emphasis tends to be on the role behaviors of a good provider and homemaker, and not on the behaviors closely associated with the development of intimacy, namely self-disclosure and emotional support (Kersten and Himle, 1990). In this case, the couple needs to be helped to become aware of these individually developed role behaviors, which are supposed to bring intimacy, but may not.

(7) "I must always have strong loving feelings toward my partner before I can be intimate." This belief usually emerges when the client is asked to change behaviors in relation to the partner. Clients who are resistant to such behavior change, have often habitually drifted along in their unhappy relationships (Ellis, 1986b). For example, they often say, "When I feel more loving, I'll start behaving differently." This type of statement is often the product of family traditions or personal rules, and is seldom reevaluated by the individual to prove or disprove the rule's present usefulness to the client, and general validity (Himle, 1989). This belief is also held by many men and women who have excessively high expectations for intimacy, and who are deeply troubled by anything less than perfection. Such excessive demands tend to discount levels of intimacy which may be less than perfect, and yet satisfying. An alternative belief, which the client may consider, is that intimacy may be viewed as a process in relationships, not a static condition, nor an all-or-nothing response. Various levels of intimacy may be satisfying in themselves, and not discounted because of imperfections due to personal limitations or stress-producing events.

(8) "I can't experience intimacy without having sex in a relationship." This belief will likely be expressed when partners are asked to define intimacy. We have found this to be a traditional male perspective of intimacy. This belief puts pressure on some men to involve themselves sexually with women to obtain intimacy, when that is not always what the woman or the man desires. This belief also prevents the person from experiencing intimate relationships which may develop without sexual relations. Sexual relationships are an important source of intimacy, but not the only one. The therapist's task is to help the client to consider if this belief is something they want to hold on to or just a traditional family rule or personal opinion which is open to challenge, disagreement, and subsequent revision.

The beliefs listed above are presented on the basis of our observations; further research is necessary to establish whether or not they can be generalized to all dysfunctional intimate relationships.

ASSESSING INTIMACY BELIEFS

In therapeutic interaction dysfunctional beliefs about intimacy seldom emerge in the precise form and expression as listed above. In many cases the information necessary for a complete cognitive belief assessment does not emerge until treatment is well underway. It requires the therapist to actively look for a person's beliefs about intimacy and ask questions to uncover these beliefs. A nonjudgmental attitude and empathic skills are critical in eliciting these private and personal beliefs. The therapist begins the process by identifying patterns and themes about earlier relationships which may have contributed to the development of basic or core assumptions about intimate relationships in general. These assumptions may be associated with rejection, loss, or trauma in the past, and are usually activated when needs for intimacy are unfulfilled in a contemporary distressed relationship. These assumptions based on early experiences may influence an individual's perception of the partner, and his/her emotional and behavioral responses to the partner's behavior. Identifying core assumptions can be accomplished by asking questions about the quality of intimacy in these relationships: "Were your family members close to each other?" or "How was intimacy expressed in these relationships?" (Waring, 1988).

It is also important to ask questions about any previous close relationships which have ended, such as "How and why did this relationship end?" and "How does the ending of this relationship relate to your expectation of future intimate relationships?" It is crucial to identify core assumptions based on earlier relationships because they often generalize to their current relationships, even though there is no clear evidence for this transfer of perspective. For example, the belief that one is totally responsible for intimacy in a relationship may have stemmed from previous relationships in which responsibility was appropriately placed on one partner, while this is not necessary in the present relationship. Certain questions can reveal these assumptions such as, "What type of expectations do you have for you and your partner in your present relationship?"

Having identified this type of information, it may be useful to begin to identify errors in processing information which may contribute to dysfunctional thinking and action regarding intimacy. The common types of cognitive errors include overgeneralization, fortune telling, arbitrary inference, all-or-nothing thinking discounting the positive, as mentioned above (Bums, 1980).

The therapist assists the client in developing the skill to identify automatic thoughts and cognitive errors through self-monitoring homework assignments. The Dysfunctional Thoughts Record, as described by Fennell (1989) and Bums (1980), can be a useful tool in monitoring these thoughts. The format of this record consists of three column headings: emotion, situation, and automatic thoughts. On a daily basis the client notes any distressing emotion, the situation in which the emotion occurred, and the thoughts underlying the emotional response. By keeping a diary of these responses during each week, the clients can become aware of the dysfunctional thoughts that are associated with the distressful feelings. For example, a wife records the feeling of anger when her husband does not respond with affection after she spends an entire weekend cleaning the house. Underlying this anger may be the expectation of belief #6, that is, "If I'm a good mother and wife (putting my family's needs before my own) then I should get intimacy in return." Or in another case a husband records extreme anxiety when his wife makes overtures toward intimacy. Perhaps a thought related to belief #1, "If I become close to someone, he/she will leave me," may be occurring in this case.

Some dysfunctional beliefs about intimacy can be defined as faulty assumptions about how intimacy works, whereas others can be categorized as unrealistic "musts and shoulds" which are excessive demands on how intimacy should function. In many instances these two ideas are combined, as in belief #7 above.

Standardized instruments previously mentioned may also be useful in detecting dysfunctional beliefs about intimate relationships. The Silencing the Self Scale (Jack, 1991) measures specific schemas about how one should behave in intimate relationships. It contains thirty-one sentences such as, "Caring means putting the other person's needs before my own" and "In a close relationship, my responsibility is to make the other person happy." The scale was developed to be utilized with women and high scores reflect greater pressure to fulfill the norms of the "good woman" in relationships. The psychometric properties indicate its reliability and internal consistency with a diverse sample of women (Jack & Dill, 1992).

The Relationship Belief Inventory (Eidelson & Epstein, 1982) is another instrument helpful in specifying beliefs about intimate relationships. It consists of forty items with the following subscales: Disagreement is Destructive, Mindreading is Expected, Partners Cannot Change, Sexual Perfectionism, and Sexes are Different. Eidelson and Epstein (1982) found the measure predictive of clients' motivation and expectations regarding treatment outcome and their desire to maintain versus end the relationship.

In the assessment process it is also important to evaluate how individuals may choose partners who conform to, and reinforce, their dysfunctional beliefs about intimacy. For example, both partners may avoid self-disclosure due to a shared belief that such disclosure may harm the relationship. In this situation the partners may not experience initial conflict, but retard the growth of intimacy due to the omission of self-disclosure as an intimacy producing behavior.

In some cases one spouse may have a dysfunctional belief about intimacy that conflicts with his or her partner's belief, which may or may not be dysfunctional. In addition, one partner may think that the other partner holds a particular belief, when this is not really happening. Therefore, each partner's beliefs about intimacy should be assessed both individually, and in combination. The assessment of such interactive beliefs and perceptions is essential for the development of appropriate treatment interventions (Israelstam, 1989). Some cognitive models of assessment, such as Fennell (1989), are very helpful in determining an individual's core assumptions and dysfunctional beliefs. However, these models tend to ignore the interactive aspects of a couple's beliefs, namely how one partner's beliefs or behavior can maintain or conflict with the other partner's dysfunctional beliefs about intimacy. A model that includes the interaction of beliefs is illustrated in Figure 20.1.

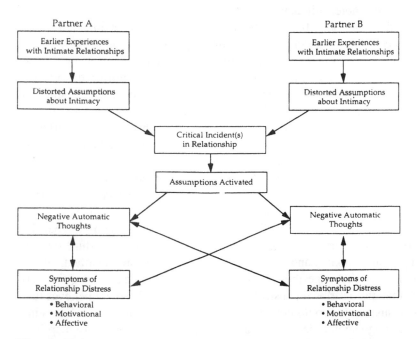

Figure 20.1 Cognitive Model for Assessing Intimacy Beliefs.

Last, a client may not be initially aware of a belief that is guiding his/ her behavior, but discovers an implicit belief only after considerable reflection. This retrieval of information can often be facilitated by asking the client to speculate about the kind of belief which might be related to a cluster of maladaptive behaviors related to intimacy problems (Himle, 1989).

INTERVENTION ISSUES

In cognitive therapy these dysfunctional beliefs are usually examined as to their accuracy and usefulness, and revisions for such beliefs are prepared using the information from the assessment process (Beck & Emery, 1985; Ellis, 1977). This revision of irrational and dysfunctional beliefs about the development, consequences, and nature of intimacy will allow the client to approach the task of intimacy with a more realistic perspective, and a greater openness to the development of intimacy skills. For example, if the client revises a belief that self-disclosure is always met with rejection, to a new belief that such disclosure may be beneficial for the development of intimacy, the client may be less resistant to the development of self-disclosure skills as part of a therapeutic intervention designed to promote intimacy.

The dysfunctional beliefs about intimacy can be changed directly through cognitive restructuring and indirectly through planned behavioral experiments. The process of restructuring dysfunctional intimacy beliefs follows the same approach as restructuring other cognitive distortions. The therapist begins treatment by giving a rationale for focusing on thoughts and beliefs. The rationale can simply be that an individual's feelings toward his/her partner are related to thoughts about the partner's behavior and what it means to him/her, rather than just the behavior itself (Schmaling, Fruzzetti, & Jacobson, 1989).

In discussing events that produced particular negative feelings, the therapist helps the couple to examine the thoughts underlying these emotional responses. The clients begin to link their thoughts to their feelings about the partner's behavior. The next step is helping them to label the type of cognitive error—overgeneralization, mind reading, fortune telling, all-or-nothing thinking, and so on. Once these thoughts are identified, clients are taught to challenge their cognitive distortions by examining the evidence that disconfirms the distortion. For example, a husband believes that because his parents could not constructively handle conflict, conflict in his own marriage should be avoided at all costs. The therapist may help him to realize that there is no compelling evidence for this assumption.

The goal is to teach clients how to evaluate their thinking for them-selves. Hence, it is crucial that the therapist elicit alternatives from the client by teaching them to ask themselves such questions as "What is the evidence?," "What alternative views are there?," "What are the advan-tages and disadvantages of this way of thinking?," and "What logical errors am I making?" (Fennell, 1989). At this point two more columns can be added to their Daily Thought Record: a fourth column entitled "More Reasonable Thoughts" and a fifth column entitled "Outcomes." This last column consists of their new feelings as a result of their more reasonable thinking. The advantage of conjoint sessions is that partners can assist each other in disconfirming erroneous thinking and, consequen-tially, reinforce the learning of new responses for each other.

In the context of couples therapy, planned behavioral experiments or assignments can be used to produce evidence that an assumption about intimacy is unrealistic. In this type of intervention, spouses agree to inter-act in a preconceived manner and then examine the outcome of this exchange (Baucom, & Epstein, 1990). It is hoped that these behavioral experiments will produce consequences that contradict the dysfunctional beliefs and further challenge their credibility. Hence, it is crucial that the therapist plan the experiment with a high likelihood of a positive out-come. For example, a wife believes that if she discloses personal feelings, her husband will minimize and discount them. After assessing the hus-band's ability to empathize with his wife's feelings, the therapist with the couple set up a behavioral experiment in which the wife is asked to appropriately disclose feelings and then monitor her husband's reaction. His reaction of acceptance and empathy will then disconfirm her dis-tortion.

Unlike the goal of behavior therapy, the behavioral change in a planned experiment is not considered an end in itself but a means for testing the validity of negative automatic thoughts (Fennell, 1989). However, there may be cases in which a skill deficit exists and a behavior change is the goal. A partner who believes that conflict destroys intimacy may need to learn appropriate conflict resolution skills along with changing thoughts about conflict and intimacy. Hence, skills training in behaviors such as self-disclosure (Jacobson & Margolin, 1983), physical touching (Barbach, 1984; Masters & Johnson, 1970), companionship (Jacobson & Margolin, 1983), and emotional support (Margolin, 1982) may be necessary to sup-plement a cognitive approach to promoting intimacy in a couple's rela-tionship. Training in these intimate behaviors, as behavioral assignments, may help the client experience closeness in relationships which may not have been predicted by his or her dysfunctional beliefs, and may strongly challenge their accuracy (Baucom, 1989; Epstein, 1982). In this latter sense, the behavioral assignment can facilitate the subsequent cognitive restructuring.

CASE SUMMARY

The following case summary presents some insights into the assessment and revision of dysfunctional beliefs in the context of marital interaction: Katie (age 40) and Russ (age 38) had been married for eight years when they decided to come for marital therapy. This was the second marriage for Katie and the first for Russ. Katie initiated the counseling. While she claimed that she was not contemplating a divorce, she felt very alienated from Russ and felt his controlling, rigid, and demanding behavior prevented them from developing a close relationship. Katie tended to behave in a quite guarded manner around Russ, not disclosing her feelings, and immersing herself in her work as a way to avoid confrontation with Russ. Russ also expressed dissatisfaction with the lack of closeness in the relationship, often blaming Katie for putting her career before their marriage. She had recently received a promotion at work and was now required to travel out of town during most weeks.

Through a series of questions regarding each spouse's family backgrounds, assumptions about intimate relationships were revealed. Katie described her family of origin as being very distant and cold. Her alcoholic father was quite intimidating and critical of the other family members. Her mother was constantly trying to maintain some semblance of family stability through appeasing her husband, often at the expense of being unsupportive of Katie. With the therapist's sensitive questioning, Katie recognized a belief that if she let her guard down and became close to Russ, he would reject her (belief #1). This belief was based on her experiences in childhood when her mother often responded to Katie's attempts for emotional closeness with indifference, and her father reacted to Katie with criticism and faultfinding. Katie shared that she had a similar experience with her first husband who was very demeaning and who, she discovered after the divorce, had been having an affair during most of their marriage. Katie also recognized her belief that any conflict in a relationship destroys the possibility of intimacy (belief #2). This belief was conveyed to her by her mother who maintained that the only way to keep the family together was by avoiding confrontation with her father. In her marriage, Katie avoided conflict by spending most of her time away from Russ—either working or socializing with her female friends.

Russ described his relationship with his parents as generally positive. However, he recalled that he was always trying to live up to his father's perfectionistic standards. As a child, Russ was often compared unfavorably with his younger brother who excelled in sports and later became a professional hockey player. Russ recognized that he believed that the only way Katie would care for him was if he maintained power in the marriage (belief #3) and by being a good provider, he would receive intimacy in return (belief #6). He felt that Katie should submit to his decisions and should be primarily responsible for the housework, regardless of her work outside the home. Russ found it difficult to accept the fact that she made a higher salary and her work became a major complaint. By weekly review of their records of dysfunctional thoughts, the therapist was able to help the couple identify errors in processing information about their interactions. The therapist helped Katie become aware of her assumptions about the role of conflict in intimate relationships based on her early experiences. She discovered that the contemporary meanings and perceptions of conflict in relationships were influenced by these early experiences. Katie believed that her mother's inability to confront conflict directly was the basis for her erroneous belief that she and Russ could not deal with conflict, either now or in the future. She began to realize that there was no compelling evidence for this assumption. Once these beliefs were challenged, Katie was open to learning alternative methods of conflict resolution that could promote closer, intimate relationships and also protect each person's basic interests in the process. Katie also began to understand that her fear of rejection was based on earlier experiences with her parents and with her first husband, and that it was an example of fortune telling when applied to Russ.

The therapist also helped Russ to challenge his thoughts that he must be in control and be the primary breadwinner in order to maintain an intimate relationship. The therapist pointed out to him that such beliefs were actually resulting in behaviors that were pushing Katie away from the relationship as opposed to creating a closer one. Behavioral experiments were planned in which Russ would agree with certain decisions made by Katie and Russ would begin doing more household chores. The results were that Katie did not lose respect for Russ but enjoyed his companionship more and spent less time at work.

CONCLUSION

In this paper, we have summarized the current literature on intimacy-related topics, and pointed out the neglect of serious research related to the specification of intimacy itself. We have identified eight dysfunctional beliefs about intimacy, and discussed the clinical implications of these beliefs for the development of intimacy. We believe that the revision of these beliefs about intimacy may facilitate subsequent behavioral change by partners, as they attempt to develop intimacy in their relationship.

It is of crucial importance to begin to specify the dysfunctional beliefs about intimacy itself, which are evident in the clinical observations of couples experiencing intimacy problems, so that meaningful revisions of beliefs can be developed (Alexander, 1988). The development of such situation-specific dysfunctional beliefs facilitates the assessment task, rather than relying on a list of generic cognitive errors or beliefs (musts and shoulds) which are thought to be sufficient for the identification of such problems in most settings.

Such belief specification is a central task for the development and usage of cognitive therapy procedures designed for the development and enrichment of intimacy. Further research is also necessary to explore and to validate the situational characteristics of the irrational and dysfunctional beliefs about intimacy as presented here, so that the mediating role of such situation-specific beliefs can be further established. Further research is needed to test the empirical validity of these beliefs about intimacy. This research should include a culturally and ethnically diverse client population. This would permit a determination of variations in beliefs about intimate relationships that may result from different cultural and socioeconomic backgrounds.

REFERENCES

Alexander, P. C. (1988). The therapeutic implications of family cognitions and constructs. *Journal of Cognitive Psychotherapy; An International Quarterly, 2,* 219–236.

Barbach, L. (1984). *For each other: Sharing sexual intimacy.* New York: Signet.

Baucom, D. H. (1989). The role of cognitions in behavioral marital therapy: Current status and future directions. *Behavior Therapist, 12,* 1–6.

Baucom, D. H., & Epstein, N. (1990). *Cognitive-behavioral marital therapy.* New York: Brunner/Mazel.

Beck, A. T., & Emery, G. (1985). *Anxiety disorders and phobias.* New York: Basic Books.

Bums, D. D. (1980). *Feeling good: The new mood therapy.* New York: The New American Library.

Chelune, G. J., Robison, J. T., & Kommor, M. J. (1984). A cognitive instructional model of intimate relationships. In V. J. Derlega (Ed.), *Communication, intimacy and close relationships* (pp. 11–40). Orlando, FL: Academic Press.

Collins, P., Kayser, K., & Platt, S. (in press). *Monitoring progress in conjoint marital therapy: A practitioner's approach to single-system evaluation.* Families in Society.

Eidelson, R. J., & Epstein, N. (1982). Cognition and relationship maladjustment: Development of a measure of dysfunctional relationship beliefs. *Journal of Consulting and Clinical Psychology, 50,* 715–720.

Eisenberg, J. M., & Zingle, H. W. (1975). Marital adjustment and irrational ideas. *Journal of Marriage and Family Counseling, 1,* 81–91.

Ellis, A. (1977). The nature of disturbed marital interactions. In A. Ellis & R. Grieger (Eds.), *Handbook of rational-emotive therapy* (pp. 170–176). New York: Springer Publishing.

Ellis, A. (1982). Intimacy in rational-emotive therapy. In M. Fisher & G. Stricker (Eds.), Intimacy (pp. 203–217). New York: Plenum Press.

Ellis, A. (1986a). Application of rational-emotive therapy to love problems. In A. Ellis & R. Grieger (Eds.), *Handbook of rational-emotive therapy Vol. 2* (pp. 162–182). New York: Springer Publishing.

Ellis, A. (1986b). Rational-emotive therapy applied to relationship therapy. *Journal of Rational-Emotive Therapy, 4,* 4–21.

Epstein, N. (1982). Cognitive therapy with couples. *American Journal of Family Therapy, 10,* 5–16.

Epstein, N. (1986). Cognitive marital therapy: Multi-level assessment and intervention. *Journal of Rational-Emotive Therapy 4,* 68–81.

Epstein, N., & Eidelson, R. J. (1981). Unrealistic beliefs of clinical couples: Their relationship to expectations, goals and satisfaction. *American Journal of Family Therapy, 9,* 13–22.

Fennell, M. (1989). Depression. In K. Hawton, P. M. Salkovskis, L. Kirk, & D. M. Clark (Eds.), *Cognitive behavior therapy for psychiatric problems: A practical guide* (pp. 169–234). Oxford: Oxford University Press.

Hatfield, E. (1984). The dangers of intimacy. In V. S. Derlega (Ed.), *Communication, intimacy, and close relationships* (pp. 207–220). Orlando, Fl: Academic Press.

Himle, D. (1989). Changing personal rules. *Journal of Rational-Emotive and Cognitive-Behavioral Therapy, 7,* 79–92.

Israelstam, K. V. (1989). Interacting individual belief systems in marital relationships. *Journal of Mental and Family Therapy, 15,* 53–63.

Jack, D. (1987). Silencing the self: The power of social imperatives in female depression. In R. Formank & A. Gurian (Eds.), *Women and depression* (pp. 161–181). New York: Springer Publishing.

Jack, D. (1991). *Silencing the self.* Cambridge, MA: Harvard University Press.

Jack, D., & Dill, D. (1992). The Silencing the Self Scale: Schemas of intimacy associated with depression in women. *Psychology of Women Quarterly, 16,* 97–106.

Jacobson, N. S. (1989). The politics of intimacy. *The Behavior Therapist, 12,* 29–32.

Jacobson, N. S., & Margolin, G. (1983). *Marital therapy: Strategies based on social teaming and behavior exchange principles.* New York: Brunner/Mazel.

Kersten, K. K., & Himle, D. (1990). Marital intimacy: A model for clinical assessment and intervention. *Journal of Couples Therapy, 1,* 103–121.

Kingsbury, N. M., & Nfinda, R. B. (1988). An analysis of three expected intimate relationship states: Commitment, maintenance, and termination. *Journal of Social and Personal Relationship, 5,* 405–422.

Levinger, G., & Snoek, J. D. (1972). *Attraction in relationship: A new look at interpersonal attraction.* Morristown, NJ: General Learning Press.

Margolin, G. (1982). A social teaming approach to intimacy. In M. Fisher and G. Stricker (Eds.), *Intimacy* (pp. 175–201). New York: Plenum Press.

Masters, W. H., & Johnson, V. E. (1970). *Human sexual inadequacy.* Boston: Little, Brown and Co.

McClellan, T. A., & Stieper, D. R. (1977). A structured approach to group marriage counseling. In A. Ellis & R. Grieger (Eds.), *Handbook of rational-emotive therapy* (pp. 281–291). New York: Springer Publishing.

McGill, M. E. (1986). *The McGill Report on male intimacy.* New York: Holt, Rinehart and Winston.

Miller, J. B. (1988). Connections, disconnections, and violations. Work in progress, No. 33. Wellesley, MA: Stone Center Working Paper Series. therapy (pp. 281–291). New York: Springer Publishing.

Miller, R. S., & Lefcourt, H. M. (1982). The assessment of social intimacy. *Journal of Personality Assessment, 46,* 514–518.

Orlofsky, J. L. (1975). *Intimacy status, partner perception and resolution of previous developmental crises.* Doctoral dissertation, State University of New York at Buffalo, 1974. Dissertation Abstracts International, 25, 3592.

Schaefer, M. T., & Olson, D. H. (1981). Assessing intimacy: The PAIR inventory. *Journal of Marital and Family Therapy, 7,* 47–60.

Schmaling, K. B., Fruzzetti, A. E., & Jacobson, N. (1989). Marital problems. In K. Hawton, P. M. Salkovskis, I. Kirk, & D. M. Clark (Eds.), *Cognitive behavior therapy for psychiatric problems: A practical guide* (pp. 339–369). Oxford: Oxford University Press.

Veroff, J., Douvan, E., & Kulka, K. (1981). *The inner American.* New York: Basic Books.

Walster, E., Walster, G. W., & Berscheid, E. (1978). *Equity theory and research.* Boston: Allyn and Bacon.

Waring, E. M. (1988). *Enhancing marital intimacy.* New York: Brunner/Mazel. New York: Springer Publishing.

CHAPTER 21

Patterns of Attachment and the Assessment of Interpersonal Schemata: Understanding and Changing Difficult Patient-Therapist Relationships in Cognitive Psychotherapy

Giovanni Liotti

The results of empirical studies of attachment behavior in children provide the cognitive psychotherapist with powerful conceptual tools that may be profitably used in some puzzling instances of patient's behavior within the therapeutic relationship. Some patients ask energetically for the therapist's reassurance and at the same time resist the therapist's comforting responses. Others seem compelled to avoid any expression of personal vulnerability as soon as they perceive the therapist's empathic availability to listen to their painful emotional experiences. Other patients utter their requests for help in a most confused, mutable, and contradictory way. When the therapist deals with such kinds of therapeutic relationship, the knowledge of the representational models of self and the attachment figure that may be inferred from abnormal patterns of attachment (avoidant, anxious-resistant, and disorganized/disoriented) guides the assessment and change of the patient's interpersonal schemata in a most profitable way.

In this chapter I shall describe how, by using attachment theory (Bowlby, 1982), some specific difficulties in the patient-therapist relationship may become a useful starting point for the assessment of the patient's interpersonal schemata. In accordance with Safran's (1990) use of the term, I mean by "interpersonal schema" a generalized representation of self-other relationships within a given meaning domain.

It is almost a truism to state that both the patient and the psychotherapist perceive their relationship, at the very basic level, as one in which the patient needs help for his/her problems, and the therapist is, hopefully, both able and willing to provide the specific kind of help which is required. To be in the situation of asking for help means to experience feelings of vulnerability. The interpersonal schema related to the meaning domain whose emotional-behavioral boundaries are feeling vulnerable and asking for care plays, therefore, a key role in the therapeutic relationship. This interpersonal schema originates, very likely, within the child's first attachment relationships. Attachment is defined as the tendency to seek for the proximity and care of a specific person whenever one is vulnerable or distressed. Attachment behavior is displayed with full intensity during infancy and childhood (Bowlby, 1977, 1982, 1988). Research on attachment behavior in infants and children (Bowlby, 1982; Bretherton & Waters, 1985; Greenberg, Cicchetti, & Cummings, 1990), therefore, may provide the psychotherapist with very useful information concerning some cognitive, emotional, and developmental processes that are likely to be implied in the shaping of the therapeutic relationship.

Developmental psychologists have identified three major patterns of abnormal, or insecure, attachment: avoidant, anxious-resistant, and disorganized-disoriented.

AVOIDANCE OF THE ATTACHMENT FIGURE

Active visual, physical, and communicative avoidance is surprisingly prevalent in children reunited with their attachment figures following stressful and prolonged separations (Bowlby, 1982). In rejected or neglected children, avoidance of the attachment figure appears also following very brief separations, such as the ones implied in Ainsworth's "strange situation" (Ainsworth, Blehar, Waters, & Wall, 1978; Main & Weston, 1982). About 20% of one-year-olds whose attachment behavior has been observed in the "strange situation" show a pattern of attachment identified by their avoidance of the attachment figure during the episodes of reunion after a brief separation. Careful observation of this avoidant behavior provides hints that it is related to an active inhibition of the behavioral system that normally motivates children to approach their attachment figures after a separation (Main & Weston, 1982).

Mothers of avoidant children often have a rejecting or neglecting attitude toward their offspring. They show a deep aversion to close bodily contact with their children, angrily perceive children's demands as interfering with the caregiver's interests and activities, and tend to have less mobility of emotional expression than other mothers (Ainsworth,1982; Bretherton, 1985). We can, then, infer that avoidant children have constructed an interpersonal schema in which the self, when needing help and comfort from another person, is portrayed as bound to loneliness, while the other person is expected to be, if not actively rejecting, at least consistently unable or unwilling to provide help and comfort. A clinical example may show how the knowledge of this interpersonal schema and of its origins helps the psychotherapist to understand a specific class of difficult therapeutic relationships.

Paola is a depressed woman of 38. In the first four sessions of her psychotherapy, she maintained an emotionally detached attitude toward the therapist. Then, in two sessions, she showed a growing emotional participation in the therapeutic dialogue. During the seventh session, Paola started complaining that it was very difficult for her to come to the therapist's office: While it was not very troublesome for her to leave home in order to reach her office or a friend's house, she literally had to force herself in order to come to the therapeutic sessions. She was unable to explain why things were like that. She felt that she needed treatment, and was fully satisfied by the therapist's professional skills and personal interest in her case. She was not afraid of becoming dependent on the therapist. Her husband was encouraging her to go on with psychotherapy. When she thought of the possibility of interrupting the treatment or of going to another therapist, she felt anxious. All this notwithstanding, she had to overcome a sort of physical resistance in herself whenever she had to come to the therapist's office. Sometimes she vomited before leaving home to come to the session. She was unable to identify any thought accompanying or preceding the vomiting. When she was in front of the therapist, it was difficult for her to concentrate on her thoughts or on her emotions in order to report about them in any detail. She could, however, acknowledge that she was very sad during the dialogue with her therapist, and that at times she felt an acute sense of loneliness. She assented to the therapist's hypothesis that this sense of loneliness could be related to the idea that the therapist—and any other person—would eventually prove either unable or unwilling to help her.

The similarities between Paola's behavior in the therapeutic relationship and the avoidance of the attachment figure in childhood are striking. As soon as she started feeling attached to the therapist (which was shown by her emotional involvement in the therapeutic dialogue during the fifth and sixth session), the interpersonal schema related to her original avoidance of the attachment figure was activated, and she felt almost compelled to avoid meeting the therapist. An inquiry into her history of attachment revealed that she was the daughter of a paranoid father, and that her mother, suffering from an extremely troublesome marriage, had been often unavailable to her pleas for affection and care.

Depressed patients, schizoid patients, or patients suffering from psychosomatic illnesses often show a tendency to avoid visual, emotional, or verbal interactions with their therapist. In all these cases, we can formulate the hypothesis that an interpersonal schema like the one constructed by avoidant children is at work whenever the patient, feeling vulnerable or distressed, establishes an emotionally meaningful helping relationship. We can also expect that the patient has been consistently rejected or neglected from at least one parent during childhood and adolescence, and that the schema constructed through this experience of rejection or neglect has not been corrected by other relationships.

ANXIOUS-RESISTANT ATTACHMENT

A child is said to be "anxious" and "resistant" in the attachment relationship if he/she, when distressed, strongly searches for the caregiver's comfort, but is not easily calmed down when he/she receives it. This kind of attachment behavior is most easily observed during the reunion of the child with the attachment figure after a brief separation in a strange environment (Ainsworth, Blehar, Waters, & Wall, 1978). While securely attached children approach the caregiver, seek interaction with him/her smoothly, and are promptly comforted by contact with him/her, resistant children show at reunion a combination of contact-seeking and tantrum-like behavior. They require much more time and energy, in comparison with the securely attached children, to be soothed. In the attachment relationship, resistant children are usually the partners of an unpredictably available, intrusive, or overcontrolling caregiver. In contrast, the caregivers of securely attached children are consistently available to the child's requests for security, help, or comfort, and do not intrude into the child's autonomous activities (Ainsworth, 1982; Bretherton, 1985).

Resistant children are likely to construct interpersonal schemata in which the self, when distressed or frightened, is portrayed as at risk of being misunderstood while the potentially helpful other is portrayed as both unpredictable and intrusive. The self-other relationship governed by such a schema implies excessive intensity and duration of requests of help (in the face of the expected untrustworthiness of the other's responses), and also fear of the intrusiveness of the helping other into one's private space of decision and choice. Such a schema is likely to be at work in the following clinical situation.

During the first psychotherapeutic session, Mario (a 28–year-old salesman) explains his problems. He is afraid of traveling because he feels that something terrible may happen to him while alone and far from home. On the other hand, he cannot avoid traveling because of his otherwise satisfactory and well-paid job. He is also afraid of beginning psychotherapy, because he strongly dislikes being dependent. While he is mentioning his fear of dependency, Mario, whose attitude in telling his problems had until that moment been concerned but not agitated, looks almost frightened. In a trembling tone of voice, he asks me how likely it is that he may suddenly die of a heart attack: His heart—he explains—sometimes pounds as if it is going to explode. I try to reassure him: What he is experiencing is anxiety, and anxiety does not kill. Mario looks as much frightened after my reassuring response as he was before it. He goes on asking for reassurance: How likely is it—he asks—that he will lose control? When, again, I try to calm him down by saying that anxiety is not synonymous with madness, Mario shifts his attention to the idea that frequent panic attacks make for continuous stress, and continuous stress could damage the heart. Mario's attitude, while he is dwelling on all these frightening possibilities, betrays his ambivalence between the urge to ask for help and the wish to remain detached, "independent," in the therapeutic relationship.

This vignette is an extreme example of an attitude toward the therapist that is relatively common in anxious-phobic patients. When these patients feel anxious, and perceive themselves as vulnerable, they tend also to construe the therapist in an ambivalent way, i.e., as somebody who may provide the much needed comfort and help, but also as somebody from whom it would be safer to remain detached because of his/her unpredictable availability and the potential danger of falling under his/her influence (fear of dependency). The sign of this ambivalence is the patient's tendency to resist the comforting responses he or she is asking from the therapist. Attachment theory and research not only help us in assessing this schema, but also allow us to predict that the patient has witnessed, as a child, the unpredictable availability, the intrusiveness, and the overcontrolling attitude of at least one attachment figure.

DISORGANIZED-DISORIENTED PATTERN OF ATTACHMENT

Children are said to be attached in a disorganized-disoriented way when they show dazed behavior on reunion with a parent, strong avoidance following strong proximity seeking, or when they simultaneously display contradictory behavior patterns (e.g., approaching the attachment figure with the head averted, or gazing strongly away while in contact with him/her).

Disorganized-disoriented attachment behavior in the child is related to an attitude of the attachment figure toward the child that is best described as frightened and frightening, or confused and confusing (Main, Kaplan, & Cassidy, 1985; Main & Hesse, 1990; Main & Solomon, 1990). Many parents of children with disorganized-disoriented attachments show signs of lack of resolution of mourning (Main & Hesse, 1990). They are, then, grieving over a previous loss, and project the feelings of an abnormal grief in their relationship with their children. They seem to respond to their children's requests for help and comfort in terms of their painful emotions and irrational beliefs concerning loss and death, rather than in terms of an objective appraisal of the child's needs. Therefore, they may respond with fear to the child's expressions of discomfort, thereby further alarming the child instead of calming him/her down. Sometimes, these parents seem to invert the normal attachment relationship: They expect to be somehow comforted by their children, and do not seem to be fully aware that children are both unable to take care of an adult and need themselves to be cared for.

The interpersonal schema related to a disorganized-disoriented pattern of attachment portrays a self caught in an interpersonal situation in which it is impossible to decide whether the self, the other, or some ill-defined external influence is responsible for the fear, the sadness or the other distressing emotions that are experienced by both partners. Confusion, rather than ambivalence, seems the proper label for the experiences bound to this interpersonal schema, which is likely to be at work in the following clinical situation.

Regina is a 25–year-old single woman, diagnosed by three different psychiatrists as suffering from chronic anorexia nervosa, from dissociative hysteria, and from histrionic personality disorder, respectively. When I met her, she deemed her case hopeless, and stated that she was unable to commit herself to any kind of treatment. She, however, seemed to appreciate my effort to establish an empathic therapeutic relationship with her, and invited me to try to treat her. The first four sessions of the treatment were devoted by Regina to dramatically and confusingly devaluating both herself and significant others. In the fifth session, as soon as she sat down, she said that she would be unable to concentrate on whatever I might have to say, because she had just swallowed four pills of a tranquilizer. The meaning of Regina's behavior was, in my opinion, to be discovered in her wishing both to ask for help and to express her difficulty in bearing the degree of intimacy implied by the therapeutic relationship. I inquired as to whether or not Regina agreed with this conjecture, and she, very hesitantly, replied that this could be the case. Then she looked half asleep for the rest of the session, during which I repeatedly stated that I could understand her mixed feelings about our beginning relationship, and asked for her assent to calling a taxi and having her accompanied home by my secretary. Regina nodded in reply, and the session ended.

Later on in the treatment, Regina showed many instances of her mixed feelings about the therapeutic relationship. For instance, each new piece of self-disclosure was accompanied by her turning her gaze away from me for the whole session. To this, she sometimes added moving her seat away from my desk: thus, she made it clear that she wished to get a greater physical distance from me each time she decided to reduce the emotional distance in the therapeutic relationship. Also, she dramatically clung to her statement that hers was a hopeless case each time she directly, or more often indirectly, let me know that something positive was taking place in her life. Thus, when she found a job—she quit high school when she was 16 and never tried to find a job since then—she did not mention the event to me. Rather, she had her mother phone me in order to ask whether the timetable of the sessions could be changed, so that Regina could respect her office hours. During the session after her mother's phone call, Regina alternated expressions of gratefulness to me, accusations that I was not considering her problems with body weight, and requests for reassurance and self-denigrations (she kept repeating that she was just a "fat nothingness"—her weight being then 10% below normal). She looked rather confused, was a bit incoherent in her speech, often avoided eye contact by lowering her eyes or looking around dazedly, and uttered her pleas for reassurance in a dramatic tone of voice: "Please, don't leave me!" she repeatedly cried, interrupting here and there her self-denigration.

Interpersonal behavior in the therapeutic relationship in which patients display multiple (mutable, or simultaneous and contradictory) attitudes toward themselves and toward the therapist is not infrequent when the diagnosis is of dissociative reaction, multiple personality, or borderline or histrionic personality disorder. It is tempting to construe this confused and confusing behavior in the therapeutic relationship as an example of disorganized-disoriented attachment behavior. This suggests that we look for any condition in the patient's parents (depression, unresolved mourning, personality disorders) that may have prompted them to try to invert the normal parent-child relationship and/or to play the role of a frightened/frightening partner in their child's attachment relationship (Main, Kaplan, & Cassidy, 1985; Main & Hesse, 1990).

Regina's mother treated her child, even when she was a toddler, as if she were to comfort an extremely and chronically distressed adult. Here is an example of Regina's mother's way of inverting the normal parent-child relationship. Regina's maternal aunt was collapsing under the burden of her husband's mental illness. Regina's mother found it altogether normal to allot her two-year-old daughter the role of her aunt's consoler. Regina spent most of her third year of life in her aunt's house. The little child started suffering from *pavor nocturnus,* but nobody seemed to consider this as a sign of her neglected needs for attachment, or as an indication that the burden that had been placed upon her was unbearable. This experience may have prompted Regina to expect to be exploited within attachment relationships and, as a result, to build up the self-presentation of a hopeless and helpless person, from whom nothing could be expected.

A disorganized-disoriented pattern of attachment may be the origin of an interpersonal schema, which is activated within any further attachment relationship, in which both the self and the other are represented as utterly suffering, while any causal attribution for this suffering is confused and easily changeable. Without stable causal attributions for one's own and other people's deepest emotions, the self-other relationship is bound to be represented at the basic level as both meaningless and "void." This "void" is likely to be filled up with every momentary attribution of meaning that may be at hand—either positive or negative, but in any case highly inconsistent attributions.

FROM PATTERNS OF ATTACHMENT TO INTERPERSONAL SCHEMATA

To summarize what has been stated concerning the correlations between patterns of attachment and patterns of caregiving: 1) securely attached children are likely to be the offspring of parents who are consistently available to the child's needs for help and protection without being intrusive into the child's need for autonomous exploration of the environment; 2) anxious-resistant attachment is related to a style of caregiving that may be described as both unpredictable and overcontrolling or intrusive; 3) avoidance of the attachment figure is related to rejecting, neglecting, or hostile attitudes of the caregiver toward the child; 4) disorganized-disoriented attachment is related to a confused and confusing, or frightened and frightening, pattern of caregiving.

Thus, children seem to behave, in the attachment relationship, according to their expectations concerning the caregiver's behavior. These expectations, in turn, are the result of learning from previous interactions with the caregiver. According to these learning processes, children seem to have constructed interpersonal schemata, by which any partner in any future attachment relationship is likely to be construed, at least at the beginning of the relationship, as the former attachment figures have been construed. If no corrective experience of attachment intervenes during the life span between childhood and adulthood, and if a person does not reflect on his/her beliefs concerning vulnerability, dependency, attachment, etc., it is likely that the interpersonal schemata corresponding to the original patterns of attachment will persist unmodified in adult life. These schemata will be activated whenever the person feels vulnerable and asks for help (feeling vulnerable is the condition for the activation, during the whole life span, of the behavioral-motivational system of attachment (Bowlby, 1977, 1982, 1988).

This is, in a nutshell, the theoretical basis for applying our knowledge of insecure patterns of attachment to the analysis of therapeutic relationships such as the ones portrayed in the above clinical vignettes (see also Bowlby, 1977, 1988; Liotti, 1986, 1988). In order to properly apply attachment theory to clinical issues, it is important that the clinician not force any aspect of the patient's behavior into any preexisting schematic categories of early attachment patterns, but rather use his/her knowledge of these patterns as a guide for a proper priming, through careful questions, of the patient's memories. Let us now dwell briefly, in order to exemplify this way of applying research on attachment to clinical problems, on the case of patients who, like Mario, are afraid of dependency. We may start by asking our patients why they are so afraid of dependency and how they predict the future behavior of the therapist on whom they would eventually come to depend. Do they somehow expect the therapist to exploit their dependency and intrude upon their private space of decisions? Do they expect the therapist to become unpredictably unavailable after they come to need his or her comfort—and therefore expect themselves to suffer for being neglected or rejected by the therapist? Do they expect that the therapist will criticize their dependency? Guided by our knowledge of the results of attachment research, we can match our patients' answers to these questions with the information we possess concerning the behavior of the caregivers of anxiously attached children. If, for instance, patients state that they expect to be rejected from the person they come to depend on, we may ask whether and when they have been rejected by an attachment figure. If they say that they expect the therapist to be only sporadically available when they will need his/her help, we may inquire about the possibility that they have perceived their former attachment figures as unpredictable in their responses to their needs. If they express the fear of becoming unable to assert themselves in the relationship with a person on whom they depend, we may ask if they have been intruded upon by their parents when they were trying to assert their needs for autonomy. And so on. The patients' answers, then, not only provide cues to the way they construe the person to whom they address themselves when they need help, but are also the basis from which one can start for a reconstruction of the behavior of the patient's former attachment figures (Bowlby, 1988; Liotti,1988). In this historical perspective, one can better grasp (a) the learning process that has led to the construction of the patient's interpersonal schemata related to care-eliciting behavior, and (b) the function played by these schemata both in past and in present interpersonal relationships.

CONCLUSION

The advantages of this way of analyzing the therapeutic relationship, assessing the patient's interpersonal schemata and reconstructing the patient's history of attachment are manifold.

First, the clinician can quickly grasp how the patient construes the self, the therapist, and the therapeutic relationship.

Second, by taking an exploratory attitude toward the patient's reasons for finding the therapeutic relationship troublesome, the therapist can avoid arousing the patient's resistance and reactance: Resistance and reactance are more likely activated within a therapeutic relationship in which the therapist takes a directive or pedagogical attitude (Dowd, 1989; Liotti, 1989).

Third, by reconstructing how the difficult therapeutic relationship is related to the former experience of an insecure attachment, the therapist comes to know how to avoid the unwitting repetition of the behavior of the patient's former attachment figures. In this way, the confirmation of the patient's negative expectations concerning the self-other relationship can more easily be avoided within the therapeutic relationship.

Fourth, the reconstruction of the patient's history of attachment may foster the revision of the patient's interpersonal schemata without attacking the related beliefs and expectations as mere irrationalities. When the patient sees how a counterproductive model of the self-other relationship has been constructed stemming from past transactions with the caregivers (in which context beliefs that now appear irrational and detrimental might have seemed quite plausible and adaptive), his/her confidence in the basic efficiency of his/her own mind is likely to be preserved (Liotti, 1989).

Finally, if the therapist straightforwardly confronts the patient with his/her irrationalities at the beginning of a difficult therapeutic relationship, he/she will, very likely, do so from a dominant position in the relationship. The patient may, then, either fight for dominance or accept the subordinate role (see Chance, 1986, and Trower & Gilbert, 1989, for an analysis of dominance-submission in human relationships, and for an evolutionary study of the "agonic" mode of interaction that leads to the definition of ranks). If the patient is forced into one-down-manship, the development of a "hedonic" mode of interaction (as opposed to the "agonic" one, Chance, 1986; Trower & Gilbert, 1989) will be hindered. In other words, the pedagogical attitude of the therapist hampers the development of a truly collaborative relationship such as the one advocated by most cognitive therapists (Liotti, 1988, 1989). An exploration of the patient's history of attachment, as soon as difficulties in the therapeutic relationship are perceived, helps assessing and revising the patient's interpersonal schemata while at the same time preserving equality and cooperation in the therapeutic relationship.

ACKNOWLEDGMENT

A modified and shorter version of this paper was read at the World Congress of Cognitive Therapy, Oxford, June 28–July 2, 1989.

REFERENCES

Ainsworth, M. D. S. (1982). Attachment: Retrospect and prospect. In C. M. Parkes & J. Stevenson-Hinde (Eds.), *The place of attachment in human behavior* (pp.3–30). New York: Basic Books.

Ainsworth, M. D. S., Blehar, M. C., Waters, E., & Wall, S. (1978). *Patterns of attachment: A psychological study of the strange situation.* Hillsdale, NJ: Erlbaum.

Bowlby, J.(1977). The making and breaking of affectional bonds. *British Journal of Psychiatry, 130,* 201–210 and 421–431.

Bowlby, J. (1982). *Attachment and loss, Vol.1: Attachment. Second Edition.* London: Hogarth Press.

Bowlby, J. (1988). *A secure base.* London: Routledge.

Bretherton, I. (1985). Attachment theory: retrospect and prospect. In I. Bretherton & E. Waters (Eds.), Growing points of attachment theory and research. *Monographs of the Society for Research in Child Development, 50,* 3–35.

Bretherton, I., & Waters, E. (Eds.) (1985). Growing points of attachment theory and research. *Monographs of the Society for Research in Child Development, Serial n. 209,* Vol. 50.

Chance, M. (1986). The social formation of personality systems. *American Journal of Social Psychiatry, 6,* 199–203.

Dowd, E. T. (1989). Stasis and change in cognitive psychotherapy: Client resistance and reactance as mediating variables. In W. Dryden & P. Trower (Eds.), *Cognitive psychotherapy: Stasis and change* (pp. 139–158). London: Cassell.

Greenberg, M., Cicchetti, D., & Cummings, M. (Eds.) (1990). Attachment in the preschool years. Chicago: University of Chicago Press.

Liotti, G. (1986). Structural cognitive therapy. In W. Dryden & W. Golden (Eds.), *Cognitive-behavioral approaches to psychotherapy* (pp. 92–128). London: Harper & Row.

Liotti, G. (1988). Attachment and cognition: A guideline for the reconstruction of early pathogenic experiences in cognitive psychotherapy. In C. Perris, I. Blackburn, & H. Perris (Eds.), *Cognitive psychotherapy: Theory and practice* (pp. 62–79). New York: Springer Publishing.

Liotti, G. (1989). Resistance to change in cognitive psychotherapy: Theoretical remarks from a constructivistic point of view. In W. Dryden & P. Trower (Eds.), *Cognitive psychotherapy: Stasis and change* (pp. 28–56). London: Cassell.

Main, M., & Hesse, E. (1990). Lack of resolution of mourning in adulthood and its relationship to infant disorganization: Some speculations regarding causal mechanisms. In M. Greenberg, D. Cicchetti, & M. Cummings (Eds.), *Attachment in the preschool years* (pp. 161–182). Chicago: University of Chicago Press.

Main, M., Kaplan, N., & Cassidy, J. (1985). Security in infancy, childhood and adulthood: A move to the level of representation. In I. Bretherton & E. Waters (Eds.), Growing points of attachment theory and research. *Monographs of the Society for Research in Child Development, Serial No.209,* Vol. 50, 66–104.

Main, M., & Solomon, J. (1990). Procedures for identifying infants as disorganized/disoriented during the Ainsworth Strange Situation. In M. Greenberg, D. Cicchetti & N. Cummings (Eds.), *Attachment in the preschool years* (pp. 121–160). Chicago: University of Chicago Press.

Main, M., & Weston, D., (1982). Avoidance of the attachment figure in infancy. In C. M. Parkes & J. Stevenson-Hinde (Eds.), *The place of attachment in human behavior* (pp. 31–59). New York: Basic Books.

Safran, J. (1990). Toward a refinement of cognitive therapy in light of interpersonal theory: 1. Theory. *Clinical Psychology Review, 10,* 87–105.

Trower, P., & Gilbert, P. (1989). New theoretical conceptions of social anxiety and social phobia. *Clinical Psychology Review, 9,* 19–35.

CHAPTER 22

Cognitive Therapy with an HIV-Positive Depressed Gay Man

Vicki L. Gluhoski

Clinicians may be increasingly called upon to work with HIV-positive clients. Although cognitive therapy has proven efficacious with a broad range of populations, limited information is available on the application of cognitive therapy to HIV-positive clients. This chapter will describe the case of an HIV-positive gay man seen for cognitive therapy as part of a research protocol. This case was chosen for several reasons: (1) to demonstrate how to address specific HIV-related issues in cognitive therapy (e.g., disclosing to family, coping with illness progression), (2) to illustrate how to work with multiple levels of cognitions in a short time period, and (3) to show how to work with long-held beliefs within the context of HIV.

CASE DESCRIPTION

The client, Tom (pseudonym given to protect confidentiality), was randomly assigned to receive 16 sessions of cognitive therapy as part of a psychotherapy study for depressed HIV-positive individuals. Tom was a 34-year-old gay White male. When first evaluated for the study, he reported a six–month history of increasing depression (Beck Depression Inventory = 29), difficulty sleeping, and intrusive thoughts about HIV. He had a history of alcohol dependence but had been in remission for eight years. He had two previous experiences with psychotherapy: he had seen a therapist 15 years earlier, for eight months, following a charge of driving while intoxicated and another therapist for three years, approximately eight years earlier, when he began his remission from alcohol. He described the model of these previous therapists as "supportive"; he had no prior experience with cognitive therapy.

When treatment began, he was working as a counselor and resident manager at a group home for developmentally disabled individuals. He was a college graduate and had also taken several advanced courses. He learned that he was HIV-positive one year before he began cognitive therapy. At his initial evaluation, he reported that his T-cell count was approximately 19, indicating full-blown AIDS. He reported an ulcer and vague gastrointestinal problems; it was unclear if these symptoms were related to HIV. He was taking several medications: AZT, DDC, D4C, Zovirax, Mycobutin, Diflucan, and Pentamidine. He believed he had been infected approximately ten years earlier.

INTRODUCTORY SESSIONS (SESSIONS #1 AND #2)

In the initial sessions, Tom was introduced to the cognitive model. He described increasing symptoms of depression and anxiety. Negative automatic thoughts were identified in the domains of self ("I can't do anything," "I don't have strength," "I'm helpless"), personal world ("My entire life is work," "It's hard for me to socialize"), and future ("I don't know if I'll live," "I won't see my nieces and nephews grow up") and their connection to depressed mood was highlighted. He also noted that loneliness was a significant problem—he had not had a romantic relationship in over ten years.

He completed a Dysfunctional Thought Record for homework following the first session, which focused on a work incident in which he thought "I don't have control." The second session focused on the association between a lack of perceived control and anxiety, as well as teaching him strategies for developing alternative responses. The relationship between catastrophic predictions and anxiety was also described. He noted that this style of thinking pervaded multiple domains of his life: work, friends, and health.

INITIAL FOCUS ON HIV (SESSIONS #3 AND #4)

Tom continued to be highly compliant with homework assignments, completing Dysfunctional Thought Records and reading *The Feeling Good*

Handbook. Session #3 began with a discussion as to why he had not told his family and most of his friends about his HIV status. Multiple levels of beliefs were identified. He initially stated that he had not told his family because "They'll think I deserve it." Further questioning led to uncovering several self-blaming statements: "I brought this on myself . . . I drank and wasn't careful" and "If I weren't gay, I wouldn't have it." These beliefs were associated with feelings of shame and guilt. Core schemes were also identified at this time: "I'm bad, unlovable, and not a good person." Historical events, including growing up gay in a Catholic household, with critical, unaccepting parents, and in a conservative community, were discussed as factors which may have led to developing these beliefs.

To begin to alleviate his self-blame, links were made between his core beliefs and his previous compensatory strategy of alcohol dependence. He saw that beliefs of "I'm unlovable" led to social anxiety. He used alcohol to avoid activating these beliefs in social situations, such as meeting men in bars. Although the alcohol temporarily numbed his core beliefs and he was able to socialize, it led to unsafe sexual encounters. This model provided Tom with a great deal of comfort and diminished his self-blame for contracting HIV. He saw that although he had engaged in risky sexual activities, he now had a framework for understanding why it occurred. This was an initial step in making sense of why he was HIV-positive.

By the next session, therapy had to switch from beginning to identify and modify long-held beliefs to AIDS. In that week Tom learned that his T-cell count was 3, he was anemic, and he had developed Kaposi's Sarcoma. Automatic thoughts included "This (the KS) is a concrete manifestation of the disease—I have AIDS, I'm not just HIV-positive," and "I don't know how much longer I have." Subsequently, his anxiety was elevated. He was particularly worried about his medical coverage and his ability to pay his bills. We decided that the goal of the session would be regaining a sense of control. Problem-solving techniques, such as identifying specific problems, and generating and evaluating solutions were employed. Enrolling in a specialty HIV clinic and getting insurance information were top priorities. Strategies for meeting these goals were collaboratively outlined (e.g., call insurance company, contact different clinics in the area). The advantages and disadvantages of particular programs at different hospitals were discussed so that he could make the best choice for his care. The decision of whether or not to leave his job, an ongoing struggle, was also evaluated. Advantages of the job (money, daily pattern, rewarding aspects) were compared with the disadvantages (stress, long hours). The benefits of leaving (more time to see friends and pursue pleasurable activities) versus the disadvantages (less money) were also discussed. Finally, more concerns about disclosing his status to his family were identified: "They'll be devastated," "They're still not over my sister's death (she had died in an accident several years previously)," and "Telling them makes it more real." The association between these thoughts and his avoidant behavior was pointed out.

LIFE CHANGES DUE TO HIV (SESSIONS #5 AND #6)

Despite significant and realistic health concerns, Tom reported that his mood had improved (BDI = 23). This was traced to thoughts of "I'm doing something to take control" and "I'm not just letting bad things happen to me." These thoughts occurred because he had obtained information about different hospitals and programs, and had scheduled a doctor's appointment with an AIDS specialist. Because a belief of uncontrollability was prominent, it became clear that a goal of therapy would be for Tom to gain a sense of mastery, where possible, within the context of his disease. Although he could not control the disease progression, he began to see that he could control aspects of his care, his mood, and future plans. This realization brought him a sense of relief.

At this time, he brought up fears of being hospitalized which centered on two domains: health ("I won't come out") and interpersonal ("No one will visit me"). His fears of not surviving a hospitalization developed from past negative experiences with hospitals, in which both his sister and grandfather died. Thus, he had strong evidence to support his belief. The differences between his circumstances (e.g., he knew many people with AIDS who experienced multiple hospitalizations) and the others (e.g., his sister was brought in after a car accident, his grandfather was elderly) were highlighted. These distinctions lessened his anxiety. The expectation that no one would visit was tied to underlying beliefs of "I'm not worth it and I'm unlovable." We began to generate alternative responses to these beliefs, such as evidence of friends and family who truly cared for him and had been available and supportive in the past. In addition, Tom generated explanations for why they really cared that focused on his unique attributes (e.g., he's kind, a good friend). Focusing on his attributes was necessary and promoted schema level work, as his first inclination was to believe they would visit just to be polite. This exercise led to a discussion of schemas, focusing on his beliefs of worthlessness, being unlovable, vulnerable, and without control. A core belief log, in which he would note evidence contrary to these beliefs, was assigned for homework. In addition, he was instructed to develop alternative responses when the negative beliefs were activated. Schema dialogues, in which the individual argues back to counteract the negative belief, were demonstrated and encouraged.

At the sixth session, Tom reported that he had given up his on-site apartment at his job which led to a tremendous sense of relief. He wanted to discuss asking his boss for a raise. We completed a thought record in session and identified his usual beliefs, behaviors, and consequences in situations where his desires were unmet. Typically, he believed "I will be rejected, my needs won't be met" which led to holding in his desires and an avoidance of requesting anything. Subsequently, he would feel frustrated and mistreated, which perpetuated his core beliefs. It was pointed out that if he expected to get his desires met, he would be more assertive, more likely to get his needs met, and his negative beliefs would not be activated.

A second focus of this session was continuing to identify and reframe negative thoughts about telling his family about his HIV status. At this point, his avoidance was tied to core beliefs such as "I will be rejected." By the end of the session, he planned to tell his sister first in confidence, before disclosing to his parents.

POSITIVE LIFE CHANGES (SESSIONS #7 AND #8)

Tom began to see tangible benefits of his changing belief system. He moved back into his own apartment and was pleased with this change; he reported his life was less stressful now. He asked for and received a raise. He completed Dysfunctional Thought Records between sessions and found them to be helpful in improving his mood and diminishing avoidance.

During this time he spent a week in the Caribbean with his extended family. Before the trip, he had been apprehensive as to whether he could be assertive with them. We role-played different scenarios (e.g., how to decline when they offered him alcohol) and outlined a new set of beliefs about his rights ("My needs are as important as others' needs," "No evidence that they'll reject me," "My requests are reasonable"). Subsequently, he had a wonderful time. He set limits on his family which they willingly accepted. When negative thoughts arose, he countered them quickly and effectively. He was pleased and proud of his progress. These experiences contributed to strengthening his new beliefs of controllability and worth.

INITIAL PHYSICAL DETERIORATION (SESSIONS #9 AND #10)

By the next session, two weeks later, Tom was hospitalized with Cytomegalovirus (CMV) retinitis and extensive Kaposi's Sarcoma had been found throughout his lungs. Session #9 was a phone session as he was hospitalized and in isolation, because his doctors suspected that he might have tuberculosis. The session focused on his concerns about death and outlining his spiritual beliefs. Tom stated that he was not afraid of dying, due to his religious and spiritual beliefs. He believed he would be reunited with his loved ones, and particularly found comfort in his belief that he would be reacquainted with his deceased sister and grandfather. When asked to outline his specific concerns and regrets, he stated that his predominant concern was that he would not see his nieces and nephews grow up and would not be able to have an impact on them. Additional questioning about his spiritual beliefs revealed that he believed people in heaven could observe, influence, and protect the living. Subsequently, he saw that this belief would apply to him and the children. He also stated that he realized he would be reunited with them when they died. This realization brought him much relief and peace. To further address his concern that he could not have an impact on them, it was suggested that he leave behind something tangible for them, such as a videotape, audiotape, photographs, or letters. We also discussed that he could influence how he was remembered by notifying family members of particular stories and memories he wanted the children to hear about him. He was heartened by these suggestions.

At this time, he had begun chemotherapy for the Kaposi's Sarcoma and an experimental drug for his CMV retinitis, and discussed the aversive consequences of his treatment. He mentioned his fear that he would linger in the hospital a long time. However, he was able to develop alternative responses to this expectation, such as "I have a living will. I know my family will enforce it and that my doctors will comply."

A significant issue at this time was revealing his illness to his family and friends. Contrary to his negative expectations, they were not surprised and were loving and supportive. He expressed relief at not having to be secretive anymore. The incongruity between his negative expectations and reality were highlighted to demonstrate that situations usually did not fulfill his negative predictions.

Despite such significant health changes, he stated that his mood was "upbeat" and that he felt more comfortable with himself (BDI for Session #9 = 21, BDI for Session #10 = 16). He attributed these positive changes to altered thinking: He saw that people cared about him and did not blame him for being HIV-positive, which lessened his own self-blame, and he had also learned that a hospital stay was not as negative as he had expected. He also was accepting and enjoying the support others gave him. It was suggested that perhaps this attention was easier to accept because of changes in his self-view: He was beginning to realize that he was lovable and worthy.

He discussed altered plans for his future and viewed these changes as positive, rather than threatening. He decided his most significant goal was "to live life to its fullest and not waste time." Toward this goal, he decided to leave his job and visit a sister living in France. Other fulfilling options for spending time included more contact with friends and family, perhaps volunteer work or taking a class. Although it was unclear how much he would realistically be capable of achieving, he was optimistic and these positive expectations were not challenged.

ONGOING CHANGES DUE TO ILLNESS PROGRESSION (SESSIONS #11, #12, AND #13)

Packing up his office belongings was associated with emotions of sadness and anxiety for Tom. The sadness was due to thoughts of "I have a loss of identity and friendships"; the anxiety was related to thoughts of "I've lost my insurance and income." To attack the depressive beliefs, we identified other aspects of his self-view that were still intact and that could even be enhanced, due to ending his job. These included a view of himself as a compassionate, caring friend, a devoted family member, and a person with multiple interests which could develop further (e.g., reader, exerciser, student, art lover). In addition, we generated a list of pleasurable activities he could now enjoy, due to his extra free time. The anxiety thoughts were remedied by generating evidence to show he would have financial stability (e.g., he would collect disability, was still covered for medical care). He noted that he was beginning to hold a new belief, "My negative predictions don't come true," which enabled him to face challenging situations directly.

He continued to complete homework assignments which focused on finding positive evidence which countered his negative core beliefs and on reframing information he initially interpreted as supporting his negative view. The outpouring of social support he was receiving was helpful in diminishing beliefs of unlovability and worthlessness. One particularly flattering event was his farewell party at work. He had been dreading this event because he expected it would have a funeral atmosphere and he would be uncomfortable with all the attention, due to beliefs of unworthiness. His coworkers were gracious and highly sensitive—instead of calling it a "going away" party, they labeled it an "appreciation" party. During the event, they spoke of his contributions and were generous in giving him a paid trip as a thank-you gift. He was extremely touched and able to use these factors as further evidence of his worth and lovability. He also noted that his enhanced self-view enabled him to be less avoidant and take more risks, such as being more assertive, and to pursue positive things for himself.

By the 13th session, he had established a new routine for himself which included increased socialization and self-pampering. He found a new gym to join, and spent a long weekend at a luxurious spa. He noted a concerted effort not to limit himself due to beliefs of "I'll feel worse if I do nothing" and "I don't have time to put things off."

Some friends began to distance themselves slightly at this time. He was able to change his initial thought of "They don't care" to "They're afraid and uncomfortable." The later interpretation was subsequently confirmed when he gently questioned his friends about their behavior. His self-view of worthiness had changed so greatly that he believed they should have kept in touch and he was initially angry at their behavior.

GUILT AND FORGIVENESS (SESSIONS #14 AND #15)

At this point, Tom again mentioned his sister who had died ten years earlier in a car accident and stated he felt guilty due to the thought, "I should have died instead of her." In response to my questioning about the origin and reason for this thought, he revealed that he had been arrested 15 years earlier. He had been driving while intoxicated and caused an accident in which someone was killed. He was imprisoned for manslaughter. His sister was killed shortly after his release. These events were associated with beliefs such as "It (the accident) was my fault . . . and God punishes for bad things," "(sister's death and AIDS) are God's way of punishing me," "My parents blame me for her death . . . I'm hurting them again and can't ask for their help." To diminish his guilty feelings and perceptions of ongoing punishment, we spent time developing alternative interpretations for these events and construing a different meaning for why he developed AIDS. Alternative responses included: "My punishment for the accident I caused was going to jail," "I didn't cause my sister's death," "God isn't so cruel that he'd punish my sister to hurt me," and "Her death had a positive aspect in that I stopped drinking—maybe it was God's way of starting me on the right path."

For homework he continued to develop alternatives to his guilt-producing beliefs, as well as developing a list of positive contributions he had made in his life. The purpose of the positive contributions list was threefold: to appease his guilt, to serve as a life review and aide in finding meaning, and to further diminish his negative core beliefs.

The following week he reported that he had worked on these assignments and viewed his situation differently: "I've been punished enough,"

"I've really changed my life and made significant contributions," "Everyone makes mistakes . . . I'm no worse than anyone else," and "Getting sick doesn't reflect a person's goodness; it isn't anyone's fault and isn't a punishment." He reported that these assignments contributed to self-acceptance, forgiveness, and calmness.

FINAL SESSIONS (SESSIONS #16 AND #17)

Tom's positive self-view remained strong. He attended a week-long retreat with other former substance abusers and reported that it was a rewarding experience, accompanied by a sense of peace. He attributed this to beliefs such as "People are basically good," and "I have real value as an individual with lots of worth, and much to contribute."

However, 11 days later at our next session, he had physically declined further. The Cytomegalovirus (CMV) retinitis had spread to his other eye, and the chemotherapy was increasingly difficult to tolerate. Despite these changes, his BDI remained stable (BDI at Session #17 = 18). We systematically discussed the advantages and disadvantages of continuing versus ending aggressive treatment. He concluded that he would seek more information from his doctors about the purported benefits of treatment, since his illness was so advanced, and then make a decision. In session we developed a list of specific questions that he wanted to ask his doctor.

He had written his will, and had a medical proxy, to whom he had transferred the power of attorney. He had also planned out his funeral and decided on his place of burial. He anticipated discussing this with his parents when he next saw them.

He reiterated his concerns that his nieces and nephews would not remember him. To address this fear, he agreed to a homework assignment to come up with some ideas for a videotape. We decided that we would make the video in our next session.

Unfortunately, Tom died a few weeks later. We spoke briefly on the phone a week after our final session, when he forgot to keep our next appointment. He said that he was not doing well and was moving in with his parents. Two weeks later, he died following the development of an extensive brain mass.

THE CLINICIAN'S ROLE

Tom's rapid deterioration, coupled with his significant therapeutic gains, made this a powerful and rewarding case. Only six months passed between his initial session and his death. His eagerness to learn and apply the cognitive therapy model, along with his moving therapeutic issues, makes him an unforgettable client.

At several points it was necessary to modify my own negative thoughts. Early in treatment, he had to cancel an appointment due to severe stomach pain. My catastrophic thoughts were "He sounds awful. I think something is terribly wrong with him." At our next session, when I asked about the cause of his pain, he sheepishly remarked that he had eaten a sausage and pepperoni pizza which had aggravated a long-standing ulcer. This reminded me of the importance of not overreacting to physical symptoms which may be due to relatively innocuous causes.

Second, I initially hesitated bringing up the topic of his imminent death. I thought, "He'll think that I think his case is hopeless," "Discussing his dying will be uncomfortable for both of us," and "I can't do anything to help him in this area." Of course, none of these predictions came true. He actually seemed relieved when I brought up the topic, we had meaningful sessions on the issue, and he reported comfort in talking about it.

The final area of concern is due to a thought of "I could have done more." I regret that we were unable to make the videotape he desired for the children in his family. My restructuring includes the thought "His anticipation of making a tape produced the necessary relief. At the end of his life, he was incoherent and no longer concerned about the video." I also focus on the fact that this experience was clinically enriching. Hopefully the description of this case will provide others with some viable suggestions for working with HIV-positive clients.

CHAPTER 23

Content, Origins, and Consequences of Dysfunctional Beliefs in Anorexia Nervosa and Bulimia Nervosa

Myra J. Cooper, Gillian Todd, and Adrian Wells

A semi-structured interview was used to investigate negative self beliefs in female patients with eating disorders and women without an eating disorder history. Information about possible developmental influences on these beliefs was also collected. Beliefs linking eating behavior with weight and shape and beliefs about the self were identified, but only by the patients. Self-beliefs were invariably negative and unconditional. Beliefs about eating, weight and shape were usually in the form of conditional assumptions. Most patients identified specific origins for their negative self-beliefs: usually trauma or abuse in childhood. All patients believed that dieting was a way of counteracting the negative implications associated with their self-beliefs. Bingeing seemed to provide an initial distraction in some cases from negative automatic thoughts, images, negative self-beliefs and negative emotional states. However, after bingeing, these intensified. Implications for cognitive theories of eating disorders and for clinical practice are discussed.

There are two main cognitive theories of eating disorders. One has been developed for anorexia nervosa (Garner & Bemis, 1982) and one has been developed for bulimia nervosa (Fairburn, Z. Cooper, & P. J. Cooper, 1986). Both theories highlight the importance of self-statements or automatic thoughts, disturbed information processing, and underlying assumptions, beliefs, or attitudes.

In both theories (Fairburn et al., 1986; Garner & Bemis, 1982) unusual beliefs about weight and shape are thought to have a causal role in the maintenance of the disturbed behavior characteristic of eating disorders. These beliefs hold great personal significance and are dysfunctional because they are rigid and extreme (Fairburn et al., 1986). Typical examples include "to be fat is to be a failure, unattractive, and unhappy" (Fairburn et al., 1986, p. 399) and "weight gain means that I am bad or out of control" (Garner & Bemis, 1982, p. 141).

Underlying assumptions and beliefs are reflected in self-statements or automatic thoughts about eating, weight, and shape. These thoughts are moment-to-moment thoughts that occur throughout the course of the day. Typical examples include "I can't control my eating," "I mustn't let myself gain weight" (Cooper, 1990).

Information-processing errors, i.e., systematic distortions in the processing and interpretation of events, can be detected at the level of underlying assumptions and automatic thoughts. These include dichotomous or all-or-nothing reasoning, for example, the belief "if I gain one pound I'll go on and gain 100 pounds" (Garner & Bemis, 1982, p. 137). Support for the validity of the theories includes evidence from questionnaire studies and studies using techniques from experimental psychology (Cooper, 1997).

The two theories described by Garner and Bemis (1982) and by Fairburn et al. (1986) form the basis for most of the cognitive therapy which is conducted with patients who have eating disorders. However, they are limited in their specification of cognitive variables typically viewed as central in modeling dysfunction. Guidano and Liotti (1983) and Vitousek and Hollon (1990) draw attention to two structures that may be important in patients with eating disorders and that may need to be included in a more detailed theory: cognitive structures relating to personal identity (Guidano & Liotti, 1983) and self-schemata (Vitousek & Hollon, 1990).

Personal identity structures and self-schemata seem to be identical: both are beliefs and rules around which individuals operate and around which they organize their lives, and both appear to be important in organizing and influencing experience, for example, by determining perceptions, thoughts, affect, and behavior (Vitousek & Hollon, 1990). The content of both structures appears to consist of negative beliefs about the self, beliefs that Young (1990) has called "core beliefs." For example, Guidano and Liotti (1983) note that, among other beliefs, personal identity in anorexia nervosa is characterized by beliefs in general ineffectiveness and failure. Guidano and Liotti also draw attention to the role of early experience, particularly within the family, in the formation of these structures. Detailed information about the nature of both negative self-beliefs and the role of early experience are missing from current theories.

A third missing element is detailed information about the assumptions linking negative self-beliefs to disturbed eating behavior. These assumptions are particularly important because they suggest a possible mechanism.

Although existing theories provide a few general examples and assign assumptions a causal role in the maintenance of disturbed eating, they do not explain precisely how disordered thinking manifests as disturbed eating. In particular, they do not specify in detail what the typical content and form of such beliefs might be.

Detailed information about three elements, therefore, is missing from existing cognitive models. This includes information about the nature of core beliefs, particularly negative beliefs about the self; detailed information about the content and form of assumptions linking negative self-beliefs to disturbed eating behavior; and information about the role of developmental factors or early experience in the formation of negative self-beliefs.

Our clinical work with patients with eating disorders suggests that core beliefs, particularly negative self-beliefs, may be an important aspect of anorexia nervosa and bulimia nervosa, and that certain types of early experience may play a part in the development of these beliefs. We have also observed that certain assumptions about weight, shape, and eating may provide a link between negative self-beliefs and disturbed behavior.

The aim of this study was to conduct a systematic investigation to provide detailed information about negative self-beliefs and assumptions in patients with eating disorders. Information on developmental influences which might give rise to negative self-beliefs was also collected.

METHOD

Participants

Twelve female patients with a DSM-III-R diagnosis of anorexia nervosa and 12 female patients with a DSM-III-R diagnosis of bulimia nervosa were interviewed (American Psychiatric Association, 1987) together with 12 women without a history of an eating disorder or depression.

Five patients in the group with anorexia nervosa and seven patients in the group with bulimia nervosa also had a DSM-III-R diagnosis of major depression. One patient with anorexia nervosa had a history of bulimia nervosa and four patients with bulimia nervosa had a history of anorexia nervosa. None of the patients with anorexia nervosa reported recent episodes of binge eating. All participants were screened with the eating disorder and major depression modules of the Structured Clinical Interview for DSM-III-R (SCID: Spitzer, Williams, & Gibbons, 1987) to confirm or exclude diagnosis.

Measures

Demographic Information. Information was collected on age, weight, and height, years of full-time education, diagnosis, and duration of any eating problem.

Self-Report Questionnaires. Each participant completed the Eating Attitudes Test (EAT: Garner & Garfinkel, 1979), the Beck Depression Inventory (BDI: A. T. Beck, Ward, Mendelson, Mock, & Erbaugh, 1961) and the Rosenberg Self-Esteem Scale (RSE: Rosenberg, 1967).

Semistructured Interview. A semistructured interview was conducted with each participant. The interview was developed in pilot work with four eating disorder patients (two patients with anorexia nervosa and two patients with bulimia nervosa). It was based on a semistructured interview developed to investigate core beliefs in patients with health anxiety (Wells & Hackmann, 1993).

The interview asked participants to focus on the most recent situation that they could remember and in which they had felt really worried, anxious, or bad about their eating. Patients with bulimia nervosa were asked to identify two situations, one situation that was a binge episode and one that was not a binge. All participants were also asked to identify the most recent situation in which they had felt bad but where feeling bad was not connected with eating, weight, or shape. The situations were identified and investigated in more detail, one at a time.

For each situation the interview was structured using a series of specific probe questions. Initially, specific instructions were given to remind participants of the situation they had identified (e.g., "imagine that situation") followed by probe questions to help them to get a clear picture of it (e.g., "what do you see?," "what do you hear?," "what do you feel?," "what do you smell?"). Specific probe questions were then asked to provide information for each situation on feelings (e.g., "how do you feel?"), automatic thoughts (e.g., "what thoughts do you have?") and images (e.g., "what images or pictures do you have?"). For the binge episode these details were collected before and after bingeing occurred.

Once automatic thoughts and images had been identified the most salient thought and the most salient image were investigated using the downward arrow technique described by Burns (1980) together with further, specific semistructured questions and discussion. The aim was to identify the personal meaning or assumptions together with the negative self-beliefs underlying the automatic thoughts and images. As before, specific probe questions were asked to achieve this (e.g., "what does that mean to you?," "what's so bad about that?," "what's the worst that can happen?"). The interview was then structured to provide information about the origins of negative self-beliefs, also using specific probe questions (e.g., "what's your earliest recollection of having these thoughts?"), followed by further, follow-up probe questions (e.g., "where were you?," "how old were you?," "what was happening in your life at that time?") to provide more detail. This was followed by probe questions designed to give more information about the assumptions linking these beliefs to patients' behavior, that is, information about the consequences or effect of assumptions on behavior (e.g., "is there anything you can do to change how you think?," "do you feel the thought or belief I'm . . . , image . . . or feeling are connected in some way to your dieting or to your bingeing?"). These were also followed by further specific probe questions to provide more detail (e.g., "how does that help?," "how do you think that works?").

Procedure

All participants were interviewed individually by clinicians experienced in the assessment and treatment of patients with eating disorders. Demographic information was collected and the diagnosis was operationalized using the SCID. The semistructured interview was conducted and participants completed the self-report questionnaires. Each semistructured interview was audiotaped.

RESULTS

Participant Characteristics

Information on age, years of full-time education, Body Mass Index (weight in kg/height in m^2) and duration of eating disorder can be seen in Table 23.1 together with scores on the EAT, BDI, and RSE.

Semistructured Interview

Patients. All patients readily identified a recent situation that was not a binge episode in which they had felt really worried, anxious, or bad about their eating. Twenty out of 24 of the situations identified had occurred on

Table 23.1 Participant Characteristics

Variable	FC (n = 12) Mean	SD	AN (n = 12) MEAN	SD	BN (n = 12) MEAN	SD
Age (years)	25.7	5.3	26.0	7.9	25.7	6.3
Education (years)	15.3	2.1	14.8	2.9	14.3	3.1
Duration of illness (years)	—	—	5.0	4.4	5.9	6.7
Body Mass Index	23.2	3.4	15.5	1.3	21.6	2.8
EAT	5.0	3.7	71.7	18.8	52.6	15.7
BDI	4.2	4.1	36.3	9.0	22.9	9.4
RSE	32.3	4.2	17.2	4.4	19.2	3.6

FC = Female controls. AN = Anorexia nervosa. BN = Bulimia nervosa. Body Mass Index = weight (kg)/height (m^2). EAT = Eating Attitudes Test. BDI = Beck Depression Inventory. RSE = Rosenberg Self-Esteem Scale.

the day of the interview or the previous day. All patients with bulimia nervosa were able to identify a recent binge episode. In nine out of 12 cases these had also occurred on the day of the interview or the day before. Only three patients identified a recent situation in which they had felt bad and which was not connected with weight, shape, or eating.

Controls. Nine of the noneating-disordered participants reported that they never felt really worried, anxious, or bad about their eating. Three reported concerns: in all three cases these thoughts had not occurred for several weeks. Three participants also reported situations not connected to eating, weight, or shape in which they had felt really worried. Only one of these situations had occurred recently.

Feelings, Automatic Thoughts, and Images

Patients. When questioned about the eating situation that was not a binge episode, all patients identified feelings and automatic thoughts associated with the situation they described. Thirteen patients also reported images. In nearly every case these were images of how the patient felt she would look if she were to gain weight or become fat. In every case images contained the same predictions as the associated automatic thoughts. Automatic thoughts and images were usually accompanied by feelings of anxiety or panic. The automatic thoughts, images, assumptions, and negative self-beliefs elicited from the patients in the interview are reported in Table 23.2. Automatic thoughts and beliefs are reported in the patients' own words.

Table 23.2 Thoughts, Images and Beliefs in Patients With Eating Disorders

Age	Weight, shape, eating thoughts	Images	Beliefs	
			1. Beliefs about weight, shape and eating	2. Beliefs about self
Anorexia nervosa patients:				
1.31	I'll eat more than I should. I'll put on weight.	Guests pressing her to eat more, unable to say no.	If I gain weight I can't feel happy about myself. I'll be unattractive and people won't like me. My husband might leave me. Eating more means I'm out of control.	I'm a failure/worthless/no good. I lack self-control. I'm weak.
2.35	I'm piggish/greedy. I'll get fat. I shouldn't be eating when I'm not hungry.	Fat on stomach and across thighs.	If I'm fat it means I'm disgusting/I've failed. No one will notice me/value me as a person. If I eat when I'm not hungry it means I'm out of control.	I'm a failure/not good enough/unworthy. I'm isolated/alone/abandoned. I'm not safe.
3.29	I'm too fat. I don't need this food. I've let myself get out of control.	Being fat, with a big body larger than anyone else.	If I eat I've failed. If I'm fat people will laugh at me/I wouldn't have any friends. Eating means I've let myself get out of control.	I'm useless/unlikable/unlovable.
4.27	I'm absolutely enormous. I've been a pig all day.	No images.	If I eat normally I'm not worth anything. If I eat too much I'm not in control.	I'm not worth anything. I'm all alone.
5.17	I'm fat and overweight.	Being pregnant but, instead of a baby, stomach is crammed with food.	If I'm fat I won't have any friends.	I'm all alone. I don't have any personality.
6.23	I'm totally fat again.	Body when sitting down, thighs like two circles.	If I gain weight I'll have to take on more responsibility/face things/work. I'll fail and I won't have an excuse for failing. I'll be hurt by others/rejected. If I'm getting thinner I can feel good about myself/safer.	I'm nothing/not fit to be a person. I'm useless/worthless. I'm not safe.

Table 23.2 (*Continued*)

Age	Weight, shape, eating thoughts	Images	Beliefs	
			1. Beliefs about weight, shape and eating	2. Beliefs about self
7.21	I'm very fat. I've no will-power. I'm out of control.	Huge bloating. Face, thighs, tops of arms ballooning out.	If I'm fat I've lost everything I was good at. People will notice me/think less of me/not approve of me. Eating is the only thing I can control.	I'm not very good at anything. I'll never achieve. I'm selfish/wicked. I'm all alone.
8.44	I'm getting fat. I'll get obese.	No images.	If I overeat it means I've failed/I'm not in control.	I'm a failure.
9.18	I'm eating too much. I should be able to control my eating better. I'll put on weight.	No images.	If I get fat I won't be able to feel happy with myself. I won't be able to go out and have a good time. It means I've failed to control what's happening to me/I've failed to achieve.	I'm unattractive. I've failed. I lack determination.
10.26	I want to exercise. I want to chuck my food away. I can't control my weight gain.	No images.	If my weight goes up I won't be protected anymore. I'll have to face up to everything I don't want to face up to/relation ships.	I'm rejected/not sought after. I've nothing left. I'm worthless.
11.23	I'll carry on gaining weight, get more out of control.	No images.	If I gain weight I'll isolate myself, won't have any motivation to do anything. People will expect me to be happy/cope/do well.	I'm worthless. I'm a failure.
12.18	I'm going to get fatter. People will see me as doing something wrong.	Of women with good figures. How I think I look and what I would be like if I eat.	If I eat then I'm failing/lack self-control. I wouldn't be able to get on with other things. I'd feel disgusted with myself/be unhappy/feel worthless.	I'm worthless. I'm superficial.

Table 23.2 (*Continued*)

Age	Weight, shape, eating thoughts	Images	Beliefs	
			1. Beliefs about weight, shape and eating	2. Beliefs about self
Bulimia nervosa patients:				
1.23	I want to be slim. I've got to start dieting.	No images.	If I was slim then I'd be happy. If I'm fat I'm not good enough/can't make my boyfriend happy. No one will ever love me.	I'm horrible/useless to myself, other people/not good enough. I can't achieve anything. I'm all alone.
2.21	I'm fat and unattractive.	Body growing, expanding.	If I'm fat people won't like me/they'll laugh at me.	I'm inferior/not good enough. I'm boring/not a nice person. I'm all alone.
3.35	I can't stop (eating). I'm scared where it might end. I'm a blob of a person.	No images.	If I eat I'm not in control/I hate myself. If I'm fat it means I won't be like/I'll end up all alone.	I hate myself. I'm a horrible person. I'm pretending. I'm all alone. I'm a nonentity/failure/no good/shallow.
4.33	I need something nice, for comfort. I can't stop eating.	No images.	If I eat I can't feel good about myself. I'm worthless/not in control/it's harder to cope with other things.	I don't matter. I'm worthless/helpless/trapped/weak-willed/bad.
5.36	I'll get fat. I'm greedy.	Distended stomach, bulbous shape.	Being greedy means I'm selfish. I'll lose friends/colleagues. I should put other people first.	I'm inadequate/useless/stupid.
6.20	I'll be fat when everyone is thin, they'll call me fat	No images.	If I'm fat I can't feel good about myself. I couldn't wear nice clothes/go out/meet friends/enjoy myself. I'll end up without any friends/all alone.	I'm all alone.

Table 23.2 (*Continued*)

Age	Weight, shape, eating thoughts	Images	Beliefs	
			1. Beliefs about weight, shape and eating	2. Beliefs about self
7.25	I always eat too much. I don't want to be fat. I need to lose some weight.	Eating more and more until she has to vomit.	If I eat I'm not in control. If I'm fat people will think I'm weak/not see me as a person.	I'm disgusting/inadequate/ worthless/not a person,
8.17	It's too much (food). I might eat too much and not be able to be sick. I need to lose some weight.	Round tummy after eating.	It's bad/wrong not to control something (like weight) that you've set yourself. If I were to be fat I'd have failed and it would be very hard to live with myself.	I'm a failure.
9.26	I'm fat, gross and horrible. I've let myself down because I said I shouldn't eat. I'll store it as fat.	Face round and chubby, huge hips, big legs, a big chest.	If I'm fat people won't like me/they'll laugh at me. If no one likes me I can't feel good about myself. The only thing I've got is my looks.	I'm not very intelligent/ haven't got a brain. I'm not as good as other people. I'm a piece of dirt.
10.25	It'll go onto my stomach. I'll look horrible tomorrow. I'll put weight on. I'll get fat and horrible.	Self being fat.	If I got fat I wouldn't like myself. I'd feel I didn't really deserve to be around. Other people wouldn't like me/love me/have any respect for me. Eating means I've no self-willpower.	I'm ugly/pathetic. I give in all the time. I've no self-willpower. I'm a loser/not worth it. I'm a failure.
11.28	I should eat more, I don't want to. I must force myself to eat. I'll put on weight.	No images.	If I put on weight I'll be open to criticism of being overweight. That would undermine and take away my confidence. It would mean I wasn't in control/I'm sloppy.	I've no value. I'm awful/ insignificant/worthless. I'm a failure.
12.19	I'm fat, horrible, unattractive.	No images.	If I don't look good then I don't know where else to turn to validate myself.	I'm worthless/no good at anything/not very attractive.

Controls. The three noneating-disordered participants who reported some concerns about eating all identified feelings and automatic thoughts associated with the situation they described. None reported images. In two cases automatic thoughts reflected concerns about healthy eating, e.g., "I need to eat a healthy diet," while in the third case thoughts reflected concern about a desire to eat chocolate, e.g., "I need it (chocolate)," "I must have it". All three commented that these were only passing thoughts or passing concerns rather than definite worries. Two participants reported that the thoughts were not associated with any clear negative feelings. One participant reported mild, transient feelings of guilt but, in all three cases, when the concern had occurred, it had not made the participant feel anxious or bad.

Content of Dysfunctional Beliefs

Patients. Two main types of beliefs were elicited from the patients in the interviews. These were beliefs about weight, shape, and eating, and beliefs about the self. Beliefs about the self were, without exception, negative and unconditional. They included beliefs about being worthless, useless, inferior, a failure, abandoned, and alone.

Beliefs about weight, shape, and eating were generally conditional assumptions, phrased in the form of "if . . . then" statements. They focussed on the personal meaning of being fat and thin and on the personal meaning of eating. In the chain of thoughts and beliefs elicited, in all the patients interviewed, these conditional statements provided a link between automatic thoughts and images and negative self-beliefs. Questions about the meaning of the automatic thoughts and images elicited a conditional assumption about the personal meaning of being fat or thin and the personal meaning of eating. Questions about the meaning of the conditional assumption elicited an unconditional negative self-belief. Assumptions included concerns about the relationship between weight, shape, self-acceptance, and acceptance by others, as well as concerns about control over eating.

Controls. The three noneating-disordered participants who reported automatic thoughts associated with eating were also questioned about the meaning of these thoughts. In all three cases no specific meaning could be identified: thus no beliefs about eating, weight, shape, or the self were elicited.

Origins of Dysfunctional Beliefs

Most patients were able to identify specific origins for their negative self-beliefs. These were usually unpleasant early experiences and included physical abuse, emotional abuse, neglect, and lack of attention or understanding from parents, teachers, and peers. In 13 cases these experiences occurred before the age of 13. In the remaining patients they occurred between the ages of 13 and 17. Some patients also identified specific origins for their beliefs about weight, shape, and eating. These included teasing or criticism about weight and shape from family members, peers, and teachers, or excessive emphasis on food and eating at home or at school.

Consequences of Dysfunctional Beliefs

All patients believed that dieting helped with their negative self-beliefs. Assumptions associated with dieting were generally mirror images of the beliefs that patients expressed about the meaning of being fat, gaining weight, or eating normally. They appeared to be similar to the beliefs described by Young (1990) as *schema compensation* beliefs. For example, the patients said that dieting made them feel more successful, less of a failure, more in control. Dieting appeared to be a way to make up for, or overcome, early experiences and associated negative self-beliefs. Being thin meant that less was expected of them or that other people were more likely to accept them. Being liked and accepted meant that they wouldn't end up lonely and alone in the way they feared. Like the other schema processes which Young describes, schema compensation strategies may function to maintain a schema by preventing it from being challenged.

Binge Episodes

In all the patients with bulimia nervosa bingeing seemed to intensify the feelings, automatic thoughts, and images that were identified. Thoughts and images became more accessible and harder to ignore, and were accompanied by increased distress. Bingeing appeared to occur for a variety of reasons, including hunger and habit. However, eight patients identified thoughts and/or images that seemed to be triggers for binges. Only some of these thoughts and images were related to weight, shape, and eating. Others were, for example, related to relationships or work difficulties. In all cases, questioning revealed negative self-beliefs similar to those already identified. In these eight patients bingeing appeared to be an attempt to provide distraction from thoughts, images, negative self-beliefs, and negative emotional states. This process appears similar to that described by Young (1990) as *schema avoidance,* a process that may also function to maintain a schema by preventing it from being challenged. Without exception, all patients also identified *permissive thoughts* that appeared to be similar to those described in substance abuse (A. T. Beck,

Wright, Newman, & Liese, 1993). Once eating had begun, these thoughts seemed to make it easy to continue.

CASE

The content, origins and consequences of dysfunctional beliefs in individual cases are illustrated in the case presented below. It is an example expanded from Table 23.2.

Anna: A Patient With Bulimia Nervosa

Anna had met DSM-III-R criteria for bulimia nervosa for most of the past eight years. Her score on the EAT was 56.

Recent Situations

The last time she had felt bad about her eating (not a binge episode) was during the evening two days before the interview. She had eaten a meal with friends and had eaten more than she had really wanted. Anna had last had an objective binge (Fairburn, 1987) seven days previously.

Feelings, Automatic Thoughts, and Images

Anna recalled that after eating the meal she felt her heart beating much faster than usual. She felt guilty, tense, and panicky, as well as angry. She felt angry that she couldn't vomit while there were other people in the house. Her automatic thoughts were "it (the food) will go onto my stomach, I'll look horrible tomorrow, I'll put weight on, I'll get fat and horrible." She had an image of herself being fat.

She recalled feeling nervous and frightened before bingeing, and worried about her work. Her automatic thoughts were "I've wasted the week, my work's not very good, my time's going, I'm not in control, I'm not clever." She also reported thoughts that made it easier to binge once she had started eating. These were "I deserve a reward, it's OK to eat." After bingeing she felt angry with herself and frightened. Her automatic thoughts were "I'm out of control, it (bingeing) will go on forever, I'll blow up, get fat."

Beliefs About Weight, Shape, and Eating

Anna's assumptions were concerned with what it would mean to put on weight and be fat, with weight as a means to both self-acceptance and acceptance by others, and with the importance of controlling her eating. Putting on weight and getting fat, would mean that she wouldn't like herself. She said that she would feel that she didn't deserve to be around. She also said that it would mean that other people wouldn't like her, love her, or have any respect for her. Eating more would mean that she gave in all the time and that she had no willpower.

Negative Self-Beliefs

Anna had several negative self-beliefs. She said "I'm ugly, pathetic, not clever, a failure. I'm a loser, not worth it, I don't deserve to be around. I give in all the time. I've no willpower."

Early Experiences

Two early experiences were associated with Anna's first memory of having these negative self-beliefs. When she was seven her mother had a nervous breakdown and Anna had been sent to stay with her grandparents for several months. She recalled being desperately unhappy there. Her grandparents had treated her like a much older child. They had repeatedly told her that she was extremely clever, given her adult books to read, and insisted that she was put into a class at school with children two years older. Anna was unable to understand the books they gave her and unable to keep up with her class at school. She recalled thinking that she was stupid and a failure. At the same time she became much more aware of food and weight. Her grandmother cooked large meals for her, insisted that they were eaten, and weighed her every week to see if she had gained weight.

When Anna was 10 her parents divorced, and she did not see her father for some time. She blamed herself for this, believing that her father didn't want to see her because she was "a loser" and "not worth the trouble." She recalled thinking that this meant that she didn't deserve to be around. After the divorce the family had financial difficulties and Anna was the only child in her class at school without a school uniform. This made her feel different and inferior to the other children. At about the same time Anna recalled having to change for gym in front of the boys in her class. She was an early developer and remembered feeling acutely embarrassed about this and very conscious of her body. She dated the belief that she was ugly from this time. To cope with her unhappiness Anna became a "show off," feeling inside that she didn't want to be like that but unable to stop herself. This seemed to be the origin of her beliefs that she was pathetic, had no willpower, and couldn't control her behavior.

Consequences of Dysfunctional Beliefs

Dieting. Anna was clear that dieting helped with overcoming her negative self-beliefs. Dieting was a way to make herself feel attractive, successful, less of a failure, and more worthwhile. It gave her something that she could try to control.

Bingeing. Bingeing provided an escape from Anna's negative self-beliefs and the feelings associated with them. It appeared to be facilitated by the thought "I'm not in control." Bingeing left her feeling numb and meant that she no longer had to think about herself or feel bad.

Other Situations

Anna also described a recent situation in which she had felt bad but which was unrelated to weight, shape, or eating. When she was questioned about this situation the negative self-beliefs elicited were similar to those already described.

DISCUSSION

This preliminary study has provided a detailed description of the content, origins, and consequences of dysfunctional beliefs in anorexia nervosa and bulimia nervosa. The results show that the beliefs of young women with eating disorders, unlike those of noneating-disordered women, consist of at least two types of qualitatively distinct information: negative self-beliefs and instrumental assumptions. Negative self-beliefs were unconditional and were concerned with themes of worthlessness, uselessness, inferiority, failure, abandonment, and loneliness. In contrast, assumptions were conditional and expressed relationships between negative self-beliefs, weight, shape, and eating. Three types of assumptions could be distinguished: those linking shape, weight gain, and weight loss with social- and self-desirability, those linking eating with self-control, and those linking bingeing behavior to cognitive and emotional control. In addition, all the patients with bulimia nervosa reported permissive thoughts that were activated at the onset of a binge episode. Such permission-giving cognitions might be important in temporarily suppressing the salience of beliefs concerning the dangers of eating and weight gain, and their presence and development might distinguish individuals with bulimia nervosa from those with anorexia nervosa. A recent questionnaire study provides additional evidence for the importance of negative self-beliefs, assumptions about social-and self-desirability and assumptions about control of eating in patients with eating disorders (Cooper, Cohen-Tovee, Todd, Wells, & Tovee, 1997).

Wells and Hackmann (1993) have commented on the important role of the *conjunction* of different beliefs in determining the nature of disturbance. The present data extend this concept to eating disorders. In particular, the negative self-beliefs obtained are general and likely to be found in a range of disorders such as depression and health anxiety. However, the conjunction of these beliefs with assumptions concerning weight, shape, and eating suggests that a specific behavioral and cognitive profile is characteristic of eating disorders.

Young identifies three processes that function to maintain schema or core beliefs (McGinn & Young, 1996; Young, 1990).[1] These are schema maintenance, schema compensation, and schema avoidance. In defining schema compensation Young notes that it refers to behaviors or cognitions that are attempts by the individual to redress or cope with traumatic early experience (McGinn & Young, 1996). In defining schema avoidance he notes that this process refers to cognitive, behavioral, and emotional strategies that the individual may use to avoid triggering a schema and the intense related affect (McGinn & Young, 1996). We have illustrated how, for the majority of patients here, instrumental assumptions offered a means, through particular behaviors, of compensating for negative self-beliefs.[2] In addition, bingeing behavior was used by some patients to block out negative emotions and associated self-beliefs. If our analysis is correct, it implies that eating behaviors in anorexia nervosa and bulimia nervosa may represent types of *schema compensation* and *cognitive and emotional avoidance*.

Our findings are compatible with the hypothesis advanced by Vitousek and Hollon (1990) that the core psychopathology of eating disorders is represented in weight-related self-schemata. Although no details about the form and content are provided, Vitousek and Hollon describe these schemata as organized cognitive structures that unite views of the self with views about weight. This description parallels our finding that the conjunction of negative self-beliefs and assumptions about weight, shape, and eating is the defining characteristic of eating disorders.

Clinically, the findings presented here suggest that it may be important to identify underlying assumptions and negative self-beliefs in the process of therapy for anorexia nervosa and bulimia nervosa and to include them in individual cognitive case formulations. Both underlying assumptions and negative self-beliefs may be important in the individual case. These beliefs might usefully be indentified using questions taken from the semistructured interview format used here. Other helpful techniques might include a detailed review of thought diaries to identify themes, completion of the self-report questionnaire mentioned above (Cooper et al., 1997) and, for identifying negative self-beliefs, a brief sentence-completion task (Cooper, Todd, & Cohen-Tovee, 1995). For treatment to be successful and to prevent relapse it may be important to address both negative self-beliefs and any associated schema-driven processes or assumptions. Underlying assumptions might usefully be challenged by identifying evidence for and against each assumption, examining the advantages and disadvantages of continuing to believe in it or behave as though it were true, together with carrying out follow-up behavioral experiments to put reformulated beliefs to the test. A variety of cognitive and behavioral techniques might be useful to address negative self-beliefs, including use of the core belief worksheet (J. Beck, 1995), positive data logs, cognitive-continuum and historical tests of beliefs (Padesky, 1994).

There are some limitations to the present study. The number of patients interviewed is relatively small and we have only included a noneating-disordered control group. Other appropriate control groups might include restrained eaters, or dieters and depressed patients. However, despite these limitations, our findings strongly suggest that cognitive models of the maintenance and etiology of eating disorders, and cognitive therapy based on these models, should consider the role of self-beliefs and assumptions as well as the role of schema compensation, and cognitive and emotional avoidance processes in conceptualizing anorexia nervosa and bulimia nervosa.

ACKNOWLEDGMENTS

This article is based on a paper presented at the World Congress of Behavioural and Cognitive Therapy, Copenhagen, Denmark, July, 1995. We would like to thank Esther Cohen-Tovee for her help in developing and piloting the semistructured interview used in this study.

NOTES

1. Young uses the term schema to refer to both the structure with its associated processes and the content of the structure. Technically, the term "schema" should be used to refer only to the structure, while the term "belief" should be used to refer to the content of the structure (A. T. Beck & Freeman, 1990, p. 4).

2. As well as an attempt to overcome or make up for early mistreatment, Young also notes in his definition of schema compensation, that it refers to behaviors or cognitions that overcompensate for a schema, that become dysfunctional, and that appear to be the opposite of what one would expect from knowledge of the early

schemes. Dieting is frequently carried to extreme lengths and becomes dysfunctional. As such, it might be considered to be a form of overcompensation. While dieting to overcome, for example, beliefs of worthlessness or failure is not strictly speaking the "opposite" of what might be expected from knowledge of the schemas, it is clearly unexpected and not what one might initially predict. Given this, and the fact that it meets other criteria, it seems that dieting, as investigated here, can be usefully accommodated within Young's definition of schema compensation.

REFERENCES

American Psychiatric Association. (1987). *DSM-III-R.* Washington, DC: American Psychiatric Association.

Beck, A. T., & Freeman, A. (1990). *Cognitive therapy of personality disorders.* New York: Guilford Press.

Beck, A. T., Ward, C. H., Mendelson, M., Mock, J., & Erbaugh, J. (1961). An inventory for measuring depression. *Archives of General Psychiatry, 4,* 561–571.

Beck, A. T., Wright, F. D., Newman, C. F., & Liese, B. S. (1993). *Cognitive therapy of substance abuse.* New York: Guilford Press.

Beck, J. S. (1995). *Cognitive therapy: Basics and beyond.* New York: Guilford Press.

Burns, D. D. (1990). *Feeling good.* New York: Signet.

Cooper, M. J. (1990). *Classifying thoughts from transcripts: A Manual.* Unpublished manuscript: University of Oxford.

Cooper, M. J. (1997). Cognitive theory in anorexia nervosa and bulimia nervosa: A review. *Behavioral and Cognitive Psychotherapy, 25,* 113–145.

Cooper, M. J., Cohen-Tovee, E., Todd, G., Wells, A., & Tovee, M. (1997). A questionnaire to assess assumptions and beliefs in eating disorders: Preliminary findings. *Behaviour Research and Therapy, 35,* 381–388.

Cooper, M. J., Todd, G., & Cohen-Tovee, E. (1996). Core beliefs in eating disorders. *International Cognitive Therapy Newsletter, 10,* part 2, 2–3.

Fairburn, C. G. (1987). The definition of bulimia nervosa. *Annals of Behavioural Medicine, 5,* 3–7.

Fairburn, C. G., Cooper, Z., & Cooper, P. J. (1986). The clinical features and maintenance of bulimia nervosa. In K. D. Brownell & J. P. Foreyt (Eds.), *Physiology, psychology and treatment of the eating disorders.* New York: Basic Books.

Garner, D. M., & Bemis, K. M. (1982). A cognitive-behavioural approach to anorexia nervosa. *Cognitive Therapy and Research. 6,* 123–150.

Garner, D. M., & Garfinkel, P. E. (1979). The Eating Attitudes Test: An index of the symptoms of anorexia nervosa. *Psychological Medicine 9,* 273–279.

Guidano, V. F., & Liotti, G. (1983). *Cognitive processes and emotional disorders: A structural approach to psychotherapy.* New York: Guilford Press.

McGinn, L. K., & Young, J. E. (1996). Schema-focused therapy. In P.M. Salkovskis (Ed.), *Frontiers of cognitive therapy.* New York: Guilford Press.

Padesky, C. A. (1994). Schema change processes in cognitive therapy. *Clinical Psychology and Psychotherapy, 1,* 267–278.

Rosenberg, M. (1965). *Society and the adolescent self image.* Princeton: Princeton University Press.

Spitzer, R. L., Williams, J. B. W., & Gibbons, M. (1987). *Instructional manual for the structured clinical interview for DSM-III-R* (SCID, 4/1/87 Revision). New York: New York State Psychiatric Institute.

Vitousek, K. B., & Hollon, S. D. (1990). The investigation of schematic content and processing in the eating disorders. *Cognitive Therapy and Research, 14,* 191–214.

Wells, A., & Hackmann, A. (1993). Imagery and core beliefs in health anxiety: Content and origins. *Behavioural and Cognitive Psychotherapy, 21,* 265–273.

Young, J. E., (1990). *Cognitive therapy for personality disorders: A schema focussed approach.* Sarasota, FL: Professional Resource Exchange, Inc.

CHAPTER 24

Cognitive Therapy: Current Problems and Future Directions

Robert L. Leahy

Why has cognitive therapy come so far, so quickly? It seems not very long ago that Beck and his colleagues published *Cognitive Therapy of Depression* and set off a revolution in the field of clinical psychology and psychiatry (Beck, Rush, Shaw, & Emery, 1979). Beck's original formulation (1967) argued that depression is related to the conscious cognitive biases of the patient,—including the negative triad (negative view of self, of experience, and of the future). These cognitive biases are reflected in the specific negative content of automatic thoughts, maladaptive assumptions, and personal schemas. These initial formulations are open to empirical testing, because they are potentially falsifiable. One of the significant appeals of a cognitive-behavioral model is that its credibility has depended on the fact that many of its propositions are empirically testable.

With the recent publication of Clark, Beck, and Alford's (1999) *Scientific Foundations of Cognitive Theory and Therapy of Depression,* there is now clear empirical support for the major tenets of cognitive theory. These include the role of negative cognition in depression, selective information processing, stability of cognitive processes, and the cognitive diathesis-stress hypothesis. Clark (1986), Salkovskis (1989, 1996), Salkovskis and Kirk (1989, 1997), Wells (1997, 2000), and Wells & Matthews (1996) have provided substantial support for a variety of hypotheses for the cognitive model of a range of anxiety disorders.

Over the past 20 years, the cognitive model has gained wide appeal and appears to be influencing the development of the field more than any other model. What accounts for the ascendancy of the cognitive model? I think this is an important question, even if it appears to be self-congratulatory. Ironically, the reason I say this is that I have concerns that what has made us successful may be taken for granted and that we may find ourselves tempted to abandon the scientific and rational basis in order to advance other models.

Four reasons for the success of the cognitive model are:

- Cognitive therapy is a manualized treatment. This allows for relative consistency across therapists in the adherence to the cognitive model. Therapist "competence" can be measured by specific behaviors. Findings can be replicated.
- Cognitive therapy is derived from a cognitive model of psychopathology. The advantage of this is that research and theory on cognitive processes in psychopathology can be generalized to application in clinical practice. If depression is associated with negative automatic thoughts, then modifying those thoughts may alleviate depression.
- The model has internal consistency. The concepts of schema, automatic thoughts, core beliefs, underlying assumptions, and other cognitive processes are all interrelated in an apparently logical and coherent manner.
- The concepts in the cognitive model lend themselves to operational definitions and, in most cases, to direct manipulation. Thus, we can define what an automatic thought is and manipulate it to determine its causal connection to other cognitions or symptoms.

There are also certain appeals that the cognitive model has to the consumer, that is, the patient. These include the following:

- It works. There is considerable empirical evidence that cognitive therapy is an effective treatment for depression, panic, generalized anxiety, social phobia, and a variety of other problems.
- It appeals to the assertive client. Consumers are better informed and more demanding. They want a rational, effective, focused, and practical treatment for specific problems. They do not want to lie on a

couch for years, reminiscing about memories and dreams, hoping
for insights. Cognitive therapy places the power to change in the
hands of the consumer.
- It is not mysterious and complicated. This is related to the foregoing
  point but is worth expanding upon. The cognitive model allows
  clear case conceptualization that the reasonably intelligent patient
  can comprehend. The less mysterious and complicated, the easier it
  is to transfer the knowledge of the therapist to the patient.
- Emphasis on cost-effectiveness makes cognitive therapy appealing.
  Whether it is managed care or simply the assertive consumer of
  services, there little place for the Viennese analyst stroking his beard
  and proclaiming incomprehensible statements. Patients demand results and their insurance carriers will remind them of this.

These are some of the reasons that cognitive therapy has become so
popular. But there may be directions that we find ourselves moving in—
directions that we may need to move in—-that can present some possible
pitfalls. At the risk of sounding like the dark side of the force, let me
explore some possible (mis)directions and how we might approach these
problems.

NEED FOR A DEVELOPMENTAL MODEL

Although Beck (1976; Beck et al., 1979) had proposed that maladaptive
schemas may be established during early childhood, the cognitive model has
not advanced a coherent developmental model of the affective, anxiety, or
personality disorders. Unlike the psychoanalytic model that proposes a definitive (if questionable) model of etiology, which stresses stages and processes
of development and the possibility of regression, the cognitive model offers
a vague claim that earlier development may affect current adult functioning.

I have argued that a developmental model of psychopathology must
meet certain requirements (Leahy, 1995). First, what really develops cognitive content, structure, or defenses? Second, are there stages of development or is development simply an accumulation of experiences,
information, and learning? Third, is development progressive—that is,
moving toward something more adaptive as Piaget (1934) implies—or is
it marked by movement along "deviant pathways," as Bowlby's (1980)
model would imply? Fourth, what accounts for transition or change? Is it
reward, punishment, modeling, cognitive conflict, or some other process?
Fifth, both Piaget and Bowlby argue for the "conservation of schemas" or
limitations on change. Piaget's model is one of a balance of assimilation

and accommodation—or, to put it in more popular terms, *readiness for change.* Are there self-limiting processes that maintain cognitive content or processes? Sixth, one may argue that the genetic predispositions of the child may influence the socialization practices of the parents, thereby reversing the presumed causal direction of influence (see Collins, Maccoby, Steinberg, Hetherington, & Bornstein, 2000).

Probably because cognitive therapy was advanced as an alternative to psychoanalytic theory, initially there was less emphasis on the importance of early experience. The "here-and-now" focus of cognitive therapy may imply that earlier experiences are not a focus of therapy. However, many cognitive therapists have proposed that an understanding of earlier experiences is essential for case conceptualization (J. Beck, 1996; Persons, 1989), personality disorders (Beck, Freeman, & Associates, 1990), or for modifying personal schemas (Young, 1990). However, the use of developmental data appears to lack a comprehensive or even consistent developmental model.

As I indicate further on, each Axis I and Axis II disorder (DSM-IV; American Psychiatric Association, 1994) requires a separate cognitive conceptualization regarding schematic vulnerability, triggers, epistemology and self-protective strategies. Developmental research that focuses on the earlier socialization experiences of patients should attempt to link earlier experience with these specific cognitive elements. For example, rather than examine the relationship between early childhood experience and the current existence of generalized anxiety disorder, research should attempt to link early experience (or even more recent experience) with current vulnerabilities (e.g., health, money, relationships, failure at work) and coping strategies (e.g., ruminating, worrying, reassurance-seeking). Cognitive research on development should focus specifically on cognitive content and less on the more general diagnostic categories. As an example, it may be more likely that for the individual who worries about money today, specific issues about money were emphasized earlier in life (e.g., "money is running out." "Our family lost all its money," or "having money means that you are worthwhile"). We might find that current maladaptive strategies, such as worrying or overcompensating were utilized (or even underutilized) by parents. Thus, developmental research should link earlier behavioral and cognitive strategies with current strategies, rather than replicate a more global approach to DSM-IV diagnostic categories.

THE NEED FOR A MODEL OF THE SELF

The cognitive model emphasizes a number of processes that reflect an implicit theory of the self. These include the nature of self-criticism, personal schemas, the distinction between sociotropic and autonomous functioning, and the stress on information processing, especially as related to biased processing of schematic-relevant information. But there is coherent theory of the self that has been explicated. What would such a theory require? Can cognitive theory accommodate such a theory?

Of course, the issue of the self has been a central one for psychologists since William James (1892). One can make a distinction between the self as content and process. Content aspects of the self include differentiation of domains of the self (physical, interpersonal, work, values, family, etc), as James and others have suggested (James, 1892; Damon & Hart, 1988). In addition, self-content may be assessed in terms of evaluation—good, bad, neutral. Content may also include viewing the self from different perspectives, such as from the perspective of the real-self (how I see myself), the ideal self (how I would like to be), and the social self (how I think others see me). The content of the self may be more or less accessible to consciousness, and the qualities of the self may be viewed as more or less stable over time and situations.

Process concepts of the self include those forms, structures, or phenomena that affect the functioning of the self. These include metacognitive awareness (i.e., being able to take a perspective on one's self or self-functioning), concepts of causes of the self's behavior (such as attribution processes or theories of one's own development), and self-regulatory processes that affect emotional and cognitive regulation or self-direction toward goals. Process concepts would also include models of structural integration such that certain aspects of the self would be viewed in terms of a hierarchical or organizational relationship to other aspects of the self.

Furthermore, as indicated earlier, a developmental model of the self would entail a model of qualitative change in content and processes of the self. For example, does the self-concept change with developmental level? Are there formative experiences that affect different aspects of the self? Is the self stable or unstable across time? Which aspects of the self develop first and how do they influence other aspects of the self? Do processes of self-awareness, self-regulation, and self-evaluation change with development?

I believe that many of these questions may be addressed within a cognitive theory of psychopathology and the self. Thus far, however, the emphasis has been more on a molecular level—examining specific self-content or self-functions. Beck (1997) has proposed the concept of *modes* as a superordinate construct that attempts to relate the various plans, affects, and cognitions to one another, but this needs much further exploration, especially in light of the issues of self that I have raised. Although the cognitive model of personality disorders draws heavily on inferences and mini-theories of self-other functioning—and purported antecedents——there is considerable room for theoretical and clinical development in this area.

THE NAÏVE VIEW THAT THERE IS ONE COGNITIVE MODEL OF PSYCHOPATHOLOGY

Some people who do cognitive therapy appear to think that the initial model of cognitive therapy of depression applies to every aspect of psychopathology. Thus, according to this naïve view, patients who have panic disorder would be told that they have distorted automatic thoughts and assumptions and that they simply have to do exposure treatment. However, Beck's view is considerably more sophisticated than this. Each disorder presents the opportunity and necessity of a separate cognitive conceptualization. Panic disorder is conceptualized as a specific set of assumptions about emotions, sensations, and thoughts and the need to control them lest one lose total control. Exposure, in this specific cognitive model, involves identifying the patient's beliefs about emotions, sensations, and thoughts; and eliciting predictions, inducing the symptoms, and practicing exposure to this experience in order to test out the theory of emotions and control.

Similarly, there are specific cognitive treatments for social phobia, generalized anxiety, and hypochondriasis, as well as psychotic disorders and bipolar disorder. Each disorder is characterized by the patient's implicit and explicit theory of the nature of the problem. One can take the view that pathology is due to problems in schematic bias (what schema lies dormant), activation (what triggers the schema and the mode), epistemology (how is reality known and what counts as evidence), and self-protective strategies (what specific rules, behaviors and cognitions are utilized to avoid further danger or loss). Consider health anxiety, or hypochondriasis. The patient's schematic bias is that he is vulnerable to disease. These cognitions are activated by any signs of physiological imperfection, a blemish for example. The epistemological model that is activated stipulates that any possibility of illness implies significant probability and that the inability to provide certainty as to the nonexistence of an illness confers danger. Any imperfection can count as evidence in favor of an illness and medical reassurance can be discounted because it does not rule out that possibility, so the patient is in a constant state of self-vigilance. The self-protective strategies—checking, reassurance-seeking, collecting medical evidence, or even avoiding checking and seeing doctors—are viewed as self-protective by the patient. Similar analyses may be conducted for each of the anxiety disorders and for other Axis I disorders.

The cognitive model has expanded and will continue to expand beyond the initial schematic bias model. Certainly, individuals who are anxious have schemas about threat (e.g., losing control, being hurt, being humiliated), but their specific epistemologies and their self-protective strategies are essential in understanding the nature of the cognitive psychopathology.

THE LIMITS AND PROBLEMS OF ECLECTICISM

Between the 1930s and 1950s, psychology in North America was guided by grand theories or models, including psychoanalysis, drive theory, learning theories of various kinds, and Piagetian theory. Comprehensive and far-reaching theoretical models had the appeal of offering generality and internal coherence. When attempts at integration were made, such as in the work of Dollard and Miller (1950) in their integration of psychoanalysis with learning theory, the effort was directed toward translating concepts of psychoanalysis into learning theory concepts so as to make them more accessible, testable, and open to manipulation.

Grand theoretical models began to collapse in the 1960s as psychologists found that no grand theory could encompass what it proposed to handle. Shortcomings in psychoanalytic theory, both in terms of its overemphasis on ideas that could not easily be tested and the questionable efficacy of treatment, led psychoanalysis to branch in different directions and to a gradual abandonment of the model in developmental psychology and among many clinicians. Other forces, such as the ascendance of cognitivism and behaviorism and the influence of pharmacolological treatments, also contributed to the decline of psychoanalysis as a pervasive force.

In cognitive therapy, there is an appeal to utilizing techniques and concepts from other fields. For example, Young's schema-focused therapy utilizes ideas from Gestalt therapy, object relations theory, and other approaches. Although eclectic approaches may enhance the range of problems and interventions that the therapist might consider and may provide a sense of greater depth, there may be unforeseen risks in an "unstructured eclecticism" (Alford & Beck, 1997). Too great a reliance on integration or eclecticism may—but does not necessarily—involve the risks of losing coherence of theory, of introducing hypotheses that are not testable, and ad hoc explanations. These risks may be attenuated by recognizing that a coherent theory may utilize concepts and insights from other models as long as there is consistency of language or constructs and an openness to empirical disconfirmation.

Yet just as there are problems with eclecticism, there are also problems with a reductionistic cognitive model. New developments in the field may go beyond the current cognitive model, perhaps offering new directions of inquiry, intervention and conceptualization. We need to avoid becoming "true believers" who canonize the cognitive model. For example, claiming that new concepts are similar to more traditional concepts may result in a failure to understand that new models and new ideas point to new ways of conceptualizing and treating the patient. These new ideas might not be easily developed from the traditional model. Reductionism—the approach that the learning theorists utilized to try to explain human language—ran into the pitfall of being overly simplistic.

THE LACK OF COHERENT THEORY

One of the cornerstones of any theory is its internal consistency. Internal consistency is marked by the fact that a theory does not include self-contradictory statements and that a good theory should have some inductive implication that holds separate parts of the theory together. One example of the lack of consistency in a theory is the following story that one clinician told me many years ago. He was on the staff of a predominantly psychoanalytic department, and a psychiatrist was discussing a new patient on the ward. The psychiatrist indicated that the patient had significant "Oedipal conflicts" as exemplified by his problematic family history and his relationships with authority figures. Our colleague asked, "How do you know if this is true?" and the psychiatrist went back to his diagram and pointed out symbolic Oedipal struggles. Again, our colleague remonstrated, "But how do you know if you are right?" Frustrated, the psychoanalyst said, "How can I show you?" The doubting Thomas said, "Make a prediction." The analyst said, "Okay. I predict that he will be rebellious toward ward staff, since they will represent authority figures."

The next week they called in the attendant on the ward and the analytic psychiatrist asked the attendant about the new patient's behavior. "I don't know why this guy needs to be hospitalized," the attendant said. "He has been the most cooperative patient I've seen. He wanted extra work to keep him busy." The psychiatrist dismissed the attendant, turned to the group and said triumphantly, "See. I told you he had an Oedipal thing about authority!" Bewildered, our friend replied, "But you said he'd be rebellious!" Self-assuredly, looking down from his glasses, the analyst said, "But don't you see. It's a *reaction formation.*"

Is cognitive therapy at risk of becoming a set of hypotheses that are self-contradictory and non-falsifiable? I hope not. But consider the fact that schema theory predicts that the individual with a schema of demanding standards can engage in schema maintenance, schema avoidance, or schema compensation (Young, 1990). The first question that arises is, How could it be otherwise? After all, what is left, except perhaps "schema-irrelevant behavior"? and how do we predict which individual will engage at what time in one of these three responses?

THE LACK OF TESTABLE HYPOTHESES

A theory is only as good as its ability to generate hypotheses that are open to confirmation and disconfirmation. Good theories have constructs from which one may deduce clear hypotheses, which may not be contradictory to other hypotheses derived from the theory. The hypotheses should be stated in a form that allows operational definitions and offers predictions that are falsifiable. Looking out my window as I am writing this, my theory about cloudy days in New York when the weather forecaster predicts rain is that there will be rain. I predict that it will start raining within the next 2 hours. We can falsify this prediction by observing later that it is not raining.

The problem that may arise from wholesale eclecticism is that some concepts may not be falsifiable. An example of this is the use of case conceptualization. (I am not critical of case conceptualization as a clinically useful tool, but how do we know if we are right?) Case conceptualizations are almost always developed in hindsight, and we are relying on the patient's report of his memory (both of which may be open to question). We are also attempting to organize the information we are provided by using vague and untested ideas about development and psychopathology. Because the explanation is post hoc, it does not allow for manipulation or falsification. Another example of non-testable hypotheses is the schema model that proposes that there is schema maintenance, compensation, or avoidance. As indicated earlier, how could it be otherwise?

Many explanations in the personality theories of cognitive theory rely on interpretations and inferences that are not related to empirical literature. The hypothesized origins of the different personality disorders or schemas, as exemplified in the cognitive model (Beck et al., 1990; Young, 1990) are not falsifiable nor are they based on any developmental research on socialization or personality development. We may be running the risk of reproducing the "clinical intuition" that got the psychoanalysts in trouble.

MODELS OF THE MIND

Cognitive models of depression and anxiety emphasize an information-processing model that proposes that personal schemas direct attention and memory processes. Wells and his associates (Wells, 1997, 2000; Wells and Matthews, 1994, 1996) have advanced the Self-Regulatory Executive Function (S-REF) model to explicate implicit theories of mind that affect the emotional disorders. The S-REF model proposes that there are different levels of processing, with a lower level that is relatively automatic, an "on-line" level with relative conscious awareness, and a level of self-beliefs that are held in long-term memory. Wells and Matthews distinguish between two modes—an object mode in which thoughts are relatively unexamined and are "accepted" and a meta-cognitive mode in which the individual can distance himself and evaluate the content and processing of his thought.

The area of metacognition will gain increasing importance in cognitive therapy. Metacognition refers to "thinking about thinking," an area that Salatas & Flavell (1976) and Selman (1980,1981) investigated in developmental psychology some time ago. The idea of metacognition in developmental psychology was viewed as an example of decentering, or role-taking ability—that is, the ability to stand back and examine the self from the point of view of others. One's thoughts, intelligence, or mind could then become an object of one's own cognition. The importance of metacognition in the cognitive model of psychopathology is that individuals with different emotional problems may differ in their beliefs about how their minds work.

For example, consider the issue of worry. Individuals who worry often believe that it protects them, prevents their being surprised, and allows them to solve problems that may arise (Wells, 1997, 2000). In addition, they may also believe that their worry is out of their control and might cause irreparable damage to their mental or physical well-being (Borkovec, 1994; Wells, 1997, 2000). Thus, the generalized anxiety patient who worries excessively may have a theory of worry that may cause increased anxiety and, ironically, more worry.

Similarly, individuals with obsessive-compulsive disorder may believe that they should not have bizarre or unwanted thoughts and that their thoughts may result in loss of control over action—"thought-action fusion" (Rachman, 1993; Salkovskis, 1996; Salkovskis & Kirk, 1997). These individuals may believe that once they have a thought about possible harm they are responsible then for neutralizing or preventing the harm regardless of how remote the probability may be (Salkovskis, 1996). A similar cognitive vulnerability about the nature of worry is reflected in hypochondriasis (see Salkovskis & Kirk, 1997). Thus, the obsessive individual may believe that worry, checking, and seeking reassurance are desirable—even necessary—ways of coping.

Theories of one's mind and emotions are also reflected in other coping strategies such as "safety behaviors" (Clark, 1986; Wells, 1997). These behaviors, thoughts, or images are utilized by the individual to prevent loss of control, exposure, or harm. For example, the socially phobic individual may speak softly, lower his gaze, and turn away from others in order to avoid calling attention to himself. However, these safety behaviors may lead people to think he is odd, adding further to the individual's belief that he needs to continue the safety behaviors and the avoidance. Similarly, an individual with a fear of flying may check with the pilots, check the weather forecast numerous times, rehearse prayers, and clutch the side of her seat when the plane takes off. Although the individual may have exposed herself to flying, her implicit theory is that the safety behaviors have protected her.

CHALLENGING CLINICAL POPULATIONS

Cognitive therapy has now been applied to the treatment of a wide range of clinical populations that Beck did not originally anticipate as treatable with this model. Although the nature of the treatment is modified to conceptualize the individual and his problem, the cognitive model has wide generality. There are now cognitive models for the treatment of schizophrenia, delusional disorders, bipolar disorder, dysthymia, and the various personality disorders. One set of disorders, however, still merits considerable attention, especially because it represents the most common problem in clinical practice. I am referring to patients with comorbid diagnoses, that is, patients who qualify for more than one psychiatric diagnosis. This, of course, is exactly what we see in clinical practice.

The use of empirically validated treatments for depression and anxiety disorders has revolutionized clinical practice. Clinicians may feel confident that they are using methods and treatment plans that have proven to be effective in controlled studies. However, those studies were conducted on patients who were selected as presenting with one dominant diagnosis—let's say, major depression. Yet we know from research and clinical experience that patients in clinical practice present with comorbidity: The patient with major depression may also present with generalized anxiety, social phobia, dependent personality, and compulsive personality. Clinicians are then faced with several difficult questions: (a) Which disorder do I treat first? (b) What is the relationship between one disorder and the others: Is it cause and effect? Are they determined by another, perhaps unknown factor? Will improvement on one problem generalize to improvement on other problems? (c) Are there any data on how effective the empirically validated treatments are for patients with comorbid disorders?

There are no simple answers to these important real-world questions. Some clinicians may be guided by the idea that treating a substance abuse disorder first is the most valuable strategy. Others may believe that a very severe depression should take priority before treating social phobia or panic. Many would think that treatment of Axis I takes priority over treatment of Axis II. But the nature of the treatment may or may not require modification depending on the coexisting conditions. For example, what modifications should the therapist make in treatment for two different patients presenting with major depression, where one is a dependent personality and the other is narcissistic? We know as clinicians that we do adjust the style and interventions to individual patients—therapy, in practice, is idiographic, not nomothetic. One style does not fit all. But how can we determine what the most effective approach will be? This will indeed be a significant challenge to cognitive therapy.

Of course, case conceptualization will be the most useful method to utilize. A case conceptualization for patients with comorbid disorders will require a complete diagnostic workup, developmental history, and detailed cognitive assessment. But the risks entailed in this are important to consider. They involve the possibility that more than one case conceptualization may fit the data or tell the story; there may not be any a priori way of determining the validity of the case conceptualization, the case conceptualization may change during the course of therapy as more information becomes available, the conceptualization may, at times, have more to do with the therapist than with the patient; and the case conceptualization may or may not lead to the most efficacious treatment.

NONCLINICAL APPLICATIONS

Psychoanalysts were remarkably successful in applying their theoretical and clinical ideas to a wide variety of nonclinical phenomena, including anthropology, sociology, political theory, biography, historical analysis, literary criticism, cultural studies, and organizational behavior. (This does not include the influence in popular culture, such as the films of Woody Allen!) Will cognitive theory have application beyond the field of clinical psychology?

Beck's *Prisoners of Hate* (1999) is an attempt to apply cognitive theory to an understanding of hostility at the individual and political level. Relying on his analysis of cognitive biases that lead people to dehumanize the opposition and to personalize the behavior of others as reflecting intentions of devaluation or dominance, Beck suggests strategies that may be used to overcome some of these problems. There is a potential gold mine of cognitive therapy principles to apply to nonclinical issues. For instance, one can easily imagine the development of cognitive models of conflict resolution and negotiation that build on the conflict models of Raiffa (1983) and Fisher and Ury (1981). These conflict models utilize concepts consistent with a cognitive model, such as assumptions and positions taken, information deficits, and goals and principles. A cognitive model of negotiation might propose that the two parties in a negotiation may differ as to their schemas—one is focused on pleasing others, the second on dominating. Each may have conditional assumptions: "If I don't please the other person they won't want to work with me" or "If I don't win everything, I'm a loser." It is obvious, in this case, how this dyad will develop: The dominant "winner" will take all. But imagine a case in which both parties believe that they must dominate entirely. Here we have the escalation of conflict and retransigence. A cognitive model might assist each in understanding the consequences of a rigid schematic approach, or a positional stance, in negotiation, and explore the payoffs inherent in a mutual benefit at some mutual cost. The cognitive approach to negotiation might focus on the distortions in thinking that underlie impasses in negotiation, such as mind-reading, personalizing, catastrophizing, or perfectionistic "shoulds."

Another nonclinical application of cognitive therapy is in the area of behavioral finance, a fast-growing field that integrates cognitive psychology with finance or investment models (see Thaler, 1980, 1992). An example of a behavioral finance approach is the portfolio theory of decision-making that I have advanced for understanding depression and mania (Leahy, 1997, 1999). However, one can just as readily extend this model to an understanding of how individuals engage in decisions regarding financial investments. As an example, the individual who may be prone to overestimating his ability to predict, control, or absorb risk and loss may overextend himself in spending or in risky investments. Personality styles, such as the obsessive-compulsive personality who may have high information demands, may be reluctant to place a bet on an investment, lest he regret it later. Spending styles may also be reflective of beliefs about resources, over- or underestimation of hedonic value, focus on myopic need-gratification, and assumptions about gaining approval from others.

Finally, organization psychologists, who already rely on the importance of cognitive psychology, may find that there are many new applications of cognitive therapy to management, motivation, conflict resolution (see earlier remarks), and organizational systems. For instance, it may be possible to characterize organizational systems in terms of fundamental schematic content ("We are superior" or "We are worthless"), maladaptive coping styles (devaluing the competition rather than knowing the competitor and competing effectively), or avoidant strategies ("Don't tell me anything that will upset me"). Management theory may be better informed by relying on examining the underlying maladaptive assumptions of workers and managers. For managers, these assumptions might include "Everyone should be motivated without my having to tell them," "They're just being spoiled," "They shouldn't be so lazy," or "I have to punish them to teach them a lesson." For workers, maladaptive assumptions or thoughts include "I should be appreciated all the time," "Everything should be fair,"" "They're doing this to me personally," or "I should always be able to do what I want to do." It is remarkable how often one can observe that someone has been placed in a position of management without any training in dealing with human behavior. This in itself is an example of the need for cognitive therapists to provide their knowledge to the real world of business, management, and labor.

CONCLUSIONS

The last 20 years of cognitive therapy have been marked by an incredible growth in the field. Cognitive therapy is now an effective treatment and provides a credible model of a range of disorders, including depression, social phobia, panic disorder, generalized anxiety, hypochondriasis, bipolar disorder, psychotic disorders, and many other problems. Yet despite this success, we should be careful that we do not become so comfortable with our ideas that we begin to believe we can pontificate rather than test out our new ideas.

I know that the way I did cognitive therapy 10 years ago is not how I do it today. My thinking has changed, partly as a result of new advances made by our colleagues and partly as I have learned more about being a therapist and how I fit into the process. Today I rely more on case conceptualization, utilizing emotions and validation, individual models of

Axis I disorders, a recognition of resistance and countertransference, and an appreciation of the difficulty in making progress. In fact, as I have become more experienced, I am more impressed with the complexity of the patient's problems, more aware of the limitations of change, and more open to the ideas advocated by noncognitive therapists. It may be that "true-believers" in cognitive therapy may find themselves starting out with a devotion to a formulaic model but will move toward integrating cognitive therapy with more awareness of the complexities and limitations of the model.

REFERENCES

American Psychiatric Association. (1994). *Diagnostic and statistical manual of mental disorders (4th ed.).* Washington, DC: Author.

Alford, B., & Beck, A. T. (1997). *The Integrative Power of Cognitive Therapy.* New York: Guilford.

Beck, A. T. (1967). *Depression: Causes and treatment.* Philadelphia: University of Pennsylvania Press.

Beck, A. T. (1976). *Cognitive therapy and the emotional disorders.* New York: International Universities Press.

Beck, A. T. (1997). Beyond belief: A theory of modes, personality, and psychotherapy. In P. M. Salkovskis (Ed.), *Frontiers of Cognitive Therapy* (pp. 1–25). New York: Guilford.

Beck, A. T. (1999). *Prisoners of hate: The cognitive basis of anger, hostility, and violence.* New York: HarperCollins.

Beck, A. T., Freeman, A., & Associates. (1990). *Cognitive therapy of personality disorders.* New York: Guilford Press.

Beck, A. T., Rush, A. J., Shaw, B. F., & Emery, G. (1979). *Cognitive therapy of depression.* New York: Guilford Press.

Beck, J. (1996). *Cognitive therapy: Basics and beyond.* New York: Guilford.

Borkovec, T. D., Roemer, L., & Kinyon, J. Disclosure and worry: Opposite sides of the emotional processing coin. In J. W. Pennebaker (Ed.), *Emotion, disclosure, & health* (pp. 47–70). Washington, DC: American Psychological Association.

Borkovec, T. D. (1994). The nature, functions, and origins of worry. In C. L. Davey & F. Tallis (Eds.), *Worrying: Perspectives on theory, assessment and treatment* (pp. 5–33). Chichester, England: Wiley.

Bowlby, J. (1980). *Attachment and loss: Vol. III. Loss: Sadness and depression.* London: Hogarth Press.

Clark, D. M. (1986) A cognitive approach to panic. *Behavior research and therapy, 24,* 461–470.

Clark, D. A., Beck, A. T., & Alford, B. (1999). *The scientific foundations of cognitive theory and therapy of depression.* New York: Wiley.

Collins, W. A., Maccoby, E. E., Steinberg, L., Hetherington, E. M., & Bornstein, M. H. (2000). Contemporary research on parenting: The case for nature and nurture. *American Psychologist, 5,* 218–232.

Damon, W., & Hart, D. (1988). *Self-understanding in childhood and adolescence.* New York: Cambridge University Press.

Dollard, J., & Miller, N. (1950). *Personality and psychotherapy.* New York: McGraw-Hill.

Fisher, R., & Ury, W. (1981). *Getting to yes: Negotiating agreement without giving in.* Houghton-Mifflin.

James, W. (1892). *Psychology: The briefer course.* New York: Henry Holt

Leahy, R. L. (1995). Cognitive development and cognitive therapy: *Journal of Cognitive Psychotherapy, 9,* 173–184.

Leahy, R. L. (1997). An investment model of depressive resistance. *Journal of Cognitive Psychotherapy, 11,* 3–19.

Leahy, R. L. (1999). Decision-making and mania. *Journal of Cognitive Psychotherapy, 13,* 1–23.

Persons, J. (1989). *Cognitive therapy in practice: A case formulation approach.* New York: Norton.

Piaget, J. (1934). *The moral judgment of the child.* New York: Free Press.

Rachman, S. J. (1993). Obsessions, responsibility, and guilt. *Behavior Research and Therapy, 31,* 149–154.

Raiffa, H. (1983). Mediation of conflicts. *American Behavioral Scientist, 27,* 195–210.

Safran, J. (1998). *Widening the scope of cognitive therapy: The therapeutic relationship, emotion and the process of change.* Northvale, NJ: Jason Aronson.

Safran, J. D., & Muran, C. (2000). *Negotiating the therapeutic alliance.* New York: Guilford Press.

Salatas, H., & Flavell, J. H. (1976). Perspective taking: The development of two components of knowledge. *Child Development, 47,* 103–109

Salkovskis, P. M. (1989). Cognitive-behavioral factors and the persistence of intrusive thoughts in obsessive problems. *Behaviour Research and Therapy, 23,* 571–583.

Salkovskis, P. M. (1996). The cognitive approach to anxiety: Threat beliefs, safety-seeking behavior, and the special case of health anxiety and obsessions. In P. Salkovskis (Ed.), *Frontiers of cognitive therapy* (pp. 48–74). New York: Guilford.

Salkovskis, P. M., & Kirk, J. (1989). Obsessional disorders. In K. Hawton, P. M. Salkovskis, J. Kirk, & D. M. Clark (Eds.), *Cognitive behaviour therapy for psychiatric problems: A practical guide.* Oxford: Oxford University Press.

Salkovskis, P. M., & Kirk, J. (1997). Obsessive-compulsive disorder. In D. M. Clark & C. G. Fairburn (Eds.), *Science and practice of cognitive behaviour therapy* (pp. 179–208). Oxford: Oxford University Press.

Selman, R. L. (1980). *The growth of interpersonal understanding.* New York: Academic Press.

Selman, R. L. (1981). The development of interpersonal competence: The role of understanding in conduct. *Developmental Review, 1,* 401–422.

Thaler, R. (1980). Toward a positive theory of consumer choice. *Journal of Economic Behavior and Organization, 1,* 39–60.

Thaler, R. (1992). *The winner's curse: Paradoxes and anomalies of economic life.* Princeton, NJ: Princeton University Press.

Wells, A. (1997). *Cognitive therapy of anxiety disorders: A practice manual and conceptual guide.* Chichester, England: Wiley.

Wells, A. (2000). *Emotional Disorders and Metacognition: Innovative Cognitive Therapy.* Chichester, England: Wiley.

Wells, A., & Matthews, G. (1994). *Attention and emotion: A clinical perspective.* Hillsdale, NJ: Erlbaum.

Wells, A., & Matthews, G. (1996). Modeling cognition in emotional disorder: The S-REF model. *Behaviour Research and Therapy, 34,* 881–888.

Young, J. E. (1990). *Cognitive therapy for personality disorders: A schema-focused approach.* Sarasota, FL: Professional Resource Exchange.

Index

Springer Publishing Company

Six Therapists and One Client, *2nd Edition*

Frank Dumont, EdD
Raymond J. Corsini, PhD, Editors

"Comparative studies in psychology are very rare and much needed. This comprehensive and well-written book certainly fills a gap in the clinical literature. Its organization, in which the various theories are applied to a single case study, makes the volume particularly helpful in evaluating various modalities of treatments..." —**Florence L. Denmark,** PhD
Robert Scott Pace Dist. Prof.r and Chair
Psychology Department, Pace University

" [This book] promises to be an exciting and gripping read for intelligent lay persons hungering for an inside glimpse into the world of psychotherapy, a world that each of us, ourselves, or our friends and families, will be destined to enter sooner or later in our lives." —**Robert Perloff,** PhD
Distinguished Service Professor Emeritus
Department of Psychology, University of Pittsburgh

This volume demonstrates how six therapists working within the structures of six different major theoretical orientations would treat the same person. Approaches include: Ericksonian Hypnotherapy (Lankton), REBT (Ellis), Multimodal Therapy (Lazarus), Individual Psychotherapy (Corsini), Person-Centered Therapy (Zimring), and Cognitive Behavior Therapy (McGrady). Each therapist explains the logic that underpins his or her critical interventions. This think-aloud methodology will have great appeal for students and clinicians.

2000   352pp   0-8261-1319-2   hard

536 Broadway, New York, NY 10012 • **(212) 431-4370** • **Fax (212) 941-7842**
Order Toll-Free: (877) 687-7476 • *www.springerpub.com*

Springer Publishing Company

Empirically Supported Cognitive Therapies
Current and Future Applications

William J. Lyddon, PhD
John V. Jones, Jr., PhD, LPC, NCC, ACT, Editors

In the spirit of disseminating some of the most recent research on empirically supported treatments, this volume brings together distinguished practitioners and researchers in the field who use a cognitive model as the basis of their research and practice.

Cognitive techniques for common clinical problems such as depression, bipolar I disorder, phobias, panic disorder, obsessive compulsive disorders, post traumatic stress disorders, and eating disorders are described in clinical detail. Newer applications for anger management and antisocial behavior in children and adolescents are also reviewed. Illustrative case examples are integral to each discussion.

Including recent trends, current limitations, and new directions and developments, this text offers a fundamental knowledge base for students and practitioners alike.

Contents:
Section I: Mood Disorders
- Depression, *I. Blackburn & S. Moorhead*
- Bipolar I Disorder, *M. R. Basco*

Section II: Anxiety Disorders
- Phobias, *E. T. Dowd & D. Fahr*
- Panic Disorder, *W. C. Sanderson & S. A. Rego*
- Obsessive Compulsive Disorder, *S. Wilhelm*
- Posttraumatic Stress Disorder, *S. A. Falsetti & H. S. Resnick*

Section III: New Directions and Developments
- Anger Management, *E.R. Dahlen & J. L. Deffenbacher*
- Antisocial Behavior in Children and Adolescents: Expanding the Cognitive Model, *L. Hanish & P. H. Tolan*
- Eating Disorders: Enhancing Effectiveness Through the Intergration of Cultural Factors, *N. L. Wilson & A. E. Blackhurst*
- Empirically Supported Treatments: Recent Trends, Current Limitations, and Future Promise, *W. J. Lyddon & D. K. Chatkoff*

2001   272pp   0-8261-2299-X   hard

536 Broadway, New York, NY 10012 • Telephone: 212-431-4370
Fax: 212-941-7842 • Order Toll-Free: 877-687-7476
Order On-line: www.springerpub.com